The Law of Journalism and Mass Communication

The Law of Journalism and Mass Communication

Contributors

Israel Udomisor, Anthony Paul Udoh et al.

AURIS
Reference

www.aurisreference.com

The Law of Journalism and Mass Communication

Contributors: Israel Udomisor, Anthony Paul Udoh et al.

Published by Auris Reference Limited

www.aurisreference.com

United Kingdom

Notice

Contributors, whose names have been given on the book cover, are not associated with the Publisher. The editors and the Publisher have attempted to trace the copyright holders of all material reproduced in this publication and apologise to copyright holders if permission has not been obtained. If any copyright holder has not been acknowledged, please write to us so we may rectify.

Reasonable efforts have been made to publish reliable data. The views articulated in the chapters are those of the individual contributors, and not necessarily those of the editors or the Publisher. Editors and/or the Publisher are not responsible for the accuracy of the information in the published chapters or consequences from their use. The Publisher accepts no responsibility for any damage or grievance to individual(s) or property arising out of the use of any material(s), instruction(s), methods or thoughts in the book.

The Law of Journalism and Mass Communication

ISBN: 978-1-78154-737-3

British Library Cataloguing in Publication Data
A CIP record for this book is available from the British Library

Printed in the United Kingdom

Exclusively distributed by CBS Publishers & Distributors Pvt. Ltd.

Contents

List of Abbreviations

AU	African Union
CEELI	Central European and Eurasian Law Initiative
CIMA	Center for International Media Assistance
CMLP	Citizen Media Law Project
CPJ	Committee to Protect Journalists
ECtHR	European Court of Human Rights
EFF	Electronic Frontier Foundation
FCC	Federal Communications Commission
FOI	Freedom of Information
FOIA	federal Freedom of Information Act
FPÖ	Freedom Party
ICFJ	International Center for Journalists
ICTY	International Criminal Tribunal for Yugoslavia
IMLA	International Media Lawyers Association
IPI	International Press Institute
IREX	International Research & Exchanges Board
ISLP	International Senior Lawyers Project
ISPs	interactive computer services
NDE	National Directorate of Employment
NPC	Nigerian Press Council
NUJ	Nigerian Union of Journalists
OSCE	Organization for Security and Cooperation in Europe
PI	Privacy International
POW	Prisoner of War),
RAF	Red Army Faction
RTDNA	Radio Television Digital News Association
UFO	Unidentified flying objects
WAN	World Association of Newspapers
WSIS	World Summit on the Information Society

List of Contributors

Israel Udomisor
The Department of Mass Communication, University of Maiduguri, Maiduguri, Nigeria

Anthony Paul Udoh
The Department of Communication Art, University of Uyo, Uyo, Nigeria

Günther Pallaver
Innsbruck School of Political Science and Sociology University of Innsbruck

Theo Hug
Faculty of Education, Faculty Member University of Innsbruck

Bonachristus Umeogu
Department of Philosophy, Faculty of Arts, Nnamdi Azikiwe University, Awka, Nigeria

Ifeoma Ojiakor
Department of Mass Communication, Faculty of Social Sciences, Nnamdi Azikiwe University, Awka, Nigeria

D. Weisenhaus
Hong Kong University

Ifeoma Dunu
Department of Mass Communication, Nnamdi Azikiwe University, Awka, Nigeria

Gregory Obinna Ugbo
Department of Mass Communication, Nnamdi Azikiwe University, Awka, Nigeria

Caroline Fishe
Journalism, Faculty of Arts & Design, University of Canberra, Canberra, Australia

Preface

The mass media or the press occupies a central position in the society. It is basically involved in the information, education, and entertainment as well as cultural transmission. The enormity of the functions of the press makes it imperative for a guiding principles or code of ethics which includes objectivity. The Law of Journalism and Mass Communication provides students with the intellectual tools they will need to resolve legal issues arising from the ongoing dramatic reshaping of the media. It includes new material on matters such as anonymity and foreign law which have become more urgent because of the transformation of media industries. First chapter is based on the framing analysis theory and the agenda setting theory of communication. Using the documentary or historical survey method in the collection of data, it is observed that the media are naturally attracted to conflict and some journalists or media organization use their position to fight individual or group battle while others blow some seemingly innocuous issues out of proportion thereby generating conflict in these society. It is also noted that the media sometimes play down, frame or slant some facts to avoid escalation of conflict. In second chapter the proposition to be tested is whether the political elites' attempt to exert influence on day-to-day news coverage and thus on political journalism is increasing and whether as a result political journalism's autonomous leeway is continually diminishing. Third chapter looks at sycophancy in the Nigerian media by looking at the reasons for its unbridled spread, effects on the public, media houses, individuals and the government of the day. Fourth chapter explores on media law education for journalists in Hong Kong. Fifth chapter undertakes an assessment of the Nigerian journalists' knowledge, perception and use of the FOI Law in the discharge of their (information) responsibility to the public. Sixth chapter reports on a selection of findings from wider inductive, qualitative research into the transition from journalism to political media advising and back again. Seventh chapter emphasizes on media law.

Chapter 1

PROFESSIONAL DEMAND OF OBJECTIVITY AND ITS EFFECT ON MEDIA OBJECTIVITY IN CONFLICT MANAGEMENT IN JOURNALISM

Israel Udomisor[1], Anthony Paul Udoh[2]

[1]The Department of Mass Communication, University of Maiduguri, Maiduguri, Nigeria

[2]The Department of Communication Art, University of Uyo, Uyo, Nigeria

ABSTRACT

The mass media or the press occupies a central position in the society. It is basically involved in the information, education, and entertainment as well as cultural transmission. The enormity of the functions of the press makes it imperative for a guiding principles or code of ethics which includes objectivity. However, current practices in the media especially as pertains to conflict management negate this ethical standard or code, hence the imperative of this study which seeks to investigate how the media can engage in conflict management without breaching this cherished and longstanding principle. This study is based on the framing analysis theory and the agenda setting theory of communication. Using the documentary or historical survey method in the collection of data, it is observed that the media are naturally attracted to conflict and some journalists or media organisation use their position to fight individual or group battle while others blow some seemingly innocuous issues out of proportion thereby generating conflict in the society. It is also noted that the media sometimes play down, frame or slant some facts to avoid escalation of conflict. All these negate the principle of objectivity. It is therefore recommended that the media should at all times value, uphold and apply objectivity in all its reportage, by separating facts from comments, for effective conflict management. The media should also embrace proactive conflict management approach, peace journalism, investigative journalism and agenda setting for peaceful resolution of conflicts.

INTRODUCTION

In recent past, there have been serious controversies over the practice of the mass media vis-a-vis adherence to ethical codes of the profession. These controversies have made many, both within and without the media circle, to lose confidence as well as have serious doubt on the mass media. The credibility which was earlier enjoyed by the media inspired early communication theorists to assume the position that the mass media are capable of creating a very powerful effect on the audience compared to that of a bullet released from a gun—the magic bullet theory. However, with an increasing media literacy coupled with the understanding that some of the media activities are nothing but make belief with the tendency of conferring undeserved status on some members of the society, the audience members became more selective in terms of exposure, attention, perception and retention. Moreover, some attempts by communication scholars to restore the media image by enhancing the credibility through enforcement of the media ethics, especially as pertains to objectivity, have become more challenged due to current demands of the media in conflict management, hence the imperative of this study to assess how the media can maintain objectivity while at the same time involving in conflict management both within the media industry and in the larger society.

MEDIA OBJECTIVITY

Journalism is a discipline of collecting, analysing, verifying, and presenting news regarding current events, trends, issues and people, (Hasan, 2013) . Mcquail cited in Hasan defines journalism as paid writing for public media with reference to actual and on-going events of public interest. It is a term used both in the print and electronic media as both are involved in the collection or gathering, analysing, verifying and the presentation to the public through the newspapers, magazine, radio, television, and the internet among others.

It has been seen to wield so much influence in the social system. It could engender unity, peace and development as well as create serious security threat, conflict, crisis and other undesirable situation in the society. This explains why some communication scholars regard journalism or mass communication as a double edge sword having the ability to construct and or destroy, make and or mar a social system. In collaboration, Baran (2004) notes that since almost all conflict involve communication problem, the medium, style or attitude of the communicator, plays a sensitive role in either escalating or managing the conflict.

Conflict

Chamberlin is a renowned pastor in one of the Pentecostal churches in South-South Nigeria. Although he was not a born again Christian from birth, childhood or in his youthful age, he became such a devout Christian in the later part of his life both in teaching and dealings. Married with four children evenly segmented in terms of sex, Chamberlin trained his children in a godly way predictive of his calibre. A civil servant though, but he created ample time for his flock and derived joy in the happiness of others either due to vocation, temperament or both. His status in the society in terms of wealth measured in landed property, estates or bank account balance has never bothered him or deters his philanthropic disposition.

However, Chamberlin's wife, Stella, who probably is the reveres of Chamberlin's disposition enjoyed accumulation of wealth and superlatively exhibited the psychological id. Stella wanted to have an estate, a fleet of cars having different colours to match her dresses, manicure and pedicure. She wanted to have a holiday in Palm Island and medical checks in Germany, India, or Saudi Arabia. Sadly though, but Chamberlin's disposition made her dreams a perpetual foetus and this did not get down well with Stella, hence conflict was an unseen but unavoidable resident of their home.

The above sad experience of Chamberlin, probably informs Elliot, Timothy, and Robin's (2004)position which holds that people have incompatible goals placing them in conflict with each other. This can be true of two groups, such as romantic partners who disagree about who should clean the kitchen, or two groups such as a labour union and company management who disagree over wages and working conditions.

Freud in Elliot et al. (2004) argues that conflict is an inevitable by-product of civilization because the goals and needs of individuals often clash with the goals and needs of their fellow human beings.

Every human being has a peculiar perception of certain phenomenon formed through socialization, experiences, etc. Therefore, exposure to stimuli that is at variance with an individual's perception creates disequilibrium—CONFLICT.

Simply put, conflict is a perceptual incompatibility. To Owens-Ibie (2002) , conflict is a product of life and living while Ibrahim (2002) says that conflict is a state of disagreement or argument between people, groups, or countries. Udomisor (2002) views conflict as the by-product of plurality in a free environment which allows opinions and feelings to be fully and freely expressed. This definition seems to situate conflict in a democratic environment probably oblivion of conflicts and even crises which often take place within other systems of government. For instance, the military era in Nigeria witnessed series of conflicts some of which claimed lives and properties. The Buhari's junta experienced lots of conflicts especially with the press due to his attempt to trim down the tentacles of the media. Ofor (2004) noted that on the assumption of office, Buhari enacted the Decree No. 4 (DN4) of 1984 which was entitled, "Public Officers Protection against False Accusation." This decree was later used to sentence the duo of Tunde Thompson and NdukaIrabor of Guardian Newspaper to one year jail term and their newspaper fined N50000 for being nuisance to the government.

The Babangida's junta was not an exemption to this conflict which resulted in the grotesque murder of a veteran journalist, Mr. Dele Giwa, the first Editor-in-Chief of News Watch magazine. Although there are quite a number of them within and outside the country, these are just a few instances within Nigeria.

In a more holistic approach, Udomisor (2002: p. 87) defines conflict as "the result of differences in opinion, attitude and behaviour, differences in philosophical, psychological, sociological, political and economic orientation of interactors in a given system".

Statement of the Problem

Journalism is a profession which is guided by some legal and ethical codes. These codes direct the practice of journalists and enabled them to distinguish between right and wrong, good and bad actions. Hasan (2013) , states that the code of ethics is an attempt to achieve a just balance between freedom and responsibility. He listed some of the ethical codes of journalism to include: objectivity, accuracy, truthfulness or the non-misrepresentation of facts. Contrarily, the concept of management entails the controlling of the media content to prevent or resolve a conflict and this suggests or implies subjectivity. Also there is an assumption that conflict management practices by the mass media negate the cherished and long standing journalistic ethics—objectivity.

Therefore, media objectivity and the expectation of the media to involve in conflict management are conflicting hence the imperative of this study.

Objective of the Study

The objectives of this study are basically to:

§ To assess the possibility of media objectivity.

§ To assess media approach to conflict management.

§ To examine how journalist can adhere to this ethical demand of objectivity while engaging in conflict management.

Research Questions

In order to achieve the objective(s) of this study, the following questions were asked:

§ Is there media objectivity.

§ How do the media manage conflict.

§ How can the media mange conflict in the face of objectivity principle?

Theoretical Framework

This study is rooted in the framing and the agenda setting theory of communication due to their relationship and explanation of the concept of the concept of study.

Framing theory or frame analysis theory as developed by Goffman is micro-level theory focussing on how individuals learn to routinely make sense of their social world. According to Baran and Davis (2009) , the theory implies that journalism's role should be to provide a forum in which ideas about a social world are routinely presented and debated. "As it is now, this forum is dominated by social institutions having the power to influence frames routinely used to structure news coverage of the social world. These institutions are able to promote frames that serve to reinforce or consolidate an existing social order and to marginalise frames that raise questions about or challenge the way things are." The duo noted that the practice of frame was startlingly evident in internal marine memos that surfaced during the 2007 murder and dereliction of duty trials of men involved in the 2005 killing of twenty-four Iraqi men, women, and children in Haditha. In response to a series of questions posed by Time reporter Tim McGirk as he worked to confirm the official account that the deaths "occurred during combat and were justified, if regrettable," the commanding officers of the unit involved met and developed "Talking Points" designed to shape McGirk's account. One common tactic used by reporters is to spin a story in such a way that it is easily recognised and remembered.

Also, the agenda setting theory, according to Baran and Davis (2009) , holds that the media may not be successful much of the time in telling the people what to think, but it is stunningly successful in telling its readers what to think about. This largely implies that the media publication on war, killings, destruction of property and other similar activities by a particular section of a country or state would form the discussion and action of the people in the larger society. If emphasis was on war, then the society would base their comments and opinions on war and if the media lay emphasis on peace, the societal opinion would follow thus.

Media Objectivity and the Demand of Conflict Management in Journalism

Media is the simple plural of medium which relates to the vehicle, means and institutions for publishing and broadcasting information. The media is a world of its own which is peopled by professionals schooled in the different areas of the field. These professionals who make up this world must be guided by some codes of conduct (ethics) which according to Ernest Greenwood is one of the qualities which an occupation must possess before it is termed a profession.

Hasan (2013) , states that the code of ethics is an attempt to achieve a just balance between freedom and responsibility. He listed some of the media ethics to include objectivity, accuracy, truthfulness or the non-mis- representation of facts.

Objectivity means that the reporter tries to transmit the news untainted by conscious bias and without personal comment or coloration (Dominick, 2011) . Corroborating Dominick's view, Hasan (2013: p. 183) notes that the term which has become frequently held to be essential to journalistic professionalism was not applied to journalistic work until the 20th century, saying that the concept of objectivity has always been somewhat ambiguous, and both journalists and the public tend to identify objectivity in its absence. "The belief in objectivity is a faith in fact. It means that journalists should have something like a neutral point of view, not taking a stand on any issues on which there is some disagreement. Instead, journalists are simply to report what 'both sides' of an issue told them."

The 1998 codes of ethics for journalists provides for accuracy and fairness which explains that the public has a right to know and that factual, accurate, balanced and fair reporting is the ultimate objective of good journalism. Dominick (2011: p. 403) states, "the journalist's primary loyalty is to the audience to report fully the fact of a story." Similarly, McQuail (2005: p. 200) highlights three features of objective journalism. One is that it adopts a position of neutrality towards the object of reporting," secondly, there is a lack of partisanship, which he explains as not taking sides in matters of dispute or showing bias. Thirdly, objectivity requires strict attachment to accuracy and truth.

Hasan emphasized that the facts of the news must be presented as they are as any deletion or interpretation on the part of the news writer will tend to make the presentation of facts in favour or against a person or any organisation.

In contrast, conflict management entails the collating, coordinating, controlling, and shaping certain facts, materials and resources to prevent the escalation of conflict as well as resolving existing ones.Akpan (2005) noted that conflict management involves efforts or strategies aimed at resolving an already existing conflict. It is a process of handling conflict, to avoid conflict escalation.

In discussing the role of the media in conflict management, John Langlois cited in YII & Parajon (2007) framed the discussion within four parameters. He firstly, asked how the media contribute to or dampens potential conflict situation, and whether the media play a role in setting agenda for potential third party interveners. The group was also asked to ponder the differences between local media and the international media in reporting on conflict events. They noted that the group was prompted to think about the degree to which media are not root cause of conflict itself.

"International media sources such as the BBC, CNN, al Arabiya, and al Jazeera have global reach, and as such have an 'agenda setting effect.' This effect, as Steven Livingston explained, revolves around the ideological components of political disagreements, and more specifically the way key actors in conflict seek to manipulate public perceptions of the disagreement. That is actors in any conflict will seek to either minimise or exaggerate the conflict, depending upon their relative position of power. Weak actors will want to 'socialise' the conflict—that is, to enlist allies in their cause against a greater power and to increase the perception of suffering. Actors in positions of dominance seek to 'privatise' the conflict and limit attention to or awareness of the conflict. Those who are weak will seek to draw media coverage to the conflict while those who have power will seek to minimise the extent of the problems," (Ibid).

They are of the view that whereas international media giants are juggernauts in the policy-setting arena, local media play a different role in conflict prevention. Often, local media can contribute to peace merely by restoring levels of trust and self-worth in a population on the brink of or emerging form of violence. George Papagiannis' work in Chad speaks of the ability of the local media to give voice to those who were previously silenced by conflict. Papagiannis shared his impression of running radio stations in refugee camps in Chad. "Genocide is about silencing a people. So when you give someone a microphone and ask them to tell you something, it is like giving something back."

Papagiannis showed the value of the media in building community, Kemal Kurspahic drew upon his experience in the Balkans to emphasise that the media can just as easily have a deleterious effect and cause an escalation of violence and hate speech. According to Kurspahic account, the media's action in the Balkans is a prime example of how the media can be a source of antagonism and an instigator of conflict rather than a source for peace. Each side (Serbian and Croatian) propagated an "us versus them" mentality among their respective populations to a point of inventing crimes in addition to fanning the flames of ethnic tensions, the media was also guilty of obstructing peace-making efforts by failing to objectively present views of the minority.

YII and Parajon (2007) noted that the media can give voice to those who are advocating tolerance, peace, and negotiation. In Belgrade, those who opposed the war were signalled out as traitors. Had their voices been heard, others might have been inspired to non-violent means of resistance and channels for negotiation could have opened before violence ensued.

Although conflict is seen by many scholars as majorly, a disagreement resulting from a breach in communication, it is also worthy of note that the way and manner as well as the content of certain communicated information could trigger conflicts in a society. For instance, the 2002 newspaper comment involving the Islamic Pro- phet Muhammad which sparked major religious riots and caused a fatwa to be issued on the author, Isioma Nkemdilim Nkiruka Daniel.

On November 16, 2002, Isioma wrote a piece on Miss World beauty pageant that was to be held in Nigeria later that year. Reacting to opposing views about the contest, she remarked that, "the Muslims thought it was immoral to bring 92 women to Nigeria and ask them to revel in vanity. What would Muhammad think? In all honesty, he would probably have chosen a wife from one of them."

This publication triggered violent religious riots that left more than 200 dead and 1000 injured, while 11,000 people were rendered homeless. Ten days after, an Islamist government of Zamfara State, issued a fatwa against Isioma Daniel. This publication, undoubtedly generated ripples that unsettled the country.

Similarly, a serious sectarian violence was sparked in 2006 following cartoons first printed in September by a Danish newspaper and reprinted in European media and later other countries.

The caricatures which angered some Muslim extremist saw some youths in Nigerian northern city of Potiskum armed with machetes and clubs, attacking shops belonging mostly to Christians and burning five churches. The violence reportedly followed a weekend protest over the publication in Europe of controversial cartoons of the Muslim Prophet Muhammad that enraged Muslims worldwide. The killings and destruction of property was fully reported in both the print and electronic media. These reports disclosed the killings of some southerners in the northern part of Nigeria and triggered the retaliation of the southerners. It was reported that about 127 people were killed at the north while 80 died in the south-eastern city of Onitsha. An eye witness (a journalist), had told this researcher that while some of the northerners in Onitsha were burnt to ashes, brutalised, and slaughtered, others ran into the River Niger and those who could swim survived while others drowned.

It would be recalled that the incident made the Hausa community in Onitsha to shift their base and market to its present location at Asaba, Delta State.

It could rightly or wrongly be said that the news of the killings and destruction of property in the north would not have been heard in the southern part of the country and the multiple killings would have been averted. To this effect, some proponents of the conflict management have suggested that the mass media should suppress or under report some issues which are likely to generate ripples in parts of the country. That is, the media should, for public good, suppress some facts as well as keeping blind eyes to others (subjective/ emotional reasoning). It is unarguable that a media report of, "300 Nigerians or southerners killed in any part of Nigeria" would trigger the wrath and retaliation that could lead to war. This explains why some conflict management scholars advocate a play down on such reports by adopting the framing theory by framing the story in a manner that would not incite the public or generate further crisis. The use of number, especially when very large, is also discouraged by conflict management experts.

However, Baran and Davis (2009) state that framing theory challenges a long accepted and cherished tenet of journalists—the notion that news stories can or should be objective. Overtime, some scholars have shifted grounds to argue that objectivity is not realisable in journalism as man is naturally subjective due to his emotions. These scholars also argue that news angle and dictions are subjected to the writer hence the impossibility of objectivity. This dominating subjective position which the media have assume informs (YII & Parajon, 2007) , to note that media, and the way in which they select material to report, are simply not a reliable catalyst for policy change and that the international community would do well to recognise the danger of calibrating its responses to the substance and timing of the information it receives from the media reports.

It should be stated here that proponents of the above argument of subjectivity probably do not have a full understanding of the objectivity concept and tenets. This explains why Dominick (2011), stressed that Objectivity simply means that the reporter tries to transmit the news untainted by conscious bias and without personal comment or coloration.

Although Dominick agrees that complete and total objectivity is not possible because the process of reporting itself requires countless judgement, each influenced in some way by the reporters value system, but he emphasised that journalists have traditionally respected the truth, refused to distort facts deliberately, and consciously detached themselves as much as possible from what they were reporting. Similarly, C.P. Scott, a famous editor of Guardian (Britain) stressed on factual reporting in compliance with the objectivity principle. To celebrate the centenary of the Guardian and his 50thanniversary as editor, C. P. Scott wrote "A Hundred Years" in 1921. The essay's famous sentence "comment is free, but facts are sacred" has endured as the ultimate statement of value for a free press and continues to underpin the traditions of the Guardian newspaper today.

Therefore, journalists as well as newspaper or media organisations should endeavour to separate facts from comments as the objectivity tenet entails facts, accuracy, truth, and balance. In the words of Hasan (2013) , journalists who hold unto objectivity should endeavour to separate facts from opinion, while also treating opinion as relevant.

In whole, YII and Parajon (2007) summarised the role of the media in conflict management into three by saying that that:

- International media have the potential to influence governments and international organisations, and as such can have an agenda-setting effect. These reports, however, are not always the most accurate reflection of the relative severity and risk of a particular conflict.
- Donors that are interested in conflict prevention and sustaining stability should support local media. Local media often yield non-tangible results in war-torn communities, such as increased levels of trust, increase hope in the future of the country, and the ability to contribute to a peaceful society.
- Guarantees regarding the media and freedom of the press—as well as efforts to promote professional, objective, unbiased reporting—should be an integral part of any successful peace agreement.

METHODS

This study employs the documentary or historical survey method in the collection of data. This is a method where data are collected through books, journals, documents and the internet.

DISCUSSION OF FINDINGS

Here, the researchers answered the questions raised in the study by discussing the findings gathered in the course of the study. The questions are analysed sequentially.

Is There Media Objectivity?

Using the method stated above, it was discovered that there is longstanding and cherished principle of media objectivity which still forms the bases of good journalism practice. Although some scholars and practitioners tend to ignore it, that does not undermine its existence or its inevitability in good and professional practice of journalism.

How Do the Media Manage Conflict?

Media are naturally attracted to conflict because conflict situations provide the media with a ready source of raw materials used by them for the production of news stories and documentaries for their target audience, (Udomisor, 2013) . Put differently, Botes (1996) cited in Udomisor (2013) notes that conflict is the bread and butter of journalism because it is the source of sensation, which sells for the media. This probably explains why the mass media blow seemingly innocuous event and issues out of proportion thereby precipitating and igniting crisis all in an effort to make commercial success of their publication or station. There are criticism that the mass media are sometimes used to fight individuals or group battle by rich and powerful people, and the sometimes mislead public through hasty publication due to inadequate research and impatience.

In attempt to spell out the roles of the media in conflict situation, Botes presents five posers which are:

1) How should those involved in public communication respond to potential and actual conflict?

2) What roles should journalist play in covering conflict?

3) Should professional journalist merely report, comment on or interpret conflict or should they be actors in the resolution and particularly the prevention of conflict?

4) What are the moral and social responsibilities of journalists involved in reporting conflict situations?

5) Should a journalist who covers conflict play a role in their mediation and resolution?

In an effort to resolve these posers, Cousins (1996) in Udomisor (2013) explains that we have problem in distinguishing what is management problem from dispute and conflict, and it is equally very problematic in separating problem of competing interests from problem deeply rooted in the questions of culture and identity that may be at stake.

The media have over the years involved in the management of conflict due to the central role which they play in the socio-economic development of every society. They have however, employed different ways of carrying out this task including but not limited to:

- Framing: this involves the controlling or shaping of news in a pattern that will not incite others into expanded or multiple conflicts. This is sometimes achieved through either a play down on certain information, choice of words or a slant toward a safe ground that will neither aggravate nor incite conflicting parties into crises or war.
- Provision of platform through which various options are considered for the resolution of conflict.

How Can the Media Manage Conflict in the Face of Objectivity Principle?

While it is expected that the mass media should be involved in conflict management, their efforts or attempt to manage conflict should not negate the long standing and cherished principle of journalism—objectivity. This can be achieved through the following ways:

- Proactive conflict management: in recent past, some conflict management experts have observed with dismay that organisations pay less attention to potential conflict situations but relaxed till the conflict snowballed into crisis. Proactive management approach entails the act of carefully thinking ahead as well as employing all necessary strategies to ensure that all potential conflict situation and impending conflict are nipped in the bud. This has been seen as the best approach to all forms or types of management, though it might not always be successful but it gives no scar to an organisation and the organisation continues to luxuriate in an enviable reputation.
- Investigative journalism: As earlier state, most conflicts are as a result of a lack of effective communication, lack of vital and accurate information as well as a breach in communication. These therefore, make investigative journalism a very important part of effective conflict management.Hasan (2013: p. 235) notes that investigative journalism is a kind of journalism in which reporters deeply investigate a topic of interest, often involving crime, political corruption, or some other scandal. "investigative and interpretative reporting is not necessarily getting 'scoops' and sensationalising them but rather 'situation reporting' in place of event or personality reporting."
- Peace journalism: This is activist news writing engaged to promote

peace. In practice, peace journalism is a linguistic and action orientation that frames stories to encourage conflict analysis and a non-violent response. It pursues these goals—focusing on conflict resolution, complex truths, non-elite actors affected by war, and potential solutions. A Norwegian Sociologist, Galtung Johan reportedly proposed the idea of peace journalism for journalists to follow when covering war and conflict. Galtung stressed that Peace journalism is contrary to a typical war journalism that focuses on violence, propaganda, elite actors, and victory, emphasising the current conflict while ignoring the causes or outcomes.

- Gate keeping: One important characteristic of the mass media organisation is the presence of gatekeepers. The gatekeepers control the nature and content of information that gets to the public domain. Hasan (2013) observes that the enormous scope of mass communication demands some control over the selection and editing of the messages that are constantly transmitted to the mass audience. Whether done by individuals or organisations, gate keeping involves setting certain standards and limitations that serve as guidelines for both content development and delivery of a mass communication message. An effective gate keeping would have guarded against the religious riots that resulted from Isioma's comment as well as that of the Danish cartoon.
- Enlightenment: This is another important approach to a good conflict management. The media can engage in enlightenment programmes or publications that will highlight the interest of each of the conflicting parties. This approach gets the public informed on the danger of conflict, the impact or number of lives which the conflict had caused and the need for the parties to come to a negotiation table.
- Agenda setting: This is where the mass media wield lots of influence on the public. Whether through investigation, proactive management strategy, gate keeping, peace journalism or enlightenment, the media has the ability to shape the public opinion hence they should seize this opportunity to manage conflict in the society. This can be achieved through news stories, features and opinion articles, editorials, comments and cartons as well as other publications and programmes as pertains to the different types of the media.

CONCLUSION

This study has taken a look at media objectivity, conflict and conflict management as well as the role of the media in conflict management. It also reviewed some conflict situations that occurred in Nigeria in 2002 and in 2006, looking at the causes, the role played by the media and how they would have been avoided through an effective gate keeping function. It was found that the media are naturally attracted to conflict and some journalists/ media organisations use their position to fight individual or group battle while others blow some seemingly innocuous issues out of proportion thereby generating conflict in the society. It was also noted that the media sometimes play down, frame or slant some facts to avoid escalation of conflict but these negate the principle of objectivity. Media practices which undermine the ethical principles of journalism—objectivity—were analysed and better approaches to conflict management which does not negate the ethical code advocated. This study submits that the media can better manage conflict without breaching the cherished tenet of journalism through gate keeping, peace journalism, investigative journalism, and proactive conflict management approaches among others.

Recommendations

Conflict management has recently become an integral part of mass communication organisations owing to their centrality in the society. While it is imperative for the media to involve in conflict management, the longstanding and cherished principle of journalism—objectivity—must not be negated. It is therefore recommended that the media can involve in conflict management through numerous ways including:

- Investigative journalism,
- Peace journalism,
- Proactive conflict management approach,
- Gate keeping,
- Agenda setting for peaceful co-existence,
- Enlightenment of conflicting parties on the intricacies of the conflict in question.
- A journalist or/and media organisation should completely avoid a story which he is not independent of. That is a story which his interest is involved either directly or indirectly.
- In all, objective and responsible journalism should not be sacrifice at the altar of scoops to make good and sensational headlines that would sell the paper or station.
- The media should at all times value, uphold and apply objectivity in all its reportage, by separating facts from comments, for effective

conflict management. The media should also embrace proactive conflict management approach, peace journalism, investigative journalism and agenda setting for peaceful resolution of conflicts.

REFERENCES

1. Akpan, N. (2005) . Conflicts in Nigeria's Niger Delta: Issues on Response and Management. International Journal of Social Sciences, 4, 161-175.
2. Baran, S. J. (2004). Introduction to Mass Communication; Media Literacy and Culture. New York, NY: McGraw-Hillin.
3. Baran, S., & Davis, D. (2009). Mass Communication Theory: Foundation, Ferment, and Future (5th ed.). Boston, MA: Wadsworth Cengage Learning.
4. Dominick, J. (2011). The Dynamics of Mass Communication. Media in Transition (11th ed.). New York, NY: McGraw Hill.
5. Elliot, A., Timothy, W., & Robin, A. (2004). Media & Research Update: Social Psychology. Upper Saddle River, NJ: Pearson Education Inc.
6. Hasan, S. (2013). Mass Communication: Principles and Concepts (2nd ed.). New Delhi, Delhi: CBS Publishers & Distributors Pvt Ltd.
7. Ibrahim, G. (2002). Conflict in Democracies. In U. A. Pate (Ed.), Introduction to Conflict Reporting in Nigeria (pp. 18-29). Lagos: Frankad Publishers.
8. McQuail, D. (2005). Mass Communication Theory. London: Sage Publications.
9. Ofor, C. (2004). Nigerian Press: Review, Trends and Prospects. Port-Harcourt, Rivers State: Penpower Communications.
10. Owens-Ibie, N. (2002). Socio-Cultural Considerations in Conflict Reporting in Nigeria. In U. A. Pate (Ed.), Introduction to Conflict Reporting in Nnigeria (pp. 30-44). Lagos: Frankad Publishers.
11. Udomisor, I. (2002). Problems and Prospects of Reporting Conflict in a Democracy: The Editors Challenge. In U. A. Pate (Ed.), Introduction to Conflict Reporting in Nnigeria (pp. 84-98). Lagos: Frankad Publishers.
12. Udomisor, I. (2013). Media as a Party in Conflict, Conflict Management and Resolution: The Case of South Africa. International Journal of Management Sciences, 1, 245-253.
13. YII, B., & Parajon, C. (2007). The Role of the Media in Conflict. Washington DC.http://www.youtube.com/user/usinstituteofpeace

Chapter 2

POLITICAL JOURNALISM UNDER PRESSURE

Günther Pallaver[1] / Theo Hug[2]

[1]Innsbruck School of Political Science and Sociology University of Innsbruck

[2]Faculty of Education, Faculty Member University of Innsbruck

ABSTRACT

Dieser Beitrag befasst sich mit der zunehmenden Tendenz politischer Eliten, auf die journalistische Berichterstattung und den politischen Journalismus Einfluss zu nehmen. Dabei wird gezeigt, inwieweit dadurch Handlungsspielräume im politischen Journalismus eingeschränkt werden. Untersucht werden insgesamt vier Länder, nämlich die USA, die Bundesrepublik Deutschland, Österreich und Italien. Beim diesem Vergleich stellt sich die Frage nach der Bedeutung struktureller Unterschiede angesichts der verschiedenen politischen Systeme in den untersuchten Ländern (z. B. präsidentielles vs. parlamentarische Systeme, parteien- vs. medienzentrierte Systeme). Abschließend geht es um Überlegungen zu unterschiedlichen privatrechtlich organisierten oder dualen Mediensystemen im Zusammenhang strategischer Einflussnahmen und Abwehrmaßnahmen.

In this paper the proposition to be tested is whether the political elites' attempt to exert influence on day-to-day news coverage and thus on political journalism is increasing and whether as a result political journalism's autonomous leeway is continually diminishing. The countries examined are the United States, Germany, Austria and Italy. In this context the question whether there are structural differences due to the diverse political systems of the countries under consideration (presidential vs. parliamentary systems; systems centred more on parties vs. systems centred more on the media) will also be investigated. Last but not least, the role of different media systems will be considered, too (media under private law, dual systems including the Italian version).

INTRODUCTION

Over the past decades political journalism has undergone a considerable transformative process. Not only does this process operate sensitively at the crossroads of the political communication system but it also moves between the news public and the political elites – both of whom have different demands on political journalism – as well as between publishers and editors-in-chief who demand specific contributions from their journalists in order to compete effectively with other media (Blumler & Gurevitch, 1995; Conboy, 2004; Deuze, 2005).[1]

In addition, production factors such as time and resources are running short, the autonomous leeway in the media itself is narrowing, and the pressure from news management, event marketing and spin control is increasing (Bennet & Livingston, 2003). These results go well together with the results of the strategy reports on important developments in the newspaper industry globally which have been published by the World Association of Newspapers (WAN) in 2006. [2] These six strategy reports from the Shaping the Future of the Newspaper project deal with new revenue models, outsourcing, digital classifieds, new editorial concepts, advertising science and new pricing strategies, all acting as elements of regional, national and transnational network strategies. For example, the report on "New Editorial Concepts" (2006) examines several trends that are influencing newsrooms everywhere: The explosion of participative journalism, or community-generated content; The rise of audience research by media companies to learn new patterns of media usage; The proliferation of personalized news delivered online and on mobile devices; The reorganization of newsrooms optimized for audience focus; The development of new forms of storytelling geared toward new audiences and new channels; The growth of audience-focused news judgment and multimedia news judgment.

These trends affect the modes in which journalists report the news in various ways. And even if we agree that the precarious labor situation also opens up new markets and chances for journalists, it becomes obvious that especially political journalists are subject to constant pressure (Plasser, Lengauer, & Meixner, 2004).

The processes of structural transformation have led to a situation in which the editorial (political) outlook of political elites has changed. There is now also an ever increasing marked shift from decisional policies to presentational ones (Sarcinelli, 2009).

These processes of transformation and trends in media-centered democracies are discussed in various ways in academia: critical journalism vs. PR journalism, cooperative vs. conflictive journalism, production teams comprising politics, PR and journalism, meta-journalism, etc. (cf. Donsbach, 2008). At the same time, journalism has a variety of methods for reacting to the increasing influence exerted by politics (Achtner, 1996; Jarren & Donges, 2002; Swanson, 2003; Esser, Reinemann & Fan, 2001).

In this discussion, methods of *strategic influence* stand opposite methods of *strategic defense measures*: On the one hand are strategies applied by political elites to influence journalistic reporting for their own purposes. On the other hand are counterstrategies[3] applied in journalism to resist this exertion of influence. The study also requires a look at *institutional* or *governmental influences*.

This means political-regulatory measures which allow the political elites to narrow the journalistic scope for action. Such measures have different justifications (e.g. public safety) and are put in various concrete forms (e.g. laws). Ultimately they represent the selective restriction of journalistic work, thus the limitation of journalistic autonomy and the freedom of the press.

The following remarks examine this subject on the basis of isolated cases and advance the view that media-centered democracies have a creeping tendency to restrict the autonomy of journalists via the exertion of governmental-institutional influence. The study looks at three European countries, namely Italy, Austria and Germany, and at the United States.

Models for the relationship between politics and media, and basic political-institutional conditions

Hallin and Mancini (2008) differentiate three models for the relationship between politics and media in western media democracies and assign the analyzed countries to the three categories. In their view, the*Northern European or Democratic Corporatist Model* includes Austria, Germany, Switzerland, Belgium, the Netherlands, Denmark, Finland, Sweden and Norway. The *Mediterranean or Polarized Pluralist Model*applies to Italy, France, Greece, Portugal and Spain. The *North Atlantic or Liberal Model* covers the United States, Canada, Great Britain and Ireland.

The two authors compare these countries within the framework of their three models regarding the characteristics of their political and media systems and base their comparison on four criteria: Development of the communication market in special consideration of the dissemination degree of print media; Political parallelism, i.e. the intensity and type of relation between media and political parties in view of the most significant social fault lines; Development of journalistic professionalism; Intensity and type of state intervention in the communication system (Hallin & Mancini 2008, p. 23; cf. also Pfetsch

& Maurer, 2008). In the *Mediterranean or Polarized Pluralist Model,* the media system is characterized by a low reach of print media, a strong focus on electronic media, a high degree of political parallelism resulting from the management of public television companies by parliament or government, weak journalistic professionalization and instrumentalization, and strong intervention by the state. The political system is marked by polarized pluralism, a high significance of the parties, strong state influence on the economy, and a distinct welfare state.

In regard to the media system, the *Northern European or Democratic Corporatist Model* shows above all a high reach of print media, a decrease of political parallelism with increasing media autonomy, high professionalization of journalists, and strong state influence on the media system while the freedom of the press is protected. The political system is moderately pluralistic and strongly resembles concordance democracy. Moreover, it is marked by a consistent welfare state including tendencies toward the political regulation of economic activities.

The media system in the *North Atlantic or Liberal Model* is based on an average reach of the press, a strong focus on television, a highly distinctive autonomy of professional informational journalism, as well as commercial organization and deregulation. The political system in this model is characterized by moderate pluralism, competitive democracy, strong liberalism with little state influence on the economy, and a poorly developed welfare state (Hallin & Mancini 2008, pp. 62-63).

Before our analysis, we want to briefly outline two striking characteristics of the studied countries: the role of television as the most important source of information, and the political system.

In the countries we reviewed, there is a trend toward the commercialization of the media but with significant differences (cf. Thomaß, 2007). While the market in the United States is commercial and deregulated, and public television plays only a marginal role, public broadcasting is still in the lead in Europe, even though its market share is declining. In spite of all the differences among the European countries studied here, the dual system is prevalent.

As for political parallelism, Italy shows the closest relationship between politics and television (politics-over-broadcasting system), while in the United States we find the greatest distance (professional model of broadcasting governance). Germany and Austria lie in the middle (politics-in-broadcasting system; cf. Hallin & Mancini, 2008).

Differences also prevail on the level of political, party and voting systems. The United States represents the prototype of a presidential system with a two-party system. Italy, Germany and Austria are, regardless of the differences, still party-centered parliamentary systems which belong to the category of moderate pluralism (Pelinka & Rosenberger, 2007; Schmidt, 2007). In the past, Italy was considered polarized (Sartori, 1976), but today it is on the road from a fragmentedly bipolar to a moderately pluralistic party system (Chiaramonte & Di Virgilio, 2006).

In the United States, elections are based on a relative majority voting system that centers on the candidates. The European countries predominantly have party-centered proportional representation systems in different variations (barring clauses, majority bonus, direct votes, etc.).

In regard to its media system, the state can be analyzed in his roles as owner, regulating actor, and financier. This comparative study focuses on the state as regulator while regarding its role as owner whenever it seems necessary in order to explain regulatory aspects.

THE ROLE OF THE STATE AND ITS POLITICAL INFLU-ENCE ON JOURNALISM

a. Federal Republic of Germany

According to Hallin and Mancini (2008), partly because of the negative experiences coming out of National Socialism, Germany is among those countries characterized by quite articulate legislation in support of the freedom of the press, but at the same time also by a relatively high level of media regulation. For instance, there are specific rules against neo-Nazi propaganda and racial hatred, concerning the access of parties to public radio and television stations during election campaigns, etc. The public service broadcasters are controlled by the respective federal states, which is meant to strengthen the external pluralism. The board of directors is usually assembled in a politically pluralistic way in conjunction with socially relevant groups (e.g. unions, churches). This applies not only to the public service broadcasters but also to the majority of private-commercial companies. However, the state played a highly dominant part up until the 1980s and 1990s. The constitutional court has repeatedly intervened in favor of media independence and against excessive political infringement and influence on the part of the states and the federation (Hallin & Manici, 2008, pp. 144-154; cf. also Kopper & Mancini, 2003, pp. 109-130).

The state influence on the freedom of the press has increased with the onset of the 21st century in the context of the fight against international terrorism. The culmination of this development was the passage of the "Law on the

Defense against the Dangers of International Terrorism" (Anti-Terror Law), which became effective on January 1, 2009. Among other things, this law allows members of the Federal Criminal Police Office (BKA) to encroach on the professional secrecy of doctors, lawyers and journalists. Their telephones may be tapped, bugging devices and video surveillance installed in the homes of suspects, and their private computers spied on by means of Trojan viruses which are sent via e-mail or the internet. To be sure, members of the BKA need authorization by a judge and by the BKA president, but in urgent cases this requirement is waived. This part of the legislation caused major conflict among the German parties.

The law thus permits a multitude of secret investigative measures even in the absence of concrete grounds for suspicion for the purpose of preventing (terrorist) crimes. An aggravating factor is that the legal provisions also apply to occupational groups whose confidentiality is protected in the code of criminal procedure by the right to refuse to give evidence. This means that doctors do not have to testify against their patients, nor lawyers against their clients, nor journalists against their informants. This right is eroded by the new law (Prantl, 2009).

The so-called BKA Act is the preliminary peak of German security policy, which began with the measures against the Red Army Faction (RAF) and found its continuation in the legislation adopted after the attacks of September 11. The surveillance options were gradually expanded, the respective methods refined, and the number of offenses which according to the law permit the installation of bugging devices (for instance in the editorial offices of newspapers) increased. German journalists regard the BKA Act as an attack on the freedom of the press as protected by Germany's Basic Law because it violates the professional secrecy of journalists and results in the intimidation of investigative journalism (cf. Usi, 2008; Reporter ohne Grenzen, 2008).

A decision by the federal constitutional court from 2003 jeopardizes investigative journalism as well. It establishes that law enforcement agencies are entitled to monitor the telephone connections of journalists when tracking criminal actions "of considerable importance," with the latter phrase remaining undefined. Even though in individual cases the investigating judge needs to deliberate about whether to give precedence to the freedom of the press or the demands of law enforcement, this decision is a sign of the gradual tendency to restrict the protection of sources and thus also the freedom of the press (Reporter ohne Grenzen, 2003). On the other hand, in 2003 the regional court in Braunschweig, in utter contrast to the federal constitutional court, declared the tapping of journalists' phones unlawful.

The erosion of a number of rights which protect the work of journalists started even before the BKA Act. In 2006 the Freedom of Information Act came into effect. It gives each citizen the right to inspect the work of public authorities, thus facilitating journalistic research. However, even though this consolidated the freedom of the press, several individual cases have shown this freedom to be undermined. Even a year earlier there had been instances where editorial offices were searched and journalists spied on by the Federal Intelligence Service BND.

The Cicero affair is considered to be the most blatant case in point since the Spiegel affair in 1962. In the fall of 2005, officers of the Federal Criminal Police Office BKA searched the apartment of a journalist and confiscated files, tapes, computers and address directories. The reason for the search: In his portrait about the terrorist Abu Musab al-Zarqawi, the journalist had quoted from a secret BKA dossier and published information about al-Zarqawi's connections to Iran. The investigating officials justified their actions by claiming the journalist was "aiding and abetting the betrayal of secrets," even though the authorities did not find any incriminating documents (Metz, 2006).

Between 1987 and 2000, Germany saw 150 cases of surveillance, searching and confiscation in regard to journalists. Not a single journalist was proven to have committed a criminal action. In the opinion of journalist associations, this tendency has increased over the past years, which is why they have repeatedly called for strengthening the protection of information (Metz, 2006).

In 2007, the federal constitutional court decided in favor of the magazine Cicero and ruled the policy of search and confiscation in the course of preliminary investigations against members of the press unconstitutional if it serves solely or predominantly the purpose of obtaining the identity of informants. The decision was regarded as boosting the freedom of the press, though journalists in Germany can still incur a penalty for the publication of secret documents if the investigating judge "sees positive evidence for the existence of the publication of a secret that was intended by the secret carrier and which the journalist can aid and abet." The German press council sees an urgent need for action in this regard (Spoo, 2008, pp. 87-88).

Apart from the Cicero affair, the year 2006 brought more cases where the BND monitored e-mail communications (of the magazines *Spiegel* and *Stern*, the television channel ZDF, and the *Financial Times Deutschland*). The observations were primarily aimed at journalists who had investigated the activities of the intelligence service (Reporters without borders, 2007).

Apart from legal regulations and, to some extent, the decisions of the federal constitutional court, the "war against terror" has brought about increased political pressure on critical journalists. To oppose critical coverage on the war in former Yugoslavia, for example, political pressure on a journalist working for the ARD was so strong that, before long, he apologized for his critical analyses (Spoo, 2002, pp. 99-105). The same kind of pressure was exerted on the confirmation of the editor-in-chief at the ZDF who took a critical and independent line (Ulrich, 2009).

b. Austria

Like Germany, Austria is among those countries within the *Northern European or Democratic Corporatist Model* in which the media are more decidedly regulated. This pertains not only to issues of the media system such as the strong presence of the state in public service broadcasting, the legal liberalization of the media market and the promotion of cross-media concentration (Kaltenbrunner& Fallend 2006, p. 333), but also to the access of political parties to public media and generally the rules concerning campaign practices in the media context.

The Austrian Broadcasting Corporation ORF, the national public service broadcaster, still holds a special position in Austria, after having had a monopoly in the area of electronic media for decades. Only Austria's looming conviction by the European Court of Human Rights in the early 1990s led to the passage of the Regional Radio Act in 1993 and the Cable and Satellite Broadcasting Act in 1997, which ended the television monopoly. Nevertheless, the ORF was able to maintain its virtual monopoly in the area of political information services (Plasser & Ulram, 2004, p. 63). Additional characteristics are the high press concentration (compared to other European countries) and the above-average market dominance of one daily newspaper (Seethaler & Melischek, 2006).

Like the other member countries, Austria is forced to implement within its territory the guidelines of the European Union regarding the fight against terrorism. On the basis of these requirements, Austria has begun the process of reforming its security police law, which enables the police to monitor e-mail and telephone communications and/or retain personal data. As a result of a simple police inquiry, internet and telephone providers are thus obliged to release private data and IP addresses of their clients without awaiting a judge's decision. In contrast to Germany, these legislative measures have not caused a major debate about the potential restriction of the freedom of the press (Reporter ohne Grenzen, 2009).

The most intense discussion was about the political influence on the public service broadcaster ORF, which, also because of being anchored in the individual provinces, is largely considered to be a political "Proporzrundfunk," i.e. a broadcaster based on proportional political representation, which is illustrated by its supervisory board, called the "Stiftungsrat." Among other things, this panel appoints all high officials, approves the budget and controls the financial conduct. Of the thirty-five members, fifteen are appointed by the federal government, six of which in consideration of the proportional strength of the political parties represented in parliament. Furthermore, each province nominates a representative (for a total of nine), six members are chosen by the Viewers' and Listeners' Council, five by the ORF's Workers' Council (ORF-Kundendienst, 2009).

During the coalition governments between the conservative People's Party (ÖVP) and the right-wing populist Freedom Party (FPÖ, later BZÖ) between 2000 and 2007, the political influence on the ORF became enormous. Already in 2001, journalists at the ORF referred to the exertion of pressure and attempts at intimidation and interference, and they warned against the loss of independence of the ORF. Political interventions limited the interior pluralism at the ORF, achieved the broadcasting of self-serving courtesy shows and thus violated journalistic standards in a blatant manner.

In 2001, Reporters without Borders criticized the increasing censorship and self-censorship and the constraints on the freedom of the press in Austria. In 2006, the criticism by ORF journalists (Wolf, 2006) resulted in the formation of the "SOS-ORF" initiative, a citizens' group attempting to change the political circumstances and demanding the ORF comply with its public service mandate (derFreiRaum, 2006).

Against the will of the governing majority, the ORF management was replaced in 2006, leading to a significant decline in political pressure on the editorial staff (Wolf 2007). However, the governing parties left nothing undone to influence the editorial line by means of the politically appointed supervisory board (SOS-ORF, 2007).

Under the new 2008 SPÖ/ÖVP coalition government, the recently gained independence again became more of a target for regulation (Wolf, 2008). In view of the discussion about a new "ORF law," journalists at the ORF strongly rejected all attempts at using the broadcaster's current financial crisis as a reason to subject it to increased party control (APA, 2009). They demanded political independence (less influence by government and parties, no direct or indirect decisional authority for the federal chancellor, objective evidence of qualification for executives), economic independence and high-quality programming (SOS ORF, 2009).

c. Italy

In the countries attributed to the *Mediterranean or Polarized Pluralist Model,* the state has always had an important role, which is the consequence of a certain authoritarian political culture and, at the same time, the democratic tradition of an existing welfare state (cf. Kopper & Mancini, 2003, pp. 93-108). And yet, state control sometimes lags behind this ambition because the financial means and political consensus are often lacking (cf. Hallin & Mancini 2008, p. 107). In Italy, the media are considered to be social institutions which can be regulated for the purpose of public interest. This applies in particular to political coverage and the rules during election campaigns (e.g. *par conditio,* release of survey results, etc.; cf. Bettinelli, 1995; Cuperlo, 2004).

The Italian print media have always been characterized by their political affiliations. The public service broadcaster RAI has all along been subjected to proportional political representation and heavy political influence. Deregulation only came as of 1976, after the Italian constitutional court ended the RAI's national monopoly. Until 1990, the "wild" years prevailed due to the absence of laws regulating commercial television broadcasters (Achtner, 1996).

In those licentious times, the Italian broadcasting system and its advertising market were revolutionized. This led to the rise of Silvio Berlusconi, who, thanks to his relations to Prime Minister Bettino Craxi (1983-1986), seized the opportunity to legally protect and expand his market-dominant position (Mazzoleni & Vigevani, 2005, p. 193). The foundation of his personal party, Forza Italia, in 1994, based on his business ventures, as well as his meteoric political rise rested solely on his media empire.

The current television market has two main players, the state-owned RAI with three national TV channels, and Berlusconi's private media company, Mediaset, with three national networks as well (and additional print media). Due to the duopolistic system, the two basically divide the advertising market among themselves. Other television providers like channel La 7 are only marginally important.

The European Parliament, the European Council and other international institutions which advocate pluralism and freedom of information have responded with a series of warnings and calls urging Italy to resolve the anomaly represented by its media system. The European Council pointed out the negative effects of the "concentration of political, commercial and media power in Italy in the hands of one person," called attention to shortcomings in the independence of public service television, and showed concern about the freedom and pluralism of media in Italy (Mazzoleni & Vigevani, 2005, p. 195).

The Berlusconi government reacted by passing legislation concerning the conflict of interest which regulated everything but Berlusconi's conflict of interest. Although the prime minister ceded the management of his empire to other family members, the independence of the editorial offices at his television broadcasters and print media is not guaranteed as long as he remains the principal stockholder of Fininvest and thus of Mediaset.

As prime minister, Berlusconi has broadened his influence on public television while still informally in control of his own television media (Mazzoleni, 2003). Following his request, several critical journalists (Enzo Biagi, Michele Santoro, Marco Travaglio) were laid off or marginalized by the RAI. Massive attacks and intimidations directed against critical journalists are commonplace under the Berlusconi government and affect not just the RAI but also print media (Ulrich, 2009a, p. 1).

The editor-in-chief of the *Corriere della Sera*, the most influential Italian daily paper, had to resign in 2003 because of his critical reporting on Berlusconi's trials. Italian journalists continue to be a preferred target of criminal charges, which compromises their criticism of the government's performance. And when it is not possible to control the flow of information or buy the media, Berlusconi as the wealthiest person in Italy and his staff have at their disposal the information media, economic resources and vast number of lawyers it takes to muzzle inconvenient journalists (Lane, 2005, p. 207). That lesson also applies to star journalists working for Berlusconi's television companies (Mentana, 2009). In addition, the number of police inspections of editorial offices and private homes of journalists has sharply increased over the past years (Lane, 2005, p. 206).

Beside the severe attacks on journalists, the government influence has a massive impact on the reporting. Television broadcasters display anticipatory obedience and manipulate the news coverage to go with the prime minister's agenda. For instance, Italians watching the evening news saw Berlusconi address a full UN General Assembly. In reality, Berlusconi had talked in front of a sparse crowd, but the RAI had added archive footage (Giordano, 2003). Alternatively, news regarding the prime minister is simply suppressed when it is about his trials, his (sex) scandals, poor election results, or strikes at one of his television companies (Bongi, 2009, p. 3; Dipollina, 2009, p. 7). Furthermore, the distribution of airtime on Italian networks (with few exceptions) is highly asymmetrical, favoring the government and putting the opposition at a disadvantage (r.pol., 2009, p. 3). The protest and resignation of several members of the RAI board of directors in reaction to the political interventions by Berlusconi came to nothing.

During the center-right coalition governments (1994-1995; 2001-2006; since 2008), a whole range of measures was introduced to shape the media system in favor of Berlusconi's media. Among them is the so-called Gasparri Act which was passed in December 2003 in order to reorganize the Italian media system. Thereby Berlusconi bypassed antitrust regulations by the constitutional court which would have forced one of his channels to be broadcast via satellite. Moreover, the government provided Berlusconi with 130 million Euros in public money to subsidize consumer purchase of digital decoders which were distributed by Berlusconi's brother (Valentini, 2005, p. 18).

President Ciampi had sent the Gasparri bill back to parliament since he thought it did not guarantee the pluralism of information and impaired advertising in print media (De Marchis, 2003, p. 22). After minor modifications, the law came into effect in 2004, ensuring the unlimited expansion of Berlusconi's television companies on the advertising market as well as his economic involvement in the print media sector, which under the old regulations was possible only to a very limited degree (Cordero, 2004, p. 16). Above all, Berlusconi awards his TV networks with institutional advertising (Lopapa. 2009, p. 9).

The picture becomes even more complicated because the competences for controlling the RAI are divided up among a parliamentary control commission, the ministry of communication and the competition authority. Starting a few years ago, the regions have also been granted certain control functions. In spite of all this, the members of the RAI board of directors, the editors-in-chief, directors of programming and other important officials are nowadays designated in Berlusconi's home (De Marchis, 2009, p. 2; Bartocci, 2009, p. 2-3).

At the beginning of 2009, parliament was about to vote on a bill which journalists have called a "muzzle law." Since judicially approved wiretapping of Berlusconi's phone calls unveiled patronage, behind-the-door agreements, and political blueprints, the prime minister instructed the parliamentary majority to pass a law that would eliminate such legal options. Among other things, investigating judges are severely limited in their use of such methods (with the exception of investigations against the mafia), while journalists are prohibited to publish tapped conversations in their entirety or in summary form. The sentence for publishing such information anyway is up to thirty days in prison, which may be cumulated with a fine of up to 5,000 Euros. The publication of wiretap transcripts that have been ordered to be destroyed may now lead to a prison sentence between six and twelve months (D'Avanzo, 2009, p. 9).

In a mutual appeal to parliament by journalists and editors called "Duty to information – Right to knowledge," the FIEG (Federazione Italiana Editori

Giornali) and FNSI (Federazione Nazionale della Stampa Italiana) protested against the restriction of the right to reporting and the disproportionate penalties at the expense of journalists and editors (FIEG/FNSI, 2009). It is not only due to this law, soon to become effective, that Italy is identified as a country with significant democratic deficits, which are mainly attributed to the lack of both media pluralism and freedom of the press (Ginsborg, 2003). Not without good reason was Italy ranked 44th on the Press Freedom Index 2008 (Reporters without borders, 2008).

d. United States

In standard liberal democracies, the role of the state is rather limited compared to the role of the market and the private sector. The same logic applies to the development of the media in the *North Atlantic or Liberal Model*. Nevertheless, even in the United States the function of the state cannot be ignored, for example in regard to the transparency of ownership structures, cartel issues, press concentration, or the right of journalists to protect their confidential sources. The dominance of the private over the public sector is particularly evident in the American television market, which did not see the introduction of (to this day) weak public television until 1967. Nevertheless, beginning in the 1980s, the operating conditions for American television were increasingly regulated (license renewal, fairness doctrine, consideration of public interests, etc.), resulting in a trend toward neutral and pluralistic reporting. The 1990s brought a reversal of this regulative approach and, for instance, the granting of licenses as a mere formality, the abandonment of the fairness doctrine, and using the market logic as the only yardstick (Hallin & Mancini, 2008, pp. 204-206). And yet, the state has (informally) relatively strong influence on the media industry by determining its rules of operation. It is not by chance that there is a consistent flow of money from the media industry to political players (Lewis, 2000; Chomsky, 2006, p. 141).

The close relationship between media and state comes to the fore whenever national security issues are concerned. In the past, a result of the "culture of national security" was that politics and the media moved in lockstep to pursue the "national" interest even without formal regulations, and that in this context the political pressure on the media was occasionally stronger than, for instance, in European countries with a different political culture (Newton & Artingstall, 1994).

This (formal and informal) pressure on the media has significantly increased since legislation like the Use of Force Resolution (September 14, 2001) or the USA Patriot Act (Providing Appropriate Tools Required to Intercept and Obstruct Terrorism, October 26, 2001)[4] were passed in reaction to the attacks on the World Trade Center in New York and the Pentagon in Washington, D.C. on September 11, 2001 (Dadge, 2004). The new measures served the purpose of simplifying investigations by federal agencies in case of a terrorist threat, restricting civil rights under the pretext of national security. Among other things, the right of the FBI to wiretap conversations was broadened considerably. The responsible judge needs to be informed of the surveillance but at the same time must authorize it. Telephone and internet providers must disclose customer data (Patriot Act, 2001). In practice, this means that investigators may collect e-mail addresses and the date and time of e-mail communications of suspicious persons. Electronic communications are treated in the same way as telephone communications. The content and length of such communications may be recorded and used as evidence. When "electronic crimes" go through American lines, US authorities are entitled to take appropriate action at home and abroad. The FBI uses software called Magic Lantern to decode and decipher all protected data on individual computers and thus allows a look at the entire content of the "captured" devices. Another method called Carnivore intercepts e-mail and decodes its content, which does not require judicial authorization anymore. Since 2004, several federal courts have ruled unconstitutional those provisions of the USA Patriot Act which concern house searching and phone tapping without judicial order or initial grounds for suspicion.

Right from the beginning, the measures to fight terrorism resulted in partly voluntary, partly imposed restrictions on the freedom of the press. One example is the silent agreement among many media to avoid overly critical reporting on political actions such as the antiterror legislation, in keeping with the political culture of national security. The explicit cue was given by the executive branch when Condoleezza Rice, national security advisor under President Bush, convened the most important editors to remind them of their "responsibility" concerning information in times of crisis. Moreover, President Bush, with reference to national security, instructed his cabinet members in early October 2001 to stop passing on certain information to members of Congress, although it would have been vital for the latter in order to execute their mandate. Bush's action was prompted by the fear that some of the information might be leaked to the press (AG Friedensforschung, 2002). This new kind of reporting had a strong impact on public opinion and thus greatly facilitated the Iraq war, for example, because the population was provided with one-sided information. Regardless of that, President Bush's press secretary warned the press in a show on CNN: "You better watch what you say" („Sie passen besser auf, was Sie sagen“) (Vidal, 2004, p. 16). The intimidation of the media became the norm in the years after 2001, and journalists increasingly practiced self-censorship (Dennett, 2004, p. 32). Nevertheless, renowned daily papers adhered to investigative journalism and contributed to publicizing the abuse of power by authorities in the "war against terror" (cf. Werhan, 2008). Journalists who did not comply with the new security logic felt the blow of politics. Peter Arnett, famous star reporter for NBC News (the network is owned by General Electric, a military supplier) was fired after he had told on Baghdad television that the original US war plan had failed (Chomsky, 2006, p. 38). Measures of this kind aimed at domestic and foreign journalists (Ospina, 2009).

In the first year after the passage of the Patriot Act, the United States dropped in the ranking of Reporters without Borders to 17th place among 139 countries included in the list, even behind Costa Rica. The reason for this result was the imprisonment of several journalists for refusing to reveal their sources in court or allegedly violating security requirements implemented after September 11 (Kulick, 2002). Reporters without Borders viewed this as a threat to an important pillar of press freedom in the United States.

One of the most familiar among the many cases in which the freedom of the press was disregarded and journalists were imprisoned for contempt of court regarded Judith Miller of the prestigious *New York Times*, who was sentenced to prison because of her refusal to identify her confidential source. Reporters without Borders sparked a worldwide protest campaign and pointed out that the protection of sources is an important principle of journalism and that the current conditions would render investigative reporting like in the Watergate scandal impossible (ngo-online, 2005).

Miller had refused to disclose her informants for an explosive story about which official in the Bush administration had uncovered Valerie Plame, the wife of former US ambassador Joseph Wilson, as a CIA agent. Wilson had been a harsh critic of the president on the issue of the Iraq war. Journalist Matthew Cooper from *Time* magazine, who also faced imprisonment for contempt of court, had evaded it only because his informant explicitly consented to the disclosure of his identity. The case of Judith Miller had caused severe protests (cf. Baden, 2005).

It was not only the practice of purposefully imprisoning journalists for contempt of court that caused fears for the freedom of the press in the United States, but more generally the massive intimidation campaigns against media the administration disliked. Among the latter was the *New York Times*, which in President Bush's second term revealed several spying activities by the White House. The reporting did not just lead to a Pulitzer Prize but also to allegations by Bush and other administration officials that the paper aided the terrorists and thus caused serious damage to the United States. There were even calls to indict the *New York Times* on the basis of anti-espionage legislation. On the other hand, hundreds of government records were sealed under the authority of the security doctrine, among them information about arrests and criminal cases and, in general, many questionable operations by the administration (Pitzke, 2006; cf. also Kleinsteuber, 2003).

The passage of the Free Flow of Information Act in 2008 brought new rules for the right of journalists to protect their sources but largely subjected it to the administration's security requirements (cf. Reporters without borders, 2008).

A collateral restriction of the freedom of the press and the freedom of information was embedded journalism, which was introduced in 2003 when the Iraq war started. It is regarded as a new form of military-controlled war propaganda, especially since in some cases the journalists are themselves members of the armed forces. The journalists' information is filtered by the military, and the reports may be censored (Dennett, 2004, p. 37).

COMPARISON AND SUMMARY

In their analytical study of communication systems, Hallin and Mancini present four criteria for comparison, the fourth of which concerns the intensity and kind of state intervention in the communication system (2008, p. 23). According to their analysis, state intervention in the media system is lowest in the *North Atlantic or Liberal Model* and highest in the *Mediterranean or Polarized Pluralist Model*, with the *Northern European or Democratic Corporatist Model* approximately in the middle.

Based on these empirically supported differences, we argued at the outset of this article that in the media-centered democracies we studied, namely Germany, Austria, Italy and the United States, there is a creeping tendency toward restricting the autonomy of journalists by means of formal and informal state and institutional influence and thereby curtailing the freedom of the press.

The analysis of the four countries permits a number of conclusions which substantially confirm our argument. To point out a few details:

· In all four countries, a historical cesura – the terrorist attacks in New York and Washington on September 11, 2001 – was the starting point for the trend toward new restrictive measures by the state in the media sector. Freimut Duve, OSCE representative on Freedom of the Media, commented on this cesura: "Shortly after September 11, the rule of law ended in the United States and in Europe" (qtd. in Ramonet 2001, 6, FN13).

· In the United States, this restrictive course is represented by the Patriot Act, in Europe, by the antiterror measures of the European Union (Europäische Union 2002, 2009) which every member country must implement within its territory.

· In all countries, "public security" was the rationale behind a number of constraints on the media of an informal (pressure on journalists) as well as formal nature (e.g. legal measures). However, there were variations in the public perception and subjective concernment of the journalists as well as their reaction to these restrictive measures which give security precedence over freedom of the media. In countries such as Austria this is rarely seen as a problem but very much so in the United States.

· Hallin and Mancini's ranking of the intensity and type of state intervention in the media system was established in 2001 and requires slight revisions. As the Media Freedom Index (Fig. 1) shows, in 2008 the United States placed third among the four countries of our study (36th overall) but still ahead of Italy (44th). Germany and especially Austria are near the top of the field in 20th and 14th place respectively.

Table 1: Media freedom Index

	2002	2003	2004	2005	2006	2007	2008
Germany	7	8	11	18	23	20	20
Austria	26	16	17	16	16	16	14
Italy	40	53	39	42	40	35	44
USA	17	31	22	44	53	48	36

Source: reporters without borders.Press freedom Index 2002-2008

From this it can be concluded that the evaluation of the influence on media freedom in these four countries depends neither on the political system, nor the voting system, nor the party system, but on the national political culture which is embodied by the particular government.

It is striking that all countries with stronger restrictions on the freedom of the media (political-economic pressure, legal provisions, etc.) were governed by conservative right-wing parties at the time when the various security measures were approved. In the United States, it was under President George W. Bush (2001-2009), in Italy, under Silvio Berlusconi (1994/95; 2001-2006; since 2008). The same trend could temporarily be noticed in Austria during the coalition government between People's Party (ÖVP) and Freedom Party (FPÖ) under Chancellor Wolfgang Schüssel (2000). It was less evident in Germany (1998-2005: SPD and Greens; since 2005: CDU-CSU and SPD). In Italy, this peculiarity is accompanied by the anomaly that the owner of the biggest television provider is also prime minister and, in that function, has strong influence on the public service broadcaster RAI. Finally, it is noticeable that monitoring and controlling the new electronic media, above all the internet, has caused especially strong reactions because it affects the "professional privacy" of journalists.

In our opinion, the significance of institutional and state intervention should not be underestimated, and not merely due to the lasting impact of the legal regulations. There are several other reasons why these interventions need to be taken quite seriously: First, because this kind of influence occurs subtly and gradually and its effects are not recognized as such by a large number of recipients. Second, because in the corresponding processes of their legitimation, reasons are blurred with pseudo-reasons (rationalizations). Third, because in the process, the emotional side tends to follow a "politics of emotion ("Politik der Gefühle"; Haslinger, 2001), and unconscious dynamics are seldom caught up with in a reflexive manner. Fourth, because paradox effects are easily misjudged, for example in the aspect that the realization of institutional regulations itself follows those modalities of staging events in the media which suggest closeness yet, upon closer inspection, represent distance and control. Accordingly, the modalities of dealing with closeness and distance in those communication processes which become significant in the context of state interventions, also suggest new forms of proximity management for journalism. Finally, the amplifying effects should not be underestimated either: When we consider for instance that processes of inter- and intra-institutional news coherence run parallel to the dynamics of media concentration and media convergence (cf. Schudson, 2003, p. 109), it is obvious to assume that these processes tend to not only be stabilized but also amplified in the course of state interventions. On the other hand, these results are not meant to hide the fact that limitations to state influence need to be considered as well. In view of the complex dynamics of media change (cf. Rusch, 2007; 2008), it is unlikely that the effects the state desires of the measures are permanently stable.

NOTES

1. The article is a revised version of the paper given at the International conference on "Journalism in the 21st Century: Between Globalization and National Identity," held at the University of Melbourne, Australia,

2. July 16-17, 2009. Translated by Mag. Susanne Toelken-Mettauer.

3. See http://www.wan-press.org/ or http://www.wan-press.org/rubrique49.html

4. Most recently, counterstrategies are also emerging in conncection with open content and open source developments (cf. http://publicmarkup.org/).

5. In March 2006 the so-called sunset clauses of the USA Patriot Act, which were due to expire in 2005, were made permanent. In August 2007 Congress passed the "Protect America Act of 2007" at the instigation of George W. Bush, which allows bypassing the FISA (*Foreign Intelligence Surveillance Act of 1978)* in regard to surveillance (internet, telephone, etc.). In 2008 Congress additionally approved the "FISA Amendments Act of 2008." All these laws follow the USA Patriot Act. In 2009 more sunset clauses are due to expire. In 2004 a federal judge had declared parts of the law unconstitutional (cf. Wieser, 2008).

REFERENCES

1. Achtner, Wolfgang (1996): Penne, antenne e quarto potere. Milano: Baldini Castoldi Dalai.
2. AG Friedensforschung (2002): Pressefreiheit in Gefahr: 120 Tage Angriffe auf die unveräußerlichen Freiheiten. [http://www.uni-kassel.de/fb5/frieden/themen/Innere-Sicherheit/bericht.html (June 17, 2009)].
3. APA (2009): ORF - Redakteursausschuss warnt vor wachsendem politischen Druck. [http://www.sos-orf.at/show_content2.php?s2id=22 (March 27, 2009)].
4. Baden, Franz (2005): Im Land der begrenzten Pressefreiheit [http://www.sueddeutsche.de/politik/625/356453/text/ (June 18, 2009)].
5. Bartocci, Matteo (2009): Del parlamento me ne frego. il manifesto, May 21, 2-3.
6. Bennet, Lance W. & Livingston, Steven (2003): A Semi-Independent Press: government Control and Journalistic Autonomy in the Political Construction of News. Political Communication, 20 (4), 359-362.
7. Bettinelli, Ernesto (1995): Par condicio. Regole, opinioni, fatti. Torino: Einaudi.
8. Blumler, Jay G./Gurevitch, Michael (1995): Journalist's Orientation to Political Institutions. In: Blumler, J.G., & Gurevitch, M. (Eds.), The Crisis of Public Communication (pp. 49-58). London: Routledge Chapman & Hall.
9. Bongi, Micaela (2009): Così la notizia viene censurata. il manifesto, May 23, 3.
10. Chiaramonte, Alessandro & Di Virgilio, Aldo (2006): Da una riforma elettorale all'altra: Partiti, coalizioni e processi di apprendimento. Rivista Italiana di Scienza Politica, 3, 363-391.

11. Chomsky, Noam (2006): America: il nuovo tiranno. Conversazione con David Barsamian. Milano: Rizzoli.
12. Conboy, Martin (2004): Journalism. A Critical History. London: Sage.
13. Corbero, Franco (2004): E nel 2004 va in onda l'inganno dell'etere. La Repubblica, January 9, 2004, 16.
14. Cuperlo, Gianni (2004): Par conditio? Storia e futuro della politica in televisione. Roma: Donzelli.
15. Dadge, David (2004): Casualty of war. The Bush administration's assault on a free press. Amherst/New York: Prometheus.
16. D'Avanzo, Giuseppe (2009): Intercettazioni, ossessione del Cavaliere tra donne, televisione e dolci di mafia. La Repubblica, June 11, 9.
17. De Marchis, Goffredo (2003): Anche Sartori spera in Ciampi. "Questa legge è vergognosa", in: la Repubblica, December 2, 2003, 22.
18. De Marchis, Goffredo (2009): RAI, nomine a casa del premier, in: la Repubblica, April 18, 2009, 2.
19. Dennett, Charlotte (2004): Das Große Spiel ums Öl. Die bruchstückhafte Berichterstattung im Kampf gegen den Terror. In: Borjesson, Kristina, et al. (Eds.), Zensor USA. Wie die amerikanische Presse zum Schweigen gebracht wird (24-61): Zürich: Pendo.
20. derFreiRaum (ed.) (2006): Der Auftrag. Öffentlich Rechtlicher Rundfunk. Positionen-Perspektiven-Plädoyers. Wien: Sonderzahl.
21. Deuze, Mark (2005): What is journalism? Professional identity and ideology of journalists reconsidered. Journalism 6 (4), 442-464 [www.firstmonday.dk/issues/issuei0_7/deuze/index.html (May 29, 2009)].
22. Dipollina, Antonio (2009): Sui TG è arrivato il giorno del blackout. La Repubblica, June 21, 2009, 7.
23. Donsbach, Wolfgang (2008): Journalismusforschung im internationalen Vergleich: Werden die professionellen Kulturen eingeebnet? In: Melischek, Gabriele; Seethaler, Josef & Wilke, Jürgen (Eds.): Medien & Kommunikationsforschung im Vergleich. Grundlagen, Gegenstandsbereiche, Verfahrensweisen (271-289): Wiesbaden: VS.
24. Esser, Frank; Reinemann, Carsten & Fan, David (2001): Spin Doctors in the United States, Great Britain, and Germany: Metacommunication about Media Manipulation. The Harvard International Journal of Press/Politics, 6 (1), 16-45.
25. Europäische Union (2002): Beschluss 2003/48/JI des Rates vom 19. Dezember 2002 über die Anwendung besonderer Maßnahmen im Bereich der polizeilichen und justiziellen Zusammenarbeit bei der Bekämpfung

des Terrorismus gemäß Artikel 4 des Gemeinsamen Standpunkts 2001/931/GASP. [http://eur-lex.europa.eu/LexUriServ/LexUriServ.do?uri=CELEX:32003D0048:DE:NOT (June 21, 2009)].

26. FIEG/FNSI (2009): Appello al Parlamento di giornalisti ed editori. La Repubblica, June 11, 2009, 11.

27. Ginsborg, Paul (2003): Berlusconi. Ambizioni patrimoniali in una democrazia mediatica. Torino: Einaudi.

28. Giordano, Attilio (2003): L'informazione ai tempi di Raiset. Il Venerdì di Repubblica, November 7, 2003, 30-36.

29. Hallin, Daniel C & Mancini, Paolo (2008): Modelli di giornalismo. Mass media e politica nelle democrazie occidentali. 4th ed., Roma-Bari: Laterza (first published in 2004):

30. Haslinger, Josef (2001): Politik der Gefühle. Ein Essay über Österreich. Frankfurt/M.: Fischer (first published 1987).

31. Jarren, Otfried & Donges, Patrick (2002): Politische Kommunikation in der Mediengesellschaft, vol. 2: Akteure, Prozesse und Inhalte. Wiesbaden: VS.

32. Kaltenbrunner, Andy & Fallend, Franz (2006): Editorial. Österreichische Zeitschrift für Politikwissenschaft. Schwerpunktthema Medien und Politik, 4, 331-334.

33. Kleinsteuber, Hans J. (2003): Pressefreiheit in den USA - zwischen „Marketplace of Ideas“ und „The people's Right to Know“. Publizistik. Vierteljahresheft für Kommunikationsforschung, 4 (Special Issue: Die Kommunikationsfreiheit der Gesellschaft), 72-95.

34. Kopper, Gerd & Mancini, Paolo (2003): Kulturen des Journalismus und politisches System. Probleme internationaler Vergleichbarkeit des Journalismus in Europa - verbunden mit Fallstudien zu Großbritannien, Frankreich, Italien und Deutschland. Berlin: Vistas.

35. Kulick, Holger (2002): USA nur auf Platz 17. [http://www.spiegel.de/kultur/gesellschaft/0,1518,219574,00.html (June 21, 2009)].

36. Lane, David (2005): L'ombra del potere. Roma-Bari: Giuffrè.

37. Lewis, Charles R.E. (2000): Media Money. How Corporate Spending Blocked Political Ad Reform and Other Tales of Influence. Columbia Journalism Review, 9/10, 20-27.

38. Lopapa, Carmelo (2009): E Berlusconi premia le sue TV, boom di pubblicità istituzionale. La Repubblica, June 16, 2009, 9.

39. Mazzoleni, Gianpietro (2003): Medienpluralismus in Italien zwischen Politik und Marktwettbewerb. Media Perspektiven,11, 517-529.

40. Mazzoleni, Gianpietro & Vigevani, Giulio Enea (2005): La televisione in Europa: regolamentazione, politiche e indipendenza. Italia. In: Open Society Institute (Ed.), La televisione in Europa: regolamentazione, politiche e indipendenza. Rapporto di analisi 2005 (pp. 188-280): Budapest/New York 17. [http://www.eumap.org/topics/media/television_europe/national/italy/media_ita2.pdf (June 21, 2009)].

41. Mentana, Enrico (2009): Passionaccia. Milano: Rizzoli.

42. Metz, Johanna (2006): Journalisten im Visier des Staates. Pressefreiheit unter Druck - aber nicht prinzipiell bedroht. Das Parlament 4, 17. [http://www.bundestag.de/dasparlament/2006/04/themaderwoche/001.html(June 21, 2009)].

43. New Editorial Concepts (2006): WAN report vol. 5, no. 4 17. [http://www.wan-press.org/article11168.html(June 6, 2009)].

44. Newton, Kenneth & Artingstall, Nigel (1994): Government and private censorship in nine western democracies in the 1970s and 1980s. In: Budge, Ian, & McKay, David (Eds.): Developing Democracy. Comparative research in honor of J.F.P. Blondel (pp. 297-321): London: Sage.

45. Ngo-online (2005): Menschenrechtler fürchten um Pressefreiheit in den USA, ngo-online. Internet-Zeitung für Deutschland (August 24, 2005). [http://www.ngo-online.de/ganze_nachricht.php?Nr=11696 (June 18, 2009)].

46. ORF-Kundendienst (2009): Stiftungsrat. [http://kundendienst.orf.at/unternehmen/menschen/gremien/stiftung.html (June 7, 2009)].

47. Ospina, Hernando Calvo (2009): The criminalization of journalism (progress weekly, May 21-27, 2009). [http://progreso-weekly.com/index.php?option=com_content&task=view&id=922&Itemid=1 (June 17, 2009)].

48. Patriot Act (2001). [http://thomas.loc.gov/cgi-bin/query/z?c107:H.R.3162.ENR (June 17, 2009)].

49. Pelinka, Anton & Rosenberger, Sieglinde (2007): Österreichische Politik. Grundlagen, Strukturen, Trends. Wien: Facultas Universitätsverlag.

50. Pfetsch, Barbara & Maurer, Peter (2008): Mediensysteme und politische Kommunikationsmilieus im internationalen Vergleich: Theoretische Überlegungen zur Untersuchung ihres Zusammenhangs. In: Melischek, Gabriele; Seethaler, Josef & Wilke, Jürgen (Eds.): Medien & Kommunikationsforschung im Vergleich. Grundlagen, Gegenstandsbereiche, Verfahrensweisen (pp. 99-119): Wiesbaden: VS.

51. Pitzke, Marc (2006): Bush-Kampagne gegen «New York Times». [http://

www.spiegel.de/kultur/gesellschaft/0,1518,424205,00.html (June 18, 2009)].

52. Plasser, Fritz; Lengauer, Günther & Meixner, Wolfgang (2004): Politischer Journalismus in der Mediendemokratie. In: Plasser, Fritz (Ed.): Politische Kommunikation in Österreich. Ein praxisnahes Handbuch (pp. 237-308): Wien: Facultas Universitätsverlag.

53. Plasser, Fritz & Ulram, Peter A. (2004): Öffentliche Aufmerksamkeit in der Mediendemokratie. In: Plasser, Fritz (Ed.): Politische Kommunikation in Österreich. Ein praxisnahes Handbuch (37-99): Wien: Facultas Universitätsverlag.

54. Prantl, Heribert (2009): Gegen den Sicherheitsstaat. Ex Minister Baum will in Karlsruhe BKA-Gesetz stoppen. Süddeutsche Zeitung, April 4, 2009, 6.

55. r.pol (2009): Par condicio inesistente. il manifesto, May 23, 2009, 3.

56. Ramonet, Ignacio (2001): Aus einer neuen Welt. Le Monde Diplomatique (German edition), December, 6.

57. Reporter ohne Grenzen (2003): Urteil des Bundesverfassungsgerichts gefährdet investigativen Journalismus, Pressemitteilung. [http://www.reporter-ohne-grenzen.de/archiv/pressemitteilungen/archiv-pressemitteilungen-single/period/1041375600/31535999/archived/browse/5/select/pressemitteilungen/article/39/urteil-des-bundesverfassungsgerichts-gefaehrdet-br-investigativen-journalismus.html (June 2, 2009)].

58. Reporter ohne Grenzen (2008): Rangliste der Pressefreiheit 2008: Nur Frieden schützt die Pressefreiheit, Pressemitteilung. [http://www.reporter-ohne-grenzen.de/fileadmin/rte/docs/2008/08_Pressemitteilung_de_lang.neu.pdf (June 3, 2009)].

59. Reporter ohne Grenzen (2009): Jahresbericht 2008 Österreich. [http://www.rog.at/JB2008_Austria.pdf (June 6, 2009)].

60. Reporters without borders (2007): Germany - Annual report 2007. [http://www.rsf.org/article.php3?id_article=20814 (June 2, 2009)].

61. Reporters without borders (2008): Annual Report. [http://www.reporter-ohne-grenzen.de/fileadmin/rte/docs/2008/ROG-Jahresbericht_2008.pdf (June 18, 2009)].

62. Reporters without borders (2009): Press Freedom Index 2008. [http://www.rsf.org/en-classement794-2008.html (June 20, 2009)].

63. Rusch, Gebhard (2007): Mediendynamik. Explorationen zur Theorie des Medienwandels. Navigationen. Zeitschrift für Medien- und

Kulturwissenschaften, vol. 7, issue 1, 2007, 13-93.

64. Rusch, Gebhard (2008): Medienwandel zwischen Evolution und Revolution. In: Hug, Theo (Ed.): Media, Knowledge & Education. Exploring new Spaces, Relations and Dynamics in Digital Media Ecologies (pp. 15-35): Innsbruck: Innsbruck University Press.
65. Sarcinelli, Ulrich (2009): Politische Kommunikation in Deutschland. Zur Politikvermittlung im demokratischen System, Wiesbaden.
66. Sartori, Giovanni (1976): Parties and Party Systems: A Framework of Analysis. Cambridge: European Consortium for Political Research Press.
67. Schmidt, Manfred G. (2007): Das politische System Deutschlands. München: Beck.
68. Schudson, M. (2003): Sociology of News. New York: WW Norton & Co.
69. Seethaler, Josef & Melischek, Gabriele (2006): Die Pressekonzentration in Österreich im europäischen Vergleich. Österreichische Zeitschrift für Politikwissenschaft, 4, 337-360.
70. SOS-ORF (2007): SOS-ORF kritisiert ORF-Programm und ORF-Stiftungsrat. [http://www.sos-orf.at/show_content2.php?s2id=12 (June 6, 2009)].
71. SOS ORF (2009): ORF MitarbeiterInnen wehren sich. [http://www.sos-orf.at/show_content.php?sid=204(June 6, 2009)].
72. Spoo, Eckart (2002): We made a good show. Wie die Informations- und Meinungsfreiheit dem Krieg zum Opfer fällt. In: Müller-Heidelberg, Till et al. (Eds.): Grundrechte-Report 2008. Zur Lage der Bürger- und Menschenrechte in Deutschland (99-105): Frankfurt/M.: Fischer.
73. Spoo, Eckart (2008): Cicero-Urteil: Durchsuchungen beeinträchtigen Pressefreiheit. In: Müller-Heidelberg, Till et al. (Eds.): Grundrechte-Report 2008. Zur Lage der Bürger- und Menschenrechte in Deutschland (87-88): Frankfurt/M.: Fischer.
74. Swanson, David L. (2003): Political News in the Changing Environment of Political Journalism. In: Maarek, Philippe J., & Wolfsfeld, Gadi (Eds.): Political Communication in a New Era. A Cross-National Perspective (11-31): London/New York: Routledge.
75. Thomaß, Barbara (Ed.) (2007): Mediensysteme im internationalen Vergleich. Konstanz: UVK.
76. Ulrich, Bernd (2009): Schwarz vor Augen (DIE ZEIT, February 26, 2009 Nr. 10). [http://www.zeit.de/2009/10/01-ZDF (June 6, 2009)].
77. Ulrich, Stefan (2009a): Schluss mit lustig. Berlusconi droht Medien, die sein bizarres Benehmen kritisieren. Süddeutsche Zeitung, April 6, 2009,

78. Usi, Eva (2008): Deutschland beschließt umstrittenes Antiterrorgesetz. [http://treff3.net/?p=2095&lang=de(June 2, 2009)].

79. Valentini, Giovanni (2005): Decoder di Stato scandalo annunciato. La Repubblica, December 17, 2005, 18.

80. Vidal, Gore (2004): Vorwort zur amerikanischen Ausgabe. In: Borjesson, Kristina et al. (Eds.): Zensor USA. Wie die amerikanische Presse zum Schweigen gebracht wird (pp. 15-18): Zürich: Pendo.

81. Werhan, Keith (2008): Rethinking Freedom of the Press After 9/11. Tulane Law Review, Vol. 82, 1561-1605.

82. Wieser, Marion (2008): Freiheit sieht anders aus – Sicherheit auch! Über den „Kampf gegen den Terrorismus“, die Auswirkungen auf die Bürgerrechte und die Debatte um Freiheit und Sicherheit in den USA. In: Ooyen, Robert C. van & Möllers, Martin H.W. (Eds.): Jahrbuch Öffentliche Sicherheit 2008/2009 (61-84): Frankfurt/M.: Verlag für Polizeiwissenschaft.

83. Wolf, Armin (2006): Rede. [http://www.sos-orf.at/show_content2.php?s2id=6 (June 2, 2009)].

84. Wolf, Armin (2007): Kommentar. [http://www.sos-orf.at/show_content2.php?s2id=11 (June 6, 2009)].

85. 86.Wolf, Armin (2008): Rettet den ORF vor seinen Rettern. Der Standard, December 17, 2008, 35.

Chapter 3

SYCOPHANCY AND OBJECTIVE JOURNALISM

Bonachristus Umeogu[1], Ifeoma Ojiakor[2]

[1]Department of Philosophy, Faculty of Arts, Nnamdi Azikiwe University, Awka, Nigeria

[2]Department of Mass Communication, Faculty of Social Sciences, Nnamdi Azikiwe University, Awka, Nigeria

ABSTRACT

Objective journalism is the desire and aim of every society and media house. However, such noble aspiration is beclouded and usurped by sycophancy and sycophantic reporting. This development denies the public the right to true information and invariably leads to loss of reputation by the media house. This paper looks at sycophancy in the Nigerian media by looking at the reasons for its unbridled spread, effects on the public, media houses, individuals and the government of the day

INTRODUCTION

Despite the time and attention given to ethical issues, our society is still riddled with different types and manner of ethical maladies. The journalist who is a product of the society is willingly or unwillingly affected by the sorry situation. One of such problems is sycophancy which is chief among the ethical problems in Nigeria. The issue of sycophancy is important to be addressed because it affects objective journalism as it is. Barry white, a renowned singer has one of his lyrics as "practice what you preach". This goes a long way to resound that talk is cheap. It is one thing to know the right thing and a different ball game to do the right thing. These days, everybody knows the slogan of a free but responsible press. Good a thing that everyone knows that; but is it really practiced? Is objective reporting attainable in this era besieged by sycophantic reporting? Every member of a democratic society has the right to know; since nobody wants to be fed with trash, the summum bonum becomes objective reporting or journalism. Overtime, the press has been riddled with all forms of ethical issues which have invariably affected what goes down to the public as news or information. Such issues include plagiarism, brown envelopism, moon lighting, and of course sycophancy. One thing that is logical is that unethical reporting results to subjective journalism. The question now is why is Nigerian journalism bedeviled with sycophantic reporting? What are the causes and inherent dangers of this ethical problem? Does it have any ethical implication for the journalist, the government and the society at large? What can be done to remedy the situation to avoid repeating the same old story?

DEFINITION OF ETHICS

What is ethics? For a word that occupies such a central place in communication, there abound definitions as there abound communication scholars. That notwithstanding, Omole (2000) in Okunna (2003: p. 2) defines ethics as the shared normative values, which any society holds dear and are used to judge the behaviour or performance of any member of that society. It sets out the minimum of acceptable behaviour which any member should attain to be regarded as a good ambassador... Ethics is a concept that borders on morality and consequences of human actions. It also recognizes the fact that man as a rational being has the ability to discern what is good or bad and in line with the approved standard of behaviour in a given society. Thiroux 1980 in (Okunna 2003) concurs by explaining that: when we speak of people as moral or ethical, we usually mean that they are good people and when we speak of them as immoral or unethical, we mean that they are bad people. When we refer to certain human actions as moral, ethical, immoral or unethical, we mean they are right or wrong. Another important characteristic of ethics is that it is voluntary in nature. That is, an individual chooses to do right or wrong. Despite associations and bodies that regulates the activities of its members; the decision to be ethical or not depends solely on the individual. That is the relativity of ethical principles. According to Ozumba (2001: p. 2), ethics as a science of good conduct can hardly on its own make good men out of bad men. Its job is to instruct us on how to be good men if we wish to be. This means that the decision is all ours.

However, that decision to be or not to be might collectively or individually be influenced by variables like sex, level of exposure, orientation, religious background and what have you. Contextualizing them, Okunna (2003) lists them "as cultural socialization, personality differences and situational contingencies". From the vast definitions of ethics, it can be summarily deduced that ethics is a set of moral principles or values dealing with what is good or bad. It has also been seen as that branch of knowledge that is concerned with the standards of good or bad conduct in society. Journalistic ethics, according to Okunna 2003, is that branch of philosophy which aids journalists in determining what is right to do and is ultimately concerned with providing moral principles or norms for journalistic actions. Oloruntola (2007: p. 58) also shares his opinions;

Every profession of repute has for its practitioner's codes of ethics that guide the conduct of members in the performance of their duties. Journalism as a profession is not an exception as such codes of journalistic ethics have been established all over the world both by members of the profession and media organizations. It holistically recognizes man as a rational being and attempts to maximize the positive inner potential of man for the greater good. Rationality has to do with the ability to make decisions and judgments based on reason. I think that is one of the things that make man a higher animal.

ETHICS AND THE JOURNALIST

The journalist just like every human being needs an ethical guideline to gauge its activities. The journalist who is like the information house; the eyes and ears of the whole citizenry, particularly needs to be ethically active so as not to misinform or disinform the public. From time immemorial, man has been under one form of rule or the other. However, journalistic ethics came into the scene following the excesses of journalists during the libertarian era. Ethics as an offshoot of social responsibility theory maintains that in media work, certain standards of performance should not just be stated but followed. This led to the emergence of journalistic codes of ethics for a more responsible conduct. Moemeka 1991 in (Okunna 2003: p. 38) captures this by writing that "this theory places due emphasis on the moral and social responsibilities to persons who, and institutions which operate the mass media". In the same vein, Merril & Lowenstein (1979) in (Okunna 2003, p. 48) summarized the importance of ethics in the practice of journalism thus: ethics—at least a concern for ethics—instills in the journalist a continuing sensitivity to his every action, to his every decision; It integrates or blends with his total search for truth, and it gives him greater awareness of himself, of others, of the consequences of interpersonal relations. A concern with ethics is the key plank in any journalistic platform; it is the "alpha and omega" of public communication.

PURPOSE OF ETHICS

The aim of ethics in journalism is to maintain quality in the media. Ethics is fundamental to journalism because mass media practice is based on a set of essentially ethical concepts of truth, objectivity, honesty, privacy etc. The role of journalism is to provide information for the enlightenment, education and entertainment of the people and this raises ethical question on the quality of the intelligence disseminated, manner of its acquisition and the objective for which it is used in the socio-economic and political processes. According to Ebeze (2004) journalists have actually derailed from the objective work they are meant to do hence ethnic reporting, wrong information, sycophantic journalism, fallacies reporting; thus, this contributed to the invention of ethics. In a nutshell, the purpose of ethics for the journalists is

- To protect the consumer, reader, listener or public in general. In fact, it also helps to protect the journalists themselves before they get drowned in the sea of societal immorality.
- Provides the journalist with standards and principles that will guide the journalist in making moral decisions. Depending on the different ethical theories and individual differences, ethics will ensure uniform standards of behaviour. This is necessary as some will believe in the rightness of their actions despite the resulting consequence(s); while other will believe that the consequence of the action determines its rightness or wrongness. That being the case, ethics spells out what is expected in a particular situation.
- Provides a duty for yourself and others. There are individual who play by the books as a matter of principle; ethical provisions or codes of conduct as the case may be helps them to play ball and effectively at that.
- Encourages responsible action in mass communication. This is the thrust of this paper as ethics has a sole purpose; to encourage free and responsible press so that the consumers have a stable platform to make decisions as rational beings.
- For Everybody
- It enables man to appreciate good or bad.
- Helps individual's live a more virtuous life.
- Promotes and stabilizes social harmony.
- Enables you to look at both sides of the coin before you judge.

OBJECTIVE JOURNALISM

What is objectivity and objective journalism? According to Ayodele (1988)

Objectivity is the state or quality of not being influenced by personal bias, prejudice, feelings and opinions. Objective news-reporting is that which is devoid of inferences, judgment and slanting. Objectivity in journalism is all about stating the obvious devoid of personal emotions and bias. It is more like saying or writing it as it is and not what the journalist will like it to be. In fact, it really takes a disciplined mind to be objective because the temptation to embellish a story is always on the high side. Again, objectivity comes with a great responsibility. Little wonder why Okunna (2003) is of the view that objectivity has a strong affinity with responsibility as far as mass communication is concerned". Corroborating this is Edeani (1993) in Okunna (2003: p. 76) who explain that objectivity and responsibility are two of the most important concepts in mass communication, in view of the central position occupied by each of them in the performance of the press. Very rarely is press ever criticizes or congratulated on its performance without at least one of these concepts coming into play. This goes on to show that being objective and responsible is the highest state any press could attain. More like the biblical injunction of "seek to be responsible and objective and every other thing will be added unto you". Despite the Importance, Gilmore & Root (1975) in Okunna (2003) describe objectivity as the "short dead-pan news ac-count" particularly in the reporting of complex events in which a little interpretation and evaluation are necessary for understanding and assimilation by the publics. This does not deduct from the value of objectivity because interpretative journalism can still be done objectively. This point is buttressed by Edeani (1993) in Okunna (2003: p. 77) when he wrote that the analysis and interpretation do not detract from, but rather strengthen objectivity if they are done with honesty, fairness and impartiality. It is agreed that there are cases and stories that requires a kind of interpretation and analysis for better understanding by the consumers. Yet, this does not negate the fact that objectivity is a virtue that should not be compromised in any way. One can still be objective as can be while interpreting. It all boils down to how well you put rein on your emotions. If that is the case, objectivity is not a myth or unattainable but relative to the journalist in question and the principles he/she upholds as ideal. In other words, Objective journalism acknowledges the public as rational and capable of handling the truth despite how much it hurts. This does not negate the fact that some situation might call for censorship but not at the expense of objectivity. Writing on the place of objectivity in journalism, Ayodele (1988) opines that Objectivity in the collating and presenting of news is the goal of the reporter, and a major principle of Journalism. In spite of the fierce competition among newspapers, newsmagazines, radio, television, or wire services, in regard to who gets a story first and is fastest in making such news items public property, objectivity in the disseminating of news is acknowledged as a significant hallmark of modern Journalistic practice. In the face of intervening variables like pressure, is objectivity really attainable? An answer can be seen in the words of Ayodele (1988) that …that objectivity in news reporting is a definitely attainable goal, but that one must strive for it even in the face of opposing realities. Adherents of attainable objectivity in the media claim that the reporter need not shy away from his prejudices, pre-conceptions, feelings and ambitions. He need not pretend to be an automaton—unthinking, unfeeling, unemotional; "saying it as it is", with bland facts and figures, and no analyzing nor interpreting. Rather, the journalist is to struggle to place under leash his biases. It all sums up my earlier premise that objectivity is attainable and relative to the journalist who chooses to be ethical or not in the face of challenges. I also want to reiterate that in journalism, there is no room for ethical flexibilities; either you are ethical or you are not ethical.

Ethical Problems

The society directly or indirectly influences the people negatively or positively. The journalist who does not exist in a vacuum is also a product of that society. In the course of being professional, the journalist is confronted by demons in the form of ethical problems and they include sycophancy (which is the thrust of this paper), pressure, character assassination, bribery, plagiarism, moonlighting and what have you. Sycophancy Sycophancy is one of the most depressing problems in mass communication. According to Obaze & Fasahnu (2006: p. 138), sycophancy is a situation whereby a medium continues to praise government or individuals despite ills or incompetence in office. Again, it has been defined by (Okunna, 2003) as false praises of those in power. Locally and internationally, this has been a source of concern to both practicing and budding journalists. The second principle in the international code of ethics has it that the foremost task of the journalist is to serve the peoples' right to true and authentic information through an honest dedication to objective reality whereby facts are reported conscientiously in their proper context, pointing out their essential connection and without causing distortions, with the deployment of the creative capacity of the journalist so that the public is provided with adequate material to facilitate formation of an accurate and comprehensive picture of the world in which the origin, nature and essence of events, processes and state of affairs are understood as objectively as possible. Coming back to Nigeria, NUJ knowing the relevance of Accuracy has it as one of its principles and it reads thus:

- The public has the right to know. Factual, accurate, balanced and fair reporting is the ultimate objective of good journalism and the basis of earning public trust and confidence.

- A journalist should refrain from publishing inaccurate and misleading information. When such information has been in advertently published, prompt correction should be made.
- In the course of his duties, a journalist should strive to separate facts from conjecture and comments.

If the above is religiously followed, what the consumer gets will be nothing short of objective and factual reports. Objective reporting on the other hand is that report that is devoid of inferences, judgments and slanting. It is the absence of objectivity that invariably leads to sycophantic reporting.

According to Okunna (1995), "a sycophant reporter is a journalist who flatters political leaders, wealthy citizens and owners of media houses who as employers have formidable power over journalist". For instance Jacque Chirac, a onetime president has been found guilty of two count charges of corruption and misappropriation of public funds. According to a media report on Aljazeera network, he employed ghost workers at the city hall and diverted the money for his campaign. This is the same man who the media while in power never criticized. Despite the political immunity covering government officials, my question is if the press never knew he was siphoning and diverting funds at the time he was in office? From previous happenings, I want to believe that they were aware but choose to be mute about. How do they live with their conscience highlighting praises of someone who has committed a crime but rather chose to sweep it under the carpet or turn a blind eye? In Nigeria, this is more pronounced in the political sphere where journalists use the media to confer status on their favored politicians and also to set agenda that will also favour the favored ones, Okunna (1995).

CAUSES OF SYCOPHANCY

There are many possible causes of sycophancy but this paper will look at the following.

Lack of Experience on the Part of the Political Leaders

In civilized countries or the developed world, leaders are well versed and more mature and so appreciate constructive criticism as against their counterparts in developing countries where criticism is a no. For instance Barak Obama of the United States of America knows that criticism sharpens one's initiative while Nigerian leaders will see such writer as the worst enemy of the State, and one would not be surprised if the writer is silenced forever. This being the case considering the immaturity of the leaders and the promise of death, the journalists will praise them despite their ratings so as not to be at loggerheads with them. Look at what happened to Dele Giwa all in a bid to be true to his profession. He was murdered through letter bombing all in a bid to silence his honest voice. Also considering the fact that most journalists in Nigeria and other developing countries are uninsured, they will not like to lose their life in exchange for a colorful and lengthy oration at the funeral ceremony. However, in the developed countries, they will dare the odds even at the expense of their life as their names will be written in the sand of time but in a country like Nigeria, who really cares about the sand of time?

PREVAILING SITUATION OR ENVIRONMENTAL CONTINGENCIES

The journalist in Nigeria does not operate in a social vacuum. If the society is morally deficient, how is the journalist expected to rise above the moral decay. The journalist according to Olomuyiwa (1988) is a product of the society. According to this writer, the African society with its various facets-tradition, beliefs, images, goal, constraints etc must inevitably influence and be influenced upon by the journalist. The journalist helps to shape the size and direction of what is communicated to the different publics of the media. As far as information flow is concerned, they are the major gate keepers in mass communication. They in turn, indirectly sets his/her own agenda; what he/she finally select to communicate. You can see that both the powers of the journalist and the public's are interwoven to an extent. Explaining this, Olomuyiwa writes that this dual yet interactive rolc has its implications for the constant barrage of charges of bias, prejudice, partisanship, untruth and especially sycophancy leveled against the media and its staff. That is to say that the level of unethical practices among Nigerian journalists is a reflection of what is happening in the larger society. Lai Oso (2001). In other words, journalists tend to succumb to the prevailing situation because when the society is immoral, objectivity and truth is thrown to the winds.

LACK OF PROFESSIONAL EDUCATION OR TRAINING OF JOURNALIST

The right formal education is one powerful tool for the making of ethical profession. When you pass through the rigorous processes of training, then you will learn to appreciate your profession and yourself; and will guard its prestige jealously. In fact, studies have revealed that journalists with higher education exhibit more professional orientation in performing their duties. Oso (2001) observes that a good number of those who go about these days as journalists have either not received any education/training in journalism or are not adequately trained and equipped for the challenges of the profession. What this shows is that the more educated one is, the more confident and secured the journalist will feel to take on the challenges that are bound to surface.

POVERTY

This is the chief cause of ethical misconduct; the mother that gave birth to other problems. An averaged journalist lives below the poverty line; and until the issue of poverty is seriously addressed with realizable solution, then no amount of constitutions or codes of conducts will have any meaningful impact. Nothing is perhaps more important than a good pay to keep the reporter on the ethical path. According to Garba (1998) "Abiola used to say that when you do not pay your journalist well, someone else will pay them and they will work for him". This is dangerous because as an employer, you will be unaware that your employee is moonlighting which poses a threat to both employers but a bigger threat to the one that do not give fat salary. This invariably aids moonlighting as an option to dealing with poverty. Worthy of note is the fact that moon lighting is also an ethical problem in Nigeria that has been generating great concern. Nigerians are known to be survivors and the journalist must also strive to survive even in the face of abject poverty to the extent of cutting corners. However, this depends on individual because the sycophantic tendencies of a journalist are to a great extent determined by the bias, prejudice and constraints personal to him. What I am trying to say is that there are still people who believe that "a good name is better than riches.

INFLUX OF GOVERNMENT OWNED MEDIA

If the saying that "whoever pays the piper dictates the tune" is anything to go by, then we must empathize with journalists that work in the government owned media. They are like birds in a cage that have their wings clipped and their legs chopped. They can only move when their owner wants them to. In other words, they do not have a will of their own; more like automated robots that move only when commanded to. What a life! One can now understand why they conveniently play the role of praise singers for the government of the day as if it is the "natural" thing to do. In reality, journalists have a duty to be objective at all times. The concept of duty therefore entails the necessity of acting from respect for the law. This implies that we have a moral obligation to do the right, remaining indifferent to the consequences. Saying or writing things as they are might bring the reporter and the government at loggerheads but Kantian opinions of duty is deontological or obligatory. According to Kant in (Ojiakor, 2004), acting from a sense of duty rather than concern and consequences is the basis for establishing one's moral obligation".

SYCOPHANTIC REPORTING

Each passing day brings modifications to the already powerful effects of the mass media. This absolute power calls for a check to ensure that the public's right to true information is not compromised. In other to be fair and truthful, the watchword is objectivity. However, is Nigerian press objective? To attempt to answer that question, several national dailies in Nigeria were content analyzed to pin point the instances of sycophantic reporting. Comparatively, old and current dailies were compared to see if the trend has remained the same or if there has been a change in the status quo. Again, garland for the oriental Amazon—this report highlighted and extolled the achievement of Dame Virgy Etiaba or "Mama Anambra" as she was popularly known by the citizens of Anambra State where she served as an executive governor. They recalled that she awarded contracts for 500 kilometers of roads, paid leave allowances of civil servants from 2003-2006, recruited teachers and what have you. No mention was made of the millions of naira siphoned during her short stay as the governor. The impression was that she initiated the contracts conveniently neglecting the part that her predecessor called the shots before a legal battle that saw our "mama" to the highly coveted seat. She may have done all that and more but the story read like a PR insert to praise her while indirectly character assassinate her predecessor. The story would have been balanced if they had brought in her weaknesses even if they downplay them a bit (The Guardian, 2007: p. 61).

Second example was in National Mirror newspaper with the headline as "the man the cap fits" and another story on the same paper that ran as "Sam Egwu: the father of modern Ebonyi State". It went on to explain how he transformed Ebonyi State into veritable heaven as the then governor of the State. No one gets it all considering that the worst part of management is human management. As a human and rational being, he must have made bad decisions and had his own share of bad moments. I suppose that aspect is on a need to know basis. Was it an objective report? A look at the Guardian paper of 9th October, 2007 will see this headline "Unizik: the making of a modern university". To be truly objective, effort would have been made to get the views and opinions of the students and staff. Such revelations no matter how bad they may seem at that time will help to know the important areas to address. For instance, what about the transportation problems of students, the frustration of students by unethical lecturers, and the politics of admission process which by the way is common among tertiary institutions?

A balanced report will have signaled more significant development processes. In the electronic media especially the State owned stations, that is the order of the day. Even when a government has become unpopular, their mouth piece in the name of the press still sings their praises. One can now understand why some citizens prefer to watch and listen to "serious" networks like Aljazeera for objective news. Objective news according to Ayodele (1988) is news that is undistorted by personal prejudice. It is news that is fair, accurate, and factual. Nevertheless, it is not news that has been gathered and presented by an unthinking, unfeeling professional. Objective news is devoid of inference, judgment, and Slanting". Comparatively, let us examine some current dailies before arriving at a conclusion. Purposively, this researcher chose to choose dailies from 1st November 2011 to 30th December, 2011. This was to content analyze with a view to fishing out sycophantic reports. The dailies are the Guardian, This Day, The Sun and The Vanguard Newspapers. I want to draw your attention to Daily Sun of December 29, 2011 with the headlines as "Obi's strides in Anambra State. The writing was on the efforts and impacts of ANIDS on the development of the State. I quote "it is fairly reasonable to argue that Governor Peter Obi of Anambra State is a handworker. This fact is not constable, at least to keep observers of development progression in the State within the last five years".

He went on to list the remarkable improvements made in the education, health, judiciary, transportation, environment, industrialization, security, roads etc. I want to make it clear that the researcher does not agree with the writer but to an extent, I beg to differ. Let us look at education sector for an instance; reformation in the education sector is at whose expense? How much do State owned universities pay as tuition fees? In the secondary school section, there is inadequate teachers which led to a situation where teachers are employed by the school management with the consent of the Parents Teachers' Association who pay the salaries of those teachers PTA levies, and not the government. If the school excels in academics, the government takes the credit. I do not want to believe that the writer did not conduct a research before this write up, if he did, then he would have found a way to applaud the concerned parents who are pulling their weight to reform the education sector for the betterment of their children and the society at large. Coming to the transport sector, I want to ask; does the state of roads affect the transportation fares? My answer is yes! Way before the price hike as a result of the removal of fuel subsidy, passengers have been paying more than usual owing to bad roads especially the Onitsha-Awka expressway. No, I do not want to go into whether it is a federal or State road because it does not change the fact that it is a death trap. Surprisingly, this reporter wrote in from Onitsha yet conveniently left out the state of the roads when he was commenting on the transport sector. If this is not a sycophantic report, then why not call the attention of the object of your praise to what the masses are going through as a result of the roads. Some of the aftermath of the roads on the masses are; lateness to work since they have to avoid the potholes and the bumps, ill health because bumpy rides always have their toll on the body, holes in their pockets since they spend supposed savings on transportation etc.

At this juncture, I want to refer you to a report on National mirror of December, 12 where the State Assembly decried the deplorable state of Nneogidi—Agulu Nise road, passing a motion on the State governor to give out the contract for the road construction. I can go and on to fault this report, but let us look at other dailies. There was also a report on Guardian of November 15, 2001 with the headline as "Chime reassures Enugu youths of employment opportunities. It was a report of the Governor of Enugu State, Mr Sullivan Iheanacho Chime, reassuring the people in Lagos that he is on the verge of creating employment opportunities in the State. It also mentioned his efforts towards that by registering job seekers, collaboration with National Directorate of Employment (NDE) and what have you. I am curious to know how he intends to achieve all this when it is difficult for him to pay the minimum wage to his workers. If you cannot pay the workers you already have, with what are you going to pay the new recruits? Well, unless the job opportunities will be for the artisans; if that is the case, what happens to the graduates? Are they over qualified to be meaningfully engaged by the government at all levels? What we were not told was if it was a press conference or a social function because a smart journalist or a courageous member of the audience would have asked this question. This writer should have questioned this development.

However, it was observed that the two months selected had something in common; they were filled with stories about and on the death of the CEO of guardian newspaper, Alex Uruemu Ibru and Chief Odumegwu Ojukwu; the National Awards by the Presidency on the selected few; and the pros and cons of the removal of fuel subsidy. Almost half of the selected newspapers were filled with stories of the above mentioned issues and/or congratulatory message to the award recipients and even birthday messages to the Nigerian president, Dr. Goodluck Ebele Jonathan. As a result of this observation, it calls for an in-depth content analysis of the publications prior to the November/ December issues.

DANGERS OF SYCOPHANTIC REPORTING

The inherent dangers of sycophancy have been outlined below:

- It makes the entire profession to lose its credibility or to be irritating to the public who often see through the masks. This could be the reason why Aljazeera network is preferred when it comes to objective news. This shows that the audiences are active and knows which station carries correct news and those that air doctored news. Explaining that the publics are no fools, Ajayi-Gbadabo (2000) writes that "protecting citizens against unfair media reports is the responsibility of the press to ensure that citizens are protected from media excesses that can amount to assault on the sensibilities of the people".

- It is now virtually impossible for the journalist to effectively discharge his duty while he is so much involved in over-praising.
- It is difficult for those being praised to perform impressively. This is because the praises will becloud their vision. According to Okunna (2003), sycophancy leads to dereliction of duty because they are not allowed to see the mistakes and correct them. Even when they realize that they are not doing well, they are content to hide behind the misinformation by the press under the illusion that the public will be none the wiser.
- It leads to abuse of power of the mass media. According to (Okunna, 2003: p. 87), during elections, unethical journalists use the media to confer status on their favorite politician and to set the political agenda in favour of these politicians even when they lack legitimacy and do not deserve the praise heaped upon them". The electorate who is powerless in the face of the all powerful effect of the media is deliberately manipulated into adopting that candidate. In Okunnas' opinion, this manipulation is one of the negative effects of sycophancy. On a second thought, does sycophancy have any positive effect? Ÿ It denotes the public their right to true and correct information. Using the report on Obi as an example, if I have been none the wiser, could you imagine the noise I will making
- in the course of arguing that the governor have performed above expectations. To people that knew the true state of things, I will sound like an empty drum. That is why the public needs to be given true and correct information so that they can make their judgments.
- It has no redress in court. Unlike libel and slander for which one can sue a publication, there is no constitutional provision for sycophancy. If there is, journalists would have been careful not to be dragged into a legal battle.
- False praises bring about false behaviour.
- To make it clearer, let us divide it into ethical implication for the journalist, government and the society.

ON THE JOURNALIST

The implication of sycophancy on the journalist is that it does not allow the journalist to criticize the government. But then, what do you expect since who pays the piper dictates the tune and dance steps as the case may be. Furthermore, the journalist who is no longer objective irritates the media audiences who often see through the falseness of the media content packages by the unethical praise singer, Okunna (1995). This ultimately leads to loss of credibility and respect for the media. The situation is clearly put in the biblical proverb that "of what use is salt if it loses its taste except to be thrown outside and trampled upon". In addition, since the journalist is so much involved in over praising, when will he/she have the time to report other things that are happening around him to the detriment of the public. On listening to State owned media, the news package is always what the State governor did or is planning to do. What about those events that are happening in the State that the public need to know about? When the lens of the press is one the government officials and newsmakers, who watches the State?

ON THE GOVERNMENT

As noted earlier, false praises bring about false behaviour. This means that if you are not doing it right and the media is saying that you do, you will now relax and overlook your duties. In the words of Okunna (1995), it leads to dereliction of duty on the part of the recipient of the false praises. This over praising acts as a curtain where they hide behind the flattering, but thankfully, the people are no fools. Whenever a government comes to power, there are expectations on the part on the electorates; so when the road are in bad condition and the press is telling them that the government is building roads, are they trying to play on their intelligence. After all, "you can tell a blind man that there is no oil in the soup and not pepper", in this case, we have eyes to know when a government is making good of his promises.

ON THE PUBLIC

The public has a right to know and to true information but sycophantic reporting denies them this right. It is a known fact that the result of sycophancy is mis information/dis information as facts are distorted and information is doctored to please an egocentric sponsor. Furthermore, as the game of praise singing goes on, the journalist fails to do the job that needs to be done which is catering for the diverse informational and communication needs of the public in a conscientious and responsible manner—a failure which is a betrayal of the trust which the public places on the press to champion public interest (Edeani in Okunna 1995).

RECOMMENDATIONS

Decades after Nigerian renowned musician cum evangelist Sunny Okosun asked which way Nigeria in one of his songs, no definite answer has been given rather, our society is still heading downwards socially, economically, morally etc. That notwithstanding, all hope is not lost if only there will be reorientation in our beloved country. There are things that were a taboo in the past that have come to be recognized as a "natural" or "normal" thing in our society. For instance, advance free fraud or 419 as popularly known in Nigeria have come to be seen as the profession of smart and intelligent people. I remember growing up that when men that made money comes back home, people are generally reluctant to accept any form of gifts from them. That has changed because such people are now besieged by their community to accept titles. Yes! That is how far we have morally derailed. If there should be a kind of mind management package to alter the current picture in our heads that the end justifies the means, maybe, the society in general and the journalist in particular will wake up to the clarion call of objective journalism.

In addition, if the press should say, when a government is still power, what they say when they have left power; we may be nipping sycophancy in the bud. For instance, when Ngige was in power, everyone including the State owned media knew he has a stolen mandate but kept quiet about it. The moment he stepped down, the media became over flogged with negative stories about him. Another instance is that of Jacque Chirac who has been convicted on two counts charges of corruption and embezzling of public funds. The press knew this was happening and kept mute. Had it been they subtly hinted that Chirac has been busted, the level of the embezzlement would not have been so high as to earn a conviction. There is a way of stating the obvious without being hurtful. It all goes down to choice of words and presentation which the journalist is expected to be familiar with. In addition, I also recommend that the issue of sycophancy having no legal implication should be urgently addressed so as to cut down its presence in Nigerian journalism. In as much as it is fair to acknowledge when someone does a noble thing or delivers on his manifesto; it should be a serious crime to overdo it. Constitutionally, there should be a boundary when praising; and when it is false praise singing, it leads to distortion of facts with the intention to deceive and that, should be a serious crime if the fight against corruption is expected to hold sway

On a lighter note, this paper recommends that government and corporate bodies should create platforms to honor the journalist who have been true to their profession. When one knows that all actions are on the radar, they will be forced to dance in line; with time, it will feel like the "natural" way to act and everyone becomes a winner. Finally, I will like to add better remuneration and condition of service of journalists. I will like to point out that this will work in conjunction with a reorientation. This is because according to Ebeze (2007), how much is really enough? What this means is that it is not about money but about re orientation. This is because if you are paid millions of naira, that tendency to cut corners will still be there. Furthermore, how much is really enough considering the fact that "more money attracts more problems"? Also writing on remuneration, Mohammed 1996 in Oloruntola 2007explains that "while journalist in the west may be well paid, insured, endowed with state of the art equipment and facilities and are highly mobile; their third world, and particularly Nigerian counterparts are poorly paid, uninsured, immobile and with poor working environment". No wonder such job insecurity makes them vulnerable and susceptible to corruption and abuse of professional ethics. If poor remuneration makes them to be unprofessional, then it is logical to assume that a better pay packet will alleviate the problem.

CONCLUSION

I wish to start my conclusion with the wise saying of N. N. Evarts that "as there is nothing great in the world but man, there is nothing truly great in man but character". Objectivity in journalism is not an abstract concept or an unattainable feat. Truth be told, it is supposed to be the goal of practicing reporters and budding journalists to strive for objectivity which is contained in the larger ideal of truth. Again, also considering the enormous power vested in the media, the press owe it to the people to rise and live above the sea of corruption that is threatening to drown this country as we know it. As always, they will be solidly backed by the agenda setting and all powerful effects theories of communication effects. Every journalist in particular and every member of the society should embrace morality and ethics as an unbreakable principle. By so doing, it will ensure that future generations are brought up with a sense of responsibility and impartiality. Again, there should be no room for ethical flexibilities; either you are ethical or not. The ethical ones should be applauded and encouraged so as to sway the unethical one into being morally firm. This is in appreciation of the fact that people change from time to time. It is about time to change for the good. I understand that re orientation and subsequent erasure of pictures in our heads will not happen overnight; but it has been said that a journey of a thousand miles begins with not only a step with that determined person. Will you be that someone?

REFERENCES

1. Adum, A. (2008). New media: The ethical question. In International Journal of Communication (No. 9, pp. 423-432). Enugu: Ebenezer

Productions.

2. Daily Sun (2011). Obi's strides in Anambra. 29 December 2011, 20.
3. Ebeze, V. (2007). Unpublished lecture notes. Awka: NAU.
4. Garba, S. (1998). Corruption in the media. Abuja: Nigerian Press Council.
5. National Mirror (2007). The man the cap fits. 8 November 2007.
6. National Mirror (2007). Sam Egwu: The father of modern journalism. 8 November 2007.
7. National Mirror (2011). State assembly calls on the governor. 12 December 2011.
8. Obaze, A., & Fashanu, F. (2006). Mass communication law and ethics. Ibadan: Safinos Publishers.
9. Ojiakor, I. (2004). Ethical journalism: A critique of Immanuel Kant's ethical philosophy. Awka: NAU.
10. Okunna, S. (2003). Ethics of mass communication. Enugu: New Generation Ventures Ltd.
11. Olomuyiwa, A. (1988). Objectivity, sycophancy and the media reality in Nigeria. Africa Media Review, 3, 106-120.
12. Oloruntola, S. (2007). Mass MEDIA ethics in Nigeria: The problem facing the Nigerian journalist. English Studies, 1, 58-68
13. Oso, L. (2000). Inculcating ethical standards through education and retraining. Ibadan: MFD/IF Seminar.
14. Ozumba, G. (2001). A course text on ethics. Lagos: Obaroh & Ogbinaka Publishers Limited.
15. The Guardian (2007). Again, garland for the oriental Amazon. 3 November 2007.
16. The Guardian (2007). Unizik: The making of a modern university. 27 October 2007.
17. The Guardian (2011). Chime reassures Enugu youths of employment opportunities. 15 November 2011.

Chapter 4

MEDIA LAW EDUCATION FOR JOURNALISTS IN HONG KONG

D. Weisenhaus
Hong Kong University

INTRODUCTION

An anti-corruption agency raids seven newsrooms. The government considers national security legislation with far-reaching repercussions for journalists. Privacy laws targeting paparazzi and others in the media are proposed. A broadcaster is admonished for comments made on air to public officials. An editor is jailed for contempt of court. These events and others in Hong Kong over the past several years demonstrate the volatility of media law developments in the Special Administrative Region, now part of the People's Republic of China. Since the 1997 return of the former British colony to Chinese sovereignty, Hong Kong has been struggling to define and shape the legal terrain on which journalists operate. The imposition of the Basic Law, Hong Kong's mini-Constitution; a dramatic rise in libel suits; new laws and proposed legislation attempting to rein in an active media, and the fact that Hong Kong no longer has to automatically apply British common law to issues that arise have resulted in a Byzantine environment for the evolution of media law. Media law education for journalists has long been recognized as essential. In the United States, media law is a required course in most accredited journalism and mass communications programs. An increasing number of programs in Asia are now teaching media law also. In July 2002, at the annual meeting of the International Communication Association in Seoul, South Korea, a panel on "Education in Mass Communication Law in Asia" surveyed such efforts in the Philippines, Singapore, South Korea and Hong Kong. In November 2004 a media law conference at Beijing's Communication University of China (formerly Beijing Broadcasting Institute) also examined media law education. As a lecturer in media law at the Journalism and Media Studies Centre at the University of Hong Kong, I participated in both conferences. We discussed the challenges of teaching media law and I addressed the particularities of educating journalists about the uniquely intricate legal landscape of Hong Kong. These intricacies include:

- The legacy of harsh media laws that remain from more than 150 years of British rule and that relate to official secrets, defamation, sedition and reporting on court proceedings.
- The big shadow China casts on press freedom, despite the "one country, two systems" principle that governs its relations with Hong Kong – a shadow made darker by the PRC's direct intervention in constitutional matters in Hong Kong.(In 2004, the National People's Congress Standing Committee in Beijing interpreted key provisions of the Basic Law to prohibit universal suffrage for Hong Kong elections in 2007 and 2008).
- Hong Kong's own legislation and regulations of the media, formed largely under an undemocratic political process.
- Increasing litigiousness that has seen dozens of major court cases in the past decade against the media in Hong Kong, the emergence of large jury awards that has encouraged even more lawsuits and the unusual propensity of local media companies to sue each other.
- The growing globalization of media law in such areas as jurisdiction, libel and copyright that affect journalists here.

In August 1999, I visited Hong Kong for the first time. As a U.S.-trained lawyer and city editor of The New York Times, I was asked to help launch a new English-language, international journalism program at the University of Hong Kong and to teach media law, among other topics. I came for a week to assess whether to assume the post.

Shortly after my arrival, I saw evidence of the complicated media law terrain. A government-linked think tank released a proposal to create a statutory press council that would have authority to single out and impose fines against newspapers for what it considered to be violations of privacy. In support of its proposal, the think tank cited numerous laws and cases from around the world, including the United States. After reading the proposal, I saw that some of the U.S cases were cited out of context or inaccurately described. I quickly contacted Floyd Abrams, a leading First Amendment litigator in the U.S., whom I had gotten to know in my years as a legal journalist. I asked Abrams, who had argued some of these cases before the U.S. Supreme Court, to help prepare a response; his analysis was submitted to the government and was published in the leading Chinese-language newspaper, Ming Pao. This newspaper and other media organizations loudly criticized the proposal and the think tank went back to the drawing board.1

I soon concluded I would find many such interesting challenges if I worked in Hong Kong and made plans to return in January 2000 to start teaching graduate students, most of whom were local working journalists. My experience in law and journalism was as a prosecutor and as a reporter, editor and producer in print and television in the United States, including as legal editor of The New York Times Magazine and as editor-in-chief of The National Law Journal, a newspaper for lawyers. What could I bring with me? I could not just import my U.S. cases into Hong Kong, where the laws are largely based on British models, but as the Hong Kong proposals for new privacy laws demonstrated, knowledge of U.S. law would be a critical component for any program that must reflect the increasingly global media law environment. Returning to Hong Kong, my challenge was how to adapt to the local environment. In Hong Kong at that time, media law was being taught at the undergraduate level at Chinese University by Kevin Lau, senior editorial writer and senior legal officer for Ming Pao who has law degrees from HKU and the London School of Economics and Politics.(Hong Kong Baptist University offered a broader media law and ethics course for its journalism and communication students). Media law was not being taught at the two law schools in Hong Kong,2 nor was there a current textbook. The last one, available only in Chinese, was published in 1995 before the handover. I met with Lau, who generously shared his undergraduate curriculum and materials; his contributions helped me understand some of the parameters of Hong Kong media law.

The difficulty though was to find the right approach for my graduate students, mainly working journalists, who would bring their practical experiences to the classroom and who could take their classroom training back to the newsroom on a weekly basis. I needed to construct a course that gave immediate practical information but also provided skills and a theoretical framework that would be useful long after they left the classroom.

Who are my students? Then, as now, they range in age from early 20s to late 40s. Many work in television, newspapers, wire services, radio and the Internet. About a quarter to a third are in other professions and are looking to enter journalism but at a higher level. They have included teachers, lawyers, engineers, bankers, government civil servants, financial analysts, flight attendants, a pediatrician and an architect. They have widely varying abilities and skills in the English and Chinese languages. In the beginning, they were mostly from Hong Kong, but increasingly over the past five years, they come from other countries such as the United Kingdom, Australia, New Zealand, Canada, South Africa, India, Singapore, Portugal, Japan, Taiwan, the United States and mainland China. Most have undergraduate degrees from outside Hong Kong from such schools as Oxford, Harvard, Yale, Peking University and the University of New South Wales. Hong Kong is an international center for journalists, as represented by our students. They have worked for CNN, BBC, Associated Press, Bloomberg, Reuters, Dow Jones, Star TV and Yazhou Zhoukan, the Chinese language newsweekly for the Chinese diaspora.

The diversity of the students also reflects the international outlook of the professionally oriented program at our Journalism and Media Studies Centre. Media law is one of the program's three core courses; the others focus on ethics and reporting and writing.3

One of the program's key principles is that courses are taught from the perspective of the journalist, so that students gain insight into the issues professional journalists face on a regular basis. Thus, the goals for the 12 three-hour long classes that comprise the media law course were to demystify and explain the law, the legal process and its players and, by doing so, empower the students. The course had to work on several basic levels. First, as almost none of the students had legal training, the course had to provide an overall introduction enabling them to acquire an understanding of legal language and concepts and the ability to read court cases and conduct legal research. I wanted to share some of the skills I had learned in law school and as a prosecutor in the U.S. that would help them feel more confident when they ventured into legal thickets. Second, the course had to work across cultures. Much Chinese secondary and undergraduate education is based on a traditional lecture format and while most of my classes would feature a lecture component, other parts were designed to encourage students to be more independent, to talk more in class and to analyze on their feet. Third, as the practice of law is essentially specialist in nature, the course had to introduce students to experts who could provide up-to-date, intimate knowledge of their specialties. Over the years, these experts have included law professors, solicitors, barristers, media company counsels, legal journalists, and even a sitting judge. Finally, and most important, students had to receive a firm grounding in media law, primarily as practiced in Hong Kong, but also incorporating key international developments.

To accomplish these goals, we start with such basic legal concepts as the nature of law, rule of law, common law, civil code systems, civil vs. criminal law, enacted law, adversarial vs. inquisitorial systems and jurisdiction. We examine the origins, definitions and sources of law on freedom of expression and freedom of the press, which are not necessarily the same thing. We look at the wordings of constitutions for Hong Kong's own "mini-Constitution," known as the Basic Law, and those from the U.S., Europe, Asia and the People's Republic of China. We look at international conventions and covenants to dissect their influence on Hong Kong and elsewhere. Only by actually reading constitutions can we begin to assess how much value a nation places on freedom of expression. Later, we see how those values play out in actual court cases.

This past year, while waiting for the judge to arrive, many students rushed over to sit in the jury box; others positioned themselves in the barristers' seats or stayed back in the press area. The judge started the session by talking for an hour or so about his work and giving insights into cases and the process; he led them through the forests of the many constitutional issues that have come before him and other judges. He impressed on them that the system of rule of law would fall apart without a thinking, responsible press to make it transparent. Then, he opened himself to a freewheeling Q & A session providing students a rare opportunity to question a Hong Kong judge. Before they left, the judge brought out his horsehair wig for the students to examine; several even tried it on! Later, during the semester, when they saw news articles about the judge's rulings in this or that case, we discussed what they learned that day and how it applied in the latest instance. This courtroom visit remains one of the course's popular components.

Early on in the course, tutorials are arranged for the students on how to conduct legal research. A senior law librarian and a trainer from Westlaw, one of the commercial legal publishing companies, are enlisted to help students learn how to update their legal knowledge. Furthermore, as part of the course requirements, they use these new skills for group or individual reporting projects on media law developments. In 2002, they had the opportunity to do legal research for a real-life purpose: they produced a 16,000-word response to the Hong Kong government's controversial proposal for national security legislation, otherwise known as Article 23, the provision in the Basic Law that requires Hong Kong to have laws on treason, secession, sedition, theft of state secrets and subversion. In their submission to the government, the students provided examples of alternative approaches to national security taken by other Asian nations such as South Korea, which eliminated its seditious libel laws during legal reforms in the late 1980s. Theirs joined hundreds of submissions to the government, which shelved its proposals in 2003 after more than 500,000 Hong Kongers marched in protest.

In just about every journalist's life, he or she needs to know how to read a court case, so students are assigned oral presentations on key media law cases to show they can discern what is important in a court's rendering. They must identify the salient facts, the key arguments of both sides, the court's analysis and its ruling. They are expected to compare this case to others and to bring in other references and applications. After each presentation in class, I follow up with comments and analysis. During the course, students are responsible for reading more than 30 court cases selected for their value in understanding aspects of media law important to the practice of journalism. They are many of the same issues journalists face all over the world and include freedom of expression, defamation, privacy, contempt of court, official secrets, access to information, court reporting restrictions, copyright, obscenity and laws affecting newsgathering practices, including the protection of sources. For other readings, students have one required textbook, An Introduction to the Hong Kong Legal System, 4 and dozens of law review articles and chapters from legal texts examining media issues in Hong Kong, the U.K., the U.S., and the PRC, among other jurisdictions. The biggest drawback to many of these readings is that they approach topics from a lawyer's point of view. I am writing a Hong Kong media law textbook5 that will parse these topics from the journalist's point of view.6

While I give lectures for almost all of these topics, over the five years I have taught this course I also have brought in more than 20 guest lecturers. I am grateful to members of the Faculty of Law at HKU for making multiple appearances, especially Johannes Chan, dean and barrister for many media law cases who has discussed official secrets, contempt of court and, most recently, the legality of government newsroom raids. Other law faculty members who have spoken to the class include Jill Cottrell, the leading academic on libel in Hong Kong; Raymond Wacks, a prolific writer on privacy now retired, and Hualing Fu, who co-wrote a leading textbook on media law of the mainland. It also is important for the students to hear from local practitioners, including lawyers representing media (or suing them!); those in government who enforce the regulations, such as the deputy director of the intellectual property department, and others with particular insight, such as a former president of the Hong Kong Bar Association and now a member of the Legislative Council who was a leading opponent of the proposed and since-shelved anti-subversion legislation. For mainland China, in addition to Fu, we have been fortunate to have as speakers Wei Yongzheng, a professor in the Department of Law for Communication University of China in Beijing who has written widely on PRC media law, Pu Zhiqiang, a libel litigator in Beijing, and Jerome Cohen, an international lawyer specializing in Chinese law and China's foreign relations and a former director of East Asian Legal Studies at Harvard Law School. One of my favorite speakers was the first one, Patrick Yu, first Chinese crown counsel in Hong Kong, who gave a frank and witty appraisal of the evolution of Hong Kong's legal system.

Some of these speakers are part of an informal group with whom I discuss new challenges in media law. The group also includes Jane Kirtley, former director of the U.S.-based Reporters Committee for Freedom of the Press and now the Silha Professor of Media Ethics and Law at the School of Journalism and Mass Comminication at the University of Minnesota; Kyu Ho Youm, Jonathan Marshall First Amendment Chair, University of Oregon School of Journalism and Communication; Mark Stephens, a leading media lawyer in London who gives seminars at Oxford's Centre for Socio Legal Studies, and Mei Ning Yan who teaches media law and ethics at Hong Kong Baptist University. The course continues to evolve. I turn to the students for assistance on research and for recommendations on improvements. The courtroom visit was among the many suggestions so far. Every year, the curriculum is revised and updated to make it the most current; typically one-third of the readings are changed.

The JMSC student intranet website is used for additional study aids, power points for lectures, speaker notes (and contact information), study questions/ guidelines for the readings, additional readings, student presentations, class schedules, guidelines for term projects, previous final exams and model answers. The students are not shy about their evaluations. Some feel the coursework is too heavy (they may be right), while others have cited it as "immensely practical and thought provoking" and beneficial for "critical thinking." In response to the charges of overwork, I tell the students that the subject matter may be one of the most important they will ever study. The course's journalistic and international perspectives help prepare them for the global media world. Its case studies and their participation in research give them hands-on experience. If journalists are to fulfill their watchdog role, then they must become skilled at understanding and reporting the law, including media law.

REFERENCES

1. On December 9, 2004, the Hong Kong Law Reform Commission released its final reports recommending privacy legislation and the creation of a statutory press commission. http://www.info.gov.hk/hkreform
2. In 2003, the University of Hong Kong Faculty of Law added media law as a course for its law students.
3. Master of Journalism students are required to take a total of seven taught courses and complete a Master's Project, a 4,000-6,000-word magazine-length article that is a deeper journalistic exploration of a topic.
4. Peter Wesley-Smith, An Introduction to the Hong Kong Legal System,

Oxford 1998.

5. Contributors for this book, Hong Kong Media Law: A Handbook for Journalists, will include Yan Mei Ning, who teaches media law and ethics for undergraduates at Hong Kong Baptist University, and Jill Cottrell, recently retired from the HKU law faculty.

6. The approach would be similar to a chapter I wrote, "Article 23 and Freedom of the Press: A Journalistic Perspective," for a HKU law faculty book, National Security and Fundamental Freedoms: Hong Kong's Article 23 Under Scrutiny, HKU Press 2005.

Chapter 5

THE NIGERIAN JOURNALISTS' KNOWLEDGE, PERCEPTION AND USE OF THE FREEDOM OF INFORMATION (FOI) LAW IN JOURNALISM PRACTICES

Ifeoma Dunu and Gregory Obinna Ugbo

Department of Mass Communication, Nnamdi Azikiwe University, Awka, Nigeria

ABSTRACT

The imperativeness of the freedom to access information, express opinions and active participation in governance by the general public has been recognized by a good number of democratic governments across the globe; hence, the adoption and enactment of the Freedom of Information Act by such democratic governments (Nigeria inclusive). However, there seems to be gross under-utilization of this enormous power bestowed on the media (and on the journalists working in the media) as both the purveyors of public information and watchdog of the society. This study, therefore, undertakes an assessment of the Nigerian journalists' knowledge, perception and use of the FOI Law in the discharge of their (information) responsibility to the public. With respondents drawn from four Nigerian Union of Journalists (NUJ) chapels, precisely, Enugu and Anambra, Imo and Ebonyi South-East zone, this study employing survey research methodology, finds that the FOI law as it applies in principles is still not symmetrical with pragmatic access to information. This perhaps accounted for the ambivalent responses got from the respondents - all are aware of the law; some consent an improvement in access to information but ironically, greater majority have never made use of the law in the discharge of their journalistic responsibilities. The researchers, therefore, recommend that the different journalistic, media bodies and media right groups must deliberately plan and monitor workshops and conferences synergetically and must be willing to firmly support journalists who may be hindered by bureaucratic bottlenecks that may result in litigations.

INTRODUCTION

In 2011, the Nigerian Government signed the FOI Bill into law, thereby making Nigeria the ninth country in Africa and among the over 90 countries in the world to have passed this bill. The Act, according to Media Rights Agenda (2011), is indeed very explicit in its mission, which is simply to: Make public records and information more freely available, provide for public access to public records and information, protect public records and information to the extent consistent with the public interest and the protection of personal privacy, protect serving public officers from adverse consequences for disclosing certain kinds of official information without authorization and establish procedures for the achievement of those purposes and; for related matters.

Described as a legal instrument that would not only radicalize reportorial engagement of journalists, FOI Act, it has been argued, will foster a greater opportunity for investigative journalism, promoting the democratic process. The FOI Act has indeed created high expectations from the public concerning journalism practice in the country - expectations of truthful and adequate information from the media on all spheres of the society; a broader window of opportunity to practice unfettered journalism and a powerful investigative tool that empowers the media to hold public officers accountable to the people. However, these expectations become a reality only when the media practitioners put this powerful investigative tool to use. As Enonche (2012) observes 'Nigerians finally have vital tools to uncover facts, fight corruption and hold officials and institutions accountable'. Given the enabling power of the FOI instrument, the critical question now is: are the Nigerian journalists making use of this important tool? This supports the argument that 'a law is useless or ineffective if not put to use/operation'.

In the light of the foregoing, we argue that, for the FOI Act to meet the high expectations and achieve the objectives of ensuring a more open and transparent society as well as enthroning democracy and responsible governance in Nigeria, the media must move beyond the euphoria that accompanied the establishment of the FOI Law, to come to terms with the provisions of the Act and begin to harness some of the expectations therein through the appropriate utilization of the Act. The Executive Secretary, of the Nigerian Press Council (NPC), Mr. Bayo Atoyebi explained how the media can harvest the benefits of the FOI Act as he clarifies: 'by first understanding the law and making bold to use it and grow our reportage from speculative to the factual'. The media should use FOI Act request to assess the level of compliance with relevant laws including the Fiscal Responsibility Act, the Public Procurement Act (PPA, 2007), the Electoral Act (especially aspects of it dealing with political finance monitoring) among others. FOI Act can also be deployed by the media as a tool to carry out its oversight functions as envisaged by section 22 of the 1999 Constitution. In this way, FOI becomes an indispensible tool in the reporting of accountability and anticorruption issues. The burning question is, do Nigerian journalists see and use the FOI Act as an investigative instrument to grow reportage from speculative to factual?

Beginning from mid 2012, training workshops were organized in different Geopolitical Zones in the country. The main objective was to familiarize the journalists with the essential elements of the FOI Act and how they can use the Act to conduct investigative reporting in the country. Having undergone these series of workshops and trainings in the use of the Act, it becomes pertinent then that we interrogate Nigerian journalists' knowledge, perception and use of the (FOI) law as an investigative tool in their day-to-day practices. This raises the concern of this paper as to whether the Nigerian journalists have adequately began to use the Act to protect the people's right to know, or to contest encroachment by government. Do the media understand their right under the FOI Act or even have a passing idea of how a request might be framed? Several other questions begging for attention could be summed up as follows: Since the enactment of the law has there been a noticeable improvement in the way the job of journalism is being done in the country? Are there cases of more in-depth, investigative journalism being put in place? Are the Nigerian media ensuring that the Nigerian publics maximize the benefits of the act by taking the lead in approaching governmental agencies and organizations for information they need to do their work? These questions are germane to this study given the fact that the trend that seems to pervade the practice currently is still the popular parlance of 'business as usual' without any seeming significant change. Given the above perceptions and observations, this study interrogates whether and how the Nigerian journalist - at this dawn of 'unrestricted access so to 'seek and say' virtually any information - are rising up to the challenge of this new dawn in the Nigerian journalism practice.

Through a lens of history: Journalists' experiences in the face of freedom of information acts

Journalists' age-long struggles for emancipation from restrictive and oppressive legislations have not been without unpleasant experiences and even extreme cases of martyrdom. Instances of oppressive measures against the press and journalists date as far back as the fifteenth century. Finkelstein (2012), in his Report of the Independent Inquiry into the Media and Media Regulation, observes that the restrictive measures on journalists and the press date as far back as 1476 when the newlyinvented printing press came to England and revolutionized communication possibilities. The press then, faced lots of prosecutions for treason and seditious libel. These repressive legislations reigned supreme till the mid-18th century when the struggle for liberation became apparent (Keane, 1991; Curran, 2010), cited in Finkelstein (2012, pp.25-26). Democratic governments realized the need for liberty and enthronement of the 'Marketplace of Ideas'. Steyn (2000) buttressed this point with the assertion that 'Freedom of speech is the life blood of democracy' With the concept of democracy becoming the order of the day, (perhaps courtesy of the frantic efforts of the United Nations), many countries realizing the fact that information is key to strengthening government-citizen relations and a means of enthroning a transparent and accountable government, made deliberate efforts to implement Freedom of Information (FOI) laws (acts) - the legislation that empowers or enables the citizens of a country to demand free access to certain specified documents or information - to give the press freer hand to operate within the ambits of journalistic ethics. To this end, several countries have adopted various forms of the FOI Laws (or similar legislations) (Schenkelaars and Ahmad, 2004; Ojo, 2010). Schenkelaars and Ahmad (2004) further observe that there was a sharp rise in the number of countries that adopted various forms of FOI legislations from 1980 to 2001, and that 80% of the Organisation for Economic Cooperation and Development (OECD) member countries now has legislation on this subject

The presence of these legislations and the claims to democracy notwithstanding, journalists' experiences keep oscillating from favourable to awfully unpleasant. To this end, scholars have documented several cases of torture, maiming, detention, assassination et cetera, meted on the journalist world over (and which in most cases extended to their family members) (Ellick, 2007; Jallow, 2008; Same, 2008) (Dombo, n.d). The reports given by these scholars are particularly disturbing as these countries already have or had claimed to have 'functional' FOI Act enshrined in their constitutions. The Nigerian situation was not far from those of other countries of the world. The editorial page of The Punch Newspaper (2008) has it that 'several cases of arrested journalists were reported in Nigeria even during democratic dispensations'. Generally, state restriction of freedom of expression and police brutality were regular threats to members of the press. Police raided editorial offices and arrested employees of press organizations including the Daily Independent, The News, and The Observer during the 1999-2003 democratic dispensation (The Punch, 2008; Onadipe, 2002, in Akinwale, 2010). The police action was said to be the result of press publications considered critical of the Nigerian government. As such, the power of the press to check government institutions was been curtailed... (Akinwale, 2010). Other accounts of repression in Nigeria are given by Ohiagu, (2010). Bush (2008) asserts that Nigeria, China, Cuba and Eritrea were among the countries with high prevalence of arrested and jailed journalists in 2007. The list is inexhaustible. However, this paper did not dwell on this, as this is not the main focus of this study. The researchers deemed it necessary to undertake the cursory look on these harrowing experiences so that we could better appreciate the FOI law and why journalists must strive at all cost to imbibe the principles of the law and put them into maximum use. Perhaps, prior to this time, the inaccessibility of information and the journalists' seeming non-performance could have been blamed on the Nigerian government's initial adamant position to the demands of the FOI Bill, but now that the FOI Law has been passed, the study interrogates why the law (save for a few cases of use) remains largely viable on paper rather than in practice. It is obvious from the foregoing analogies, that the crux of the matter herein is not a question of whether the FOI law exists, but how the journalists have been able to put this power conferred on them (by the law) into use. Consequently, to put the Nigerian FOI experience in context, this study explores Nigerian journalists' use and perception of the FOI as an investigative tool. In a nutshell, this paper seeks to ascertain Nigerian journalists' familiarity and usage of the Act as an investigative journalistic tool in their day-to-day functions as purveyors of public information and watchdog of the society. In the light of the above arguments this study interrogates the following objectives:

- To ascertain the journalists' level of awareness of the FOI law and its contents.
- To determine how knowledgeable these journalists are pertaining to the FOI law and its implications to their duties.
- To ascertain their perception of the FOI law in relation to their job as purveyors of information.
- To determine if they enjoy more access to information where hitherto they did not.
- To examine how they have been using this access to information to facilitate their jobs.

A REVIEW OF LITERATURE

Freedom of information law: An overview

The modern concept of Freedom of Information (FOI) could be said to be the brainchild of the United Nations Universal Declaration of Human Right (UNDHR) as enshrined in article 19 of 1948 Declaration thus: Everyone has the right to freedom of opinion and expression; this right includes freedom to hold opinions without interference and to seek, receive and impart information and ideas through any media and regardless of frontiers. FOI law since then has become a technical term that describes a particular class of legislation that defines and supports the rights of citizens to demand access to specified types of documents (Schenkelaars and Ahmad, 2004). Schenkelaars and Ahmad further maintain that 'access to information requires sound legislation, clear institutional mechanisms for its application, and independent oversight institutions and the judiciary for enforcement. It also depends on the citizens knowing and understanding their 'right to know'; and being willing and able to act upon it (2004). Arnold (2005) delineates the concept of Freedom of information as:

An extension of freedom of speech, a fundamental human right recognized in international law, which is today understood more generally as freedom of expression in any medium, be it orally, in writing, print, through the Internet or through art forms. This means that the protection of freedom of speech as a right includes not only the content, but also the means of expression (Arnold, 2005).

The World Summit on the Information Society (WSIS) Declaration of Principles adopted in 2003 reaffirms democracy and the universality, indivisibility and interdependence of all human rights and fundamental freedoms. The Declaration also makes specific reference to the importance of the right to freedom of expression for the 'Information Society' in stating:

We reaffirm, as an essential foundation of the Information Society, and as outlined in Article 19 of the Universal Declaration of Human Rights that everyone has the right to freedom of opinion and expression; that this right includes freedom to hold opinions without interference and to seek, receive and impart information and ideas through any media and regardless of frontiers. Communication is a fundamental social process, a basic human need and the foundation of all social organization. It is central to the Information Society. Everyone, everywhere, should have the opportunity to participate and no one should be excluded from the benefits the Information Society offers (Klang and Murray, 2005). Mendel (2005) contends that the right to access information is most commonly associated with a right to request and to receive documents…, equally important, particularly given recent technological advances, is the obligation on public bodies to actively publish information of key importance, thereby placing an obligation on public bodies to take specific measures to ensure a free flow of information to the public (Mendel, 2005). Interestingly, a good number of countries across the globe have toed the trend of the United Nations Universal Declaration of Human Rights of 1948 (as stated earlier in this paper), although scholars have conflicting record as regards the exact number of countries that have adopted the FOI law (Mendel, 2005; Neuman,

2010; Organization for Security and Cooperation in Europe (OSCE), 2012). Also, the Commonwealth Law Ministers Meeting in Trinidad and Tobago, 1999, formulated and adopted the Commonwealth Freedom of Information law.

Also on the African scene, the African Commission on Human and Peoples' Rights, 2002, adopted the Principles on Freedom of Expression in Africa. This is encapsulated in Article 9 of the African Charter on Human and Peoples' Rights Freedom of Information. Nigeria, however, was not left out in the entire process. Hence, the quest for the adoption of FOI law eventually saw the light of the day on 28th May, 2011. Mendel (2005) captures the scenario thus: Campaign on freedom of information has been active since early 1999, dating from the beginning of the postAbacha era. Legislation has been put forward on various occasions since that time, with strong support from civil society groups. On 25 August 2004, the House of Representatives, the lower House of Parliament, passed the third reading of the Freedom of Access to Information Bill.

Suffice to say from the foregoing that Nigeria toed the trend of other democratic countries and eventually adopted the FOI Act after decades of struggle obviously because the Act has been globally acknowledged as a veritable investigative instrument with proven potential to revolutionize, revitalize and radicalize journalism practices and democratic processes in Nigeria.

The Precepts of Nigerian FOI Law

As stated previously, the National Assembly of the Federal Republic of Nigeria recognized the FOI law as: An Act to make public records and information more freely available, provide for public access to public records and information, protect public records and information to the extent consistent with the public interest and the protection of personal privacy, protect serving public officers from adverse consequences of disclosing certain kinds of official information without authorization and establish procedures for the achievement of those purposes and; for related matters (FOIA, 2011).

The FOIA stipulates inter alia: 1

(i) Notwithstanding anything contained in any other Act, law or regulation, the right of any person to access or request information, whether or not contained in any written form, which is in the custody or possession of any public official, agency or institution howsoever described, is established.

(ii) An applicant under this Act needs not demonstrate any specific interest in the information being applied for.

(iii) Any person entitled to the right to information under this Act shall have the right to institute proceedings in the Court to compel any public institution to comply with the provisions of this Act.

Prior to the passage of the FOI bill into law, access to information especially of Hybrid Public Authorities was no go areas for the journalists. People view some information as being sacred with the belief that it was not meant for public consumption. Journalists or media houses that had at one point in time exercised their rights on issues bordering on 'sacred information' have dearly paid for it. Afolayan (2012) notes that there have been cases of assault on journalists, arbitrary detention and mass confiscation of newspapers. For instance, in 1986 and 1995 the renowned journalists - Dele Giwa and Saro Wiwa - paid the ultimate price for being too daring in the face of corruption and injustice. Also in 2005, two newspaper offices - Daily Independent and The News - were ransacked after they had published stories about corrupt behaviour by the wife of the then president, Olusegun Obasanjo. In fact, Nigeria then had a corrupt, obdurate and highly secretive bureaucracy. Transparency and accountability were strange bedfellows to then administrations. However, Enonche (2012) sees light at the end of the tunnel for journalists. He maintains that the newly enacted Freedom of Information Act among others: Guarantees the right of access to information held by public institutions, irrespective of the form in which it is kept and is applicable to private institutions where they utilize public funds, perform public functions or provide public services; Provides protection for whistleblowers.

Critics have maintained that the viability of the FOI laws and citizens' access to information is contingent upon several factors. These include among others: how bureaucracy and citizenship are conceived. In African nations, additional hindrances include the fragility of postcolonial state formations, cultural and ethnic diversity, violent conflict and inadequate economic and social infrastructure. Demand-driven state compliance with the requirements of transparency and freedom of information is therefore rare (Neuman and Calland, 2007). They explain further:

A government's implementation of an Access to Information (ATI) law is often related to their original motivation for supporting it, and the way in which the law was passed. Where the law was passed as part of an integrated policy or to meet civil society demand, progress has been good. However, where the law was passed to satisfy conditions of loans from international donors, commitment has been questionable (Neuman and Calland, 2007).

In most countries, government documents are categorized into classifications including 'Secret', 'Top Secret' and 'Confidential' and under such circumstances, the courts usually have no recognized jurisdiction under existing law to require or compel even limited access to state information. To this end, the activist group Media Rights Agenda posits that a veil of secrecy surrounds the conduct of government affairs. Officials of government do not only routinely deny citizens, whom they supposedly serve, explanations for actions undertaken on their behalf, they also block citizens' access to even the most mundane of publicly held information (Ackerman and Sandoval-Ballesteros, 2010).

Sandoval-Ballesteros, 2010). Little wonder some critics have cautioned that access to information does not necessarily lead to greater citizen participation, state accountability and state responsiveness. Rather, (especially) in many developing countries, there are real structural and political barriers which hinder both the capacity and incentives of governments to produce information, and the ability of citizens to claim their right to information and to use it to demand better governance and public services (Daruwala and Nayak, 2007). One of these barriers as identified by different studies is the inability of journalists to put effectively the FOI instrument into use, and the complicated processes involved in the usage of the Act. Coronel (2012) in the study titled Measuring Openness: A Survey of Transparency Ratings and the Prospects for a Global Index, listed the findings from the studies conducted by different media bodies and transparency groups (amongst others) (Media Rights Agenda (MRA), 2008-2010). The findings point to the fact that public institutions were mostly unwilling to release information even in the face of the FOI Act. This study will lend credence to the efficacy or otherwise of the FOI laws by examining the correlation between the empirical evidence found in the study above and the present Nigerian situation in the face of the FOI law. Furthermore, Darch and Underwood (2010) in their paper Struggles for Freedom of Information in Africa, state that the advance of information rights in Africa has been limited but lowkey activity indicates that some awareness exists. This study will seek to ascertain if similar awareness exist in Nigeria.

Nigeria was also one of the countries surveyed by the Open Society Justice Initiative and reported in 2006. Predictably, in the absence of any freedom of information legislation and given the powerful tradition of bureaucratic secrecy, the results were not encouraging (Ackerman and Sandoval-Ballesteros, 2010). If this was the case when the FOI bill was yet to be signed into law, it is our expectation that there would be a remarkable improvement with the present legislations pertaining to freedom of access to information, bearing in mind the aims and objectives of the Act . Empirical evidence as already stated indicate that in a number of countries of the world, there appears to be a significant low access to information by the citizens of such countries especially the African countries, even with the FOI Act in these places. The journalists on their part appear to be silent or perhaps not knowledgeable enough as regards the contents of the FOI law and/or its implications to their duties to the public. Although Mendel (2005) notes that 'Freedom of the press should not be regarded simply as the freedom of journalists, editors or proprietors alone to report and comment, rather, it should be regarded as the embodiment of the public's right to know and to participate in the free flow of information'; the remark portends even greater responsibilities for the journalists. As have been argued by different school of thoughts access to information via the FOI Act represents both a right and a responsibility for the journalists. It provides the media with a valuable tool to meet its responsibilities as it offers independent access to government information. FIO in principles is ultimately beneficial for journalists as part of their broader democratic and accountability role.

Available literature seems to indicate that FOI Act has not been adequately utilized by journalists to protect the people's right to know or to contest encroachment by government, in most African countries (Bildstein, 2004; Akinwale, 2010; Coronel, 2012); it is important to determine whether such findings would be made in Nigeria and why. Robert Hazell, director of the Constitution Unit, posits that 'The media is the conduit through which most of the public learn about FOI' (http://www.ucl.ac.uk/ constitution-unit/ foidp/). Consequently, the journalists have whole gamut of roles to play in sensitizing and galvanizing the citizenries to become active participants in their own governance; to question government activities and non-activities; take decisions in choosing their leaders and representatives; demand access to certain specified documents, etc. But can all these be feasible if the informants (journalists) are not by themselves knowledgeable and informed on the principles and contents of the FOI Law? This issue amongst others will be looked into in line with the postulations of the social responsibility theory upon which this study is anchored (Christians, 2004).

Theoretical framework: social responsibility theory

The Social Responsibility theory takes the stance that the social roles of the press - of enlightening the people, promoting the democratic process, safeguarding the liberties of the individual, etc. should take precedence over its role of servicing the economic system (Oloyede, 2005). Also one of the obligations of the press under the social responsibility theory as spelt out by the Hutchins Commission (1947) is: providing 'full access to the day's intelligence'. Consequently, the choice of this theory is informed by the fact that the FOI law is not an exclusive reserve of the Journalists rather it extends to the rights of the general public to access any information that is of interest to them, principally through the media. The media, therefore, owes a duty to the public - to sensitive and galvanize them to fully utilize the principles of the FOI law. It is in line with this that Robert Hazell clearly points out that 'the media is the conduit through which most of the public learn about FOI', this by implication suggests that the public have the right to or are expected to have access to information, particularly through the media in democratic governments. Although this theory falls short in the areas of expressing over confidence on the media and media operators in meeting their responsibilities using the 'self-righting' process and overly underestimated the power of profitorientation and competition in driving the media to selfish ends; the theory is adjudged most suitable for this study given the intents of this study. One of which is ascertaining how the legislations on freedom to access information have perceptibly enhanced journalism practices in Nigeria, in satisfying the public's information needs. The social responsibility theory recognizes the media's right to scrutinize and criticize the government and other institutions but not without responsibility to preserve democracy by properly informing the public. The media and media operators are not free to do as they will; they are obligated to respond to society's needs. The theory, therefore, challenges the journalists to strive at all times to keep the public informed (among other duties) within the ambits of the journalistic code of ethics and legislations. It is against this backdrop that this study seeks answer to the following questions:

- How knowledgeable are the Nigerian journalists pertaining to the FOI law and its implications to their responsibilities?
- What are their perceptions of the FOI law in relation to their job as purveyors of information?
- Has the FOI law made any significant impact on the Nigerian journalists in accessing and disseminating information? In other words, has the FOI perceptibly improved journalism practice in Nigeria?
- Do they enjoy more access to information where hitherto they did not?
- How have they been using this access to information it to facilitate their jobs?

METHODOLOGY

This study adopts a combined approach to explore the critical questions and other discourses raised in the reviewed literature. Hence, the survey research methodology was used while employing indepth interview to follow up the critical issues arising from the answers given in the questionnaire. The population of this study comprises journalists in Nigeria with the sample size drawn from four Nigerian Union of Journalists' (NUJ) Chapels in Enugu, Anambra, Ebonyi and Owerri states, all in the Southeastern zone of Nigeria, the choice of which is informed by the chapels' propinquity. The total number of registered journalists in these four chapels was 180 and they constituted the sample size for the study.

Analysis of data

From the total of 180 questionnaires that were distributed to respondents from the four NUJ Chapels, in Southeastern Nigeria, 136 questionnaires were validly returned and analyzed accordingly. Data generated from these responses are presented using the major themes explored in this study.

The demographic profile of the respondents

The researchers explored the demographic profiles of the respondents. The results show that 70.6% are males while 29.4% are females. Findings also show that all the respondents are between the ages of 26-30 years (26.5%) and 31 years and above (73.5%); and that all have acquired one form of tertiary education's qualifications or the other with the least qualification being OND. 33.8% of the respondents have Masters Degree, HND/OND (40.4%) and other tertiary qualifications at 22.1%. The data above suggest that most of the journalists are adult males with tertiary qualifications (Table 1).

These data show the percentage distribution of respondents' awareness and knowledge of FOI Act.

Table 1: Respondents' awareness and knowledge of FOI law

	Awareness of FOI Law	Knowledge of the contents of FOI Law
Yes	100%	74%
No	-	26%
Total	100% (n = 136)	100% (n=136)

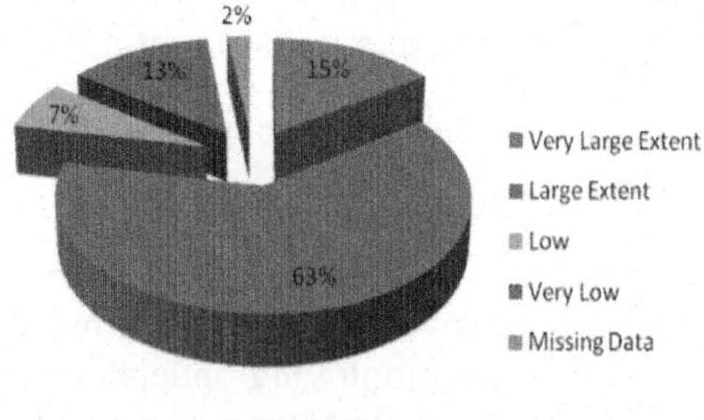

Figure 1: Respondents' level of understanding of FOI principles.

Table 2: Respondents' perception and use of FOI law

	Do journalists view the FOI Law as an investigative tool in news gathering?	Has FOI Law enhanced their access to information?	Do journalists utilize FOI law in discharging their duties?
Yes	82%	34%	15%
No	18%	66%	85%
Total	100% (n = 136)	100% (n=136)	100% (n=136)

The Nigerian journalists surveyed showed high level of awareness of the FOI Law, as all the respondents agree that they are aware of the existence of the Freedom of Information law. 100 per cent of them affirmed their awareness of the FOI Law, while only under two thirds (26%) indicated lack of knowledge of the FOI Act, an indication that awareness and knowledge of the FOI Act is high among the journalists (Figure 1).

To ascertain the level of knowledge of the Act, the respondents' level of understanding of the Act was also analyzed. The data in Figure 1 clearly indicate that the degree or extent of this awareness and understanding of the principles of the FOI law is high among the sampled journalists, considering that 78% of the respondents fully understand the principles of the Law, while 13% of them do not have such understanding even though they know the law exists. Similarly, 7% of the journalists showed low understanding of the FOI law. The analysis clearly demonstrates that majority of Nigerian journalists are knowledgeable about the precepts of the FOI Act (Table 2).

Since journalists' perception of the Act is of interest in this study, to ascertain whether their view of the Act affect their usage for reporting, we now sought their opinion of the Act as an investigative instrument for news gathering, and found out that slightly more than three-fourths (82%) of the journalists see the Act as an investigative tool for journalism practice. Meanwhile, two thirds (66%) identify that the Act improves their access to information; this is against 34% who do not agree. Even though majority of the journalists view the Act as an investigative tool and also admit that it increases their access to information, more than three-fourth (85%), an overwhelming majority, indicated they have not been using the Act. The data suggest that although all the journalists sampled are aware of the FOI Law and its potential to enhancing access to information, greater majority of the journalists have not made use of it as their responses indicated, in the discharge of their duties.

Next, we tried to compare the media situation now with what obtains in the past before the existence of the Act (Figure 2). This is to determine if there is any improvement or not. Slightly more than a half of the respondents (51%) were of the view that the situation of denial of access to information has improved compared to what obtained in the past, while 33% declared no improvement;

12% were undecided while 4% did not respond to the question. This data at first glance could be interpreted to mean improvement. But, a closer look will suggest indications to the contrary. A more critical examination will suggest ambivalence, an indication that clearly points to the fact that journalists are not capable of making the comparisons since they have not been using the act.

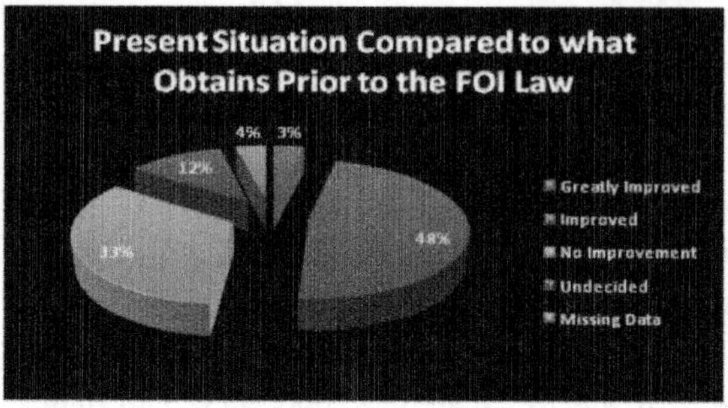

Figure 2: Present situation compared to what obtains prior to the FOI law.

Table 3: Challenges to the use of FOI law

	Do principal parties comply with the principles of the law?	Are there challenges to the use of FOI law?
Yes	19%	85%
No	81%	15%
Total	100% (n = 136)	100% (n=136)

The data go to support the earlier finding that indicates that Nigerian journalists are presently not making use of the act; therefore, they cannot adequately compare situations and make valid deductions.

Compliance with the principles of FOI law by all parties concerned and other challenges

The researchers went further to find out if all parties concerned comply with the principles of the FOI Law and to also determine whether there are challenges in the implementation of the law for journalists. The data from Table 3 show that (19%) are of the opinion that concerned parties comply, while a greater majority (81%) did not agree. Further, on the issue of challenges, threefourth (85%) of the respondents indicate the existence of challenges in the use of the law, while 15% did not. Reading this data, one will be tempted to just say 'yes! Challenges exist' as countless studies have proven. In this case however, what comes through is the fact that majority that indicated the existence of challenges may as well be those that have found it difficult to use the Act in their day to day practice of journalism- that is, those journalists that have never used it. While, the small minority that may have used it going by these data did not encounter much challenges. Again, this goes further to show that majority of Nigerian journalists sampled have not applied the law as an investigate tool in their journalism profession.

This is not surprising, when we recall the journalism culture of Nigeria has tended towards 'routine arm-chair reporting' instead of the more rigorous investigative journalism culture. To examine respondents further on the use of the Act, they were asked open- ended questions as a follow up. From the open-ended questions that the researchers used to prod the respondents further, the respondents attributed the seeming reluctance to the use of the FOI law to the following factors which they saw as challenges:

Respondent 1: some government officials despite the law still hoard information claiming that their bosses have not permitted them to release same. Also a lot of people especially those in government offices are yet to fully embrace the new law Respondent 2: the FOI law has never made any change in getting information for effective journalism Respondent 3: the challenges have to do with lack of adequate awareness and enforcement as most journalists are still very ignorant of the principles of the law. Respondent 4: the problem of privacy laws and official secret acts still hinder adequate accessibility to information Respondent 5: Inadequate enforcement-despite the bill being passed into law, it is not yet practicable. There is the need to equip information managers with information on how to address issues of non-compliance.

Respondent 6: Some journalist may use it as an opportunity to behave anyhow and some issues not meant to be public consumption may be tampered with. Respondent 7: There is no cooperation at government level. This is reflected in the attitude of civil servants particularly to freedom of information. Some civil servants and other educated elites sit on the information which they ought to dish out freely to the journalists for objective reporting. Respondent 8: socio-cultural background and government bureaucracy is a major challenge. The government at all levels still disobey the laws of the land and we Nigerians are yet to fully embrace and imbibe the principle of democracy.

From the responses above, we could deduce that the problem boils down to the issue of non-compliance. The respondents further mentioned the civil servants, judiciary, gate-keepers/news makers, government, public and private institutions as not complying with the FOI law. It is therefore obvious from the list that all parties are directly involved and points to the fact that the law has not been fully implemented especially for the few journalists who have tendered one form of request or the other pursuant to the Act. This finding on non compliance by the government and other public institutions coincides with Coronel's (2012) observation that government and public institutions fail to comply with the principles of the FOI Act and that the few that eventually comply, either delay in the stipulated duration of compliance or comply after a long process of litigation.

The Right-to-Know group maintains that this dragging of requests for information through the long appeal process from the High Court all the way to the Supreme Court has a potentially negative effect on the utility of the information requested. On the other hand, some of the respondents mentioned lack of adequate knowledge on how to operate with the Act. This worrisome fact undermines the previous suggestion that non compliance by government and other public institutions are responsible for low usage of the Act by Nigerian journalists, although the possibility does exist. This particular finding supports and points to the near absent usage of the Act by the journalists. It also suggests widespread ignorance both on the side of the journalists and the general public of the FOI Act as a veritable, legal investigative tool at their disposal. This seems to be the precursor to the underutilization of the law. The Right to Know group in her 2012 review of the level of implementation of the FOI law posits that the value of a law can only be seen when it is tested. Again, a law can only be tested by citizens who are aware of their rights under the law.

DISCUSSION AND CONCLUSION

The findings derived from the study present no new discovery but rather reinforced previous research findings regarding the use of FOI Act by journalists in different countries (Bildstein, 2004; Neuman and Calland, 2007; Calland, 2010, cited in Coronel, 2012). The study has shown that Nigerian journalists understand and value the FOI Act as an investigative tool, as Darch and Underwood, (2010) also observed, but the Act is generally not often used by them. From the findings, it was apparent that Nigerian journalists seem not to have imbibed the culture of routine investigative journalism but rather still lean on speculative arm- chair reporting, which has continued to be the bane of journalism practice in Nigeria. The findings of the study suggest that the FOI Act is yet to create an impact in Nigerian journalism traditions. While in the past, journalists have had greater personal access to politicians and their aides as primary sources of information, the FOI should now substitute for such access, but going from what we found, that seemed not to be the case; the FOI has not been adequately put to work by journalists. What seems to prevail regarding journalism practice is 'business as usual' without the Act making any notable difference. What this suggests, is that the use of investigative and analytical skills considered as the most critical for ensuring professionalism in journalism practice is still an area of serious challenge for the Nigerian journalists. It seems probable, that the Nigerian media's reluctance in the use of FOI Act among other factors stems from a preference for alternative sources or a hesitancy to undertake investigative journalism as opposed to speculative practice.

Considering the fact that the FOI Act is still a recent development in the Nigerian media terrain, one will not be too surprised with the findings of this study. This notwithstanding, there is an urgent need for training and retaining of journalists on the use of the FOI Act before this prevailing low usage subsists and becomes a tradition. Lack of FOI Act usage tends to have a negative spiral effect on the investigative skills with the FOI Act if left unchecked. As is widely acknowledged, erosion of skills leads to a downward trend because unskilled journalists who attempt to use the Act on an infrequent basis will achieve less useful results from the FOI request than the few who use it frequently. On the other hand, if journalists become adequately educated about the FOI, the possibility exists that they will be encouraged to use it more and government and other public would be under greater pressure to be compliant and accountable. Again, if adequate sensitization and orientation were given to the public and private institutions concerning the provisions in section 2 (3) of the Act, there certainly will be a change in the way the Act was administered such that the institutions concerned proactively and willingly disclose information in a timely and less strenuous manner, then journalist would be more likely to use the FOI. More importantly, since most government, security outfits and other corporate bodies' (like NNPC) activities are still shrouded in secrecy probably because of the Official Secret Act, there is the need to streamline the principles of the Official Secret Act and other related Acts that attach one form of clause or the other to the usage of the FOI Act. This, as the Right-to-Know group in her 2013 communiqué also recommends, will give the journalists and the general public an unfettered access to information of public interest.

Also, the different media organizations and media right groups must deliberately plan and monitor workshops and conferences synergetically and must be willing to firmly support journalists who may be hindered by bureaucratic bottlenecks that may result in litigations. The Nigerian journalists as a matter of exigency must triple their efforts to ensure that this all-important instrument is judiciously utilized by all. Until these issues are addressed and changes made, the Freedom of Information Act and the journalists in Nigeria will remain but 'toothless bulldogs' and by extension continue to underutilize the Act.

Since this study was conducted in the Southeastern part of Nigeria, the sample may not have captured all registered journalists in the country. However, the sample does contain the requisite elements through which generalizations could be made. We, therefore, recommend further investigation into the challenging situations pointed out by the journalists surveyed in comparison with what obtains in other zones of the country. This study has succeeded in revealing that in reality, the passing of the FOI Bill into Law does not suggest concomitant pragmatic access to information, perhaps due to the gross underutilization by the journalists.

REFERENCES

1. Afolayan A (2012). A Critical Analysis of Freedom of Information Act in Nigeria. Akinwale AA (2010). Repression of Press Freedom in Nigerian.
2. Democratic Dispensations.Council for the Development of Social Science Research in Africa. Africa Dev. 35(3):47-70.
3. Arnold H (2005). Freedom of Expression. Essentials Human Rights. p.128.
4. Bildstein KL (2004). Raptor migration in the Neotropics: Patterns, process, and consequences. Ornitol. Neotrop. 15:83-99.
5. Bush GW (2008). 'Statement on World Press Freedom Day', Weekly Compilation of Presidential Documents, 5 May, 44(17):636-637.
6. Christians C (2004). Social Responsibility Worldwide. Philadelphia: Lawrence Erlbaum Associates.
7. Coronel S (2001). Fighting for the right to know. In: Coronel S (Ed.), The right to know: Access to information in Southeast Asia. Quezon City: PCIJ.
8. Darch C, Underwood PG (2010).Freedom of information and the developing world: the citizen, the State and models of openness. Oxford: Chandos.
9. Enonche E (2012). What to Expect from the Newly Signed Freedom of Information Bill. A Conference Paper delivered at the Media Rights Agenda (MRA) Workshop. Retrieved on 27th April 2013, from http://www.allin.africamediaright.com.
10. Finkelstein R (2012). Report of the Independent Inquiry into the Media and Media Regulation. ISBN: 978-0-642-75425-7 (DOC version). Freedom of Information Act (2011). Retrieved on 1st May, 2013, from http://www.nassnig.org/nass2/acts.php.
11. Klang M, Murray A (2005). Human Rights in the Digital Age. U.S.A.: Routledge
12. Mendel T (2005). Parliament and Access to Information: Working for Transparent Governance Stock No.37247 Ojo E (2010).
13. Freedom of Information: Current Status, Challenges and Implications for

News media. Retrieved on 1st May, 2013, from www.unesco.org/new/.../multimedia/.../wpfd2010_background.

14. Oloyede IB (2005). Press Freedom: A Conceptual Analysis. J. Soc. Sci. 11(2):101-109.
15. Organization for Security and Co-operation in Europe (2012). Comments on the Draft Law on Transparency, Access to Information and Good Governance of Spain.
16. Right to Know Group (2012). Implementing the Nigerian Freedom of Information Law: the Journey so Far. Accessed on 5th July, 2013, from http://www.google.com.ng/url?sa=t&rct=j&q=&esrc=s&source=web&cd=4&ved=0CD4 QFjAD&url=http%3A%2F%2Fr2knigeria.org% 2Findex.php%2Fdownloads%2Ffoi-assessmentsa-reports%2Fdoc_download%2F84-implementing-nigerias-foi-act-2011-the-journey-so-far&ei=Ep4qUvGIIMSa1AWN3IGgDQ&usg=AFQjCNHzSiIH- Zww8hlFr8MQZVNZL5lxTw&bvm=bv.51773540,d.d2k.
17. Schenkelaars F, Ahmad I (2004). Transparency and Accountability in the Public Sector in the Arab Region
18. Steyn L (2000) Secretary of State for the Home Department, Ex parte Simms.
19. United States of America (1947). Report of Press Freedom Commission (Hutchins Commission).

Chapter 6

THE DISCLOSURE DILEMMA: RETURNING TO JOURNALISM AFTER POLITICAL MEDIA ADVISING

Caroline Fishe

Journalism, Faculty of Arts & Design, University of Canberra, Canberra, Australia

ABSTRACT

The principle of transparency in journalism, including disclosure of journalistic processes and reporters' personal interests, has been enthusiastically embraced. However there has been little focus on the possible harm disclosure can have on a reporter's reputation. This paper reports on a selection of findings from wider inductive, qualitative research into the transition from journalism to political media advising and back again. Semi-structured interviews with twenty-one journalists who had moved between the two roles revealed the interviewees faced a dilemma about disclosing their previous political work history because of concern about inviting a suspicion of partisanship from others. In response, the interviewees adopted five key strategies to disclosing their political employment: Being 'up front'; 'Flying below the radar'; 'Keeping it a secret'; 'Selective disclosure; and, 'Overcompensation'. Based on these findings this paper argues that the seemingly simple principle of transparency can have complex ramifications which need to be considered when advocating disclosure of interests by journalists.

INTRODUCTION

Transparency advocates contend disclosure of journalistic processes, including a reporter's personal interests and biases, will help improve the credibility of journalism in the eyes of the public (Hayes, Singer, & Ceppos, 2007; McBride & Rosenstiel,2014). This trend toward transparency is not isolated to journalism practice. It is part of a wider push for greater openness and scrutiny of governments and international institutions to increase accountability in public affairs (Baume & Papadopoulos, 2013; Grimmelikhuijsen, 2012; Hood, 2006). The origins of the transparency ideal in relation to governing is commonly traced back to the work of philosopher Jeremy Bentham in the eighteenth century and his promotion of the notion of 'publicity', which he saw as the most effective way to prevent abuses by government (Baume & Papadopoulos, 2013; Hood,2006; Ward, 2015). Over the past 30 years the term transparency has come to be seen as 'indispensible for accountability and good governance, for preventing corruption and improving performance, for increasing trustworthiness and trust' (O'Neill,2006, p. 76).

Similarly, in journalism which has 'wrestled with public trust' (McBride & Rosenstiel, 2014, p. 89) the ideal of transparency has been embraced as a central value for reporting in the digital age (McBride & Rosenstiel, 2014). The emergence of countless new online information sources means the boundary between traditional acts of journalism and other types of published information is blurring (Gillmor, 2010; Hayes et al., 2007; Kovach & Rosenstiel, 2010; McBride & Rosenstiel, 2014; McNair,2006). The rise of infotainment, the blending of opinion and straight news reporting, fact and fiction, have raised questions about the credibility of information being published (Gillmor, 2010; Hayes et al., 2007; McNair, 2006), making it difficult to tell 'who is a journalist let alone what types of information are acting as journalism' (McBride & Rosenstiel, 2014, p. 90). As Dan Gillmor explained it, the age of 'information abundance':

> Feels more like a deluge, drowning us in a torrent of data, much of whose trustworthiness we can't easily judge. You're hardly alone if you don't know what you can trust anymore. (Gillmor, 2010, p. xv)

Advocates for transparency argue that if reporters reveal the way they make decisions about the stories they write it will boost public trust in journalism and help the public distinguish between verified information and rumor (Gillmor, 2010; Kovach & Rosenstiel, 2010).

In the age of interactive online journalism, the ideal of transparency is also seen by advocates to addresses concerns about the contentious journalistic norm of 'objectivity'. The objectivity ideal requires a reporter to put his or her biases to one side, remain detached, impartial and fair when reporting and guide 'journalists to separate facts from values and report only the facts' (Schudson, 2001, p. 150). Critics of objectivity argue that such a separation cannot be made and the inherent subjective and selective nature of journalism means objectivity is a 'deception...promoting an external truth or ideal...that doesn't exist' and is unachievable (Maras, 2013, p. 1). In its stead, transparency is seen as 'the new objectivity' (Weinberger, 2009) allowing the reader to access source materials via hyperlinks and assess the evidence on their own without having to blindly trust that the reporter has given a fair account of events.

What we used to believe because we thought the author was objective we now believe because we can see through the author's writings to the sources and values that brought her to that position. Transparency gives the reader information by which she can undo some of the unintended effects of the ever-present biases. Transparency brings us to reliability the way objectivity used to. (Weinberger, 2009)

For the purposes of this discussion, the concept of transparency in journalism has been roughly divided into two parts. The first is editorial transparency, which is concerned with journalists and editors being open about the decision making and production processes. The second goes beyond openness about editorial processes to include disclosure of a reporter's personal interests, his or her preconceptions toward the story being written, their professional history, affiliations and biases (Hayes et al., 2007, p. 271). This article is primarily concerned with this latter form of disclosure, specifically a reporter's previous work history as a political media adviser, and concern about the possible negative impact disclosing that work history could have on his or her reputation.

While the disclosure of personal interests can engender trust and inspire confidence in a person's integrity, it can also pose a risk. In his work on conflict of interest, ethicist Michael Davis (1998) says disclosure is one of the key remedies for actual and potential conflicts of interest. However, he explained it can also invite a suspicion of bias toward that person, even if the conflict of interest no longer exists, and thereby harm the person's reputation (Davis, 1998, p. 591). The journalists in the paper were aware of this risk and it presented some of them with a dilemma. Concern about attracting perceptions of bias if they disclosed their work history as political media advisers led them to question whether or not they should reveal that information when they returned to work in the newsroom. In response to this challenge, the interview data revealed five main strategies that were adopted by these former media advisers to manage the disclosure of their political work history and thereby minimize possible damage to their reputation when they re-entered journalism. In doing so, their reflections highlight a tension between the simple ideal of transparency and the possible risks and complexities of putting that ideal into practice.

LITERATURE REVIEW

In the digital age when 'everyone can be a publisher' (Hayes et al., 2007, p. 262) the adoption of more transparent practices, as part of the broader principle of accountability, is being advocated by scholars and practitioners to help increase journalism's credibility and stave off threats from bloggers and citizen journalists (p. 271). Hayes et al. (2007) stated the transparency principle is made up of two main forms: 'personal disclosure' and 'evidentiary support'. 'Evidentiary support' referred to the ability of journalists to connect readers to primary information sources and supporting evidence for their stories and thereby increase the veracity of the journalist's work in the eyes of the public. Hayes et al. (2007) argued this ability to connect to primary information sources embedded in a story also meant that journalists could provide their readers with additional information about the editorial decision making process for that story. 'Personal disclosure', the authors said, involved openness about a journalist's personal interests and biases, something that has been eagerly embraced by bloggers, but less keenly adopted by reporters (Hayes et al., 2007, p. 272).

Reporters have been more reluctant to embrace this practice, the authors argued, because traditional journalists have less organisational autonomy and have been trained in the ideal of objectivity which requires the suppression of personal biases. Hayes et al. (2007, pp. 272–3) said adoption of both evidentiary and personal disclosure practices boosted journalism's accountability through explaining editorial decision making and humanizing reporters in the eyes of the public. These benefits of transparency have been echoed by other journalism scholars. In order to maintain the trust of the public, Kovach and Rosenstiel (2007, p. 92) argued that journalists needed to be 'presenters' of truth as well as 'seekers' of truth. The best way of doing that they said was for reporters to tell the public as much as possible about where they got their information from and how they went about constructing the story.

The principle of transparency in the digital age is 'so essential a part of how modern journalism attains credibility' that McBride and Rosenstiel (2014, p. 2) have advocated for it to be included in a new journalism ethics for the twenty-first century. In addition to the traditional principles of truth, accuracy and fairness, the proposed new code stipulates that a journalist should include how they went about their work, acknowledge any errors, and explain the journalist's point of view in relation to the story they are writing. Gillmor (2010) also included 'transparency' in his list of five key principles for creating trustworthy media. He wrote that news organizations 'have a duty to explain' how they go about their news work and that journalists must also be more open about their world views and motivations, just as bloggers should be required to reveal their biases (Gillmor, 2010, p. 71).

One journalism scholar, blogger and transparency advocate, who went to great lengths to achieve this on his blog,*BuzzMachine*, is Jeff Jarvis (2005). In what he described as an 'obnoxious' display of transparency (Jarvis, 2011),

Jarvis (2005) declared every job and business connection he had, as well as his religious and political beliefs and the way he had voted in every US election. Despite Jarvis' exhaustive interpretation of what personal transparency by journalists and bloggers could look like, there is no uniform approach to personal disclosure in journalism. Research shows that different levels of transparency are adopted by journalists in their use of social media, such as Twitter (Lasorsa, 2012; Revers, 2014).

In contrast to the voices championing the benefits of transparency in journalism, there is a range of literature assessing the efficacy of the transparency principle in lifting journalism's credibility in the eyes of the public. One of the most recent contributions to this discussion has been made by Ward (2015) who traces the history of the concept from the late sixteenth century to the present. In his examination of the ideal, Ward (2015) said 'transparency' had become a 'magical concept' that is hard to argue against. The problem with that he said is 'when norms become magic, they raise unrealistic expectations' (Ward,2015, p. 49). In the case of transparency the unrealistic expectation is that it will be a cure-all for issues of accountability and public trust, but in reality transparency falls short of those expectations. As an illustration of this, Ward (2015, p. 50) and O'Neill (2006, p. 75) both note that a rise in the adoption of transparency practices by public institutions has not been met with a corresponding rise in public trust.

A similar point was made by Karlsson, Clerwall, and Nord (2014) who argued that despite the enthusiasm for transparency in journalism there was little empirical evidence to prove whether it is effective in improving the standing of journalism in the eyes of the audience. Based on research involving 1320 respondents designed to test whether disclosure did affect the way stories and reporters were perceived by the public, the three researchers concluded that transparency practices had 'almost no effect on source and message credibility' (Karlsson et al., 2014, p. 674). Though some minor positive effects were found, primarily in relation to direct linking to primary source material, the authors did not see it as 'revolutionizing' journalism's credibility in the short or longer term (Karlsson et al., 2014, p. 675). Rather than having a limited impact, Allen (2008, p. 323) suggested that disclosure of journalistic decision making processes might have the opposite effect to that being sought and unintentionally 'increase criticism rather than understanding'. Though, the push for greater disclosure in journalism is a 'valuable and important ideal', Allen (2008, p. 323) argued that 'little attention has been given to whether there is such a thing as too much transparency' and what impact that might have. He warned that greater levels of transparency can also bring greater levels of scrutiny that 'might in the end, run counter to the very goals they seek' (Allen, 2008, p. 336). In addition to literature specifically about transparency in journalism, this article draws on the work of ethicist Michael Davis (1998, 2001, 2013) about conflict of interest in the professions. In his examination of conflict of interest he described the benefits and problems of disclosure as a remedy for conflict of interest. On the one hand, he explained, the act of disclosure 'prevents deception ...and avoids betrayal of trust' (Davis, 1998, p. 593), but on the other it can also 'harm the reputation...of the individual in question' by inviting others to question the reliability of his or her judgment (Davis, 1998, p. 591). It is this tension between the benefits and possible risks of disclosure identified by Davis (1998) that lies at the heart of the dilemma discussed in this paper.

APPROACH

The aim of this article is to provide a greater understanding of the complexities surrounding the journalistic ideal of transparency, particularly in relation to the disclosure of a journalist's personal interests. This paper has been written from a phenomenological perspective and reports on a selection of findings that emerged from wider inductive, qualitative research of journalists' perceptions of their lived experience of making the career transition from journalism to political media advising and back again (Fisher, 2014). The motivation for that wider research grew out of the author's own experience of moving between these two roles. Based on the contributions of practitioners who have experienced this particular career phenomenon, this paper examines the way journalists perceived and managed issues of disclosure about their previous political employment when they entered journalism after working as a political adviser.

Drawing on the philosophical traditions of phenomenology, hermeneutics (Heidegger, 1927/2008; Husserl, 2002) and symbolic interactionsim (Blumer, 1969/1998) the aim of the wider study and this paper has been to document journalists' perceptions of their experience shifting between the two roles and treat the first-person perspective of that experience on its own terms. This perspective is useful in helping to understand the diversity of the interviewees' perceptions of their experience of making the transition from political media advising to journalism and navigating their way through managing the dilemma of disclosure about their previous employment.

To identify journalists who had been both journalists and political media advisers, purposive and snowballing sampling techniques (Bryman, 2008, pp. 458–9) were used. This resulted in twenty-one semi-structured, in-depth interviews being conducted about their individual experiences of moving back and forth between the two roles. An 'aide memoire' (Minichiello, Aroni,

Timewell, & Alexander, 1995, p. 83) was used to guide the direction of the interviews, which included discussion of conflict of interest and the way in which the practitioners managed their return to journalism. In recognition of the value of individual perception, each of the interviewees in the study and this paper has been as treated as an 'expert' or 'lay theorist' (Furnham, 1988) based on their 'intense experiences' as 'key operators' in the career transition under investigation (Herbst,1998, p. 31).

In analyzing the interview data, a general inductive approach was taken (Bryman & Burgess, 1994; Thomas, 2006), which involved a process of multiple close readings of the data, during which categories, key themes, commonalities and differences in the material were identified, interpreted and selections made, while simultaneously working back and forth between the data, extant theory and literature. In doing so, the process of analysis drew out the 'common themes' and 'unique stories' (Karp, 1996, p. 12) that highlighted the most compelling conceptual stories.

FINDINGS & DISCUSSION

Each of the interviewees in this paper was forced to confront the issue of whether to disclose their previous employment as a political media adviser when they attempted to return to the newsroom. In deciding if and how they would disclose that information, the transcripts revealed five main approaches to transparency were adopted by the interviewees when they re-entered journalism to deal with this professional challenge. Those approaches have been categorized based on the willingness and or hesitation the interviewees expressed toward disclosure: Being up-front; Flying below the radar; Keeping it a secret; Selective disclosure; and, Overcompensation. As will be discussed, the willingness or reluctance of the interviewees to disclose their previous political employment was influenced by the level of concern they had about inviting perceptions of partisanship and bias and causing possible harm to their professional reputation. Each of the five approaches is described below.

Being up-Front

'Being up-front' describes a confident approach taken by several of the interviewees to simply disclose their previous employment in a politician's office. This was seen by those practitioners as the best way of tackling possible accusations of conflict of interest and perceptions of bias once they became journalists[1]. By 'being up-front', the interviewees hoped to avoid a 'betrayal of trust' (Davis, 1998, p. 593) by revealing their employment history to the people relying on their judgment, namely the editor and the public. In doing so, 'being up-front' allows the audience to 'adjust their reliance accordingly' and take the journalist's comments with a grain of salt, or seek a second opinion (Davis, 1998, p. 593). By being up-front the journalist avoids deception and increases their credibility in the eyes of the audience. One senior newspaper columnist put it this way:

Firstly… I am up front. When I put my bio on the website or write for someone, where it is relevant to a piece that I write, I chuck in my personal experience up front. Yes I have worked for a number of liberal politicians, have even been a member of that party. What do you want to do? Put me up against a wall and shoot me? I have that and it gives me an enormous insight into the way politics works …and I am not ashamed of it. I am proud of it in fact… So I think that is the best way to attack it: to be completely open and honest with your readers.

Instead of damaging his career, the journalist said his experience working in conservative politics had become a professional strength and part of his 'shtick' in his new role as a columnist, editorial and opinion writer and had allowed him to develop an audience attracted to his political views. Not only had the interviewee worked as a political media adviser, he had also run as a candidate for the Liberal Party. Because of this overt display of partisanship, he said he accepted that he could not return to straight political news reporting: 'For appearances, I wouldn't do that'. However, none of the other interviewees ran for political office and less than half became political party members and did not consider themselves to be partisan. For those people, 'being up-front' was not a straight forward option because of the risk of being perceived as partisan and the harm that could cause to their reputation as journalists. Instead, they adopted more discrete approaches to disclosure of their previous political employment.

Flying Below the Radar

'Flying below the radar' describes an approach taken by other interviewees who did not want to draw attention to the fact they had recently worked for a politician. They said they were not hiding it, but they were not volunteering the information either. Two of the interviewees described their disclosure strategy this way:

I kept my move very low key…I didn't tell the press gallery I was coming back…People in my bureau knew, but there wasn't a lot of comment on it.

If anyone asks me I'm never backward…I mean I don't advertise it.

By not advertising it, they adopted a low-visibility strategy to disclosure because of their concerns about possible to harm to reputation resulting from perceptions of bias, and possible accusations of conflict of interest.

Keeping it a Secret

Instead of taking a low profile, one interviewee attempted to keep her past hidden in a bid to avoid the perception of being seen as partisan and thereby harming her reputation. When the interviewee returned to work for her former employer, she did not tell her hiring editor that she had been a political media adviser:

Very few people know that I worked… for the Labor Party… I don't even know if the editor of the newspaper knows. I sort of really kept it pretty much to myself.

Researcher: Why did you do that?

Well, I don't want to be type cast. I guess I think I'm doing a journalist's job and I'm doing that with my journalist's cap on … but I would be prepared to bring it up if there was something there, if there was either an appearance of conflict of interest or where there was genuine conflict of interest.

However, because the interviewee actively avoided reporting on politics when she returned to journalism, she said her previous employment as a media adviser had not presented her with an ethical challenge. In the areas she now reported on, the interviewee felt her political experience was not relevant and therefore did not feel under any obligation or pressure to disclose her political work history.

Selective Disclosure

The question of relevance regarding their previous employment as political advisers was central to the approach taken by many of the interviewees. For the majority of the practitioners, their time in politics took place more than a decade ago. In discussing the issue of disclosure, several of them felt their employment as a political staffer was no longer relevant to their contemporary journalism role and therefore they did not want to invite an unnecessary perception of bias, and thereby harm their professional reputation by disclosing that information if it was not relevant. For instance, at the time of interview, one of the journalists had not included his work history as a political staffer in his online workplace profile. His employer knew of his political work history, but the reporter said he had not disclosed it on the website because he did not consider it was relevant to his current role and did not want to alienate sections of the public by revealing it:

I don't want my audience to look at me any differently… because everyone has their pre-formed political views and I don't want to ostracize half the audience because I once worked for a Liberal [Party] government. I want them to accept me on my performance as a presenter or journalist without any preconceived notion on their part… I think if I presented myself as a political journalist or analyst with a political role it's far more relevant. In my current role I don't think it's relevant to what I do at all, but you know, as soon as that appears on your CV people might think differently of you.

However, in the context of an individual story where he could be accused of having a conflict of interest, the reporter did declare his previous employment as a media adviser. When he was required to do a story about one of the politicians he had worked for, the reporter explained that 'in the context of a longer, more personal profile piece it needed to be included'.

What these different approaches demonstrate is the ambivalence that the interviewees felt about disclosing their time as political advisers once they returned to journalism. It is an ambivalence caused by a tension between the benefits and risks of disclosure identified by Davis (1998). On the one hand disclosure of interests can avoid deception and help build trust with those who rely on the person's judgment, such as the audience, but it can also undermine trust in the reporter by inviting a suspicion that he or she has become partisan as a result of being employed as a political media adviser, and therefore rendered their judgment on political matters unreliable.

This tension between possible reputational harm and disclosure of their previous political employment also points to interviewees' desire to be seen as 'objective' non-partisan practitioners who are able to put their personal beliefs and biases to one side. Trained in the journalistic norms of independence and objectivity the interviewees were wary of disclosing personal information that might colour people's perception of their professionalism and no longer consider them to be impartial. This adherence to the norm of objectivity was identified by Hayes et al. (2007, p. 272) as one of the reasons why journalists were less open to modes of personal disclosure than bloggers, who were not bound by organizational constraints and journalistic norms.

Overcompensation

The fifth approach to dealing with the dilemma of disclosure was 'overcompensation'. When the interviewees returned to journalism after media advising, not all of them returned to political reporting. Several actively avoided political journalism and chose to report on unrelated areas, such as international news. However, those who did return to political reporting said they strived to be balanced in their reporting and were mindful of the risk of overcompensating in a bid to counter any possible perception of bias from the audience, their peers and politicians of a different persuasion:

After twelve months being back in the gallery, I felt OK, fine, I have proved my credentials. I have taken my time to be seen to be balanced. I can relax. No one has accused me of bias.

I am very conscious of where I think there is a conflict and acknowledging it to myself and really trying to balance things. To try and step outside and to ask myself 'am I making an impartial judgement here? – Am I dealing with this issue any differently than I would deal with an issue that didn't involve someone I knew in politics or some party position that I personally have some sympathy for? More of the issue here is I might be harder on someone that I know or on a Labor Party position and I have to ask myself 'am I being too hard? Am I putting too much of the opposite counter argument in an effort to be balanced? Am I overcompensating?' I have had that going on in my head about some of the decisions I have made.

Certainly early on ...I was being scrupulously fair. I don't think I was overcompensating. Although some people in the Labor Party thought I was. You do feel an increased pressure on you to be fair and even-handed. If you are going to make criticism, especially commentary, about the conservative side of politics, then it has to be soundly based. It can't just be a rant or something like that.

Yeah, certainly compensating. If I was doing a story ...and it was not a good story for the government I would certainly think 'OK, have I got that right? Have I covered myself by making sure I've got the corresponding view' and, as I say, the test of that is that I never had to deal with any complaints. Now that could be that I over compensated too much. I don't know.

These candid reflections from the interviewees reveal a strong perception of being under increased scrutiny when they returned to political reporting after working for a politician. Because of this they said they were aware of the risk of overcompensating in their reporting to counter any expectation of bias or partisanship from the audience, their journalism colleagues and other political staffers. This risk of overcompensation was identified by Gladstone (2011, p. 114) who argued that one of the benefits of disclosure was that it can increase a reporter's incentive 'to be scrupulously fair'. However, that incentive can also be undermined if the journalist reacts to the heightened scrutiny 'by suspending all judgment or overcompensating with fake balance that distorts coverage' (Gladstone, 2011, p. 114).

By injecting the distortion of overcompensation into his or her work, the journalist's attempt to appear more credible by countering possible perceptions of partisanship is ultimately undone. This risk of distortion through overcompensation and the possible damage to the reporter's reputation, points to Allen's (2008, p. 323) argument, that the act of transparency might unintentionally have the opposite effect of the one being sought and 'increase criticism rather than understanding' of the journalism process, its practitioners and the complexity of the act of disclosure.

Based on the transcripts, the issue of disclosure of previous political employment was clearly perceived as more complex by the interviewees than simply including it on their curriculum vitae. As the interviewees said: 'I don't want to be type cast', 'I don't want my audience to look at me any differently… I don't want to ostracize half the audience' because they once worked for a politician. On the face of it, a reporter including his or her political work history in their CV seems simple enough. As a single entry in a list of previous occupations it would bluntly convey the position title, job description and the period of employment. However, it would not convey the contextual circumstances of the employment, such as the journalist's motivation for taking the job and the impact the experience had on his or her perceptions of politics and the politician he or she worked for. However, that simple blunt entry on a CV could invite the suspicion that the journalist might have become partisan and therefore breached the journalistic ideal of independence and could now be biased in his or her reporting. In some cases that might be true, but in others it might not. As one interviewee explained it:

It's so hard to generalise. There are people I know who have left being press secretaries and have left with a burning desire to kick out the government they were working for because they were so corrupt… In short, what I am saying is that there is an assumption that if you have stopped being a press secretary for the government that you are still going to carry around a candle for it and that's not really true. It's not always true in every respect. What's important is that it is different in each experience.

It is the absence of contextual understanding of individual circumstances that makes it easy for people outside of the situation to assume a simple position of moralism or judgmentalism and suspect the former adviser-turned journalist of partisanship. Because of that risk, some of the interviewees opted not to advertise their time as political staffers. However, choosing not to disclose information is also risky, especially in an online environment. The decision about what personal information to disclose can be taken out of an individual's hands, such as anonymous online users being 'outed' or 'doxxed' by others (Jurgenson & Rey, 2013, p. 69). Attempts to keep certain information private can even lead to greater publicity, a phenomenon Jurgenson and Rey (2013, p. 71) referred to as the 'Streisand effect' after an attempt by celebrity Barbara Streisand to have photos of her house taken off the internet, which inadvertently made the images go viral. If the information the individual wanted to keep hidden is revealed, then the individual also runs the risk of betraying the trust of those who were relying on their judgment and thereby undermining their credibility and damaging their reputation.

The interview data revealed yet a further complication of disclosure, that being, a perception of an un-even playing field or a double standard. By double standard some of the interviewees said they perceived different levels of accountability were applied to reporters who had previously worked as political media advisers and reporters who had strong personal political leanings but had not been employed by a politician. Some of the interviewees perceived themselves to be more vulnerable to suspicions of bias and partisanship because they had worked as political staffers, whereas other reporters with undeclared sympathies for particular causes or political leanings, would remain unchallenged.

I have thought about this quite a bit before I came back in and my view is there are two important elements. One is that all journalists carry their own ideological baggage – though many of them who have never worked for any political party have extremely political views and I see it coming through in their coverage sometimes and I don't like it – but they tell you and their audiences that they are completely political neutral. They are neutered. They are political eunuchs, which is a non-sense. Some journalists are like that. You really wouldn't know. They are just straight up and down and good on them. But there are a lot of political journalists who pretend to be political eunuchs and we all know that they are not.

Some of the interviewees argued that because these journalists had not disclosed their personal political leanings, they did not feel a pressure to be 'scrupulously fair' (Gladstone, 2011) in their reporting and compensate for their personal beliefs because no one was watching them suspiciously, so they were free to push their own agenda through their journalism. This attracted criticism from some of the interviewees who felt it was wrong for reporters to use their position for personal advocacy, something they perceived other political reporters doing:

Everything about (that journalist) would tell you (their) opinion about a certain issue. 'Oh, this is terrible, how could Labor do this?' Save it for a dinner party… If you want to be an activist join a lobby group. Don't masquerade as a news journalist to press your personal views. Maybe that's why people would look at somebody like me and say he shouldn't have been allowed to be a journalist. All I can say is that is never what I was doing as a news journalist. After years of being acculturated into it, I think I get the objectivity required to do a news story.

However, because the journalist referred to in the interviewee's comment had not worked for a politician, the interviewee believed that reporter had not faced the same level of scrutiny that he did. Whether the reporter did or did not face the same degree of scrutiny is irrelevant. The purpose here is not to establish the truth of the interviewee's perception. The role of the above reflections is to demonstrate some of the complexities around the act of disclosure, such as the perception of a double standard around the declaration and concealment of personal interests by journalists and different levels of scrutiny that were perceived to be applied.

The issue of a double standard points to an important question about how the ideal of transparency should be implemented. What information should reporters disclose? Should there be a uniform requirement for all journalists to disclose every bank share, job and voting intention, like the approach taken by Jeff Jarvis (2005)? And what does it mean once the reporter has declared that information? Does it mean they can then go and report in a biased manner with a clear conscience simply because they have been open about their personal beliefs and interests? According to Ward (2015) the act of transparency alone is not enough. It does not trump the other central journalism norms of accuracy, fairness and independence. Ward (2015, p. 55) argued that independence in journalism should not be replaced by transparency because it 'insists that journalists not let allegiances and sources weaken their commitment to independent journalism. Independence, not transparency, distinguishes journalism and propaganda'. This is echoed by Gladstone (2011, p. 114), who argued that 'reporters who reveal themselves still have a duty to report responsibly', not just disclose their biases and then disregard the other principles of ethical journalism practice.

The question about implementation of the transparency ideal through the disclosure of personal interests goes beyond debate about what information a journalist should reveal about him or herself. It also includes questions about the practical mechanics of making the disclosed information available to the public. For instance, online based journalists can easily provide a hyperlink to a list of disclosures – much like Jeff Jarvis' (2005) entry 'About Me & Disclosures' on his blog *BuzzMachine*– because of online technology. However, it is not so easy for traditional television and radio reporters broadcasting live from the field to alert the audience to their previous employment history, biases and preconceptions about the story they are reporting on. As Ward (2015, pp. 51–2) described, there are many methods of implementing transparency in journalism, including 'about' pages, explanatory boxes, links to background information, primary sources, interviews, and live streaming of editorial meetings. Despite this range of approaches, Ward (2015, p. 56) said journalists and ethicists still need to be 'specific' about what is required. The lack of a uniform approach, he argued, needs further research with a view to developing 'concrete guidelines on how much weight to give transparency in different types of stories, and in different forms of journalism' (Ward, 2015, p. 56). No matter what method or methods are finally adopted across the different media platforms, ultimately every reporter will have to face the personal dilemma and professional challenge of deciding what information he or she wants to disclose or conceal about their interests and biases, their approach to journalism and the story at hand. Even if a uniform implementation framework is established in the future, questions still remain about the efficacy of acts of transparency on increasing audience trust in journalism, an area that needs more research in the future (Hayes et al., 2007; Karlsson et al., 2014; Ward, 2015).

CONCLUSION

This paper has argued that while the push for greater transparency and disclosure of personal interests is designed to lift levels of public trust in journalism and journalists in the digital age, it can also pose a dilemma for journalists about what information they wish to reveal and conceal. For the journalists in this paper who had worked as political media advisers, the decision to disclose their previous political employment was embraced by one journalist who considered 'being up-front' about his political experience and leanings as a professional advantage. However, others perceived the act of disclosing their work history as a political media adviser as inviting perceptions of partisanship and thereby risking damage to their reputations once they returned to journalism. As one interviewee explained, while some journalists might become and remain partisan in response to their experience of working for a politician, others will not. Despite this variation in individual experience, the same generalized suspicion of bias might be applied, regardless of whether the reporter is partisan or not.

In dealing with this challenge, the interviewees adopted five main approaches to personal disclosure: Being 'up front' about their past employment; 'Flying below the radar'; 'Keeping it a secret'; 'Selective disclosure'; and, 'Overcompensation'. In an online environment, where private information can be made public, choices about what personal information to reveal or conceal are even more important. It must be stressed that this paper does not argue against the broad ideal of transparency in journalism and the practice of disclosure of personal interests by journalists. It does however suggest that greater consideration needs to be given to the possible negative impacts the act of disclosure can have on individual journalists, such as the risk of possible harm to reputation, and the reluctance that can engender in some journalists to embrace the principle of transparency. As reflected in the comments of the journalists in this paper, concern about perceptions of partisanship and damage to reputation can result in some reporters choosing to be 'up-front' about their personal interests and biases and others preferring to 'keep it a secret'.

DISCLOSURE STATEMENT

No potential conflict of interest was reported by the author.

ACKNOWLEDGEMENTS

This article is derived from the author's Ph.D.: *From 'watchdog' to 'spin-doctor': An examination of the transition from journalist to parliamentary media adviser and back again.*

NOTES

1. For more on conflict of interest by media advisers once they return to journalism see Fisher, C. (2015) (in press) Managing conflict of interest: Shifting between political PR and journalism, *Journalism Practice*. doi:10.1080/17512786.2015.1027786

REFERENCES

1. Allen, D. (2008). The trouble with transparency. *Journalism Studies*, 9(3), 323–340. doi:10.1080/14616700801997224 [Taylor & Francis Online]
2. Baume, S., & Papadopoulos, Y. (2013). *Transparency as a requirement of good governance: A historical perspective*. Paper presented at the CAST Workshop 'National Security, Risk Management, and the Transformation of Bureaucratic Ethics', Boston, MA. Retrieved from http://cast.ku.dk/national-security-risk-management-and-the-transformation-of-bureaucratic-ethics/download/Baume___Papadopoulos_2013.pdf
3. Blumer, H. (1969/1998). *Symbolic interactionism: Perspective and method*. Berkley: University of California Press.
4. Bryman, A. (2008). *Social Research Methods*. Oxford: Oxford University Press.
5. Bryman, A., & Burgess, B. (1994). Developments in qualitative data analysis: an introduction. In A. Bryman & B. Burgess (Eds.) *Analyzing Qualitative Data* (pp. 1–17). London: Routledge. [CrossRef]
6. Davis, M. (1998). Conflict of Interest. In R. Chadwick, (Ed.) *Encyclopedia of applied ethics* (2nd ed., Vols 1 A-D, pp. 589–595). San Diego, CA:

Academic Press.

7. Davis, M. (2001). Introduction. In M. Davis and A. Starck (Eds.), *Conflict of interest in the professions* (pp. 3–19). New York: Oxford University Press.
8. Davis, M. (2013). Conflict of interest. In *The international encyclopedia of ethics*, Wiley online library: Blackwell Publishing.
9. Fisher, C. (2014). *From 'watchdog' to 'spin-doctor': An examination of the transition from journalist to parliamentary media adviser and back again*. Unpublished doctoral thesis. University of Canberra.
10. Furnham, A. (1988). *Lay theories: Everyday understanding of problems in the social sciences*. Oxford: Pergamom Press.
11. Gillmor, D. (2010). *mediactive*. Retrieved from http://www.mediactive.com
12. Gladstone, B. (2011). *The influencing machine: Brooke Galdstone on the media*. New York, NY: W.W. Norton & Company.
13. Grimmelikhuijsen, S. (2012). Linking transparency, knowledge and citizen trust in government: An experiment. *International Review of Administrative Sciences*, 78(1), 50–73. doi:10.1177/0020852311429667 [CrossRef]
14. Hayes, A., Singer, J. B., & Ceppos, J. (2007). Shifting roles, enduring values: The credible journalist in a digital age. *Journal of Mass Media Ethics: Exploring Questions of Media Morality*, 22(4), 262–279. doi:10.1080/08900520701583545 [Taylor & Francis Online]
15. Herbst, S. (1998). *Reading public opinion: How political actors view the democratic process*. Chicago, IL: University of Chicago Press.
16. Heidegger, M. (1927/2008). *Being and time*. Translated by J. Macquarrie and E. Robinson. New York: Harper Perennial Modern Thought.
17. Hood, C. (2006). Transparency in historical perspective. In C. Hood & D. Heald (Eds.), *Transparency: The key to better governance?* (pp. 3–24). Oxford: Oxford University Press. [CrossRef]
18. Husserl, E. (2002). Pure phenomenology, its method and its field of investigation. In D. Moran & T. Mooney (Eds.) *The phenomenology reader* (pp. 124–133). London; New York: Routledge.
19. Jarvis, J. (2005). *About Me & Disclosures*. Retrieved from http://buzzmachine.com/about/
20. Jarvis, J. (2011). *jeff-jarvis-on-transparency-in-journalism*. Retrieved from http://videos.huffingtonpost.com/jeff-jarvis-on-transparency-in-journalism-517158953
21. Jurgenson, N., & Rey, P. J. (2013). The fan dance: How privacy thrives

in an age of hyper-publicity. In G. Lovink & M. Rasch (Eds.), *Unlike us reader: Social media monopolies and their altneratives* (pp. 61–75). Amsterdam: Institute of Network Cultures.

22. Karlsson, M., Clerwall, C., & Nord, L. (2014, February 25). You ain't seen nothing yet. *Journalism Studies*, 1–11. doi:10.1080/1461670X.2014.886837 [Taylor & Francis Online]
23. Karp, D. (1996). *Speaking of sadness: Depression, disconnection and the meanings of illness*. New York: Oxford University Press. [CrossRef]
24. Kovach, B., & Rosenstiel, T. (2007). *The elements of journalism: What newspeople should know and the public should expect*. New York, NY: Three Rivers Press.
25. Kovach, B., & Rosenstiel, T. (2010). *Blur: How to know what's true in the age of information overload*. New York, NY: Bloomsbury.
26. Lasorsa, D. (2012). Transparency and other journalistic norms on Twitter. *Journalism Studies*, 13(3), 402–417. doi:10.1080/1461670X.2012.657909 [Taylor & Francis Online]
27. Maras, S. (2013). *Objectivity in journalism*. Cambridge, UK: Polity.
28. McBride, K., & Rosenstiel, T. (2014). *The new ethics of journalism*. Thousand Oaks, CA: CQPress.
29. McNair, B. (2006). *Cultural chaos: Journalism, news and power in a globalised world*. London: Routledge. [CrossRef]
30. Minichiello, V., Aroni, R., Timewell, E., & Alexander, L. (1995). *In-depth interviewing: Principles, techniques, analysis* (2nd ed.). Melbourne: Longman.
31. O'Neill, O. (2006). Transparency and the ethics of communication. In C. Hood & D. Heald (Eds.), *Transparency: The key to good governance?* (pp. 75–90). Oxford: Oxford University Press. [CrossRef]
32. Revers, M. (2014). The twitterization of news making: Transparency and journalistic professionalism. *Journal of Communication*, 64, 806–826. doi:doi:10.1111/jcom.12111 [CrossRef]
33. Schudson, M. (2001). The objectivity norm in American journalism. *Journalism*, 2(2), 149–170. doi:10.1177/146488490100200201 [CrossRef]
34. Thomas, D.R. (2006). A general inductive approach for qualitative data analysis. *American Journal of Evaluation*, 27(2), 237–246. [CrossRef]
35. Ward, S. (2015). The magical concept of transparency. In L. Zion & D. Craig (Eds.), *Ethics for digital journalists: Emerging best practices* (pp. 45–58). New York, NY: Routledge.

36. Weinberger, D. (2009). *Transparency is the new objectivity.* Retrieved fromhttp://www.hyperorg.com/blogger/2009/07/19/transparency-is-the-new-objectivity/

Chapter 7

MEDIA LAW

INTRODUCTION

Thoughtful people disagree about the proper role of the news media. Some believe that journalists should support government and supply the public only with information the government deems appropriate. Some believe the press instead should be the government's watchdog, searching out and reporting on abuses of power.

Some want the press to be an advocate, to champion causes, and to take political positions. Others believe the press should be objective and nonpartisan. Some believe that the press should respect and reflect social institutions and traditions. Others believe that the press should question and challenge them. This book suggests that despite these disagreements there are standards that describe the privileges and responsibilities of a free press in a free society.

1. A free and independent press is essential to any free society. But what do we mean by a free press? In this book, we mean a press that is not subject to undue government control and regulation, one that is free from undue financial influence from the private sector, including advertisers, and economic or business pressures from private sector businesses A free and independent press provides its readers, viewers, and listeners with the information they need to participate fully as citizens in a free society
2. A free press is courageous and will pursue those stories that are important to its readers and viewers, without fear or favor. It will challenge assumptions, it will question authority, and it will seek truth, no matter where that search may lead—to the highest corridors of power, to the owners of the news organization, or even if it leads to death, as was the case with investigative Russian journalist Anna Politkovskaya, gunned down in a contract killing in Moscow in 2006.
3. A free press is responsible. Perceptions of responsibility vary from country to country, and even from year to year. For many, the standard in times of peace and stability may seem very different than in time of war or national emergency. For example, just a few months after the

> September 11, 2001, attacks in the United States, a survey conducted by the Freedom Forum's First Amendment Center reported that 46 percent of Americans polled believed that the press had "too much" freedom, a figure that certainly was higher than before the attacks, or the 39 percent reported in the 2009 survey. Yet some essential principles remain constant. A free press must seek truth and report it. It must be tireless in seeking and achieving accuracy. The press must never knowingly publish a falsehood. Most societies would agree that even the most free press must exercise its freedom with a clear understanding that actions and editorial decisions have consequences, some of them significant. The press has great power to affect the lives of millions of people. Like any other powerful institution, it must be prepared to listen to complaints, to explain its decisions to readers and viewers, and to acknowledge and correct mistakes. But it must also be prepared to take unpopular positions and to face critics bravely when important principles are at stake. Some may call this arrogance. I call it courage.

Freedom of Speech and a Free Press I n the United States, where I live and where I do most of my research and teaching, the press is for the most part free from government controls as a matter of law. The First Amendment to the U.S. Constitution prohibits Congress, or state legislatures, from passing any statute that abridges freedom of speech or freedom of the press. That absolute language was drafted by revolutionaries shortly after the American War of Independence (1775–1783), during a time of great optimism, but also of great uncertainty. Thc nation's courts have, over the two hundred-plus years that followed, interpreted the First Amendment as powerful, but perhaps not quite absolute. The United States Supreme Court has made clear that certain types of speech are not protected by the First Amendment: publishing details about troop movements in wartime, for example. Other exceptions would include restrictions on obscene speech or on so-called fighting words that could predictably incite violence or criminal actions. And the news media are almost always subject to laws of general applicability—that is, laws that apply to everyone but that do not single out the press for special obligations or punishment. For example, laws that prohibit the interception of telephone conversations without permission apply to journalists as much as they do to corporations.

But even these exceptions are tempered by a strong tradition that there always will be a presumption against any government attempt to stifle the free press. As an American judge once wrote, the default position for the press is to publish. Government should bear the burden of justifying any restraints. This formula preserves the watchdog role of the press and facilitates government accountability laws of general applicability—that is, laws that apply to everyone but that do not single out the press for special obligations or punishment.

Above: Andrew Hamilton defended John Peter Zenger, publisher of the New York Weekly Journal, who was charged in 1735 with seditious libel for criticizing the Royal Governor. Hamilton argued the truth of Zenger's publication was a defense against seditious libel. The jury acquitted Zenger; an action Hamilton praised: "You have laid a noble foundation for securing to ourselves that to which Nature and the Laws of our country have given us a Right—The Liberty—both of exposing and opposing arbitrary power by speaking and writing Truth."

For example, laws that prohibit the interception of telephone conversations without permission apply to journalists as much as they do to corporations. But even these exceptions are tempered by a strong tradition that there always will be a presumption against any government attempt to stifle the free press. As an American judge once wrote, the default position for the press is to publish. Government should bear the burden of justifying any restraints. This formula preserves the watchdog role of the press and facilitates government accountability.

Press Accountability

But who watches the watchdog? Who ensures that the press will be accountable? In some countries, the answer is the government. Laws, statutes, and codes spell out in detail the conduct required of news organizations. In these nations, journalists' rights often depend upon fulfillment of responsibilities. The rub is that the government's definition of responsibility may differ greatly from that of the press itself, or even the public. In other countries, the answer is, the press itself, and its readers and viewers. In some parts of the world, news organizations or individual journalists subscribe to ethical codes of conduct, like that of the National Union of Journalists in the United Kingdom. Other countries impose ethical standards as a matter of law. In the United States, individual news organizations have adopted their own ethical guidelines. Typically, these codes or guidelines set out the institution's rules governing financial and other conflicts of interest. For example, an ethical guideline may prohibit a reporter from covering a company for which her spouse works. Or it may forbid a reporter to take part in a protest march, or to display a political sticker on the fender of his car or a placard in his front garden, or to wear a national flag in her lapel as she reports the news. Or it may prohibit a reporter from accepting even a nominal gift from a news source. Guidelines like these are intended to maintain both the reality and the appearance of journalistic independence. It would seem unnecessary for ethical guidelines to address the necessity for accuracy and truth-telling. But after journalists like Jayson Blair of the New York Times either fabricated or plagiarized the news stories they submitted to their editors, many organizations have revised their ethics guidelines to make clear that neither practice can ever be accepted or condoned by a responsible news organization. Sometimes ethics and the law intersect. In Northern Ireland, for example, Suzanne Breen, the Belfast-based editor for Dublin's Sunday Tribune, faced a legal and ethical dilemma.

Breen had been telephoned by an individual who claimed responsibility for murdering two soldiers at Massereene Barracks in Antrim. The police demanded that she turn over her cell phone, computer records, and notes about her contacts with the paramilitary Real IRA organization. Breen resisted, arguing that to do so would breach her professional obligation to protect the confidentiality of her sources. She also candidly acknowledged that complying with the law enforcement demands could endanger her life, and the lives of her family members. But if she defied the order, Breen faced the prospect of up to five years in jail for contempt. In June 2009, a judge in Belfast ruled that compelling Breen to surrender her news-gathering materials would put her life at risk in contravention of the European Convention on Human Rights

By contrast, in the United States, New York Times reporter Judith Miller refused to cooperate in a criminal investigation seeking the identity of a government official who had revealed the identity of a covert intelligence agent. Miller defied orders to testify, even after judicial rulings that journalists possessed no special privilege to decline naming confidential sources. She spent 85 days in jail in 2005. Some judges and members of the public argued that journalists can never hold themselves above the law. But the ethics policies of most news organizations would require a reporter to honor a promise given to a source, even if it means going to jail. Legal and ethical provisions vary from country to country. Reasonable people— and even journalists themselves— may disagree on how they should apply in a particular situation and whether they strike the proper balance between competing societal interests.

Privacy and Libel

Is it ever appropriate for a reporter to violate an individual's privacy? In the United States, the Supreme Court has ruled that it is lawful for the press to publish the name of an individual who has been sexually assaulted. But is it the right thing to do? Is it right for a journalist to make fun of a public official or to lampoon a name or image that is sacred to a particular ethnic or religious group? In the United States, after the pornographic Hustler magazine satirized the outspoken clergyman Rev. Jerry Falwell, the Supreme Court ruled that a free society must tolerate even "outrageous" speech in order to guarantee robust public debate and discussion. As one justice once wrote, "There is no such thing as a false idea. However pernicious an opinion may seem, we depend for its correction not on the conscience of judges and juries, but on the competition of other ideas." On the other hand, in March 2008, the United Nations Human Rights Council adopted a resolution condemning "defamation of religions." And many countries retain, and enforce, statutes that make it a crime to insult or "offend the dignity" of any person, even a public official—even if the underlying facts are true. The Supreme Court of the United States has never upheld a government attempt to stop the press from publishing classified information. Fierce debates over whether journalists can be criminally prosecuted under espionage laws arise periodically. In China, for example, theft of state secrets is a crime regardless of who does it, and the definition of state secrets is an expansive one. But even assuming that they do not break the law, is it right for journalists to publish classified information, especially when it is claimed that doing so will alert terrorists to surveillance techniques and undermine intelligence efforts to maintain safety and security?.

Above: New York Times reporter Judith Miller was jailed for contempt of court for refusing to reveal a confidential source. Miller, accompanied by her legal team, leave the U.S. District Court in Washington, DC, on June 29, 2005.

Transparency

Despite these concerns, the term "transparency" has become a watchword in civil society. Both public and private institutions are exhorted to be more forthcoming about their operations, funding, and governance. The digitization of data and the ubiquity of the Internet can help. But universal access to information raises new issues about security and privacy, and it compounds the difficulties of protecting proprietary or copyrighted information. Ironically, some regard the technology that maximizes access to information as a threat to other fundamental rights, such as the right to a private life or, as an American jurist once wrote, "to be let alone." Add to this volatile mix the legions of unidentified and seemingly ungovernable bloggers and citizen journalists, operating with gusto but without prior training or certification of any kind. There is no question that they contribute a lively counterpoint to the mainstream media. But will their tendency to challenge conventions and flout the rules lead to greater attempts to regulate the press? These are not easy questions. Nor are there easy answers. It is not easy to live with a free press. Doing so means that one is being challenged, dismayed, disrupted, disturbed, and outraged—every single day. A free press is fallible and at times fails to live up to its potential. But developing democracies around the world demonstrate every day that they have the courage and confidence to choose knowledge over ignorance and truth over propaganda by embracing the ideal of a free press. It is not easy to live with a free press. But I know I couldn't live without it.

Whereas recognition of the inherent dignity and of the equal and inalienable rights of all members of the human family is the foundation of freedom, justice and peace in the world.

A G OOD ENV I RONMENT FOR FOSTERING JOURNALISTS

National legal systems vary. Civil law nations like Germany and France often adopt detailed and precise statutory schemes that govern the rights, duties, and obligations of journalists. In common law nations like the United Kingdom and the United States, a mix of statutes, regulations, and case law establishes broad legal principles that encompass press freedom, even if these laws do not always directly address journalists.

Regardless of the particular legal approach, good journalism flourishes where society respects and enforces the rule of law. The work of legal, theoretical, and philosophical thinkers, including Confucius, Milton, Rousseau, Meiklejohn, and Mill, among others, supplies the intellectual underpinning for contemporary media law and media ethics.

International Standards

International standards supply guarantees of free expression. But these standards also typically acknowledge certain legitimate grounds for the state's restriction of free expression. The Universal Declaration of Human Rights, proclaimed by the United Nations General Assembly in 1948, pronounces in Article 19 that: Everyone has the right to freedom of opinion and expression; this right includes freedom to hold opinions without interference and to seek, receive and impart information and ideas through any media and regardless of frontiers. Article 29 then qualifies this right as: ...determined by law solely for the purpose of securing due recognition and respect for the rights and freedom of others and of meeting the just requirements of morality, public order and the general welfare in a democratic society. Similarly, Article 10 of the European Convention on Human Rights states: Everyone has the right to freedom of expression. This right shall include freedom to hold opinions and to receive and impart information and ideas without interference by public authority and regardless of frontiers. This Article shall not prevent States from requiring the licensing of broadcasting, television or cinema enterprises. However, that absolute language is qualified further in this convention:

The exercise of these freedoms, since it carries with it duties and responsibilities, may be subject to such formalities, conditions, restrictions or penalties as are prescribed by law and are necessary in a democratic society, in the interests of national security, territorial integrity or public safety, for the prevention of disorder or crime, for the protection of health or morals, for the protection of the reputation or rights of others, for preventing the disclosure of information received in confidence, or for maintaining the authority and impartiality of the judiciary. Many international documents, conventions, and treaties embrace a similar approach, among them the International Covenant on Civil and Political Rights, the African Charter on Human and Peoples' Rights, and the American Convention on Human Rights, as well as many others. The details differ, but all recognize freedom of expression as a fundamental right, but one that can be limited by duly enacted laws tailored to protect equally compelling societal interests.

National Standards

National constitutions also frequently guarantee press freedom. For example, Article 25 of the Belgian Constitution, which dates from 1831, provides that: The press is free; censorship can never be established; security from authors, publishers or printers cannot be demanded. When the author is known and resident in Belgium, neither the publisher, nor printer, nor distributor can be prosecuted. The First Amendment to the United States Constitution, ratified in 1791, is similarly absolute: Congress shall make no law respecting an establishment of religion, or prohibiting the free exercise thereof; or abridging the freedom of speech, or of the press; or the right of the people peaceably to assemble, and to petition the Government for a redress of grievances. Other national constitutions acknowledge the right of free expression but do not regard it as absolute. For example, Article 8 of the Senegal Constitution guarantees freedom of expression and opinion "subject to the limitation imposed by laws and regulations."

Similarly, Article 36(1) of the Constitution of the Kyrgyz Republic explicitly declares that the "mass media are free" but then qualifies that statement in Article 17(2): Restrictions to the exercise of rights and freedoms is allowed by the Constitution and laws of the Kyrgyz Republic only for the purposes of ensuring the rights and freedoms of other persons, public safety and order, territorial integrity and protection of constitutional order. But in doing so, the essence of constitutional rights and freedoms shall not be affected. It is probably fair to say that no country in the world regards the cherished universal or fundamental right of free expression as absolute. It is subject to limitation and modification when competing rights are deemed to outweigh it. As a result, some press freedom laws can weaken rather than strengthen the protections afforded a free press

Bill of Rights
Congress OF THE United States,
begun and held at the City of New-York, on
Wednesday the fourth of March, one thousand seven hundred and eighty nine.

Above: Freedom of the press is explicitly protected under the First Amendment of the Bill of Rights in the U.S. Constitution.

Laws That Discourage Journalists

Censorship—government-imposed restraint on freedom of speech and expression—poses the greatest single threat to a free press. Censorship can take many forms:

- compulsory licensing schemes;
- mandatory pre-publication review;
- imposition of gag orders during the pendency of a legal proceeding;
- extraordinary taxes or fees;

- With drawl of legal protection that would ordinarily be granted to other businesses or citizens.

The threat of post-publication sanctions, such as criminal fines or incarceration, can be as intimidating and crippling to the ability of a news organization to operate as any prior restraint. More subtle, but equally problematic, are mandates that impose certain duties or responsibilities on the press. Some autocratic countries and democracies require that the press publish "checked facts" or "the truth." For example, Article 20(d) of the Constitution of Spain states, "The rights are recognized and protected...of freely sending or receiving true information by any medium" [emphasis added]. Government desire for accurate reporting is understandable. In former dictatorships, where propaganda and the promulgation of falsehoods were commonplace, the public is eager to learn a variety of facts from many different sources. And it is a basic tenet of ethical journalism that no reporter wants knowingly to disseminate an untruth. But requiring accuracy only raises more questions:

What is truth? Who decides? The government? Certainly all journalists should aim to be accurate. But often the perception of truth will change over time. As a breaking news story unfolds, what initially appeared to be a fact may turn out to be false?

A spectacular example occurred on September 11, 2009, when the CNN and Fox cable television networks reported that the U.S. Coast Guard had opened fire on a suspicious vessel in the Potomac River in Washington, D.C., not far from the Pentagon, where President Barack Obama was attending commemorative services. Relying on information obtained by listening to police scanners, CNN also used the social-networking application

Twitter to report, "Coast Guard confronts boat as Obama visits Pentagon, police scanner reports say shots fired." The Chicago Tribune reported that it took almost 30 minutes for the networks to determine that they had overheard open radio transmissions—during which personnel made "bang bang" noises and stated, "We have expended ten rounds"— that were part of a routine training exercise, not an attack. White House Press Secretary Robert Gibbs chided the networks for causing panic, observing, "Before we report things like this, checking would be good." CNN claimed that before reporting the incident, it had contacted the Coast Guard's public affairs office and been told that the Coast Guard was unaware of any activity on the river. The Coast Guard did not apologize for its part in the incident, other than to promise that it would review both "our procedures and the timing of this exercise." Commentators criticized the news media for rushing to disseminate the story, suggesting that the networks should have withheld it until they were able to verify the details.

But this example illustrates the difficult tightrope that news organizations walk when reporting breaking news. In an increasingly competitive media marketplace, the pressure to be first with a story is intense. The old Associated Press maxim, "Get it first, but get it right," seems almost quaint in a 24/7 world, where not only mainstream media, but bloggers and other "citizen journalists" can observe and report events instantly. Should CNN and Fox have been subject to government sanction for having made a good-faith error in their reporting? In the United States, the answer would be "no." But in other countries, such a mistake might lead to a fine or the loss of a license.

As troubling as the Coast Guard incident may be, at least the factual discrepancies were quickly resolved. With issues like global warming or the financial or health crises, the facts emerge more gradually. How can journalists determine the truth at any given point? And what is the responsibility of the government, or of the public, to define and interpret the facts? The reality is that journalism is only one means of ascertaining truth. In a free society, it is up to members of the public, not a governmental entity, to review the facts from a wide variety of sources before deciding what is true. In one prominent example, the U.N. Security Council in 1996 called on Rwanda to identify and close radio stations it contended had fomented hatred and incited acts of mass violence there. The case raised an important question: Should the media be held responsible for the violent acts of their viewers, listeners, or readers? Punishment may also await those who challenge the accepted wisdom concerning historical incidents.

Above: Ernst Zündel, author of The Hitler We Love and Why and publisher of Did Six Million Really Die?, was handed the maximum allowable sentence under German law in 2007 for inciting hatred and denying the Holocaust. Holocaust denial is a specific criminal offense in several European countries.

In Turkey, it is a crime to refer to the mass killings of Armenians during World War I as genocide. In 2007, the neo-Nazi Ernst Zündel was imprisoned in Germany after publishing statements denying that the Holocaust occurred, a violation of the German Criminal Code. A corollary to the problem is created when the government declares what the truth is in the enactment of insult laws that prohibit criticism of monarchs, politicians, or other public officials, national symbols, or a particular race or religion.

Dozens of countries throughout the world, including some in the European Union, former Soviet Union, Asia, Africa, and Latin America, have enacted such statutes. Although the precise language varies, it is invariably both broad and vague, easily manipulated by governments to punish dissent and to silence criticism. Another dimension arises when the effort to suppress unwelcome publications crosses national boundaries or is initiated by non-state actors. Most notoriously, in February 1989, the Iranian spiritual leader Ayatollah Ruhollah Khomeini issued a fatwa offering a bounty for the death of the British author Salman Rushdie, whose novel The Satanic Verses Khomeini declared "blasphemous against Islam." In September 2005, the Danish newspaper Jyllands-Posten published editorial cartoons depicting the Prophet Mohammad. Again blasphemy was charged. Violent protests and threats on the lives of the cartoonist followed. Blasphemy charges are not leveled only by Muslims. Not until July 2008 did the British House of Lords vote to abolish the common law crimes of blasphemy and blasphemous libel.

Compulsory Licensing

Another mechanism to discourage journalists is the use of compulsory government licensing. This usually is justified as helping to ensure that only those with appropriate qualifications engage in the profession of journalism. But, as Leonard Sussman of the New York-based.

Freedom House writes, "Governmental licensing of the press is the old blunderbuss of censoring weapons." Government licensing both determines who may be a journalist and circumscribes the parameters of acceptable reporting and commentary. In short, it encourages self-censorship and stifles dissent and debate. Even in countries where any individual has the right to engage in journalism, those who seek to operate broadcast, cable, Internet, or even print news organizations may be subject to compulsory licensing. By their very nature, broadcast and cable franchises are limited in number and scope within a particular geographical area. Most countries have concluded that some governmental authority will be the "traffic cop" that allocates operating frequencies in the broadcast spectrum, or assigns to certain operators the "natural monopoly" of cable or Internet service providers.

Above: Flemming Rose, center, commissioned the controversial cartoons caricaturing the Prophet Mohammad published by the Danish newspaper Jyllands-Posten in 2005. The cartoon sparked heated public debate about the balance between satire and censorship

Without this type of licensing, anyone might, to use one example, broadcast on the same radio frequency as his neighbor. The result would be complete cacophony and chaos. Even so, when the state chooses who will be allowed to operate the electronic media, there is a real danger of inhibiting the free flow of information. In some countries with a tradition of stateowned public broadcasting, it is difficult, if not impossible, for independent media to secure a place in the broadcast spectrum. In nations where privately owned commercial media predominate, questions about how much the state may inquire into programming and editorial decisions when reviewing initial license applications or renewals remains a nagging problem. On the one hand, some argue, broadcast airwaves are a public resource that should be operated essentially as a public service or, in the words of the Communications Act of 1934 (U.S.), in "the public interest, convenience or necessity." The uniquely pervasive nature of electronic media, it is said, justifies greater government interference in content. On the other hand, broadcasters should enjoy the same editorial autonomy as the print media, subject only to laws of general applicability governing expression, such as libel, invasion of privacy, and obscenity.

Regulation and the Internet

With each new medium of communication, government efforts to control information appear. Some countries, including China, Iran, Saudi Arabia, and Tunisia, have blocked access to Web sites based on their political or cultural content, monitored individuals' activities on the Internet, and imposed stringent restrictions on Internet service providers. Even mature democracies, including Australia, France, India, and the United States, have blocked access to or punished publication of online material that they deem to be objectionable. The Internet provides individuals an unprecedented ability to communicate without relying on newspapers, television, or any other traditional media. But many countries retain legislation from the era when, in the words of New Yorker magazine contributor A.J. Liebling, "Freedom of the press belongs to the man who owns one." Some countries grant an individual an enforceable right of reply to an article concerning her that she deems false, inaccurate, defamatory, or misleading. The logic of these laws is that because radio and television stations and newspapers are in the hands of a few, the free exchange of ideas requires that they provide those who disagree an opportunity to be heard. Predicated on the idea that a news organization has an obligation to be fair, a statutory right of reply usurps a news organization's editorial authority by requiring an editor to publish material he otherwise would not. When editors tone down their coverage to avoid being compelled to publish replies, the result is more self-censorship and less publication of controversial material. As a U.S. Supreme

Court justice wrote, in a case striking down a Florida state right-of-reply statute, "A newspaper or magazine is not a public utility subject to 'reasonable' governmental regulation in matters affecting the exercise of journalistic judgment as to what should be printed." Ironically, the Internet, which empowers anyone with access to be a publisher, has nevertheless encouraged right-of-reply measures directed at bloggers and other digital journalists. In 2006, the European Parliament adopted a Council of Europe recommendation that a right of reply be imposed on the online media. The council argued that the physical limitations of space and time that exist in conventional forms of media like newspapers or television do not apply in cyberspace, lowering drastically the cost of affording a reply privilege. In 2009, the Philippine legislature was considering bills requiring anyone who speaks on the Internet, including bloggers and posters on socialnetworking sites, to grant a right to reply to anyone who considers herself wronged. Compelled publication arguably is another form of censorship.

Balancing Legitimate Competing Interests

The most insidious aspect of censorship is that at first glance it can seem justifiable, or reasonable.

- Why shouldn't a government authority have the power to stop a news organization from publishing classified material in the name of protecting national security?
- Why shouldn't a court be allowed to prohibit a journalist from reporting the prior criminal history of a defendant facing a murder charge?
- Why shouldn't an individual have the right to demand that a broadcaster refrain from airing footage that would reveal intimate personal information, such as the identity of a child who has been sexually abused?
- Why shouldn't a licensing board have the authority to stop the distribution of a book or film that it deems contrary to public morality?
- Why shouldn't laws proscribing racist or "hate" speech be upheld? Regardless of how a society resolves these hard questions, the danger is that, all too frequently, these seemingly reasonable restrictions are utilized as a means of restricting press freedoms and ultimately to restrict the dissemination of unpopular opinions and ideas.

This is not to suggest that freedom of the press will, or should, inevitably trump other fundamental values. The challenge is to strike a balance between legitimate competing interests. This is not an easy task.

The liberty of the press is indeed essential to the nature of a free state:

but this consists in laying no previous restraints upon publications, and not in freedom from censure for criminal matter when published.

A FRAMEW ORK FOR A FREE PRESS

A useful starting point as we set out to create a framework for a free press is to consider what rights are essential in order for journalists to do their jobs. These might include no prior restraint; protection from compelled disclosure of information; the right of access to government information and court proceedings; the right to criticize government officials and public figures; the right to gather and publish newsworthy information about individuals; limits on government licensing of journalists and news organizations; and only narrow and carefully tailored restrictions on indecent or obscene speech.

No prior restraint

The 18th-century English jurist William Blackstone argued, "The liberty of the press is indeed essential to the nature of a free state: but this consists in laying no previous restraints upon publications, and not in freedom from censure for criminal matter when published." Blackstone's was an important distinction. The English government's power to license, to control both who could operate a press and what he could publish, was the quintessential abridgement of free expression. By stopping speech even before it is uttered, government stifles discussion and dissent. But in Blackstone's view, the publisher would properly bear the responsibility for whatever he chose to disseminate. Blackstone would prohibit government from censoring speech, but he would still allow sanctions to be imposed after publication. Only rarely does a country go so far as Blackstone advocated by absolutely outlawing any and all previous restraints on the press. We will examine here a number of types of restraints that are recognized as lawful in many countries. Below are the circumstances under which a prior restraint might be considered proper:

- A compelling interest should be identified.
- The order should be narrowly tailored and no broader in scope than necessary to address the compelling interest adequately.
- The order should be precise in its terms and as limited in duration as possible.
- It should be demonstrated that the order will actually advance the compelling interest asserted or avert the identified harm.
- Notice of the order and an opportunity to be heard to contest it should

be provided prior to imposition. What types of interests might be sufficiently compelling to justify a prior restraint? Such interests could include, among others:

- confidential or proprietary business information;
- highly intimate personal information;
- copyrighted material;
- information pertaining to an on-going criminal investigation or prosecution;
- Obscene or immoral material.

But probably the most frequently invoked justification is national security. This poses a genuine dilemma for journalists. On the one hand, no journalist wants to undermine national security by disseminating information that poses a genuine threat. On the other hand, government officials can be tempted to invoke national security to justify expansive censorship. The Supreme Court of the United States considered this issue in New York Times Co. v. United States (1971), often referred to as the Pentagon Papers case. After the New York Times began publishing excerpts of classified documents about the American involvement in Vietnam, the administration of President Richard M. Nixon sought a judicial restraining order to stop further publication. The Supreme Court ruled against the government. "Any system of prior restraints comes to this Court bearing a heavy presumption against its constitu- tional validity," the Court noted and concluded that in this case the government had failed to meet the "heavy burden of showing justification for the imposition of such a restraint."

The brief opinion provided little insight into the Court's reasoning. It is difficult to discern what conditions, if any, might in a future case justify a prior restraint. We only know that the government did not meet its burden in this case. The Court did not say that it never could. Practically speaking, the case of the Pentagon Papers has created a virtually insurmountable barrier to government imposed censorship on national security grounds in the United States. Never since has the Supreme Court upheld a prior restraint on the media's ability to publish national security information, not even in the post-9/11 environment. Given the limits of territorial jurisdiction, it has always been challenging for the government of a particular country to impose a restraint that will be truly effective worldwide. In the late 1980s, the British government's attempts to restrict the publication of Spycatcher, a former MI5 agent's memoirs, were ultimately futile. While an English court did ban publication, the book circulated widely in Australia, and even in Scotland, a part of Great Britain not covered by the writ of the English court.

Above: (from the right)Reporter Neil Sheehan, Managing Editor A. M. Rosenthal, and Foreign News Editor James L. Greenfield formed part of the New York Times team responsible for publishing the Pentagon Papers, excerpts of classified U.S. government documents about American involvement in the Vietnam War.

Copies poured into England from these and other jurisdictions. Eventually the English courts were forced to lift their ban on the grounds that publication elsewhere meant there no longer were any secrets left to preserve. At the height of the controversy, British editions of The Economist magazine ran a blank page with this notation: "In all but one country, our readers have on this page a review of 'Spycatcher,' a book by an ex-M.I.5 man, Peter Wright. The exception is Britain, where the book, and comment on it, have been banned. For our 420,000 readers there, this page is blank—and the law is an ass." The Spycatcher case predated the growth of the Internet. Today, the burgeoning new media pose a significant obstacle to the effective imposition of a prior restraint. An example is the Wikileaks case. In February 2008, a federal judge in California issued a permanent injunction on Wikileaks, a Web site that claims to have been founded by "Chinese dissidents, journalists, mathematicians and...technologists, from the U.S., Taiwan, Europe, Australia and South Africa," whose self proclaimed mission was to "reveal unethical behavior in...governments and corporations." Wikileaks allowed users to publish anonymously a wide variety of documents, such as rules of engagement for American troops, operating manuals for Guantanamo Bay prison, and confidential Swiss bank account information. The site claimed it was not responsible for the content of materials that users posted on its site. The injunction ordered Dynadot, the California company that had registered Wikileaks's domain name, immediately to lock and disable the domain name and to block access to the documents. But the New York Times reported that even after Dynadot placed restrictions on the site, users worldwide could still reach it and read the documents by accessing mirror sites registered in Belgium, Germany, and the Christmas Islands. Two weeks after the initial injunction had been issued, the same federal judge lifted it. "It is clear that in all but the most exceptional circumstances, an injunction restricting speech is impermissible," Judge Jeffrey White wrote. He also observed that his initial order had not only been ineffective but "had exactly the opposite effect as was intended" because the press coverage of the injunction had only increased public attention to the Wikileaks materials. Other types of gag orders, injunctions, and restraining orders will be discussed in more detail in the appropriate sections below.

Protection from Compelled Disclosure of Information

The right of a journalist to protect confidential sources and unpublished information from disclosure is essential to promoting both the free flow of information and the public's right to know. Reporters must be able to assure their sources that their identities will remain secret in order to encourage them to speak freely. They must also be able to protect the fruits of their news gathering from scrutiny by government or private entities in order to maintain their editorial independence. Without these privileges, the ability of the press to scrutinize government and to uncover corruption would be severely compromised. Most media codes of ethics require that journalists protect the confidentiality of their sources. For a reporter, this is both a matter of honor and a pragmatic necessity. A journalist who violates a promise of confidentiality will not be trusted by other sources in the future. For this reason, journalists will protect their sources, even if it means facing contempt of court.

The rationale for recognizing a reporter's privilege was persuasively set forth by the European Court of Human Rights (ECtHR) in Goodwin v. United Kingdom (1996). The case involved reporter William Goodwin, who had received a company's confidential financial information from a source whose identity he had agreed to keep secret. The company claimed that the material had been stolen and obtained an injunction restraining publication of the information, as well as an order under the Contempt of Court Act to compel Goodwin to reveal his source's identity "in the interests of justice" so that it could take legal action against the source. After the Court of Appeal and the House of Lords upheld the order, Goodwin appealed to the ECtHR, where he argued that under Article 10 of the European Convention on Human Rights (ECHR), only exceptional circumstances could justify compelling him to testify. For its part, the British government contended that no compelling public interest justified recognizing the privilege in this situation, especially given that the source had, at worst, acted irresponsibly in providing the proprietary business information to Goodwin. The court ruled in favor of Goodwin, finding that the company's interest in pursuing the source was not sufficient to outweigh the public's interest in protecting the right of journalists to keep sources confidential: Protection of journalistic sources is one of the basic conditions for press freedom. ...Without such protection, sources may be deterred from assisting the press in informing the public on matters of public interest. As a result, the vital public-watchdog role of the press may be undermined and the ability of the press to provide accurate and reliable information may be adversely affected. Having regard to the importance of the protection of journalistic sources for press freedom in a democratic society and the potentially chilling effect an order of source disclosure has on the exercise of that freedom, such a measure cannot be compatible with Article 10 of the Convention unless it is justified by an overriding requirement in the public interest. All countries that are parties to ECHR are bound by the Goodwin decision, but the decision has been influential even outside the European Union. Other international and regional bodies,

including the Inter-American Commission on Human Rights and the African Commission on Human and People's Rights, have issued declarations recognizing the right of journalists to maintain the confidentiality of their sources and unpublished information. In some countries, the journalist's privilege is included in the constitution. For example, the Constitution of Palau says, "No bona fide reporter may be required by the government to divulge or be jailed for refusal to divulge information obtained in the course of a professional investigation." Sweden's Freedom of the Press Act, which is part of the national constitution, provides an expansive privilege for journalists, subject only to a limited number of exceptions, such as if the source is suspected of espionage or treason, or if an accused person demonstrates that the information sought is essential for her defense in a criminal case.

The law also provides that a journalist who reveals a source without consent may be prosecuted. In other countries, courts have ruled that the journalist's privilege may be derived from constitutional provisions. In 2006 in Japan, for example, the Supreme Court found that Article 21 of the constitution, which guarantees freedom of expression, also protects "the freedom of gathering news," as well as the reporting of news. In Canada in 2008, the Ontario Court of Appeal struck down a finding of contempt against a reporter who refused to disclose the source of leaked confidential municipal investigative reports concerning a nonprofit nursing home. It ruled that the right to protect confidential sources is an essential part of freedom of expression as recognized under the Canadian Charter of Rights and Freedoms. "The likely effect of revealing a journalist's confidential source," the court said, "would be to discourage from coming forward other potential sources who, for whatever reason, need to conceal their identity." Although it declined to find an absolute privilege governing all confidential communications obtained in the course of reporting, the court nevertheless recognized that the contempt power should be used only as a last resort, mindful of the competing rights at stake. Some other nations have by statute granted journalists a privilege to avoid testifying under specified circumstances.

About 20 countries have adopted legislation giving journalists absolute rights to protect their sources, among them Mexico, Indonesia, Mozambique, and Turkey. More common are national laws that recognize a qualified privilege, which may be overcome under certain situations. Armenia, for example, grants the privilege but withdraws it in cases where the information sought is directly related to a heinous criminal case when the public interest in disclosure is strong. In some countries, including Germany and the United States, statutory protection has been left to the individual states. Like the national laws, these statutes can be either absolute or qualified in scope. In the United States, although 39 states, plus the District of Columbia, have enacted journalists' shield laws, Congress has considered, but has failed to pass (as of summer 2010), federal legislation recognizing a reporter's privilege. This means that state shield laws apply in some state court proceedings but not in the federal court system. (For further information on the roles of federal and state laws and court systems, see Outline of the U.S. Legal System, http://www.america.gov/publications/ books/outline-of-u.s.-legal-system.) Although each society will work out the precise contours of a journalistic privilege against compelled disclosure of information, an effective privilege would supply broad answers to the following questions:

- To whom does it apply? A broad privilege would apply to anyone who is practicing journalism— meaning anyone involved in the process of gathering, writing, editing, or publishing news or information for dissemination to the public, whether for compensation or not.

- Is it limited by media platform? The most effective privilege would not be limited to those in the print and broadcast mainstream media. It would include book authors, as well as bloggers and others who disseminate their work on the Internet.

- Which sources does it protect? A comprehensive privilege would cover not only the identity of sources but also unpublished information and documentary materials, such as photographs, notes, tapes, drafts, and other unpublished journalistic work product. In the absence of an absolute privilege, one who seeks to compel a journalist to reveal confidential sources and information should be required to show good cause. Nations have devised different standards, but the more common factors include:

- The information is unobtainable from any other nonjournalistic source after all reasonable alternatives have been exhausted.

- The information sought is material, or absolutely essential, to the disposition of the underlying case (such as exonerating evidence for an accused criminal).

- A judge must find that the public interest in disclosure outweighs the public interest in the free flow of information.

The final element is the most problematic. When does another interest outweigh the fundamental right to press freedom? In cases involving national security, for example, government authorities often argue that preserving public safety outweighs protecting editorial independence. In the United States, federal efforts to enact a journalists' shield law have been stymied for years, in part, because of fears that terrorists might use it to protect their communications from law enforcement scrutiny. War correspondents face many special challenges. Maintaining source confidentiality can be essential to protecting these journalists' safety. But what happens when the journalist is an eyewitness to atrocities and is summoned before a war crimes tribunal to give evidence? In 1993, Washington Post reporter Jonathan C. Randal interviewed Radoslav Brdjanin, a Serbian nationalist, whom he quoted in an article on ethnic cleansing. Years later, after Randal had retired from journalism, Brdjanin was charged with genocide. Prosecutors wanted to introduce Randal's article as evidence in the trial before the U.N. International Criminal Tribunal for Yugoslavia (ICTY). When the defense insisted on the right to cross-examine Randal, the former reporter was subpoenaed to appear before the court. Randal resisted, arguing that being compelled to testify would compromise his ability to gather news in war zones and could endanger his personal safety were sources to perceive him as a potential witness. In December 2002, the Appeals Chamber recognized a qualified testimonial privilege for war correspondents, even where their sources are not confidential and their information has already been published. It defined war correspondents as "individuals, who for any period of time, report (or investigate for the purposes of reporting) from a conflict zone on issues relating to the conflict." The court acknowledged that to do their jobs,

"War correspondents must be perceived as independent observers rather than as potential witnesses for the Prosecution. Otherwise, they may face more frequent and grievous threats to their safety and the safety of their sources."

The tribunal ruled the amount of protection [recognized] is directly proportional to the harm that it may cause to the newsgathering function." To compel testimony, it held, the subpoenaing party must show that the evidence is of "direct and important value in determining a core issue in the case" and that the evidence cannot reasonably be obtained elsewhere. Randal's case was a controversial one. Although more than 30 international news organizations supported his appeal, Ed Vulliamy, a British journalist who also covered the war in Bosnia and voluntarily testified at the trial of Milan Kovacevic, argued that Randal's position was wrong. "At the root of the Washington Post's objection is the supposed bedrock of the journalists' profession: neutrality," he wrote. "I believe that there are times in history…that neutrality is not neutral but complicit in the crime.

The court needs reporters to stand by their stories on oath." A related issue involves the power of governmental authorities to search media offices. Zurcher v. Stanford Daily (1978) was a U.S. Supreme Court case challenging the power of police officers to enter the office of a university student newspaper and to seize unpublished photographs of a violent confrontation between police officers and demonstrators who had seized and occupied the Stanford University hospital. Although the student newspaper argued that the First Amendment protected it from law enforcement searches of its premises, the majority opinion by Justice Byron White ruled that news organizations enjoy no special status under the First Amendment, although they would be protected by the Fourth Amendment, as any other entity would be, from "unreasonable searches and seizures." In dissent, Justice Potter Stewart wrote: It seems to me self-evident that police searches of newspaper offices burden the freedom of the press. The most immediate and obvious… injury…is physical disruption of the newspaper. …But there is another and more serious burden…imposed by an unannounced police search of a newspaper office: the possibility of disclosure of information received from confidential sources, or of the identity of the sources themselves. In response to the majority ruling, the U.S. Congress enacted the Privacy Protection Act of 1980. This statute forbids both federal and local law enforcement authorities from seizing documentary, or work product, materials in the possession of persons intending to disseminate them to the public (i.e., journalists). Exceptions include materials necessary to prevent death or serious injury, or child pornography. Similarly, in 1995, the New Zealand Court of Appeals ruled searches of journalists' workplaces appropriate only in exceptional cases when essential to promoting the interests of justice and, even then, not to be executed in a way that would impair the dissemination of news. But in other parts of the world, newsroom searches occur frequently. For example, in 2004, the Independent Commission Against Corruption in Hong Kong obtained 14 warrants to search newspaper offices and journalists' homes. The commission sought the identity of an individual who had provided a witness's name to the news organization. The Court of Appeal ruled these searches justified. Although the European Court of Human Rights holds that newsroom searches violate Article 10 of the European.

Convention on Human Rights, many European countries still permit them. Austria and Germany are two exceptions, with the German Constitutional Court ruling in February 2007 that these searches violate constitutional freedom of speech protections. Antiterrorism laws adopted in much of the world since 2001 have expanded law enforcement and intelligence authority to intercept communications through wiretapping and similar means. These laws typically afford journalists no less, but also no more, protection than other citizens. However, a few countries do grant the news media special protection. In Georgia, intercepting journalists' communications for the purpose of uncovering professional secrets is a crime. And in Belgium, the Law on Protection of Journalists' Sources imposes the same restrictions on surveillance as on an attempt to compel disclosure of a confidential source. In short, thcrc is broad rccognition that protecting journalists' confidentiality is essential to maintaining their independence

The Right of Access to Government Information and Proceedings

Why is the right of access to government proceedings and information important?

- Access helps keep government accountable to its citizens. As a U.S. Supreme Court justice once wrote, freedom of information laws allow citizens to find out "what the government is up to" in the present, and also what it did in the past. By helping to check improper conduct, access serves as a valuable anticorruption tool and helps build public trust.

- Access allows the public to tap into the vast quantities of government-collected and -maintained information, information paid for by the public's tax dollars.

- When journalists can obtain public records, they need not rely on the whims of a government source to report on government actions and activities, and they can better disclose how tax dollars are spent and how policies are made and implemented. In short, journalists' access to government information is an essential tool for building and maintaining democracy. Many international agreements embrace and promote transparency:

- Article 19 of both the Universal Declaration of Human Rights and the International Covenant on Civil and Political Rights guarantees the right to seek, receive, and impart information. This phrase has been construed to include a right of freedom of information.
- Article 9 of the African Union (AU) Convention on Preventing and Combating Corruption, a treaty signed by 40 of the 53 members of the AU, says, "Each State Party shall adopt such legislation and other measures to give effect to the right of access to any information that is required to assist in the fight against corruption and related offenses."
- The Organization of American States, the Arab Charter on Human Rights, and many other treaties, conventions, agreements, and declarations recognize freedom of information as a fundamental human right. But the reality often falls short of the rhetoric. Individual nations decide whether and how they will implement these lofty principles. The journalist who sets out to exercise her right to know may find the experience a challenging one

Freedom of information is a constitutional right in about 80 countries. Sweden's 1766 press law, often considered the first freedom of information act, is part of its constitution, and some older constitutions have been amended to include a right to know. Many developing democracies in Central and Eastern Europe and Latin America include access provisions in their new constitutions. Even when the constitution contains no explicit language, the highest courts in some countries, including Korea, Japan, and Israel, have found a right of access to information implicit in the right of freedom of the press or expression. More than 70 additional countries have enacted freedom of information statutes. These are well established in Europe and the Americas, less so in Asia, the Middle East, and Africa. But the trend is definitely toward greater transparency in government around the world.

Freedom of Information Laws

Most freedom of information laws share common principles and characteristics. Many recent examples were influenced by the U.S. federal Freedom of

Information Act (FOIA), so we will use that statute as an example. President Lyndon B. Johnson signed FOIA into law on July 4, 1966. Despite its name, the statute does not actually create a right of access to information. Rather, it establishes a presumptive right of access to existing records, in paper or digital form, held by executive branch agencies, departments, regulatory commissions, and government-controlled corporations. These include, for example, the Departments of State, Defense, and Justice, as well as the Federal Bureau of Investigation and the Central Intelligence Agency, among many others. Unlike laws in countries like Ireland, FOIA does not list covered agencies by name, nor does it categorically exclude bodies that handle intelligence and security, as in the United Kingdom. But the U.S. FOIA covers neither the legislative nor judicial branches of government. Access to state and local executive branch agency records are covered by state opengovernment laws. In the United States, as in most countries, anyone can make a FOIA request. Neither U.S. citizenship nor residency is required, and access is open to all, not just journalists. Requesters are encouraged to utilize government reading rooms, either brick-and-mortar or virtual, to gain free access to records already released under so-called E-FOIA initiatives or disclosed in response to an earlier FOIA request. They are also invited to contact the agency FOIA officer to discuss informally what types of records may be available before filing a formal access request. In the United States, no special form is necessary to file a FOIA request—just a simple letter, addressed to the pertinent FOIA officer, reasonably describing the records sought. Most agencies are prepared to accept requests in writing or electronically. Despite the presumption of openness, however, nearly every freedom of information law includes exemptions—categories of records an agency can withhold. The U.S. FOIA has nine exemptions, which, under the terms of the statute and based on guidance from the Department of Justice, should be narrowly construed:

- national security;
- internal agency rules/practices;
- internal agency memoranda (such as working papers, reports, and studies prepared as part of the agency's decision-making process);
- trade secrets;
- records made secret by another federal statute;
- some law enforcement records;
- bank records;

- oil and gas well data;
- records containing information that, if revealed, would constitute an unwarranted invasion of personal privacy.

Most of these exemptions are not mandatory. Agencies may release records if they conclude that the public interest in disclosure outweighs any harm. They must be prepared to justify any exemption and to withhold only the exempt portion of any record while releasing the balance. The necessity of withholding a particular record may evolve over time. In the case of classified records, requesters have the option to appeal to a special review board that will determine whether a previously classified record can now be made public. In some countries, although not in the United States, access laws include specific prohibitions on withholding certain categories of information

Above: U.S. President Barack Obama signed five executive orders on January 21, 2009, requiring staffers to comply with strict new rules on the Freedom of Information Act. In a memo released that day, President Obama wrote: "The Government should not keep information confidential merely because public officials might be embarrassed by disclosure, because errors and failures might be revealed, or because of speculative or abstract fears.

Although the United States does not have an official secrets act of the type found in many other countries, records properly classified in accordance with a presidential executive order can be withheld. In the post-9/11 environment, the practice of classifying information has increased in much of the world. This imposes new obstacles to citizens seeking both intelligence and law enforcement records. And as governments collect more personally identifiable information, agencies frequently invoke the privacy exemptions as grounds to withhold many government records. These exemptions are sometimes vague and difficult to interpret, and the tendency for most records custodians is to withhold the record if there is any doubt. A requester denied access to a record has a right to appeal. Under FOIA, and in most countries, she begins by seeking an internal review within the agency. This tactic sometimes, but not always, results in release of the records. The next step is to submit the appeal for external review. In the United States, that means filing a lawsuit in a federal district court, with subsequent appeals as necessary through the federal appellate courts and even to the Supreme Court. In other countries, and in some of the individual states in the United States, the requester may appeal to a freedom of information ombudsman, or to an independent tribunal or information commission. Even in those jurisdictions, a final review can be sought in the national courts. A successful requester may be able to obtain not only the records but attorney's fees, as well. In some U.S. states, and in many countries, courts can impose sanctions on government agencies and employees who willfully withhold records in violation of the law.

These sanctions can include monetary fines and, in rare cases, even a jail sentence if the violation is particularly egregious. Even where the law requires disclosure, administrative backlogs, lack of resources, or inefficiency may result in delays. Most freedom of information laws set short deadlines for initial responses but allow additional time to handle complex requests. In the United States, the National Security Archive, a private organization that conducts research on access policy, reported in 2007 that the oldest pending FOIA request was 20 years old, although many others are processed far more quickly. Under certain circumstances, as where a journalist demonstrates compelling public interest in immediate release, a requester may be entitled to expedited processing.

Agencies may be authorized to recoup costs from requesters, even if they do not fulfill the entire request. Some countries (although not the United States) assess a filing fee, regardless of the size or scope of the request. Others demand payment for administrative costs, including search time, redaction of exempt information, and copying. Under the U.S. FOIA, certain categories of requesters, including the general public and the press, are entitled to full or partial fee waivers, but commercial requesters (not including the news media) are required to pay all applicable costs, which are determined by the agency according to a fee schedule. Freedom of information laws create a presumption of public access. FOIA disclosures have empowered journalists to write thousands of stories, some embarrassing to the U.S. government. These range from the revelation of the 1968 massacre at My Lai in Viet Nam to unsanitary conditions in food-processing plants; from cost overruns by defense contractors to the most dangerous places to work in the United States. Even features about unidentified flying objects (UFOs) are based on information obtained under the FOIA. All that is required is the persistence to make use of it.

Above: U.S. American soldier Ron Ridenhour was largely responsible for uncovering the massacre at My Lai in 1968 by gathering eyewitness accounts and sending letters to 30 members of Congress and to Pentagon officials. Ridenhour later became an investigative journalist.

Access to Court Proceedings

The official activities of the judiciary have a tremendous impact on and are of great interest to the public. And yet, when journalists set out to report on court cases, it may result in an adversarial relationship. Simply put, journalists frequently want to publicize information attorneys and the judge would prefer to keep secret. Most countries at least tacitly acknowledge that court proceedings should be presumed open to the press and the public, subject to certain limitations. Article 6 of the European Convention on Human Rights provides, in part: In the determination of his civil rights and obligations or of any criminal charge against him, everyone is entitled to a fair and public hearing within a reasonable time by an independent and impartial tribunal established by law. Judgment shall be pronounced publicly but the press and public may be excluded from all or part of the trial in the interest of morals, public order or national security in a democratic society, where the interests of juveniles or the protection of the private life of the parties so require, or the extent strictly necessary in the opinion of the court in special circumstances where publicity would prejudice the interests of justice. In common law countries, the Anglo Saxon tradition since Magna Carta (1297) has presumed that trials would be open in order to protect the rights of the accused and to ensure accountability. In the United States particularly, a line of Supreme Court cases beginning in

1980 has construed broadly both a criminal defendant's Sixth Amendment right to a fair and public trial and the right of press and public under the First Amendment to attend that trial. Many courts recognize a presumed right of access to court documents, as well. But the Supreme Court also has ruled that a specifically identified state interest can outweigh the presumption of openness.

This could include a substantial threat to the criminal defendant's right to a fair trial or a compelling need to protect the privacy of a particular witness or victim during testimony. However, before closing the courtroom, the presiding judge is required to consider whether any alternative will avert the threat and must also establish that closure will be effective. In addition, any closure must be narrowly tailored—as brief in scope and duration as possible. Some countries, such as Spain and Sweden, among many others, afford similar constitutional guarantees that the administration of justice is to take place in public. However, a separate issue arises concerning limitations on what journalists may report about a pending or ongoing case.

Prior Restraints and Gag Orders

In the United States, the strong tradition against prior restraints makes it almost impossible to persuade a court to issue a gag order on the press. For the most part, restraining orders are limited to court officials and trial participants. The courts have ruled almost uniformly that dissemination of information pertaining to a case that has been obtained legally by the press cannot be restricted, whether it originated in or out of the courtroom.

The Supreme Court ruled in 1976 that a gag order would be permissible only if publication would pose a "clear and present danger" to the conduct of the trial, if the order actually would be effective to alleviate the harm, and if no less drastic means would address the problem. For this reason, journalists in the United States are almost never subjected to gag orders, and they nearly always succeed in challenging those that are imposed. A rare exception occurred in 2003. Professional basketball player Kobe Bryant was charged with rape and faced trial in Colorado. A court clerk accidentally emailed the transcript of a closed pretrial hearing to seven media organizations. The transcript included the name of the alleged victim, information that was secret under the Colorado rape shield law. Upon discovering the mistake, the presiding judge ordered news organizations to "delete and destroy any copies and not reveal any contents thereof, or be subject to contempt of Court." Although some U.S. legal authority suggests that journalists may defy transparently unconstitutional gag orders, in this case the news organizations immediately appealed the order to the state's highest court. The Colorado Supreme Court ruled that protecting the accuser's privacy and preserving the ability to prosecute future sexual assault cases constituted significant state interests justifying the order. The dissenting justices, noting that the news organizations had broken no law, observed, “It is the responsibility of the government, not the media, to protect information that lies within its control.” Ironically, within a short time, even more information, including the alleged victim’s last name, was posted on the Internet. The judge released most of the transcripts, and the media dropped their appeal to the U.S. Supreme Court. By contrast, judges in the United Kingdom and Canada enjoy broad authority to enjoin publication of material that could create a “substantial risk that the course of justice...will be seriously impeded or prejudiced,” and to hold in contempt anyone who engages in conduct that tends to “interfere with the course of justice...regardless of intent to do so.” As a consequence, from the time a suspect is arrested or charged until sentencing, journalists in these nations may attend the proceedings but are limited in what they may report. In other countries, provisions in either the civil or criminal code specify what types of information may or may not be reported. Common restrictions include the identity of crime victims, familial details in divorce or child custody proceedings, or details about an accused person’s past criminal record. In some nations like Sweden, where the law is silent, the journalists’ own code of conduct specifies that defendants should not be identified unless “an obvious public interest requires it.”

Cameras in the Courtroom

Courtroom cameras provide greater public access, but they remain a contentious issue in many nations. Coverage of the notorious O.J. Simpson murder trial in 1995 in California continues to influence judges and policymakers around the world. They cite the perceived excesses of that case as proof that cameras undermine the right to a fair trial—even though Simpson was acquitted. Concerns that cameras will disrupt the proceedings, intimidate witnesses, and encourage lawyers to act inappropriately are just a few of the justifications offered to keep electronic media from covering court cases. Nevertheless, cameras continue to be allowed in many U.S. state trial courts and in the highest appeals courts in a variety of countries—though not, as yet, the Supreme Court of the United States. In 2000, a report commissioned by the International Criminal Tribunal for Yugoslavia concluded that cameras in the court did not significantly affect the participants’ behavior and helped to provide a full and accurate court record. It noted further that cameras can inform the international community about tribunal workings and encourage a transparent and fair system of justice. It suggested that other international judicial proceedings should follow suit.

The Right to Criticize Government Officials and Public Figures

Journalists report on the activities of government officials and public figures. But, ironically, the more prominent and powerful the individual, the more she may object to criticism. During the course of their careers, many reporters find themselves facing a lawsuit, accusing them of having falsely defamed an individual. Libel is broadly defined as a false and defamatory statement made to a third party about another individual, with the potential to harm the subject's reputation. In most jurisdictions, an action for libel is a civil case, brought by the individual as a means of recovering monetary damages. Because the right to reputation is regarded as an important, though not necessarily fundamental, right, international conventions and treaties generally do not reject libel suits as necessarily violating the right of freedom of expression and the public's right to know. Article 19 of the International Covenant on Civil and Political Rights, for example, provides that:

The exercise of rights...carries with it special duties and responsibilities. It may therefore be subject to certain restrictions, but these shall only be such as are provided by law and are necessary…for respect of the rights or reputations of others [emphasis added]. The U.S. Supreme Court first grappled with the question of whether the First Amendment to the Constitution applied in libel cases in New York Times v. Sullivan (1964). The case arose after the newspaper published a paid editorial advertisement protesting the treatment of civil rights activists by law enforcement personnel in Montgomery, Alabama. Although he was not named in the advertisement, L.B. Sullivan, a city commissioner who supervised the local police, sued, claiming that the advertisement included erroneous statements and that it had defamed him. He was awarded $500,000 in damages. The U.S. Supreme Court reversed the decision. In the majority opinion by Justice William Brennan, the Court observed,

"Debate on public issues should be uninhibited, robust and wide-open," recognizing for the first time that, paradoxically, the First Amendment must protect some false statements in order to encourage truthful speech about matters of public importance. Henceforth, no public official could prevail in a libel case without proving actual malice—that the statement was published "with knowledge that it was false or with reckless disregard of whether it was false or not." In subsequent cases, the Court extended the actual malice test to include libel suits brought by public figures as well. In cases involving private individuals (not public officials or public figures), the Court permits each state to establish the requisite standard. It acknowledges a legitimate government interest in affording individuals the opportunity to be compensated when published falsehoods harm their reputations. But even then, the Supreme Court requires at a minimum that a plaintiff prove publisher negligence, a standard that affords journalists some leeway for good-faith errors. Journalists possess a variety of privileges and defenses against libel claims, even those of non-public figures. Truth, of course, is an absolute defense to libel. The fair report privilege permits reporters to republish without liability government documents, including court filings, that contain libelous allegations, as long as the report of their contents is accurate. Fair comment permits good-faith criticism of individuals involved in matters of public concern, provided it is based on facts that are truthfully stated or otherwise privileged. And, as a matter of First Amendment law, the Court has held that pure opinion—statement that can neither be proven true nor false—is absolutely protected. The laws of many nations—Canada, Australia, Japan, Thailand, Brazil, and Poland, among them—include variations on these privileges and defenses. Many countries make no distinction between public and private figures, although they may impose stricter standards of proof on plaintiffs who are also government officials. Some countries permit corporations to sue for libel, but many limit those actions to statements damaging to the company's trade or business reputation.

Many countries have abolished seditious libel and prohibit government entities from suing for defamatory statements, even though individual officials may be permitted to do so. Assuming that a plaintiff both pleads and proves the elements of libel, she then typically will seek monetary damages. Although harm to reputation will be presumed in some circumstances, such as when a statement falsely accuses an individual of a crime, in most instances, the plaintiff will be obliged to prove that she actually suffered damage as result of the publication. Many countries allow plaintiffs to recover damages to compensate them for actual out-of-pocket monetary losses, as well as impairment of reputation, loss of standing in the community or profession, or personal humiliation. In addition, where the journalist's conduct is considered outrageous, courts may award punitive damages, designed not to compensate the plaintiff but to punish the media defendant. In some countries, media defendants may mitigate or reduce their damages by demonstrating that they promptly published a full and fair retraction of the false and defamatory material. In a number of nations, a defendant's offer of amends—a claim that the libel was published innocently—will either nullify the libel action or act as a defense in a subsequent suit. An alternative to monetary damages is an injunction prohibiting publication of the allegedly libelous material. Courts in the United States and Canada have rejected injunctions as a remedy for libel, finding them to be incompatible with freeexpression principles. But many other countries permit them. Courts in India, for example, will sometimes issue prepublication injunctions, but only if the statement complained of is demonstrably false and only if the plaintiff can demonstrate that immediate injury to person or property is likely to occur. In Italy, not only can prior restraints be obtained, but under Article 321 of the Italian Criminal Code, a court can order the seizure of a defamatory publication. In many countries, a state prosecutor can bring a criminal libel suit. Many scholars view criminal libel as outdated (its original purpose was to protect the monarchy or aristocracy from criticism or insults). One rationale was to provide a legal alternative for those who might otherwise turn to dueling or vigilantism to seek satisfaction for affronts to their honor or dignity. However unrealistic these threats may be today, even some mature democracies, including the United States, retain criminal libel statutes on their books, although they are rarely used.

In Germany, criminal defamation laws have been defended as necessary to pro tect the individual's right to dignity under the Basic Law. Portugal has argued that the state has the duty to protect an individual's reputation. Article 443 of the Belgian Criminal Code permits prosecution for libel, defined as "viciously and publicly attributing to a given person fact, the legal proof of which may not or cannot be established and which is likely to harm that person's honor or to expose that person to public contempt." However, the European Court of Human Rights has overturned criminal defamation convictions based on Article 10 of the European Convention. In Lingens v. Austria, for example, it ruled that a politician who "inevitably and knowingly" opens himself to scrutiny by journalists and the public must be prepared to accept harsh criticism. The court noted that criminal libel convictions have "a chilling effect" on the press and discourage the media from practicing their role as public watchdog. Nevertheless, criminal libel laws have been justified as necessary to protect nascent democracies from damaging criticism. Azerbaijan and the Maldives are just two countries that, in the summer of 2009, prosecuted journalists for defamation. Some nations apply much looser standards that are less compatible with press freedom. Some jail reporters for erroneously reporting falsehoods about individuals. In many others, desacato laws permit criminal prosecution of journalists for insulting or offending the dignity of public officials or institutions. Turkey, for example, has 11 separate insult laws, including one to protect the memory of Mustafa Kemal Ataturk. Expressions of contempt for the president, vice president, or a foreign head of state are punishable by one to five years imprisonment, and/or a fine in Cameroon. A journalist who "dishonors or discredits" another individual can be fined or imprisoned in Argentina. And even France retains the Law of July 29, 1881, on its statute books, permitting the press to be punished for insulting the president, the senate, foreign dignitaries, and the national flag. By contrast, in the United States, the Supreme Court has said, "There is no such thing as a false idea."

In Gertz v. Robert Welch (1974), Justice Lewis Powell observed, "However pernicious an opinion may be, we depend for its correction not on the conscience of judges and juries but on the competition of other ideas." In 1988, the Court categorically rejected a cause of action for infliction of emotional distress brought against Larry Flynt's Hustler magazine by the Rev. Jerry Falwell. The magazine had published an "advertising parody" depicting the clergyman purportedly describing his first sexual encounter with his mother in an outhouse while both were intoxicated. The publication included a disclaimer that the parody was fiction, "not to be taken seriously." Falwell sued Flynt for libel, invasion of privacy, and intentional infliction of emotional distress. Although Falwell lost on the first two claims, the jury ruled in his favor on the third. An appellate court upheld this verdict, but a unanimous Supreme Court reversed. Citing the long American tradition of robust and caustic political commentary, Supreme Court Chief Justice William Rehnquist rejected Falwell's attempt to impose an "outrageousness" standard that would permit recovery. He wrote, "'Outrageousness' in the area of political and social discourse has an inherent subjectiveness about it which would allow a jury to impose liability on the basis of the jurors' tastes or views, or...their dislike of a particular expression." Absent a showing that a false statement of fact was made with actual malice, Rehnquist wrote, a public figure must tolerate such attacks, in order to give adequate "breathing space" to the freedoms protected by the First Amendment.

The Right to Gather and Publish Newsworthy Information About Individuals

In 1890, two Boston lawyers, Louis Brandeis and Samuel Warren, published an article in the Harvard Law Review entitled "The Right to Privacy." They observed that: The press is overstepping in every direction the obvious bounds of propriety and decency. Gossip is no longer the resource of the idle and vicious, but has become a trade, which is pursued with industry as well as effrontery. To satisfy a prurient taste the details of sexual relations are spread broadcast on the columns of the daily papers. To occupy the indolent, column upon column is filled with idle gossip, which can only be procured by intrusion upon the domestic circle. ...When personal gossip attains the dignity of print, and crowds the space available for matters of real interest to the community, what wonder that the ignorant and thoughtless mistake its relative importance. The lawyers' prescient observations eventually led to the recognition of a common law right to privacy in the United States. Their concerns seem remarkably timely more than 100 years later. Privacy rights are enshrined in a number of international legal documents. Article 17 of the International Covenant on Civil and Political Rights says, "No one shall be subjected to arbitrary or unlawful interference with privacy, family, home or correspondence," and Article 8(1) of the European Convention similarly guarantees "the right to respect for his private and family life, his home and his correspondence."

Above: After Hustler owner Larry Flynt, left, published a lewd parody of Virginia televangelist Rev. Jerry Falwell, right, Falwell sued Flynt for libel. The case reached the U.S. Supreme Court where Chief Justice William Rehnquist wrote that Falwell, as a public figure, must tolerate such attacks in order to give sufficient "breathing space" to the freedoms protected by the First Amendment.

On the national level, privacy rights may be guaranteed by the constitution, by statute, or by common law. Article 5 of the Constitution of Brazil, for example, declares, "The private life of an individual is natural and inviolable." The Danish Criminal Code guarantees the right to privacy by making it an offense to trespass into private homes, to access private papers, to use mechanical devices to eavesdrop, to photograph or spy on individuals when on private property, to communicate someone else's private facts to another person, or to intrude on another's solitude after having been warned to leave him alone. Germany guarantees "the right of personality" in its Basic Law. And the right of privacy is guaranteed in South Africa both in Section 14 of the constitution and by common law. Courts in the United States, however, were slow to recognize a right to privacy. Although the Supreme Court has interpreted the Fourth Amendment of the U.S. Constitution to protect individuals from unreasonable searches and seizures, as well as other unwarranted intrusions by government agents, the amendment applies to the government and not to actions by other individuals. With the exception of a handful of federal statutes that prohibit certain types of electronic interception of private communications, U.S. privacy law is almost exclusively the province of the 50 states. By 1960, the American legal scholar William Prosser had identified four distinct privacy torts:

- intrusion on seclusion;

- publication of private facts;
- depiction of another in a false light;
- misappropriation or commercial use of another's name or image.

Some arise from common law. Others are statutory. Not every jurisdiction recognizes all four torts. But each is designed to provide a remedy to an individual based not on his external reputation, as in libel, but on his own sense of violation of self. Many countries recognize some or all of them. Intrusion on seclusion most commonly arises in the context of news gathering. It includes not only physical trespass into another's private space but also eavesdropping, tape recording, or otherwise intercepting private conversations without permission. Although the Supreme Court once observed, "Without some protection for seeking out the news, freedom of the press would be eviscerated," the high court has never exempted journalists from generally applicable laws that prohibit intrusion. The use of hidden cameras, for example, is unlawful in some states, and the Supreme Court let stand a Florida ruling that statutes prohibiting the use of concealed tape recorders do not violate the First Amendment rights of the press. In most, but not all, jurisdictions, journalists are free to record or photograph anything they can observe in a public place. However, there are exceptions. Scottish author J. K. Rowling, of Harry Potter fame, successfully sued for invasion of privacy on behalf of her young son after she was photographed on an Edinburgh street while pushing him in a stroller. A young Canadian woman recovered damages from a Montreal magazine that had photographed her sitting on a door stoop after, she claimed, her friends made fun of her. Even though she was in public at the time the picture was taken, the Supreme Court of Canada found that her right to control the use of her image in the media was guaranteed by the privacy clause in the Quebec human rights charter. The publication of private facts tort presents a free-expression dilemma because it permits legal action to be brought against journalists who have published the truth. Nevertheless, many countries recognize some version of this tort.

The United States construes it narrowly, limiting actions to publication of intimate facts highly offensive to a reasonable person and of no legitimate public concern. A public figure or public official will probably be held to have a diminished expectation of privacy. The challenge for any journalist is to determine whether a court would deem a particular fact newsworthy. A news organization's decision to publish information does not necessarily mean that it is of public concern. One also must distinguish between issues that are of legitimate public interest and connecting those issues with individuals. For example, when the British tabloid newspaper The Daily Mirror published photographs of Naomi Campbell leaving a Narcotics Anonymous meeting, the supermodel was able to recover damages for invasion of privacy. The House of Lords concluded that although the general topic of substance abuse was a matter of public concern, Campbell's addiction and treatment were not.

A more extreme example involved Princess Caroline von Hannover of Monaco, who claimed that publication of photographs depicting her going about ordinary activities, including horseback riding, shopping, and skiing, violated her privacy under German law. The German courts rejected her claims, but in 2004, the European Court of Human Rights upheld them, finding that her rights as guaranteed by Article 8 of the European Convention on Human Rights had been violated. The court acknowledged that Von Hannover is a public figure but ruled the photographs involved no matter of general concern: A fundamental distinction must be made between reporting facts—even controversial ones—capable of contributing to a debate in a democratic society relating to politicians in the exercise of their functions, for example, and reporting details of the private life of an individual who, moreover, as in this case, does not exercise official functions. While in the former case the press exercises its vital role of "watchdog" in a democracy by contributing to impart[ing] information and ideas on matters of public interest,…it does not do so in the latter case. Broadly speaking, however, information that is in the public domain—for example, details that can be obtained from public records or proceedings—cannot be the basis of an invasion of privacy suit for publication of private facts. In 1989, the U.S. Supreme Court ruled that the victim of a sexual assault could not sue a newspaper that included her name as part of a criminal incident roundup. Even though Florida, the state in which she resided, prohibited news organizations from publishing the names of rape victims, the high court found that because the newspaper had obtained the information legally—from a police report form that had been inadvertently made available in the sheriff's department press room—it could not be held liable for accurately reporting the information. Similarly, individuals who consent to the release of information, or who affirmatively disclose it themselves, generally cannot complain if it is published. The tort of false-light invasion of privacy is something of a legal anomaly and is not universally embraced. A few countries, such as Hungary and South Africa, allow actions for publication of false and misleading information, but only about two-thirds of American states recognize the tort. Similar to libel, false light allows individuals to sue for depictions that imply inaccurate, but not necessarily defamatory, facts. These may arise in the context of embellishment or fictionalization, such as in a docudrama or other dramatization of a true story.

But many false-light cases arise from the publication of photographs or videotape coupled with misleading captions, headlines, or stories. For example, in 2002, an actor whose photograph appeared on the cover of Playgirl successfully sued the magazine in federal court in California by arguing that the combination of the picture and the headlines created the false impression that nude photographs of him appeared inside. Appropriation of an individual's name or image for commercial purposes is regarded in many jurisdictions as essentially a proprietary right, comparable to trademark or copyright. Others consider it an extension of the right of personality. As an Irish Law Reform Commission report put it: Where the person does not consent to such use of the photograph, she or he may feel offended and embarrassed simply because they dislike publicity or because they dislike being associated with the product. In such cases, the protected interest is not necessarily proprietary or commercial. It is human dignity. China, Australia, Austria, Canada, Germany, and France are among the countries recognizing some variation of this tort. In Italy, Article 41(2) of the constitution permits individuals to commercially exploit the image of another person, as long as consent is first obtained. In the United States, the tort is limited to unauthorized uses in advertisements or product endorsement. For example, the Texas appropriation statute, (known as the Buddy Holly Act because it was enacted in response to exploitation of the deceased singer's name and image,) specifically exempts any use in a play, book, film, radio program, magazine or newspaper article, political material, or work of art. Parodies or satirical works are also protected.

Limits on Government Licensing of Journalists and News Organizations

Mandatory licensing of reporters has been justified as a means of ensuring that only qualified individuals engage in journalism and of keeping professional standards high. Some international organizations have advocated licensing to protect journalists from government harassment or harm. But when a government asserts authority to determine who can and cannot cover the news, it claims, says Leonard Sussman of Freedom House, "a license to censor." The lack of a license can provide the pretext for arresting journalists or expelling them from a country, and regimes can arbitrarily withhold licenses from reporters whose work they wish to suppress. As the 1980 International Commission for the Study of Communication Problems, also known as the MacBride Commission report to UNESCO, concluded, "Licensing schemes might well lead to restrictive regulations governing the conduct of journalists; in effect, protection would be granted only to those journalists who had earned official approval." In 1985, the Inter-American Court of Human Rights ruled a Costa Rican journalistlicensing statute contrary to the American Convention on Human Rights and, by extension, all human rights conventions, "insofar as it denied some persons access to the full use of the news media as a means of expressing themselves or imparting information." Mandatory membership, certification, or educational requirements can prevent individuals from gathering and disseminating information and deprive others of the opportunity to receive it. Principle 8 of the Declaration of Chapultepec draws the logical conclusion:

"The membership of journalists in guilds, their affiliation to professional and trade associations and the affiliation of the media with business groups must be strictly voluntary."

Mandatory licensing or affiliation requirements for journalists remain in place in many countries in Africa, Asia, and the Middle East. Although in June 2009, the Supreme Court in Brazil abolished a legal regulation requiring a university degree and membership in a union, nine Latin American countries continue to impose some requirements. And in Zimbabwe, journalists challenged the establishment of a media accreditation authority empowered to assess licensing fees, which the journalists claimed were grossly unreasonable and restrictive of freedom of expression. Licensing conditions news organization operations upon government approval. It affords another means of controlling the press and promoting self-censorship. Article 10 of the European Convention on Human Rights guarantees freedom from "interference by public authority" but has never been interpreted to prohibit licensing requirements. Nevertheless, licensing requirements can, under some circumstances, also be viewed as censorship and, accordingly, as incompatible with freedom of expression.

Additional Government Regulation

I n many jurisdictions, the government's power to regulate content differs between print and broadcast media. In the United States, the First Amendment is held to prohibit any government licensing of newspapers and magazines, but the Federal Communications Commission (FCC) has exclusive authority to license use of the electromagnetic spectrum, which is regarded as a scarce public resource. As the Supreme Court observed in 1969: Where there are substantially more individuals who want to broadcast than there are frequencies to allocate, it is idle to posit an unabridgeable First Amendment right to broadcast comparable to the right of every individual to speak, write or publish. ...It would be strange if the First Amendment, aimed at protecting and furthering communications, prevented the Government from making radio communication possible by requiring licenses to broadcast and by limiting the number of licenses so as not to overcrowd the spectrum. U.S. law authorizes FCC control over some aspects of broadcast station ownership. It may prohibit the concentration of many outlets in the hands of a single entity or limit cross-ownership, where one company controls multiple media platforms in a single market. Nevertheless, the FCC's jurisdiction over broadcasters' content decisions is subject to the First Amendment, and in recent years has been limited primarily to regulating indecency and to requiring broadcasters to provide equal opportunities for opposing candidates for public office to appear on the airwaves during the period immediately preceding an election. The fairness doctrine, which required broadcast licensees to report on controversial issues of public importance in their communities and to provide responsible representatives of opposing views a reasonable opportunity to reply, was repealed by the FCC in 1987.

At that time, the commission concluded that because of the explosion of new media outlets, the doctrine was no longer necessary to serve the public interest in receiving "diverse and antagonistic sources of information." The commission added that: The intrusion by government into the content of programming occasioned by the enforcement of doctrine unnecessarily restricts the journalistic freedom of broadcasters ...and actually inhibits the presen- tation of controversial issues of public importance to the detriment of the public and in degradation of the editorial prerogatives of broadcast journalists. Taxation, too, presents issues. Tax laws that apply to all for-profit corporations are generally acceptable, while those singling out the news media for special obligations often are deemed unconstitutional prior restraints on speech. By the same token, restrictions on the international circulation of news media products violate both Article 10 of the European Convention on Human Rights and Article 19 of the International Covenant on Civil and Political Rights, which guarantee the free flow of information and ideas "regardless of frontiers." An extensive discussion of licensing and regulatory schemes is beyond the scope of this book. In general, it is legitimate to require news organizations to abide by corporate laws and regulations of general applicability (such as registering the names and addresses of those legally responsible for the organization's operations). Any government regulation of media operations or content decisions should be transparent; subject to public scrutiny, participation, and oversight; and no more extensive than necessary to promote identified public interests.

Only Narrow and Carefully Tailored Restrictions on Indecent or Obscene Speech

Probably the biggest challenge to evaluating government controls on indecent or obscene speech is defining the terms "indecent" and "obscene." The United Kingdom's Obscene Publications Act of 1959 (as amended), for example, provides that material shall be deemed obscene if "the effect…is, if taken as a whole, such as to tend to deprave and corrupt persons who are likely, having regard to all relevant circumstances, to read, see or hear the matter contained or embodied in it." The late U.S. Supreme Court Justice Potter Stewart, when asked to define obscenity, famously observed, "I know it when I see it." In most countries, publishing or distributing obscene materials is a criminal offense. Prior restraints on their distribution are often considered constitutional. Many laws seek to protect children from both exploitation and exposure to pornographic materials. However, national and international freedom of expression guarantees generally protect the access rights of consenting adults, except for certain specific categories. In Germany, the criminal code prohibits distribution of pornography that depicts abuse of children. In Sweden, some images of sexual violence can be banned. Child pornography, whether or not legally obscene, enjoys no constitutional protection in the United States. Many countries forbid the sales of any pornography to those under age 18. In mature democracies, obscenity laws usually raise no significant concerns for mainstream news organizations. But in some countries, outdated statutes still recognize offenses like "conspiracy to corrupt public morals" or "outraging public decency." Vaguely worded laws may proscribe indecent or obscene material without defining it, or they may lack qualifying language like that adopted by the U.S. Supreme Court in 1973, which limited obscenity to those works that, "taken as a whole, lack serious literary, artistic, political or scientific value." In these situations, journalists may run afoul of the laws if they publish sexually explicit, but newsworthy, material. Or the obscenity laws may be used as a pretext to censor other material. For example, in Vietnam, the government claims that it filters out Internet access only to sexually explicit material.

Yet a 2007 report by the Internet watchdog group OpenNet Initiative found instead that pornography remains rela- ively unfettered, while religious and political sites critical of the government routinely are blocked. Even in the United States, the Supreme Court has upheld greater restrictions on the broadcast of indecent material that would be constitutionally protected speech in the print media, on the ground that the pervasive nature of the broadcast medium makes its programming uniquely accessible to children. The best approach to regulating obscenity is a focused one. Laws should define with precision what is being banned. That way, all parties are on notice of what is impermissible. Laws should distinguish materials that are offensive but not demonstrably harmful. Content that has redeeming social, political, scientific, or artistic value should be protected. Any government body authorized to classify or restrict distribution of obscene or indecent material or to impose sanctions on publishers should operate transparently and follow clearly articulated standards.

SELF-R EGULAT ION IN LIEU OF LITIGATION

Journalists and news organizations make mistakes. Courts offer aggrieved individuals remedies. Lawsuits for libel, invasion of privacy, breach of confidence, copyright violation, and infliction of emotional distress are just a few types of civil action one can bring against the press.

But lawsuits take time, cost money, and often do not afford a plaintiff satisfactory results. For example, in the United States, constitutional protections in libel cases are so strong that some trials never reach the point of adjudicating the underlying allegation's truth. By contrast, legal standards favoring libel plaintiffs turned the United Kingdom into the "libel capital of the world" in the 1990s and first years of the 21st century, with individuals of many nationalities filing suit in London against foreign publications that they claimed defamed them. But in May 2010, the newly elected coalition government vowed to "review and reform libel laws to protect freedom of speech, reduce costs, and discourage libel tourism." The right to free expression often collides with other competing interests. Sometimes there is no legal remedy for types of journalistic misconduct that can upset readers and viewers. A courtroom is often not the best place to resolve disputes about balance, fairness, and accuracy. And there is always the risk that harsh judicial remedies, even those imposed when the underlying case involves journalistic misconduct, will inhibit the future free and open publication of controversial views. Self-regulatory mechanisms offer a valuable alternative.

Ombudsmen

Also known as "readers' representatives" or "public editors," ombudsmen act as liaisons between a news organization's staff and the public. Typically, they field complaints, investigating alleged ethical breaches. They encourage staff to respond to readers' questions, and they explain how and why news organizations make their decisions. They may write a column, or they may simply handle complaints on an individual basis. Even though ombudsmen are generally paid by the news organization, they should be assured autonomy and independence.

Press Councils

Press councils, which typically operate as tribunals that consider and adjudicate complaints about media conduct, can take many forms. Some are legislatively mandated. Many are funded by the news media. Others are underwritten by charitable foundations or nongovernmental organizations, multilateral organizations such as UNESCO, or even voluntary contributions from the public. Still others are affiliated with universities. A few receive support from governmental entities but operate independently. Press councils can have national, regional, or local jurisdiction. The members of the tribunal usually include representatives of the press and of the public, including academics, and, sometimes, of the government. Those who choose to submit their complaints to a press council for resolution are usually obliged to waive any right to pursue a law suit. Council staff screens complaints and submits those of potential merit for adjudication under council procedures. A typical model features an open hearing before the tribunal. Both the complainant and the news organization have the right to appear. After the presentations, questions, and deliberations, the tribunal issues a ruling. Some news councils require member news organizations to publish the rulings involving them; for others, publication is voluntary

Codes of Ethics

Most associations of journalists, and many individual news organizations, have adopted codes of ethics. Terms vary. Some codes are binding, and violation of a provision can lead to dismissal by an employer or expulsion from a professional journalism society. But most codes of ethics, instead, offer voluntary guidelines to help journalists make morally and professionally sound decisions. Codes thus encourage greater accountability to readers and viewers. Some codes of ethics are extremely detailed. Others offer more general principles. A good example is the Code of Ethics for the Society of Professional Journalists (SPJ), the largest voluntary association of U.S. news reporters and editors. Its code encourages journalists to abide by four core principles:

- Seek truth and report it: Journalists should be honest, fair and courageous in gathering, reporting and interpreting information.
- Minimize harm: Ethical journalists treat sources, subjects and colleagues as human beings deserving of respect.
- Act independently: Journalists should be free of obligation to any interest other than the public's right to know.
- Be accountable: Journalists are accountable to their readers, listeners, viewers and each other. By its own terms, the SPJ code is a voluntary guide to ethical behavior.

It states: "The code is intended not as a set of 'rules' but as a guide for ethical decision-making. It is not—nor can it be under the First Amendment—legally enforceable." The SPJ has a National Ethics Committee, consisting of members from throughout the United States with a special interest and expertise in ethics. Although the committee does not adjudicate specific complaints, it does provide guidance and opinions to journalists and members of the public.

THE R ESPONSIBIL IT IES OF JOURNALISTS

In August 2009, a court in Amsterdam ruled that the Associated Press (AP) violated the Dutch royal family's privacy by distributing photographs taken of them on a skiing holiday in Argentina. The presiding judge prohibited further dissemination or sale of four of the photos. She found that the pictures were taken during "a private vacation" and depicted "private activities." "The right to respect the personal sphere weighs more heavily than the right to freedom of expression," the judge wrote.

Taking the photographs was legal under Argentine law. But the judge cited a 2005 media code drawn up by the Royal House with the assistance of the Netherlands Government Information Service (RVD), requiring the Dutch news media to refrain from photographing them except during official functions or designated "media moments." Although she acknowledged that the code "cannot be regarded as a binding agreement," the judge nevertheless invoked it as the basis to threaten AP with a fine of up to 50,000 euros for any future distribution of the photos. The AP had argued that royalty's public actions are of public concern. It predicted the ruling "would have the unfortunate effect of unduly restraining the exercise of freedom of information globally." Reporters Sans Frontières (Reporters Without Borders) denounced both the ruling and the media code, contending that the system established by the code "reduces the media to PR agencies." But the judge concluded that publication of the photos served no public interest and that, in this particular case, "The right to respect the personal sphere weighs more heavily than the right to freedom of expression." This story represents the responsible journalist's worst nightmare. A nonbinding journalistic code of conduct became the basis to stop an international news agency from publishing photographs of public figures that had been taken legally. It does not always happen that way, of course. Many individual media organizations and journalists' associations voluntarily adopt codes or standards of practice. These serve not as grounds to restrict press freedom but, instead, as guideposts to help journalists determine the best way to do their jobs. As the preamble to the Code of Ethics of the U.S.-based Society of Professional Journalists says, "Professional integrity is the cornerstone of a journalist's credibility.".

Is Journalism a "Profession"?

The term "code" is usually associated with a profession. But whether journalism is a profession is a hotly contested question. In many countries, the answer is "no." Traditionally, a profession is an occupation with formal qualifications, requiring specialized training and licensing, and subject to a regulatory body with the authority to admit and discipline members. Lawyers, physicians, and members of the clergy are regarded as professionals throughout the world. So are architects, engineers, dentists, pharmacists, and accountants.

Above: Was privacy a more important right than freedom of the press? A court in Amsterdam ruled that the AP photographers violated the Dutch royal family's privacy by distributing photos taken of them during a skiing holiday in Argentina.

Journalists are sometimes subjected to similar requirements. Some countries require reporters to complete a particular training or university program. Others mandate their guild or union membership or compel them to hold a government-issued license. Most free-expression advocates oppose mandatory credentialing schemes. However well-intentioned, they argue, these impose barriers to participation and can exclude individuals who represent unpopular or minority viewpoints. Licensing circumscribes freedom of expression and undermines the public's right to receive information from diverse sources. Ideally, then, journalism codes of ethics will be aspirational rather than legally enforceable by the state. The former might allow a member news organization to discharge an individual reporter who violates the code. But even then, nothing would stop that reporter from seeking another job elsewhere or prevent another organization from hiring her. No court or licensing board could rule that reporter ineligible to practice journalism.

Ethics and Standards: More Questions

Than Answers Ethics codes aim not to impose legally enforceable standards but, instead, to offer journalists a framework to help them decide what to report and how to report it. No code of ethics can answer every question, and good ones probably raise more questions than they answer. Reasonable people, even journalists them selves, may disagree about how a specific ethical standard should apply in a particular situation.

- For example, should a journalist lampoon a name or image sacred to a particular ethnic or religious group? This is perfectly legal in many countries. But does it contribute to robust public discussion or, instead, foment hatred and promote conflict?
- Should the press publish classified information, especially where government claims that doing so will damage its efforts to protect the public? Would this be the act of an independent government watchdog or of one needlessly endangering public health and safety?
- Should a television station air graphic footage of military conflict, including scenes of violence and death? Would this convey to the public the reality of war? Or, instead, undermine morale and needlessly distress surviving family members? Readers and viewers may not agree with every choice a news organization makes. But ethical standards and guidelines can offer guidance toward thoughtful and defensible solutions.

Seeking Truth: The First Principle

Most journalism codes emphasize that telling the truth—being accurate— is essential. "Seek truth and report it" is the first core principle of the Society of Professional Journalists Code of Ethics. The British Editors' Code of Practice also lists accuracy as its first principle and states, "The press must take care not to publish inaccurate, misleading or distorted information, including pictures." The one universal ethical principle may be simply this: A journalist never knowingly publishes a falsehood. This is not always an easy standard to uphold. Of course, a journalist should make every effort to verify a story before reporting it.

Above: In 1971, the New York Times published the Pentagon Papers despite government claims that doing so would endanger national security. The U.S. Supreme Court ruled that constitutional guarantees of a free press overrode other considerations, and allowed further publication.

But facts that alter original perceptions may only be learned over time, after publication. Here, a responsible news organization publishes a correction or clarification as quickly as possible. News organizations should take great care to assure that headlines, teasers, sound bites, or quotations are not only accurate but do not oversimplify the facts or take them out of context. Photographs, audio, and video may need to be cropped or edited to address considerations of space or time but not in a way that misleads or misrepresents. The staging of photos or reenactments of news events should be avoided or, where absolutely necessary, clearly labeled. Obviously journalists should not fabricate the news, nor should they plagiarize— that is, copy without attribution—another person's work. They should not make up quotations, nor reprint a news story prepared by someone else without first obtaining permission to do so.

Sources

Areporter, it is said, is only as good as her sources. Knowledgeable ones enhance a journalist's news-gathering ability and help her publish more information. But journalists must be cautious and determine that a source is credible. This includes ascertaining a source's point of view or what his "agenda" might be. Ideally, reporters should consult multiple sources to obtain diverse perspectives on a subject. And they should make every effort to verify the accuracy of a source's information whenever possible. What about anonymous sourcing, the practice of attributing a fact to an unnamed source? It is preferable that all sources be "on the record" and that facts not be linked to "administration sources" or some other imprecise formulation. Sources who stand behind their word are more likely to tell the truth. Attributing information to a named source also helps the reader or viewer evaluate independently the credibility of the source. But sometimes a source has valid reasons to request, or demand, that his identity be kept secret. When possible, a journalist should resist making this promise. But it won't always be possible. Some news organizations require that an editor approve any promise of confidentiality. Although this can frustrate a reporter, the policy makes sense. When an unattributed piece of information is published, the news organization's reputation is at stake along with that of the individual reporter. Reporters should be very clear about their promises. Phrases like "off the record" and "on background" mean different things to different people. Journalist and source should agree on the terms governing the news organization's use of information. Once a promise is made, it must be kept. As the British Code of Practice says, "Journalists have a moral obligation to protect confidential sources of information." Should the journalist be called to testify in court about her information, keeping that promise can put the journalist at risk of being held in contempt in nations that do not recognize a legal privilege for journalists. Any reporter must be clear with the source exactly how far he is prepared to go to keep that promise.

Surreptitious and Undercover Reporting Techniques

Journalists should avoid deceptive reporting techniques, like using hidden cameras, tape recorders, and microphones, or assuming a false identity. In some jurisdictions, they are illegal. But equally important, they can undermine credibility. Readers and viewers often won't believe that a reporter who essentially lied in order to get a story will tell the truth when he reports it. Generally speaking, a journalist should identify herself as a member of the news media and make clear that she may use whatever she learns in a story. Nevertheless, there are times when a story can be obtained only through subterfuge. Journalists and their news organizations should reserve these techniques for the rare occasion when conventional methods will not work and, only then, when a compelling public interest demands it. News media should then explain their methods when the story is published or broadcast.

Objectivity in the News

Journalists in the United States strive to achieve objectivity. This model has been criticized in recent years. Some question whether objectivity is desirable. They suggest that true objectivity essentially has no moral compass and treats all facts and all viewpoints as equally deserving of respect. Professor Michael Bugeja, director of the School of Journalism at Iowa State University, disagrees. "Objectivity is not a synonym for truth," he writes, "but the process through which we seek to attain it." No one approaches any story with complete objectivity. As a reporter begins researching, it is likely that she will have a definite bias toward at least some aspects of the story. But the goal is to set aside those presumptions and prejudices and to move forward with a healthy skepticism. Suppose a suspect has been arrested and charged with a crime. In many countries, an accused person enjoys a presumption of innocence until tried and convicted. Yet law enforcement personnel often want to convince the public that the person in custody really is the perpetrator of a crime and will encourage news media reporting of information that strengthens their case. The objective journalist will, of course, report what the authorities say. But, to the extent the law permits, she also should seek independently to verify the accuracy of the information and to search for credible conflicting information from other reliable sources. She should resist simply parroting the theories of the authorities as if they are proven fact.

Encouraging Diversity of Views

In many countries, a partisan press is the norm. Readers and viewers in these nations may expect that a news organization will approach topics from its own particular point of view and select the subjects that it covers accordingly. They also know that competing news organizations may advocate different perspectives. This can be consistent with journalism ethics but only if the news organization distinguishes between advocacy and reporting. Opinion columns and editorial commentary should be clearly labeled and should neither distort nor falsify the facts that underlie the opinion. Journalists should seek out diverse voices and afford competing and, even unpopular, views an opportunity to be heard. They should support freedom of speech for all. News organizations should provide a forum for robust debate on issues vital to their community. Letters to the editor and online readers' comments are two ways to encourage public participation. But news organizations also should make every effort to keep the discussion civil and to discourage the dissemination of falsehoods or pejorative attacks on others.

Respect for the Individual

The second tenet of the SPJ Code of Ethics is to "Minimize harm…treat sources, subjects and colleagues as human beings deserving of respect." This principle recognizes that a responsible journalist sometimes unavoidably will harm someone but requires her to make every effort to minimize that damage. The SPJ code, like many similar codes, exhorts the journalist to show compassion for those who will be affected by news coverage, especially when they become the subject of attention through no fault of their own. Crime victims, the relatives of public figures and celebrities, children, and other vulnerable individuals should be treated with sensitivity. Journalists should consider carefully whether there is a genuinely newsworthy reason to report on them at all. Intrusive news-gathering techniques can cause harm. Persistence is appropriate, but aggressive tactics will not be justified in every case. Although they may be legal, making repeated telephone calls, following a person on the street, taking multiple photographs, or remaining on private property after having been asked to leave may cause distress. Even the most public person is entitled to some zone of privacy, and only an overriding public interest justifies intrusion into individuals' private lives. On the other hand, there can be good and valid reasons to report information that a news subject would prefer to keep secret. A public official may wish to keep secret details of an extramarital affair. But if public funds or other resources are used to support the affair, they become a matter of legitimate public interest. Similarly, crime victims often prefer that their identity remain confidential, and a news organization may agree, at least in the case of children or sexual assault victims. But in many countries, a crime victim plays the role of accuser in a criminal prosecution. Although an alleged victim's credibility might be a legitimate issue to explore—and one of some importance to the criminal defendant—journalists should not pander to prurient tastes by publicizing sensational facts that are not a matter of public interest. The news media should balance the rights and interests of both victims and criminal defendants with the right of the public to be informed.

Cultural Sensitivity Journalists should not reinforce stereotypes

The practice is intellectually lazy and can lead to misperceptions and inaccuracy. They should consider carefully whether it is necessary to identify an individual by race, religion, sexual orientation, or similar characteristic. Gender-neutral language is often appropriate. Reporters should remember and be sensitive to different cultural traditions. For example, adherents of some religions forbid or strongly discourage photographing individuals. Journalists should respect their preferences, unless there is a compelling reason to do otherwise. On the other hand, "cultural values" sometimes is a cloak for censorship. Repressive regimes may cite social values when their real intent is to restrict freedom of expression and to silence dissenting views. The ethical journalist should challenge attempts to suppress the truth, whatever justification is offered.

The Independent Journalist

The journalist's highest loyalty should be to the public. This means avoiding conflicts of interest that could compromise her ability to act independently and to inform the public free from other influences and considerations. Journalists should avoid accepting gifts, fees, tickets, travel, or other goods or services from news sources. Review copies of books, music, or movies should be donated to charity unless there is a journalistic reason to retain them as a resource for future reporting. Be wary of travel junkets that are little more than thinly disguised attempts to persuade reporters to write enthusiastically about a particular destination or subject. News organizations should pay their own way when sending staff to cover sporting or cultural events.

If this is not possible, a disclaimer should be included in the story. Journalists should not endorse products in return for compensation, and they should keep separate the editorial and advertising sides of the news business. Advertisers must not influence favorable coverage or suppress negative reporting. Any advertisement should be clearly labeled so there is no possibility of confusing an ad with news reporting or commentary. Memberships in clubs, associations, political parties, or religious organizations can create a conflict of interest for a journalist. Some news organizations prohibit certain kinds of political or philanthropic activities, such as running for political office or volunteering with an advocacy group. Most forbid journalists to report on organizations with which they, or close family members, are affiliated. Although an editor at the Washington Post even abstained from voting in elections, individuals obviously do not surrender their civil rights when they choose to become journalists. But it is important to remember that affiliations can be interpreted as bias. If a conflict of interest is unavoidable, it should be disclosed. Many news organizations have special rules for reporters and commentators who cover business and financial topics. Laws forbidding insider trading (buying and selling stocks and other equities when one possesses nonpublic knowledge that may affect the stock price) may apply. Journalists should not write about companies in which they own stock or have some other financial interest, particularly if their reporting might influence the market and benefit them personally. They should disclose to their editors the financial instruments they and their families own and refrain from trading stocks within a short time of writing about them. Just as journalists should not take payments intended to influence news coverage, they should not offer bribes or payments to news subjects. To the outside observer, news that has been "bought and paid for" is suspect. In certain situations, such as when a source is asked to travel to a particular location to appear on a radio or television program, it may be appropriate to reimburse her reasonable expenses, including meals, travel, and lodging. But "checkbook journalism" and bidding for news should be avoided.

Ethical Issues

When Covering Government Reporting on government raises particularly difficult challenges. The public generally expects journalists to act as watchdogs, guarding against improper government behavior. But what about when law enforcement officials ask reporters not to report the details of an ongoing hostage situation, for example? Should journalists cooperate? If they do not, lives may be endangered. But if they do, they may compromise their own ability to hold government accountable. During war, crisis, or emergency, journalists may feel conflicting loyalties. The pressure to be patriotic can be great. Or a newly elected government may claim that it cannot afford a completely free press and will urge journalists to write favorably as a way to help solidify a fragile and emerging democracy. Sometimes journalists are asked to report propaganda as truth in the interest of protecting "national security." When editorial decisions conflict with government wishes, news organizations can be criticized for substituting their own judgment for that of elected officials. This can arise when the government claims that there is a compelling need for secrecy about intelligence and law enforcement matters. On the other hand, journalists may also be condemned for withholding information or accused of delaying publication for partisan reasons. These are difficult calls. The answers are not always easy. One guiding principle is that a journalist's loyalty is to the public, not to a particular government or regime. No journalist wants to harm his community or country. But governments may be tempted to suppress critical reporting by claiming it could damage public safety or national security. Reporters can respect these claims, but they should also be skeptical. They can give government officials an opportunity to explain why a particular story might endanger lives or a specific national interest. But journalists should scrutinize those in power and hold them to account. Sometimes, the most patriotic thing a journalist can do is question authority.

Being Accountable to the Public

An important part of a journalist's job is to hold those in positions of authority accountable to the public. News organizations have a similar ethical obligation of accountability. The news media are more transparent than many businesses because their work product is constantly available for scrutiny. Journalists regularly critique and challenge each other's work. And in most countries, the consumer has many news choices and can reject those whose standards fall short. That said, most news organizations can do more to be accessible to the public. If business or political affiliations influence their editorial choices, they should be disclosed. Did a merchant who advertises heavily in a newspaper, for instance, request favorable news coverage? Media should explain how they make editorial decisions, especially controversial ones. Deviations from usual ethical standards should be explained. News organizations should invite readers to comment and encourage them to raise concerns and complaints.

Ideally, a dedicated, impartial staff member should address these complaints. All news organizations make mistakes. They should strive to minimize these by establishing fact-checking procedures throughout the editorial process. But when errors do occur, they should be acknowledged promptly and corrected prominently.

Special Ethics Issues Raised by New Media and Citizen Journalism

Most, if not all, traditional media's ethical guidelines make sense for citizen journalists, bloggers, and other new media practitioners. But those who publish in cyberspace face additional challenges. Bloggers, unlike mainstream journalists, often publish anonymously or use a pseudonym. In some societies, those holding controversial or dissenting views withhold their identity as a matter of personal safety. But those who speak anonymously still have an ethical obligation to be truthful, accurate, and as transparent as possible about conflicts of interest. Many bloggers encourage readers to engage in the discussion and to add comments to their sites. They may invite usergenerated content and post it on their blogs. They may link to external sites. And they may excerpt others' work for the purpose of commentary and criticism. All these techniques add vitality to a blog. But bloggers should consider whether they will attempt to verify links and to moderate postings made by others, as well as whether they will establish policies for certain content types, such as sexually explicit video or personal attacks. It is wise to post these policies prominently and to apply them consistently.

Using Social Media

Many journalists, both traditional and new media practitioners, are turning to social media, such as Facebook, Orkut, and MySpace, or tapping into YouTube or other sites that allow individuals to post content. These media can provide story ideas and useful leads. They can even allow a journalist to interact with a community or to promote a journalism "brand" by encouraging readers to visit a news organization's Web site.

Above: Social media raises new questions for journalists. Facebook CEO Mark Zuckerberg delivered the keynote address at an internet conference in San Francisco on April 21, 2010.

But social media pose new challenges for the ethical journalist. Verifying postings can be difficult. Reporters should make clear when they utilize social media sites as the basis for a story. They should exercise special caution when using information concerning minors, which could damage someone's reputation, or when using information that someone else claims to own—such as a trade secret. The laws of libel, privacy, and copyright still apply in cyberspace. Some news organizations have adopted ethics policies for their employees' use of social media. Dow Jones, publisher of the Wall Street Journal, discourages its reporters from expressing personal or partisan viewpoints on their personal Facebook pages or from discussing developing stories that have not yet appeared in the newspaper. Some organizations recommend that a reporter maintain separate professional and personal Facebook pages. Journalists should remember that friending a confidential source on Facebook may reveal that source's identity to the world. They also should recall that decisions to friend or to join a fan page may be construed as evidence of bias. Finally, nothing on Facebook or similar sites is really private. Once something has been posted to the social media, there is really no way to take it back or to stop others from using it in whatever way they choose.

CONCLUSION

Many journalists believe they should not have to justify their role as government watchdogs and as conduits of public information. Surely, they think, modern recognition that freedom of expression is a fundamental right has already settled all that. Therefore, some journalists think that they must have the legal right to be wrong—sometimes. But journalists' own ethical standards can be more stringent than legal ones. They encourage journalists to examine their motivations, their methods, and their work product. They encourage reporters and editors to ask tough questions about how they make decisions. And these ethical precepts invite journalists both to consider other perspectives and to contemplate how their decisions affect others. Adopting and applying ethics principles can seem daunting. But they help journalists do the best job possible. They provide a mandate to act independently —even courageously—when seeking and pursuing truth.

NEW MEDIA

The freewheeling world of the blogosphere seems like the last bastion of truly free speech. One does not need a lot of money, an expensive printing press, or a transmitter tower. Anybody with access to a computer, a modem, and a little software can share his thoughts with the world through a weblog, or blog. And many of the intensely personal and highly opinionated weblogs proliferating on the Internet inhabit a world apart from the sometimes-dreary realm of meticulously sourced and factchecked traditional journalism. Bloggers are a law unto themselves. Or are they?

BALANCING FREE SPEECH AND COMPETING INTERNET INTERESTS

From the early days of popular use of the Internet, the rallying cry was that cyberspace was the new frontier, subject to no law. But governments around the world, shaken by the implications of the new communication technology, have tried to figure out how to harness and control its use. Gaining access to the Internet can be the first hurdle. A 2007 report by the Internet watchdog group OpenNet Initiative showed that attempts to censor the Web are spreading and growing more sophisticated. Saudi Arabia, to offer one example, uses filtering software to block everything from sites classified as pornography or gambling to religious conversion sites and sites critical of the Saudi monarchy. China has been criticized for a combination of Internet control measures, including filtering software, requiring users and Internet cafes to purchase licenses, and banning Internet cafes. In the United States, Congress, state legislatures, and the courts have struggled to balance free speech on the Internet against competing interests, like national security, copyright protection, and the right to reputation. In its landmark Reno v. ACLU (American Civil Liberties Union) decision (1997), the U.S. Supreme Court extended to communications on the World Wide Web the same First Amendment protections covering newspapers or other print media. Cyberspace, the Court ruled, is neither a "scarce expressive commodity," like the broadcast spectrum used by radio and television broadcasters, nor an invasive one that enters "an individual's home or appears on one's computer screen unbidden." With neither of these historical justifications for government licensing and control applicable, Justice John Paul Stevens wrote for the majority,

"The interest in encouraging freedom of expression in a democratic society outweighs any theoretical but unproven benefit of censorship."

The Reno decision means that Internetbased communication receives the highest level of constitutional protection, including many judicial rulings defining the scope of the First Amendment. Prior restraints are presumed unconstitutional. Successful libel suits require proof of publisher fault, even if a plaintiff proves the challenged statement false. Most invasion of privacy suits will be rejected if the publisher can demonstrate that the subject of its story was newsworthy. Copyright violations may be excused if the publication constitutes fair use. One need not be a recognized journalist to invoke these protections. As far back as 1972, the U.S. Supreme Court said, "Liberty of the press is the right of the lonely pamphleteer…as much as of the large metropolitan publisher." So bloggers have First Amendment protections. They may have statutory protection as well. Existing laws protecting reporters' confidential sources might or might not apply to a blogger, depending on the language of the statute or the court addressing the issue. Although some laws limit coverage to full-time employees of for-profit traditional news media, many are expansive, covering anyone who engages in gathering information and disseminating it to a wide audience. A California court ruled that the state shield law protected the identities of bloggers who revealed Apple Computer's trade secrets.

Their publications, the court ruled, constituted "news." But shortly thereafter, a federal court in the same state refused to acknowledge that blogger and self-described anarchist Josh Wolf was a journalist because he was not "connected with or employed by" a news organization. U.S. courts have interpreted broadly Section 230 of the Communications Decency Act, which immunizes providers of "interactive computer services" (ISPs) from defamation claims arising from third-party content. Courts have extended this protection to those who operate Web sites and listservs, even if they exercise some editorial control over that material. The same analysis logically would apply to blogs.

Holding Bloggers Accountable

So does that mean that bloggers are free to upload whatever they want, with no fear of being sued? Absolutely not. Whatever immunity may exist for links to third-party sites or to postings submitted by readers, a blog publisher can still be sued for any material he writes himself. During the course of litigation, the blogger could face a protracted examination of his news-gathering techniques. Did he attempt to verify the accuracy of the story, or did he simply repeat an unsubstantiated rumor? Did he rely on anonymous sources? Did he, in other words, act negligently or with reckless disregard for the truth? If a court finds that he did, he may lose the suit. In most countries, libel suits can be grounded only in false statements of fact. No one can be sued for statements of pure opinion that can be proven neither true nor false. But many blogs are a robust mixture of idiosyncratic opinion and unsupported allegation. It can be hard to distinguish between the two when invoking an opinion privilege, which requires showing that the underlying factual statements on which the opinion is based are true. U.S. legal protections end at the border but the Internet does not.

A blogger in the United States can brandish the First Amendment and Section 230 all she wants, but a foreign court has no obligation to pay any attention. Those courts will, for the most part, apply their own laws. Although traditional journalists long have faced lawsuits and even criminal prosecutions in other countries where their work product is distributed, it may surprise bloggers to learn they are vulnerable to suit anywhere their words are read. The Australian High Court so ruled in 2002, when it allowed "Diamond Joe" Gutnick to file a libel suit. An Australian national, Gutnick claimed that an article published online by U.S.-based Barron's magazine defamed him. When Gutnick showed that a handful of readers in his hometown of Melbourne downloaded the story, the court allowed him to file a libel suit there. The chief justice wrote, "[T]hose who post information on the World Wide Web do so knowing that [it] is available to all and sundry without any geographic restriction."

Above: Australian philanthropist "Diamond Joe" Gutnick (left) sued U.S.-based Barron's magazine in 2002 for defaming him in an article posted online. Even though the alleged defaming article was published in the United States, the Australian High Court decided any article available online can be considered published wherever it is read, thus granting Gutnick the right to sue in Melbourne.

Libel lawsuits are not all that bloggers need worry about. Statutes in many countries make it an offense, or even a crime, to "insult" or "offend the dignity" of someone, even if the criticism is absolutely true. For example, in 2008, blogger Raja Petra Kamarudin, editor of the Web site Malaysia Today, was arrested and detained on charges of violating Malaysia's Internal Security Act by criticizing Islam. Many countries enforce mandatory rights of reply, which compel publication of responses by individuals and corporations who claim they have been the subject of inaccurate reports. In 2006, the European Parliament adopted a Council of Europe recommendation to extend these rights of reply to online media, including any "service available to the public containing frequently updated and edited information of public interest." That sounds like a typical weblog. Many bloggers already take these steps.

They update their blogs, often print retractions or modifications to erroneous postings, and freely publish responses from disgruntled readers. They claim that laws are not required to make them act responsibly. But there is a big difference between making an editorial choice because you believe it enhances your credibility and doing so under compulsion of law. In addition, many bloggers engage anonymously in vituperative online commentary. Under Section 230, an ISP can be compelled to reveal an individual's identity if a judge concludes that a plaintiff has made a valid libel claim. Here, ISP includes newspapers and other media, who could be forced to unmask readers posting anonymous comments on their Web sites, leaving the posters vulnerable to retaliation or retribution.

Protecting Privacy and Copyright

Invasion of privacy presents special challenges in cyberspace. Digital technology facilitates news gathering. In theory, digitizing government records should create an unprecedented opportunity for citizen access and oversight. But many judges and legislators, driven by fear that access will facilitate identity theft, employment discrimination, or other illegal conduct, instead curtail access to electronic files. Judges also express discomfort at the prospect of someone from a distant location, with no legitimate interest in the local community, surfing through court or real estate records and publishing them online. They fear that bloggers do little except spread rumors, violate copyright laws, and identify sexual assault victims, all the while hiding behind the anonymity that the Web permits. They worry that citizen journalists with cellphone cameras and recorders will invade courtrooms and post trial footage online, a practice they find both disruptive and undignified. Gatekeepers often support access to government records and proceedings in the abstract; once access becomes cheap and easy, they may question its wisdom. Information, they think, is too valuable, or dangerous, to be online. For example, in September 2008, a California trial judge forbade the Orange County Register to report "by all means and manner of communication, whether in person, electronic, through audio or video recording, or print medium" testimony by any witness appearing in a class action wage-and-hour suit brought by its newspaper carriers.

He concluded this injunction was necessary to prevent future witnesses from being influenced by others' testimony. An appellate panel eventually overturned this order. It ruled that the risk that news reports might influence witnesses was insufficient to justify censorship. Other, less intrusive alternatives, such as admonishing witnesses not to read the paper, would accomplish the same goal. But the pervasiveness of the online media had convinced the trial judge to overlook nearly 70 years of precedent outlawing similar prior restraints. Copyright law presents separate challenges. The owners of intellectual property have always possessed the legal right to demand that violators "cease and desist" publishing and distributing infringing works. But the Internet makes copying others' work without permission easier than ever before. Should the telephone company or other ISP be liable when one of its customers uses their connection illegally to post a copy of an .mp3 file for download? The U.S. Digital Millennium Copyright Act (DMCA), enacted in 1998, was designed to address this situation without also stifling protected speech. The statute's "safe harbor" provision protects ISPs from liability if, upon receiving notice that infringing material has been posted, they "expeditiously" remove it. The problem is that a prudent ISP will choose to take down the content and leave the subscriber and copyright owner to sort out their respective rights. To facilitate the process, the DMCA permits copyright holders to use "administrative subpoenas" to compel the ISP to disclose the subscriber's identity. Although these are supposed to be issued only to curtail infringing activity, the risk is that subpoenas might improperly be used to circumvent the wellestablished First Amendment principles protecting the right to engage in anonymous speech. The emergence of the Internet as a significant communications technology and publication platform for journalists creates new legal complications. But the governing principles should remain constant. They should not depend on whether a journalist works for the mainstream media or publishes a blog. Judges and legislators should follow the principles that have long protected the press and the public's right to know, regardless of affiliation or platform.

FREE E XC HANGE OF INFOR MAT ION AND EN HANC I NG CIVIL SOCIETY

Courageous journalists all over the world have risked their livelihood, and even their lives, to report the news and to bring accurate information to the public in the face of repressive governments and other significant obstacles. But journalism thrives best where the rule of law is respected. A free press is best protected through a national constitution or by statutory or common law. However formalized, the law should, at a minimum, protect the news media from censorship and guarantee reporters access to information.

"Freedom of the press" is not just a slogan. Nor is it only for journalists. The right to receive and impart information is a universal one. But while a system of generally applicable laws benefits everyone, specialinterest legislation that singles out the news media for protection or provides the press with special rights is less desirable because it invites de facto licensing of the press. It can also create a false sense of confidence. Protection a legislature grants today can be withdrawn tomorrow. And that's the paradox. The "rule of law," however defined, protects everyone, including the press. But, of course, bad laws can also be enacted, and even the best law can be repealed or struck down. That's one of the reasons why some journalists are reluctant to lobby, even for legislation that might benefit them, like shield laws. Governments change. But public support for a free press should be constant because citizens are the ultimate beneficiary. A free press enhances the public's right to know by encouraging the free exchange of information. Protecting it requires a national commitment, by government and the public alike. The result is a stronger civil society for all. Once strong legal protections are enacted, an independent judiciary is essential to ensure they are applied and enforced equitably. No matter how clear the text of the law, confusion and conflicts may occur. When they do, the judicial branch's interpretation of the law can be decisive. Judges who appreciate the importance of a free press are the best assurance that it will be protected.

Advocacy Resources

In this section, we consider some organizations that work to strengthen and enact laws that guarantee and strengthen freedom of the press. Established in 1986, this human rights organization is named for the Universal Declaration of Human Rights provision that guarantees the rights of freedom of expression and opinion. Article XIX is based in London, England. It lobbies and litigates internationally to promote these universal rights. This NGO develops networks to raise awareness about and to improve monitoring of threats to freedom of expression. It provides legal training for other organizations, journalists, and government officials. It drafts model legislation, including freedom of information laws, and provides a searchable database of legal opinions and other resources. Its periodic reports call international attention to laws and actions that restrict freedom of information and expression. It denounces attacks on individual journalists and the institutional press alike. Among its many accomplishments, Article XIX convened the group of international law and human rights experts who adopted the Johannesburg Principles on National Security, Freedom of Expression and Access to Information in 1995.

Canadian Journalists for Free Expression

Originally established as a project of the Centre for Investigative Journalism in Canada in 1981, CJFE advocates freedom of expression throughout the world.

It conducts media training in developing countries, including Indonesia and Thailand, and has worked to rebuild key parts of the media in Sierra Leone after the conclusion of the civil war there. CJFE manages the International Freedom of Expression eXchange (IFEX) Clearing House, a virtual network of 88 organizations that monitors the state of free expression around the world and transmits that information to more than 120 countries. IFEX provides daily Action Alerts by country and region and a weekly Communique.

Central European and Eurasian Law Initiative (CEELI)

Aproject of the American Bar Association, CEELI was founded in 1990. Its mission is to provide technical legal assistance to increase professionalism among judges and lawyers in Central and Eastern Europe and the former Soviet Union. The group maintains a training institute in Prague and a number of volunteer legal liaisons. Among its goals are promoting accountability and increased awareness of international human rights standards, combating corruption, and increasing public transparency and accountability

Center for International Media Assistance (CIMA)

An initiative of the National Endowment for Democracy, a private nonprofit organization, CIMA supports programs that assist the media throughout the world. It convenes working groups, holds events, maintains a database of media assistance resources, and conducts research. It has established a network of media practitioners and experts through the Global Forum for Media Development. CIMA is funded through a grant from the U.S. Department of State.

Chapultepec Project

The Chapultepec Project began in 1994 as a special undertaking of the InterAmerican Press Association, a membership organization of more than 1,300 newspapers and magazines located throughout the Americas. Although its original mission was to increase public understanding of the importance of press freedom in civil society, the project has expanded to include sponsoring a series of international conferences with representatives of all three branches of government. These conferences have been instrumental in curtailing insult laws in several countries. The Chapultepec Project has submitted friend-of-the-court briefs before the Inter-American Commission on Human Rights on behalf of journalists in three cases, and it has sent missions and held emergency forums to protest legislation that would curtail press freedom. It published Press Freedom and the Law (1999), the first comparative study of laws related to press freedom in the Americas, and is undertaking a new initiative on the internal issues media organizations face and the values that should guide them

Citizen Media Law Project (CMLP)

Based at the Berkman Center for Internet & Society at Harvard Law School in Cambridge, Massachusetts, CMLP provides legal assistance, education, and resources to individuals involved in online and "citizen" media. It also files friend-of-the-court briefs in appellate cases. CMLP's Web site provides a variety of legal guides, as well as a "threats database" that outlines current and pending legal cases involving online media. CMLP has organized a network of lawyers and academics interested in representing individuals facing lawsuits arising from online journalism activities. It is affiliated with the Center for Citizen Media at Arizona State University.

Committee to Protect Journalists (CPJ)

Agroup of foreign correspondents from the United States created CPJ in 1981. Based in New York, but with a network of consultants in more than 120 countries, this NGO conducts its own research into press harassment. It publishes articles, news releases, special reports, and Attacks on the Press, an annual global survey of press freedom. It intervenes when local or foreign correspondents are threatened, and it provides advice to journalists on dangerous assignments. CPJ's campaigns have worked successfully to secure the release of journalists imprisoned in Iran, including Maziar Bahari, Newsweek's Tehran correspondent, and freelancers Roxana Saberi and Iason Athanasiadis.

Electronic Frontier Foundation (EFF)

Anon-governmental organization, EFF was founded in 1990 with offices in Washington, D.C., and San Francisco. It defends free speech, privacy, innovation, and consumer rights online. It has litigated many cases in U.S. courts and, through its Action Center, educates the public, mobilizes citizen responses to legislation, and provides advice to policymakers. Although much of its work is domestic, EFF also fights for digital rights around the world, and in July 2009, it published A Practical Guide to Internet Technology for Political Activists in Repressive Regimes.

Freedom House

Eleanor Roosevelt and Wendell Willkie, the 1940 U.S. presidential candidate, were the first honorary co-chairs of Freedom House, which was founded in

1941 and is headquartered in Washington, D.C. It publishes a wide variety of annual surveys, including Freedom of the Press and Freedom in the World, an annual report on journalistic independence throughout the world. Freedom House advocates globally for human rights and democracy. It works directly with democratic reformers in Cen- tral Asia, Central and Eastern Europe, the Middle East, Africa, Latin America, and the former Soviet Union to provide training, policy briefs, and support. The World Press Freedom Committee (WPFC) (http://www.wpfc.org), a consortium of 44 press freedom groups from throughout the world based in Northern Virginia, merged with Freedom House in 2009. The WPFC has monitored press freedom developments at international organizations, such as UNESCO, and published authoritative studies, particularly on insult laws, for more than 30 years. Freedom House Europe serves as Freedom House's primary European office. It is based in Budapest, Hungary (http:// www.freedomhouse.hu/).

Index on Censorship

Originally founded as a magazine in 1972 by a group of London-based writers and journalists, Index on Censorship is an NGO that promotes freedom of expression. It works with grassroots organizations to facilitate and promote this goal. In 2009, it launched projects in Tunisia, Afghanistan, Pakistan, Iraq, and Burma. It also supports the creation of new journalistic and artistic works and is undertaking a youth outreach program. Index on Censorship's Web site is a resource for current worldwide news on freedom of expression.

International Center for Journalists (ICFJ)

Anon-profit organization based in Washington, D.C., ICFJ provides hands-on training to journalists in more than 176 countries through workshops, seminars, fellowships, and international exchanges. It operates the International Journalists' Network, IJNet (http://www.ijnet. org/), which connects journalists with opportunities to obtain media training and other assistance.

International Media Lawyers Association (IMLA)

The IMLA is a worldwide network of media lawyers that serves as a clearinghouse for sharing information, strategies, and expertise on media law and press freedom. Based at Oxford University in England, it facilitates communication between public interest lawyers around the world who work to promote freedom of expression. IMLA also conducts training sessions for media lawyers and policymakers.

International Press Institute (IPI)

This Vienna, Austria-based NGO traces its history to 1950. It works to promote and protect freedom of expression. Its Death Watch publication tracks journalists and media staff who have been directly targeted for practicing journalism, and IPI recounts the stories of individual journalists through its Justice Denied Campaign. IPI conducts independent research into the state of press freedom around the world, and its Watch List monitors governments whose official actions threaten media independence. IPI has sent advocacy and fact-finding missions to Bangladesh, Nepal, Sri Lanka, and other countries.

International Senior Lawyers Project (ISLP)

Launched in June 2001, the organization applies the skills of soon-to-be retired or retired attorneys to the legal and legislative issues in the developing world, press freedom and access to information among them. Based in New York, with offices in Washington, D.C. and Paris, ISLP's volunteers have worked primarily in Eastern Europe, Russia, and India, but the group's mandate is global. Among many other projects, ISLP's lawyer volunteers have convened a con- ference that explored China's role in establishing global Internet norms and standards, provided legal briefings arguing that the Sierra Leone criminal libel law violates that country's constitution, and worked with the Center for Journalism in Extreme Situations to help that group improve its advocacy on behalf of journalists facing defamation and related legal charges in the former Soviet Union. In 2008 and 2009, ISLP provided advice on draft freedom of information and press laws in Yemen.

International Research & Exchanges Board (IREX)

Founded in 1968, IREX is a Washington, D.C.-based international NGO that works to strengthen independent media and improve the political environment for journalists. Together with its partner, IREX Europe, based in Lyon, France (http://www.europe.irex.org), IREX organizes media training programs and provides expert consultation to local partners that help support and advance civil society development in more than 100 countries. For example, it empowered local groups to lobby for change to the media laws in Slovakia and in Bulgaria. IREX's Media Sustainability Index evaluates and quantifies conditions for independent media in 76 countries.

Open Society Institute and Soros Foundations Network

This New York-based private foundation was established in 1993 by investor and philanthropist George Soros. It provides monetary grants designed to strengthen civil society. Through the Open Society Justice Initiative (OSJI), it promotes legal reform and litigates a range of human rights cases, including freedom of information and expression. It also conducts studies, including a notable 2006 survey of government responses to freedom of information requests. This study concluded that more recently adopted laws actually work better than those in some older democracies. The OSJI cites its role as a "friend of the court" in Claude v. Chile, a case argued before the Inter-American Court of Human Rights, as a factor that led to Chile's adoption of a freedom of information act in April 2009

Privacy International (PI)

Established in 1990 by a coalition of more than 100 privacy experts and human rights organizations from 40 countries, Privacy International conducts research and sponsors programs on threats to personal privacy. Based in London, PI monitors government surveillance activities and studies the implications of cross-border information flows. This NGO publishes a wide variety of books and reports, including an annual international Freedom of Information Survey. It reviews proposed legislation, particularly in developing democracies such as Albania, Moldova, and Croatia, and has studied how counterterrorism measures affect freedom of the press and the rights of journalists to protect their sources.

Radio Television Digital News Association (RTDNA)

RTDNA (formerly the Radio Television News Directors Association) is the world's largest professional association exclusively serving the electronic news profession. Founded in 1946, it promotes ethics in reporting, freedom of information, and press freedom. It advocates, lobbies, and occasionally litigates on issues affecting the electronic journalism industry in the United States and abroad. Through its foundation, RTDNA spon- sors workshops and training programs, as well as the RIAS Journalist Exchange in Germany.

Reporters Committee for Freedom of the Press (RCFP)

Founded in 1970, RCFP is an NGO located in Arlington, Virginia, that maintains a 24-hour hotline offering free legal and research assistance to any journalist working in the United States. It lobbies and advocates for press freedom and open government, files friend-of-thecourt briefs, and initiates litigation. RFCP also publishes a wide variety of legal guidebooks and handbooks on media and freedom of information law.

Reporters Without Borders (Reporters Sans Frontières [RSF])

Founded in 1985, RSF fights censorship laws and works to improve the safety of journalists, particularly in war zones. It undertakes fact-finding missions and defends reporters who have been imprisoned or persecuted. Among RSF's many publications is an annual January round-up of press freedom, a "predators of press freedom" list released on World Press Freedom Day (May 3), and the Worldwide Press Freedom Index each October. This NGO has branches in nine countries, as well as offices in Paris, New York, Tokyo, and Washington, D.C., and a network of more than 120 correspondents in other countries.

Society of Professional Journalists (SPJ)

The largest voluntary association of working journalists in the United States, SPJ lobbies and advocates for press freedom. It files friend-of-the-court briefs, initiates litigation, and speaks out on behalf of endangered journalists in the United States and elsewhere. Thousands of journalists voluntarily embrace the SPJ Code of Ethics, which is frequently cited as the most authoritative statement of media ethics in the United States.

Ujima Project

Acollection of databases, documents, and other information launched in September 2009, the Ujima Project attempts to bring greater transparency to the workings of governments in Africa, particularly those that have no freedom of information laws. It is supported by the Great Lakes Media Institute (http://www. greatlakesmedia.org/), an NGO whose mission is to encourage professional and ethical journalism in Sub-Saharan Africa.

REFERENCES

1. Working Bibliography (Last updated in December 2012)
2. Abbate, J. *Inventing the Internet.* Cambridge, MA: MIT Press, 1999
3. Adorno, Theodor. "The Curves of the Needle" (1927/1965); "Music in the Background" (1934); "The Form of the Phonograph Record" (1934); "On the Fetish-Character in Music and the Regression of Listening" (1938); "The Radio Symphony" (1941); "The Culture Industry: Englishtenment as Mass Deception" (1973 [1944]); "How to Look at Television" (1954); "The Culture Industry Reconsidered" (1975)
4. Agamben, Giorgio. 2009. *What Is an Apparatus?: And Other Essays.* Trans. David Kishik and Steefan Pedatella. Stanford: Stanford University Press.

5. Akrich, Madeleine. "The De-Scription of Technical Objects." In Wiebe Bijker and John Law, eds. *Shaping Technology / Building Society: Studies in Sociotechnical Change*. Cambridge, MA: MIT Press, 1994.
6. Anthony, David W. 2010. *The Horse, the Wheel, and Language: How Bronze-Age Riders from the Eurasian Steppes Shaped the Modern World*. Reprint. Princeton University Press.
7. Banta, Martha. 1993. *Taylored Lives: Narrative Productions in the Age of Taylor, Veblen, and Ford*. Chicago: University of Chicago Press.
8. Baron, Dennis. 2009. *A Better Pencil: Readers, Writers, and the Digital Revolution*. New York: Oxford University Press.
9. Barthes, Roland. 1985a. "An Almost Obsessive Relation to Writing Instruments." In *The Grain of the Voice: Interviews, 1962-1980*, tran. Linda Coverdale, 177–182. New York: Hill and Wang.
10. Barthes, Roland. *Camera Lucida*
11. ———. 1985b. "From Speech to Writing." In *The Grain of the Voice: Interviews, 1962-1980*, tran. Linda Coverdale, 3–7. New York: Hill and Wang.
12. Batchen, Geoffrey. *Burning with Desire: The Conception of Photography (1999)*
13. Batchen, Geoff. "Electricity Made Visible," in *New Media, Old Media: A History and Theory Reader*, ed. Wendy Hui, Kyong Chun, and Thomas Keenan (New York: Routledge, 2006).
14. Baudrillard, Jean. "Requiem for the Media." For a Critique of the Political Economy of the Sign (1981)
15. Baudrillard, Jean. 2012. *The Gulf War Did Not Take Place*. Tran. Paul Patton. Power Publications.
16. Bazerman, Charles. 1999. *The Languages of Edison's Light*. MIT Press.
17. Beetham, Margaret. 2006. "Periodicals and the New Media: Women and Imagined Communities." *Women's Studies International Forum* 29 (3) (June): 231–240. doi:10.1016/j.wsif.2006.04.002.
18. Benjamin, Walter. "The Work of Art in the Age of Mechanical Reproduction"
19. Benjamin, Walter. "Little History of Photography" in The Work of Art… ed. Jennings, Doherty, Levin. (2008 [1929])
20. Benjamin, Walter. 1969. *Illuminations: Essays and Reflections*. Ed. Hannah Arendt. Tran. Harry Zohn. first Schocken paperback edition. Schocken.

21. Benjamin, Walter. Convolutes A, B, G, K, L, N, P, Y, Z, and p in The Arcades Project
22. Bennett, Jane. "The Force of Things: Steps Toward an Ecology of Matter" *Political Theory* Vol.32, No.3 (June 2004).
23. Bergson, Henri. *Matter and Memory*, Cambridge , MA , Zone Books, 1990, Introduction and Ch. 1-2, pp. vii-169.
24. Bledstein, Burton J. and Robert D. Johnson, eds. *The Middling Sorts: Explorations in the History of the American Middle Class.* New York: Routledge, 2001.
25. Blumin, Stuart M. *The Emergence of the Middle Class: Social Experience in the American City, 1760-1900.* New York: Cambridge University Press, 1989.
26. Bolter, J. David. 2001. *Writing Space: Computers, Hypertext, and the Remediation of Print.* Taylor & Francis.
27. Bolter, Jay David and Richard Grusin, "Immediacy, Hypermediacy, and Remediation" and "Mediation and Remediation," from *Remediation*
28. Bolter, David Jay, and Richard Grusin. *Remediation: Understanding New Media.* (MIT) (Introduction: The Double Logic of Remediation, pp. 1-50).
29. Boorstin, Daniel. *The Image: A Guide to Pseudo-Events in America.* New York: Atheneum, 1961.
30. Borgman, Christine. *Scholarship in the Digital Age: Information, Infrastructure, and the Internet* (MIT Press, 2009)
31. Boyne, Roy. 2006. "Classification." *Theory, Culture & Society* 23 (2-3) (May 1): 21 –30. doi:10.1177/0263276406062529.
32. Brecht. *Brecht on Theatre: The Development of an Aesthetic.* ed. Willett (1964). (selections)
33. Briggs, Asa, and Peter Burke. *A Social History of the Media: From Gutenberg to the Internet.* 2 ed. Malden, MA: Polity Press, 2005.
34. Brown, Richard D. *Knowledge is Power: The Diffusion of Information in Early America, 1700-1865.* New York: Oxford University Press, 1989.
35. Brown, John Seely, and Duguid, Paul. *The Social Life of Information.* Boston: Harvard Business School Press, 2000.
36. Brown, Bill. *A Sense of Things* (2003)
37. Budiansky, Stephen. 2005. *Air Power: The Men, Machines, and Ideas That Revolutionized War, from Kitty Hawk to Iraq.* Penguin Books.
38. Burke, Kenneth. *Attitudes Toward History* (3rd ed.). Berkeley, CA:

University of California Press, 1984.

39. Burke, Peter. 2000. *A Social History of Knowledge: From Gutenberg to Diderot*. (Polity)
40. Bush, Vannevar. "As We May Think," Atlantic Monthly (July 1945).
41. Buzzetti, Dino. 2002. "Digital Representation and the Text Model," *New Literary History*: 61-88.
42. Carey, James W. *Communication as Culture: Essays on Media and Society*. Boston: Unwin Hyman, 1989.
43. Carey, James. "The Case of the Telegraph."
44. Carr, Nicholas, *The Shallows: What the Internet is Doing to Our Brains* (W. W. Norton, 2008)
45. Carr, Nicholas. 2011. "Situational Overload and Ambient Overload." Accessed March 8. http://www.roughtype.com/archives/2011/03/situational_ove.php.
46. Campbell, Timothy. *Wireless Writing in the Age of Marconi* (2006).
47. Cavell, Richard. 2003. *McLuhan in Space: A Cultural Geography*. Toronto: University of Toronto Press.
48. Cavell, Richard. 2010. "McLuhan and the Humanities." *ESC* 36 (2-3) (September): 14–18.
49. Cavell, Stanley. "The Ordinary as the Uneventful." Themes Out of School: Effects and Causes (1984); "The Uncanniness of the Ordinary." In Quest of the Ordinary: Lines of Skepticism and Romanticism (1988); "The Same and Different." Pursuits of Happiness: The Holywood Comedy of Remarriage (1981): The Claim of Reason: Wittgenstein, Skepticism, Morality, and Tragedy (1979) p. 463
50. Chandler, Alfred D., Jr, and James W. Cortada, eds. *A Nation Transformed by Information: How Information has Shaped the Unites States from Colonial Times to the Present*. New York: Oxford University Press, 2000.
51. Chandler, James, Arnold I. Davidson, and Adrian Johns. 2004. "Arts of Transmission: An Introduction," *Critical Inquiry* (Autumn): 1-6.
52. Cheever, "The Enormous Radio," *New Yorker* (1947).
53. Chun, Wendy Hui Kyong, and Thomas Keenan. 2006. *New Media, Old Media: a History and Theory Reader*. Psychology Press.
54. Committee, University of Edinburgh. Faculty of Social Sciences. Seminars. 1973. *Meaning and Control: Essays in Social Aspects of Science and Technology*. Tavistock Publications; distributed in the USA by Harper & Row, Barnes & Noble Import Division, New York.

55. Consuegra, David. *American Type: Design & Designers*. New York: Allworth Press, 2004.

56. Cook, Michael. 2005. *A Brief History of the Human Race*. Reprint. W. W. Norton & Company.

57. Crain, Patricia. 2003. *The Story of A: The Alphabetization of America from the New England Primer to the Scarlet Letter*. Stanford: Stanford University Press.

58. Crary, Jonathan. "Techniques of the Observer," *October (*1988).

59. Crary, Jonathan. *Suspensions of Perception: Attention, Spectacle, and Modern Culture* (1999)

60. Crary, Jonathan. *Techniques of the Observer: On Vision and Modernity in the Nineteenth Century* (1990)

61. Crookes, "Some Possibilities of Electricity," *Fortnightly Review* (1892).

62. Czitrom, Daniel. *Media and the American Mind: From Morse to McLuhan*. Chapel Hill, NC: University of North Carolina Press, 1982.

63. Darnton, "An Early Information Society: News and the Media in Eighteenth-Century Paris," *American Historical Review* (2000).

64. Deacon, Terrence. "Why a Brain Capable of Language Evolved Only Once: Prefrontal Cortex and Symbol Learning." *Zygon*, Vol. 31(4), 1996: 635-670.

65. Deacon, Terrence. *The Symbolic Species: The Co-Evolution of Language and the Brain*, New York; Norton, 1997, Ch. 3, pp. 69-101; Ch. 4, pp. 102-115; Ch. 11, pp. 321-375; Ch. 12, pp. 376-410; Ch. 13, pp. 411-419 & 423-432; Ch. 14, pp. 433-464.

66. Derrida, Jacques. "Différance", *Margins of Philosophy* , translated by Alan Bass (Chicago: University of Chicago Press, 1982), pp. 3-27.

67. Derrida, Jacques. *Paper Machine*. Trans. Rachel Bowldy. Stanford: Stanford University Press.

68. Derrida, "Freud and the Scene of Writing"

69. Deuze, Mark. 2011. "Media Life." *Media, Culture & Society* 33 (1) (January 1): 137 –148. doi:10.1177/0163443710386518.

70. Diamond, Jared. 2005. *Guns, Germs, and Steel: The Fates of Human Societies*. 1st ed. W. W. Norton & Company.

71. Drucker, Johanna. *SpecLab: Digital Aesthetics and Projects in Speculative Computing*. Chicago: University of Chicago Press, 2009.

72. Druckrey, Timothy. 1996. *Electronic Culture: Technology and Visual Representation*. Aperture.

73. Duguid, Paul and John Seely Brown, "The Social Life of Documents"
74. Dyson, George. 19978. *Darwin Among the Machines: The Evolution of Global Intelligence*. Massachusetts: Addison-Wesley Publishing Company, Inc.
75. Edgerton, David. 2011. *The Shock of the Old: Technology and Global History Since 1900*. Reprint. Oxford University Press, USA.
76. Edison, "The Phonograph and its Future" (1879).
77. Edison, History of the Kinetograph, Kinetoscope and Kinetophonograph (1895)
78. Eisenstein, Elizabeth L. *The Printing Press as an Agent of Change: Communications and Cultural Transformations in Early Modern Europe*. New York: Cambridge University Press, 1979.
79. Elias, Norbert. 2000. *The Civilizing Process: Sociogenetic and Psychogenetic Investigations*. Revised. Blackwell Publishing.
80. Engelbert, D.C. "Augmenting Human Intellect: A Conceptual Framework" (1962)
81. Essinger, James. 2007. *Jacquard's Web: How a Hand-loom Led to the Birth of the Information Age*. Oxford: Oxford University Press.
82. Fang, Irving E. *A History of Mass Communication: Six Information Revolutions*. Boston: Focal Press, 1997.
83. Feenberg, Andrew. *Questioning Technology*. New York: Routledge, 1999.
84. Fletcher, Alan. *The Art of Looking Sideways* (New York: Phaidon, 2001
85. Flusser, Vilem, *The Shape of Things: A Philosophy of Design* (1999)
86. Forty, Adrian. 1992. *Objects of Desire: Design and Society Since 1750*. Thames & Hudson.
87. Michel Foucault. "Panopticism." In *Discipline and Punish: The Birth of the Prison*, trans. Alan Sheridan. New York: Vintage Books, 1977. pp. 195-228.
88. Foucault, Michel. "Photogenic Painting"
89. Foucault, Michel. 2007. *Archaeology of Knowledge*. Psychology Press.
90. Friedberg, Anne. 2009. *The Virtual Window: From Alberti to Microsoft*. MIT Press.
91. Fuller, Wayne E. *Morality and the Mail in Nineteenth Century America*. Urbana: University of Illinois Press, 2003.
92. Fuller, Matthew. *Media Ecologies: Materialist Energies in Art and Technoculture* (2005)

93. Galison, "Einstein's Clocks," *Critical Inquiry* (2000).

94. Galison, P. *Einstein's Clocks, Poincare's Maps: Empires of Time*. New York: Norton, 2003.

95. Gitelman, Lisa. "Making History, Spelling Things Out" and "Imagining Language Machines," *Scripts, Grooves, and Writing Machines*

96. Gitelman, Lisa. 1999. *Scripts, Grooves, and Writing Machines: Representing Technology in the Edison Era*. Stanford University Press.

97. Gitelman, Lisa. *Always Already New: Media, History, and the Data of Culture*. Cambridge, MA: The MIT University Press, 2006.

98. Gitelman and Pingree, Eds. *New Media, 1740-1915* (Cambridge: MIT Press, 2003).

99. Gleick, James. 2011. *The Information: A History, a Theory, a Flood*. New York: Pantheon Books.

100. Goody and Watt, "The Consequences of Literacy," *Comparative Studies in Society and History* (1963)

101. Goudsblom, "The Civilizing Process and the Domestication of Fire,"*Journal of World History* (1992)

102. Giedion, Sigfried. *Mechanization Takes Command: A Contribution to Anonymous History* (1948)

103. Giesecke, Michael. "Literature as Product and Medium of Ecological Communication," Trans. Michael Wutz and Geoffrey Winthrop-Young,*Configurations* 10 (2003): 11-35.

104. Goudsblom, Johan. 1995. *Fire and Civilization*. Penguin Books.

105. Grossberg, Larry, Ellen A. (Ann) Wartella, D. Charles Whitney, and J. Macgregor Wise. 2005. *MediaMaking: Mass Media in a Popular Culture*. 2nd ed. Sage Publications, Inc.

106. Grosz, Elizabeth. "Introduction: To the Untimely" in *The Nick of Time: Politics, Evolution, and the Untimely*.

107. Guillory, John. 2004. "The Memo and Modernity." *Critical Inquiry* 31 (1): 108–132.

108. ———. 2010b. "Enlightening Mediation." In *This Is Enlightenment*. University of Chicago Press.

109. ———. 2010a. "Genesis of the Media Concept." *Critical Inquiry* 36: 321–362.

110. Gumbrecht, Hans Ulrich. 1994. "A Farewell to Interpretation." In *Materialities of Communication*, ed. Hans Ulrich Gumbrecht and K. Ludwig Pfeiffer, tran. William Whobrey, 389–402. Stanford: Stanford

University Press.

111. Hacking, Ian. 1990. *The Taming of Chance*. Cambridge University Press.

112. Hall, Stuart. "Base and Superstructue in Marxist Cultural Theory" in Problems in Materialism and Culture: Selected Essays (1980)

113. Stuart Hall, "Encoding/Decoding," in Stuart Hall, Dorothy Hobson, Andrew Lowe, Paul Willis, eds., *Culture, Media, Language*, London; Hutchinson, 1980, pp. 128-138.

114. Hansen, Mark B.N. Bodies in Code: Interfaces with Digital Media (2006); New Philosophy for New Media (2004); Embodying Technesis: Technology Beyond Writing (2000); "The Arche-Technics of Life (Arakawa and Gins)," Interfaces, 21/22. vol. 1 (2004): 69-85.; "'Not thus, after all, would life be given': Technesis, Technology, and the Parody of Romantic Poetics in Frankenstein," Studies in Romanticism, 36: 4 (Winter 1997): 575-609.

115. Mark Hansen, "Media Theory," Theory Culture & Society 23(2-3) (2006): 297-306.

116. ———. 2010. "New Media." In *Critical Terms for Media Studies*, ed. W.J.T. Mitchell and Mark B.N. Hansen, 172–185. Chicago and London: The University of Chicago Press.

117. Hansen, Miriam. "Why Media Aesthetics?" Critical Inquiry 30.2 (2003)

118. Harsock, John C. *A History of American Literary Journalism: The Emergence of Modern Literary Form*. Amherst: University of Massachusetts Press, 2000.

119. Harris, Stefanie. 2009. *Mediating Modernity: German Literature and the "New" Media, 1895-1930*. Pennsylvania: Penn State Press.

120. Hassan, Robert, and Julian Thomas. 2006. *The New Media Theory Reader*. McGraw-Hill International.

121. Havelock, Eric A. 1988. *The Muse Learns to Write: Reflections on Orality and Literacy from Antiquity to the Present*. New Haven and London: Yale University Press.

122. Havelock, Eric. 1982. *Preface to Plato*. Belknap Press of Harvard University Press.

123. Hawkins, Jeff, and Sandra Blakeslee. 2005a. *On Intelligence*. Macmillan.

124. Hayles, Katherine N. *How We Became Posthuman: Virtual Bodies in Cybernetics, Literature, and Informatics* (1999)

125. Hayles, Katherine N. 2004. "Print Is Flat, Code Is Deep: The Importance of Media-Specific Analysis." *Poetics Today* 25 (1): 67–90.

126. Heidegger, Martin. "The Origin of the Work of Art." Poetry, Language, Thought (1971 [1937]); Being and Time (selections) (1927); "The Question Concerning Technology [Technik]" (1954)

127. Heim, Michael. 1994. *The Metaphysics of Virtual Reality*. Oxford University Press.

128. Henkin, David M. 2008. "On Forms and Media." *Representations* 104 (1): 34–36.

129. Henkin, David M. *The Postal Age: The Emergence of Modern Communications in Nineteenth-Century America*. Chicago: University of Chicago Press, 2006.

130. Hocks, Mary E., and Michelle R. Kendrick. 2005. *Eloquent Images: Word and Image in the Age of New Media*. MIT Press.

131. Holmes, "The Stereoscope and the Stereograph," *Atlantic Monthly* (1859).

132. Holmes, Oliver Wendell. "The American Stereoscope" (1869)

133. Horn, Eva. "Editor's Introduction: 'There Are No Media.'" in "New German Media Theory." Special Issue of Grey Room, No. 29 (Winter, 2008).

134. Hounshell, David A. 1985. *From the American System to Mass Production, 1800-1932: The Development of Manufacturing Technology in the United States*. Baltimore: JHU Press.

135. Hughes, Thomas. "Technological Momentum." In Merritt Roe Smith and Leo Marx, eds. *Does Technology Drive History?* Cambridge, MA: MIT Press, 1994.

136. Huhtamo, Erkii and Zielinski, Sterling, and Druckery. *The Book of Imaginary Media: Excavating the Dream of the Ultimate Communication Medium* (2007)

137. Hui Kyong Chun, Wendy, and Thomas Keenan, eds. *New Media Old Media: A History and Theory Reader*. New York: Routledge, 2006.

138. Innis, Harold A. *The Bias of Communication*. Toronto: University of Toronto Press, 1951.

139. Innis, Harold A. 2007. *Empire and Communications*. New. Rowman & Littlefield Publishers.

140. Innis, "The Bias of Communication," *Canadian Journal of Economics and Political Science* (1949)

141. Jenkins, Henry. "Worship at the Altar of Convergence" and "Photoshop for Democracy" in *Convergence Culture: Where Old and New Media Collide*

142. John Cayley: Writing on Complex Surfaces." 2011. Accessed February 18. http://dichtung-digital.mewi.unibas.ch/2005/2/Cayley/index.htm.

143. John, Richard. *Spreading the News: The American Postal System from Franklin to Morse.* Cambridge: Harvard University Press, 1995.

144. Kasson, Joy. "At the Columbian Exposition 1893," from *Buffalo Bill's Wild West: Celebrity, Memory, and Popular History*, ''pp. 3-19; 93-121.

145. King, W. Davies. 2008. *Collections of Nothing*. Chicago and London: University of Chicago Press.

146. Kirschenbaum, Matthew G. 2008. *Mechanisms: New Media and the Forensic Imagination*. Cambridge: MIT Press.

147. Kitch, Carolyn. *Pages From the Past: History and Memory in American Magazines*. Chapel Hill: University of North Carolina Press, 2005.

148. Kittler, Friedrich. *Gramophone, Film, Typewriter*

149. ———. 1990. *Discourse Networks 1800/1900*. Trans. Michael Metteer, with Chris Cullens. Stanford: Stanford University Press.

150. Kittler, Friedrich A. 1987. "Mother's Mouth and Typewriter." *Poetics Today* 8 (3/4): 675–687.

151. ———. 1996. "The City Is a Medium." *New Literary History* 27 (4): 717–729.

152. ———. 2006. "Thinking Colours And/or Machines." *Theory, Culture & Society* 23 (7-8): 39–50.

153. ———. 2009. "Towards an Ontology of Media." *Theory, Culture & Society* 26 (2-3): 23–31.

154. ———. "The History of Communication Media." *CTheory.net.*

155. Kramer, Sybille. 2006. "The Cultural Techniques of Time Axis Manipulation: On Friedrich Kittler's Conception of Media." *Theory, Culture & Society* 23 (7-8): 93–109.

156. Kraemer, S. *Medium, Messenger, Transmission. Small Metaphysics of Mediality*. Frankfurt: Suhrkamp, 2008.

157. Krause, Monika. 2011. "Reporting and the Transformations of the Journalistic Field: US News Media, 1890-2000." *Media, Culture & Society* 33 (1) (January 1): 89 –104. doi:10.1177/0163443710385502.

158. Lacan, "The Instance of the Letter in the Agency of the Unconscious"

159. Landow, George, and Paul Delany. 2001. "Hypertext, Hypermedia and Literary Studies: The State of the Art." In *Multimedia: From Wagner to Virtual Reality*. (Norton) (selections)

160. Landow, George P. 2006. *Hypertext 3.0: Critical Theory and New Media*

in an Era of Globalization. JHU Press.

161. Landsberg, Alison. *Prosthetic Memory: The Transformation of American Remembrance in the Age of Mass Culture*. New York: Columbia University Press, 2004.
162. Jaron Lanier, *You Are Not a Gadget* (Knopf, 2010)
163. Latour, Bruno. "Visualization and Cognition: Drawing Things Together"
164. Latour, Bruno, and Tomas Sanchez-Criado. 2007. "Making the 'Res Public'." *Ephemera* 7 (2): 364–371.
165. Latour, Bruno and Jim Johnson. "Mixing Humans and Nonhumans Together: The Sociology of a Door-Closer." *Social Problems*, Vol. 35, No. 3 (1988): 298-310.
166. Latour, Bruno, and Peter Weibel. 2005. *Making Things Public: Atmospheres of Democracy*. The MIT Press.
167. Latour, Bruno. "Where are the Missing Masses? The Sociology of a Few Mundane Artifacts." In Wiebe Bijker and John Law, eds. *Shaping Technology / Building Society: Studies in Sociotechnical Change*. Cambridge, MA: MIT Press, 1994.
168. Lawrence Lessig. "Code is Law." *Code and Other Laws of Cyberspace*. New York: Basic Books, 2000. pp. 3-8.
169. Leroi-Gourhan, André. *Speech and Gesture*. Cambridge, Mass; MIT Press, 1993, pp. 187-266.
170. Lessig, Lawrence. *Code and Other Laws of Cyberspace*, version 2.0. Basic Books, 2006.
171. Levy, David M. *Scrolling Forward: Making Sense of Documents in the Digital Age*. New York: Arcade, 2001.
172. Lievrouw, Leah A., and Sonia Livingstone, ed. 2006. *Handbook of New Media: Student Edition*. SAGE Publications Ltd.
173. Lima, Manuel. 2011. *Visual Complexity: Mapping Patterns of Information*. Princeton Architectural Press.
174. *Literature & Photography: Interactions 1840-1990 : A Critical Anthology*. 1995. First Edition. University of New Mexico Press.
175. Alan Liu, *The Laws of Cool: Knowledge Work and the Culture of Information*(Chicago, 2004)
176. Liu, Alan. 2004. "Transcendental Data: Toward a Cultural History and Aesthetics of the New Encoded Discourse," *Critical Inquiry* 31 (Autumn): 49-81.
177. Liu, Alan. *Local Transcendence: Essays on Postmodern Historicism*

and the Database (2008)

178. Liu, Alan. "When Was Linearity: The Meaning of Graphics in the Digital Age."

179. Livingston, James. 1997. *Pragmatism and the Political Economy of Cultural Revolution, 1850-1940*. Chapel Hill: Univ of North Carolina Press.

180. Lovink, Geert. "Whereabouts of German Media Theory" in *Zero Comments* (2007)

181. Maas, Winy, Arjun Appadurai, Joke Brouwer, and Simon Conway Morris. 2003. *Information Is Alive: Art And Theory On Archiving And Retrieving Data*. Rotterdam: V2_Publishing/NAI Publishers.

182. Maines, Rachel P. 2001. *The Technology of Orgasm: "Hysteria," the Vibrator, and Women's Sexual Satisfaction*. 1st ed. The Johns Hopkins University Press.

183. Manovich, Lev. *The Language of New Media* (What Is New Media?", "The Interface," and "The Forms," from *The Language of New Media*)

184. Mackenzie, Adrian. *Transductions: Bodies and Machines at Speed*, London; Continuum, 2002: Introduction, pp. 1-27; Chapter 1, pp. 29-56; Chapter 6, pp. 171-204.

185. Martin, Michele. 1991. *Hello Central?: Gender, Technology, and Culture in the Formation of Telephone Systems*. First Edition. Carleton Univ Pr.

186. Marvin, Carolyn. *When Old Technologies Were New: Thinking About Electric Communication in the Late Nineteenth Century*. New York: Oxford University Press, 1988.

187. Marzio, Peter C. *The Men and Machines of American Journalism*. Washington DC: National Museum of History and Technology, 1973.

188. Marshall McLuhan, *Understanding Media: The Extensions of Man*(Cambridge, Mass.: MIT Press, 1994), pp. 3-61.

189. Marx, Leo. "The Idea of 'Technology' and Postmodern Pessimism." In *Does Technology Drive History*? ed. Merritt Roe Smith and Leo Marx (Cambridge, Mass., 1994), 238-57.

190. Marx, Leo. "Technology: The Emergence of a Hazardous Concept." *Technology and Culture, Volume* 51, Number 3 (2010): 561-577.

191. Massumi, Brian. "Introduction," "The Political Economy of Belonging and the Logic of Relation," and "Chaos in the 'total field' of vision" in *Parables for the Virtual: Movement, Affect, Sensation* (Duke UP, 2002)

192. Mauss, Marcel. "Body Techniques." *Sociology and Psychology: Essays*(1979 [1950]) also "Techniques of the Body." *Incorporations*, ed. Jonathan Crary and S. Kwinter (1992)

193. Mattelart, Armand. Networking the World, 1794-2000. Translated by Liz Carey-Libbrecht, James A. Chen, and James A. Cohen. Minneapolis: U. of Minnesota, 2000.

194. Mattelart, Armand. 1996. *Invention Of Communication*. Trans. Susan Emanuel. Univ Of Minnesota Press.

195. McLuhan, Marshall. *The Gutenberg Galaxy: The Making of Typographic Man*. Toronto: University of Toronto Press, 1962.

196. McLuhan, Marshall. 2001. *Understanding Media: The Extensions of Man*. Routledge.

197. McGann, Jerome J. 1991. *The Textual Condition*. Princeton: Princeton University Press.

198. McGann, Jerome. *Radiant Textuality: Literature after the World Wide Web*. Palgrave, 2002.

199. McGill, Meredith L., and Andrew Parker. 2010. "The Future of the Literary Past." *PMLA* 125 (4): 959–967.

200. McGill, Meredith L. 2007. *American Literature and the Culture of Reprinting, 1834-1853*. Philadelphia: University of Pennsylvania Press.

201. McKenzie, D.F. 1999. *Bibliography and the Sociology of Texts*. Cambridge: Cambridge University Press.

202. McLaughlin, Kevin. 2005. *Paperwork: Fiction and Mass Mediacy in the Paper Age*. Pennsylvania: University of Pennsylvania Press.

203. McNeely, Ian F. and Lisa Wolverton. *Reinventing Knowledge: From Alexandria to the Internet*. New York: W. W. Norton, 2008.

204. McNeill, J. R., William H. McNeill, and John Robert McNeill. 2003. *The Human Web: A Bird's-Eye View of World History*. 1st ed. W. W. Norton & Company.

205. McNamara, Andrew and Peter Krapp. "Introduction" in "Medium Cool," special issue of *The South Atlantic Quarterly* 101:3 (Summer 2002)

206. Millard, André. *Edison and the Business of Innovation*. Baltimore and London: John Hopkins University Press, 1990.

207. Misa, Thomas J. *A Nation of Steel: The Making of Modern America, 1865-1925*. The Johns Hopkins University Press, 1999. Print

208. Mitchell, William John Thomas, and Mark Boris Nicola Hansen. 2010. *Critical Terms for Media Studies*. University of Chicago Press.

209. Moretti, Franco. 2005. *Graphs, Maps, Trees: Abstract Models for a Literary History*. London: Verso.

210. Mumford, Lewis. *Technics and Civilization*. New York: Harcourt, Brace & Co, 1934.

211. Mumford, Lewis. 1967. *The Myth of the Machine: Technics and Human Development*. 1st ed. Harcourt.

212. ———. 1968. *The City in History: Its Origins, Its Transformations, and Its Prospects*. Mariner Books.

213. Myerson, George. *Heidegger, Habermas and the Mobile Phone*

214. Ong, Walter. "Writing Restructures Consciousness," from *Orality and Literacy*

215. Parikka, Jussi. *Insect Media: An Archaeology of Animals and Technology*. Univ Of Minnesota Press. 2010.

216. Parikka, Jussi. 2012. *What Is Media Archaeology*. 1st ed. Polity.

217. Peirce, Charles Sanders. "Some Consequences of Four Incapacities," *Peirce: Of Signs*. (Chapel Hill: Univ of North Carolina Press, 1991), pp. 54-84.

218. Peters, Benjamin. "And Lead Us Not Into Thinking the New is New: A Bibliographic Case for New Media History," *New Media & Society*, 11, no. 1/2 (2009): 13-30.

219. Peters, John Durham. 2001. *Speaking into the Air: A History of the Idea of Communication*. University Of Chicago Press.

220. Peters, John. 2009. "Strange Sympathies: Horizons of Media Theory in America and Germany – John Durham Peters." *Electronic Book Review*. http://www.electronicbookreview.com/thread/criticalecologies/myopic.

221. Peters, John Durham. "History as a Communication Problem," In *Explorations in Communication and History*, edited by Barbie Zelizer, 19-34. London: Routledge, 2008.

222. Peters, John D. *Speaking Into the Air: A History of the Idea of Communication*. Chicago: University of Chicago Press, 1999.

223. Peters, "Space, Time, and Communication Theory," *Canadian Journal of Communication* (2003).

224. Peters, "Helmholtz, Edison, and Sound History," *Memory Bytes* (2004).

225. Peters, "Clock, Calendar, Tower" (2007).

226. Peters, John. "The Case of the Telegraph Revisited."

227. Petroski, Henry. 1990. *The Pencil: A History of Design and Circumstance*. 1st ed. New York: Alfred A. Knopf.

228. Pfitzer, Gregory M. *Picturing the Past: Illustrated Histories and the American Imagination, 1840-1900.* Washington DC: Smithsonian Institution Press, 2002.

229. Pingree, Geoffrey B., and Lisa Gitelman, ed. 2004. *New Media, 1740-1915.* Cambridge: MIT Press.

230. Piper, Andrew. 2009. *Dreaming in Books: The Making of the Bibliographic Imagination in the Romantic Age.* University of Chicago Press.

231. Plant, Sadie. "The Virtual Complexity of Culture," in George Robertson, et al, eds., *FutureNatural* (Routledge 1996) pp.203-217

232. Polchin, James. 2011. "The Smart Set: Murky Muybridge – January 13, 2011." Accessed January 21. http://www.thesmartset.com/article/article01131101.aspx.

233. Pool, Ithiel de Sola. *Technologies Without Boundaries: On Telecommunications in a Global Age.* Cambridge, MA: Harvard University Press, 1990.

234. Pool, Ithiel De Sola. 1982. *Forecasting the Telephone: A Retrospective Technology Assessment of the Telephone.* Praeger.

235. Poster, Mark. 1990. *The Mode of Information: Poststructuralism and Social Context.* University of Chicago Press.

236. Pursell, Carroll. 2007. *The Machine in America: A Social History of Technology.* 2nd ed. The Johns Hopkins University Press

237. Ramsay, Stephen. 2011. *Reading Machines: Toward an Algorithmic Criticism.* 1st Edition. University of Illinois Press.

238. Renfrew, Colin. 1990. *Archaeology and Language: The Puzzle of Indo-European Origins.* Cambridge University Press.

239. Robertson, "The Possibility of Writing," chapter 2 in *The First Writing: Script Invention as History and Process*, ed. Houston (2004)

240. Robertson, Craig. "A Documentary Regime of Verification" *Cultural Critique* (June 2006).

241. Rosenzweig, Roy. "Scarcity or Abundance?: Preserving the Past in a Digital Era," *The American Historical Review*, 108, no. 3 (2008): 735-62.

242. Rotman, Brian. "The Emergence of the Metasubject," in *Signifying Nothing: The Semiotics of Zero* (New York: St. Martin's Press, 1987), pp. 27-56; "Absence of an Origin," pp. 87-107.

243. Marie-Laure Ryan, "The Text as World," from *Narrative as Virtual Reality*

244. Saint-Amour, Paul K. 2003. *The Copywrights: Intellectual Property and*

the Literary Imagination. Ithaca and London: Cornell University Press.

245. Saxton, Alexander. *The Rise and Fall of the White Republic: Class Politics and Mass Culture in Nineteenth-Century America.* London: Verso Books, 1990.
246. Samuels, Robert. *The Illustrated History of Copyright*
247. Sandweiss, Martha. "'The Spirit Is Wanting': Photography and the Mexican-American War," in *Print the Legend: Photography and the American West* (New Haven: Yale University Press, 2002).
248. Schudson, Michael. *Discovering the News: A Social History of American Newspapers*. New York: Basic Books, 1978.
249. Sconce, Jeffrey. 2000. *Haunted Media: Electronic Presence from Telegraphy to Television*. Duke University Press.
250. Seelye, John. *War Games: Richard Harding Davis and the New Imperialism*. Amherst: University of Massachusetts Press, 2003.
251. Seife, Charles. 2000. *Zero: The Biography of a Dangerous Idea*. Paperback Book Club. Penguin Books.
252. Sellen, Abigail J. and Richard H. R. Harper. *The Myth of the Paperless Office*. Cambridge: The MIT Press, 2002.
253. Seltzer, Mark. *Bodies and Machines* (1992)
254. Shackelford, Laura. 2005. "Narrative Subjects Meet Their Limits: John Barth's 'Click' and the Remediation of Hypertext," *Contemporary Literature* 66 (2):275-310.
255. Siegert, Bernhard. "Cacography or Communication? Cultural Techniques in German Media Studies," in Grey Room 29 (2008)
256. Siskin, Clifford, and William Warner. 2010. "This Is Enlightenment: An Invitation in the Form of an Argument." In *This Is Enlightenment*. University of Chicago Press.
257. Solnit, Rebecca. 2003. *River of Shadows: Eadweard Muybridge and the Technological Wild West*. New York: Viking.
258. Smith, Merrit Roe. "Technological Determinism in American Culture." In Merritt Roe Smith and Leo Marx, eds. *Does Technology Drive History?* Cambridge, MA: MIT Press, 1994.
259. Smith, Merritt, Gregory Clancey, and Thomas Paterson, ed. 1997. *Major Problems in the History of American Technology (Major Problems in American History*. 1st ed. Houghton Mifflin.
260. Sobel, Dava. 2007. *Longitude: The True Story of a Lone Genius Who Solved the Greatest Scientific Problem of His Time*. Reprint. Walker &

Company.

261. Stafford, Barbara Marie and Frances Terpak. *Devices of Wonder: From the World in a Box to Images on a Screen* (2001, Getty Museum)

262. Standage, Tom. 2007. *The Victorian Internet: The Remarkable Story of the Telegraph and the Nineteenth Century's On-line Pioneers*. 1st ed. Walker & Company.

263. Starr, Paul. *The Creation of the Media: Political Origins of Modern Communications*. New York: Basic Books, 2004.

264. Steigler, Bernard. "Theories of Technical Evolution." Technics and Time, 1: The Fault of Epimetheus (1998 [1994]); "The Industrialization of Memory." Technics and Time, 2: Disorientation (2009 [1996])); "Transcendental Imagination in a Thousand Points." The Prosthetic Aesthetic (2002) ed. Morra and Smith; "Technoscience and Reproduction," Parallax 13 (4): 29–45.

265. Bernard Stiegler, *Technics and Time, 1: the Fault of Epimetheus*. Stanford; Stanford University Press, 1998, Ch. 3, "Who? What? The Invention of the Human," pp. 134-179.

266. Stiegler, Bernard. March. "Teleologics of the Snail." *Theory, Culture & Society* 26 (2-3): 33 –45. doi:10.1177/0263276409103105.

267. Sterling, Bruce. 2005. *Shaping Things*. MIT Press.

268. Jonathan Sterne, *The Audible Past: Cultural Origins of Sound Reproduction*

269. Stewart, Garret. "Media Archaeology, Hermeneutics, Narratography" in*Framed Time: Toward a Postfilmic Cinema (2007)*

270. Straw, Will. "Embedded Memories," in *Residual Media*, ed. Charles Acland (Minneapolis: University of Minnesota Press, 2007).

271. Strom, Sharon Hartman. *Beyond the Typewriter: Gender, Class, and the Origins of Modern Office Work, 1900-1933*. Urbana: University of Illinois Press, 1992.

272. Strychacz, Thomas. *Modernism, Mass Culture, and Professionalism*. New York: Cambridge University Press, 1993.

273. Suisman, David and Susan Strasser, *Sound in the Age of Mechanical Reproduction*

274. Taft, Robert. *Photography and the American Scene: A Social History, 1839-1889* (1938)

275. Talbot, William Henry Fox. *The Pencil of Nature (1844)*

276. Thompson, "Time, Work Discipline, and Industrial Capitalism," *Past*

and Present (1967).

277. Thomas, Deborah. "John Wayne's Body," from *The Book of Westerns*, ed Ian Cameron and Douglas Pye (Continuum, 1996), 75-80
278. Thompson, Emily. 2004. *The Soundscape of Modernity: Architectural Acoustics and the Culture of Listening in America, 1900-1933*. The MIT Press.
279. Tofts, Darren, Annemarie Jonson, and Alessio Cavallaro. 2004. *Prefiguring Cyberculture: An Intellectual History*. The MIT Press.
280. Turkle, Sherry. *Alone Together: Why We Expect More From Technology and Less From Each Other*. New York: Basic Books, 2011.
281. Turner, Frederick Jackson. "The Significance of the Frontier in American History" (1893)
282. Urban, Greg. 2001. *Metaculture: How Culture Moves Through the World*. (U of Minnesota P), pp. 181-227.
283. Uricchio, William. "Historicizing Media in Transition," in *Rethinking Media Change: The Aesthetics of Transition*, ed. David Thorburn and Henry Jenkins (Cambridge, MA: MIT Press, 2003).
284. Vaidhyanathan, Siva. *Copyrights and Copywrongs*
285. Vaidhyanathan, Siva. 2004. *The Anarchist in the Library: How the Clash Between Freedom and Control is Hacking the Real World and Crashing the System*. (Basic Books)
286. Valery, Paul. "The Centenary of Photography." Classic Essays on Photography ed. Alan Trachtenberg (1980 [1927])
287. Valery, Paul. "The Conquest of Ubiquity" and "Art and Technology." Aesthetics (1964)
288. Vismann, Cornelia. *Files: Law and Media Technology*. Trans. Geoffrey Winthrop- Young. (Stanford: Stanford University Press, 2008).
289. Wallace, Aurora. *Newspapers and the Making of Modern America: A History*. Westport: Greenwood, 2005.
290. Wade, Nicholas. "Social Development and Weapons Propelled Human Achievement." *The New York Times* 14 Mar. 2011. Web. 16 Mar. 2011.
291. Wardrip-Fruin, Noah, and Nick Montfort. 2003. New *Media Reader. MIT Press*.
292. Weber, Max. "Bureaucratic Authority," *Sociological Writings*. Ed.Wolf Heydebrand and trans. Martin Black with Lance W. Garmer. New York: Continuum, 1994.
293. Samuel Weber, *Mass Mediauras: Form, Technics, Media* (Palo Alto, CA:

Stanford University Press, 1996)

294. Wellbery, David. "Post-Hermeneutic Criticism," Forward to *Discourse Networks*, pp.vii-xxxiii.

295. White, Lynn. 1966. *Medieval Technology and Social Change*. Oxford University Press.

296. Wiener, Norbert. 1965. *Cybernetics, Second Edition: Or the Control and Communication in the Animal and the Machine*. second edition. The MIT Press.

297. Williams, Raymond. *Television: Technology and Cultural Form*

298. Williams, Raymond. "Base and Superstructue in Marxist Cultural Theory"*in Problems in Materialism and Culture: Selected Essays (1980)*

299. Wills, David. *Prosthesis (1995) and Dorsality: Thinking Back Through Technology and Politics* (2008)

300. Winkler, Hartmut. "Geometry of Time: Media, Spatialization, and Reversibility."

301. Winthrop-Young, Geoffrey and Nicholas Gane, "Friedrich Kittler: An Introduction," *Theory, Culture & Society* 2006, Vol. 23(7–8): 5–16

302. Winthrop-Young, Geoffrey. 2006. "Cultural Studies and German Media Theory." In *New Cultural Studies: Adventures in Theory*, ed. Gary Hall and Clare Birchall, 88–104. Athens: University of Georgia Press.

303. ———. 2011. *Kittler and the Media*. Polity.

304. Langdon Winner. "Do Artifacts Have Politics?" In *The Whale and the Reactor*. Chicago: University of Chicago Press, 1988.

305. Wright, Alex. 2008. *Glut: Mastering Information Through the Ages*. Cornell University Press.

306. Wu, Tim. *The Master Switch: The Rise and Fall of Information Empires*. New York: Knopf, 2010.

307. Yates, JoAnne. *Control through Communication: The Rise of System in American Management*. Baltimore: Johns Hopkins University Press, 1989.

308. Zerubavel, Eviatar. 1989. *The Seven Day Circle: The History and Meaning of the Week*. University Of Chicago Press.

309. Zielinski, Siegfried. 2008. *Deep Time of the Media: Toward an Archaeology of Hearing and Seeing by Technical Means*. Tran. Gloria Custance. The MIT Press.

Chapter 8

MASS MEDIA AND THE IMPERATIVE OF LAW AND ETHICS

INTRODUCTION

Not a single organization in creation has been systematized without the utilization of some form of regulations or a governing body. The food industry has the Food and Drug Administration. American professional football players have the National Football League officials. The United States of America has the Constitution. The same goes for the media, both print and digital. The Federal Communications Commission (FCC) was created to govern the systematic functions of each section of the media.The most heavily government regulated entities are the broadcast media. Television and radio media professionals are subject to a host of rules and regulations that yield hefty fines if violated. The print media, such as newspapers and magazines, remain largely unregulated; however, issues involving such offenses like slander can result in large payouts to people that sue the publications. The internet is also essentially unregulated, but many of the same rules apply to certain distributors of information.

Human beings are by nature free agents that have the capacity to seek and receive information and express it in thought, word and deed through any media. In recognition of this freedom, democratic countries around the world have made copious provisions in their constitutions for people to buttress their freedom of expression. Article of the Universal Declaration of Human Rights (1984) stipulates:

Everyone has the right to freedom of opinion and expression; this right includes freedom to hold opinions without interference and to seek, receive and impart information and ideas through any media and regardless of frontiers (United Nations; 1948).

This fundamental provision gave impetus to Article of the international Covenant on Civil and Political Rights and Article of the African Charter on Human and People Rights (1981). This has been ratified and enacted in CAP 10 Laws of the Federation of Nigeria (1990). Thompson (1992) strongly argued that the freedom of expression is almost impracticable in transitional societies in Africa most of who are suffocation under protracted military rule. The handing over of power to an elected civilian government of Chief Olusegun Obasanjo on 29th May 1999 by General Abdusallam Abubakar marked a return to democratic governance, even, if in theory. Prior to the transition period, the common enemy of the media, the military, is gone. The periodization of 1999 to 2003 corresponds to the first tenure of the Obasanjo administration when there was wide spread optimism that monumental reforms would be embarked upon following the resurrection of democracy after several botched attempts at transition during protracted years of military rule.

The period is also significant in that public perception was very robust as to the proposed reforms promised by the new civilian administration. During this period, it was hoped that the foundations of Nigeria's democracy would be re-built and sustained. Arising from this feeling is that fact the period witnessed a resurgence of several civil society groups and pressure group. Besides, the return of democracy also increased international focus and attention on Nigeria because of her strategic and economic significance. The international community therefore expected much from a nation which was reduced from the status of a colossus to a pariah.

Accordingly, most democratic nations around the world sought to partner with Nigeria to assist in the building and consolidation of democratic institutions. Thus the period marked a watershed, indeed a turning point in the political development of the nation. In Nigeria even democratic regimes pay only lip service to the freedom of expression, and this is problematic to the democratic enterprise, which though fragile, is the rarest flower in the jungle of human experience. But the Social responsibility theory posits that the press must perform a public service role to warrant their existence by properly informing the public and by responding to societies needs. This is achieved through accurate presentation of facts, balanced news reporting, encouraging transparency and accountability and above all propagating democratic values. For the purpose of this study, the press and the mass media will be used interchangeably to include newspapers, magazines, radio, television, and to a lesser extent film and books.

The Nigerian media have been very vocal, vibrant and critical of government policies. The press exposes conspicuous cases of executive high handedness, mismanagement and mal-performance. Some people also finger the Nigerian press for escalating tension and instigating military intervention in politics: Uyo (2000:PP 3-6) posits that while the media fight to educate the public, government officials most often insist on the use of discretion in deciding what measured doses of information the public should know. Besides, the Nigeria federation is fraught with structural abnormalities, which have culminated in inter and intra party federation is fraught with structural abnormalities, which have culminated in inter and intra party struggles for power, lopsided fiscal federalism, resource control and executive legislative crisis.

UNDERSTANDING LAW

The relationship between individuals and groups, which results in interdependency between them, always brings about overlapping functions, conflicting rights, competing interests, and neglected duties/expectations. The interrelationships and interdependence between individuals and groups define society. It was as a result that law set in not only to define individuals' rights, interests and obligations but also to set the limit to which a right is exercised in relation to other rights and obligations. Thus, as put by Elias (1969), the law remains an umpire.

Objectives

At the end of this unit, you should be able to:

- explain the meaning of law
- state the origin of law
- explain the significant of law.

Main content

Definition And Explanation Of Law

Law is the overall guiding principles of human conducts. A law is basically a body of principles or rules which are the basis of a society. Members of a society are meant to abide by the law established by it. It is very hard to have a society without a set of laws guiding it. Human life needs a proper rule of conduct or principle at every step. It is also important for a successful society. Law according to Oyakhilomen (2009), controls, regulates, enforces and punishes. It is very uncommon to have a society absolutely free of law, i.e. a state of anarchy. Whether consciously or unconsciously; written or unwritten; observed or violated; elements of law exist in every society. Oyakhilomen (2006) writes: Society cannot exist without rules of social order. Hence every civilised society has its publicly recognised authority for declaring, administering and enforcing its laws. Can you for a moment visualise a state without law and any enforcement system (if such state ever existed). Suppose the Nigeria Police Force were to observe one day public holiday? What would you find? The state of normlessness or lawlessness is shade or two worse than the perpetual state of warfare and reign of terror and fear. This is a mirror of the state of nature where as Thomas Hobbes stated in The Leviathan: "each man was his own master; personal force alone determined each man's position. Life in these conditions was "solitary, nasty, brutish and short". This leads one to appreciate the fact that the society cannot exist without rules of social order – law. The picture of a State without law helps to bring to the fore, what the functions of law would be in the society. There are various definitions of law by various law professionals and authors. Some of them are as follows:

1. A rule of conduct or procedure established by custom, agreement, or authority.
2. A code of principles based on morality, conscience, or nature.
3 A law is a rule of conduct of any organised society, however simple or small, that are enforced by threat of punishment if they are violated. Modern law has a wide sweep and regulates many branches of conduct.
4. A body of rules of conduct of legal force and effect, prescribed, recognised, and enforced by controlling authority.

Oyakhilomen agrees that law has no universally acceptable definition because many of the definitions put forward are conceived from individuals' perspectives of law. He thereafter highlighted and discussed some definitions from which a few are extracted for the purpose of this course. According to him, law is:

a) "A set of rules governing human activities and relations." He stated that this definition appears extremely wide, accommodating rules of every game, of clubs, even of gangs of thieves. It is all encompassing.

b) "A rule of action prescribed or dictated by some superior which some inferior is bound to obey" and is applied indiscriminately to all kinds of actions, whether animate or inanimate, rational or irrational (Blackstone), or

c) A command set either directly or circuitously by a sovereign individual or body to members of some independent political society in which his authority is supreme (John Austin). He discusses Blackstone & Austin's definitions as being silent on omission or inaction. 'Description of law as a rule of action is wide enough to cover: rules of a father to his son, or rules of a husband to his spouse which are no law' he submitted.

d) A body of principles recognised and applied by the state in the administration of justice (Salmond). He asks if the state does not apply moral principles, which do not answer the descriptions of law.

e) Rules, which the courts will follow, the prophecies of what the courts will do, in fact, and nothing more pretentious (Oliver Wendell Home). This is a classic egg and the chick case.

f) Rules, which the courts – the judicial organs of that body – lay down for the determination of legal rights and duties (John Chipman Gray). In other words, law means the rules of court.

g) An aggregation of legislations and accepted legal principles and the body of authoritative groups of judicial and administrative actions. He submits that this definition is more a description than a definition.

h) A general body of such rules of conduct expressing the will of the ruling class as are established by legislation and such customs and rules of community life as are sanctioned by the government; the application of which body of rules is secured by the coercive force of the state for the protection, consolation, and development desirable for the ruling class (Vyshinsky).

i) A general body of such rules of human conduct established or sanctioned by the government power, the execution of which rules is secured by the coercive power of the state (Gsovski)

Self-Assessmentexercise

Put all various definitions above into consideration to form your own definition of law.

Origin of Law

Law, according to some scholars, is as old as man. In Qur'an chapter verses 35 and 36, God created the first man, Adam and his wife, Eve (Hawaw) and put them in the paradise. God enacted law for them (the dos and the don'ts) to serve as their guiding principles: And He said: "O Adam! Dwell you and wife in the paradise and eat both of you freely with pleasure and delight, of things therein as wherever you will, but come not near this tree or you both will be of the wrongdoers." From this Quran verse, it is established that God enacted laws for the first man and his wife, which set for them the limit in the use of the provision in the paradise. God also stipulated the measure for the violation of the laws and the punishment that goes along with it is stated in verse 36 of the same chapter. Similar quotation can be found in Bible. Another law that testify to the earlier historical record of law is Mosaic laws (10 commandments) in the Old Testament. Whether divine or man- made, law is law, once it satisfies all or any of the conditions highlighted in Oyakhilomen (2009), namely:

- controls
- regulates
- enforces
- punishes.

Law is very wide and all encompassing and that is why every profession, like every society, has its own law or form of law. The laws that affect businesses are known as business laws or company laws or law of contracts, while those that affect property are known as property laws. It therefore implies that the laws that control, regulate, enforce and punish in the operation of mass media are Media Laws.

Self-Assessmentexercise

Can the directives given by the kings and chiefs to their subjects be categorised as laws?

Importance of Law

The importance of law is discussed below.

Protection of interests

Von Ihering has said that, "the purpose of law is the protection of interests." But what is interest and whose interest? There are various interests within a society or a state competing for protection and actualisation. According to Akinfeleye (2010), interests are of two categories:

- Individual or personal interest
- Public/State/Societal interest

a) Individual interest: Each member of a society has his personal interest to protect. His interest is important to him for his personal development, protection and gains. The interest of an individual is limited by the interest of other within the same society. This means that an individual should not protect his or her interest at the detriment of violating the interest of other individual members.

b) Public/state/societal interest: Though there are arguments on whether public interest is the same thing as state interest, our focus here is likened both to mean the collective interest of individual members of a state.

The good of the individual is not itself an end, but only a means of securing the good of the society. In essence, the society is a higher conception than the individual so that the individual can desire the common interest in addition to his own. Andrei Vyshinsky's view is that law and the state are one so that any criminal act is a danger to the regime and the state. He thought that emphasis on individual was a mere cloak to shroud the exploitation of workers by the bourgeoisie. In the western philosophy, function of law is to hold a balance between interests of the individual and those of the state.

Protection of life, national security, public safety and social welfare

You can imagine a state of lawlessness, where the right of an individual is not defined and the limitation to the right in order to protect the right of another individual is not set, only those who have the will would have their way. Law protects the rights, duties of people, be it political, social, economic or cultural.

Protection of life

There are a number of incidents taking place all the time which could be harmful to people. This leads to the need of making law. People need a proper code of life. They need to know their rights as well as others' right; only then they could lead a peaceful life. According to Sohn, law is the sum of rules, which regulates the life of the people, or creates social order and organisation that are necessary for preservation of life and ordered control of the life of the community. He explained that the private law governs the rights and duties of individuals while public law regulates the relationship between the individual and the state. The essence of law is to reconcile conflicting interests of individuals and collective interests of the public such that peaceful coexistence would be ascertained. Von Ihering sees the function of preserving life from the angle of striking a balance between egoistic and altruistic motives. He said that the purpose is the universal principle of the world. The purpose of human violation is the satisfaction derivable from acts. The purpose of law is the protection of interests.

National security and public safety

National security is the protection of a state and its human and material resources against both internal and external forces. According to Elias, state security includes all the means at a government's disposal for securing or protecting the nation or state from the danger of subjugation either by an external power or through internal insurrection. Nigerian laws forbid any Nigerian or foreigner living within the country from carrying ammunitions around without legal permission to do so or rising against the constituted authority as these may constitute threat to national security.

Sometimes, individual rights are violated to ensure that the state is secured from certain danger. For example, people's right to freedom of movement may be deprived when a curfew or a state of emergency is declared in a state to let peace rein.

Since individuals constitute the public, public safety would therefore mean the safety of life and property of every Nigerian against all that may constitute threat. Emergency powers to incarcerate persons who commit or are suspected of having committed an offence, and to stop and search without warrant any receptacle suspected to contain explosives, firearms and ammunition, exist for purposes of national security and public safety. Moreover, both the military and the police have powers to order the detention of "trouble maker" whose freedom is reasonably considered prejudicial to the society.

Social welfare of state

Oyakhilomen (2009) highlights the under listed as means through which laws ensure social welfare of state:

(i) The Constitution and various statutes enhance freedom. It is by law slave trade and slavery extraction of executive bride price or discrimination against Osu caste were abolished. Law frowns at arbitrary arrest and detention, and guarantees right of freedom of movement, speech and association. Writ of habeas corpus or fundamental rights enforcement proceedings are provided by law where ones freedom is curtailed wrongfully.

(ii) Tax laws provide money for social amenities.

(iii) Traffic laws provide for orderliness on the highways.

(iv) Law of contract encourages business transactions and allows them to strive.

(v) Law of tort protects proprietary rights and freedom of property, and commands compensation, damages or other remedies in case of trespass.

(vi) Arbitration laws and rules of courts provide ways of setting disputes when they arise.

(vii) Law performs normative and social functions by pointing to direction of wrong committed by members of the public and helping or supporting state functionaries, operators and machinery of society.

Maintenance of justice and fairness in society

Justice and fairness come from nowhere other than from the application of laws. Oyakhilomen (2009) expresses the view of some writers, who equate law with justice, contending that law ought to be just. Jus naturale, jus gentium and equity and its body of rules were developed out of the desire and search for justice, fairness and good conscience, for all peoples. In contrary, justice is an absolute requirement and the judges prepossession or idiosyncrasy. The essences of law to ensure justice are as follows:

a) To hold everybody accountable in the same proportion for equal functions given to them or obligations expected of them by the law.

b) To give everybody equal chance to contest, compete or access public gains or opportunities.

c) To give equal right to all for fair trial.

d) To give equal right to all to prosecute and to appeal.

e) To give to all equal right to be heard and equal and proportion time to defend in a trial.

f) To give equal and proportionate punishment and equal and proportionate damages to the condemned and the claimant respectively especially where the same or similar interpretations of status are applicable.

Law as an agent of change and transformation

A change in any aspect of law in a society would definitely bring a change within that society. It is not all the times that a change in any aspect of law or introduction of a new law brings about positive change. For example, there was a motion moved in the Nigeria National Assembly to legalise homosexuality. If such a bill was passed to law, it might have negative effect within the state. Besides, if laws provide for adequate remedies, such laws would transform the society. Most often people are not used to change except they consider certain benefits or see deterrents, which they are also likely to be subjected to. Notion of law changes from society to society, from one generation to another even within the same society. Oyakhilomen adds that law:

........tries to maintain the established social order and at the same time, effect social change to meet modern requirements of a new society, taking cognisance of and responding to new learning, new facts, different set of prejudices, disparity in sets of questions people ask daily, in sets of values, economics, education, social achievement and ideological orientation and very importantly quest for ideals of justice and for a transformed and better society.

UNDERSTANDING ETHICS

The study of ethics is important to the mass media because journalists and other media professionals must be guided by ethical values and principles for the good of the society. The focus of this unit is therefore to introduce you to mass media ethics.

Objectives

At the end of this unit, you should be able to:

- define ethics
- differentiate between law and ethics
- explain the importance of ethics to the society.

Main Content 3.1 Definition Of Ethics

Ethics is derived from the Greek *ethos,* meaning "custom," "usage," or "character." It is often thought of as a rational process applying established principles when two moral obligations collide (Day, 2006). Ethics is "the liberal arts discipline that appraises voluntary human conduct in so far as it can be judged right or wrong in reference to determinative principles" (Christians et al, 1998). Ethics is a set of principles of conduct governing an individual or group (Bowles and Borden, 2004).

Ethics is the science of rightness and wrongness of conduct. Conduct is purposive action, which involves choice and will. It is the expression of character which is a settled habit of will. The will is the self in action. Thus ethics is the science of human character as expressed in right or wrong conduct. But rightness or wrongness refers to the good which is the ideal of human life. Thus ethics is the science of the highest good. It is the science of morality. Ethics is concerned with the origin and growth of conduct like psychology. It is concerned with evaluation of conduct with reference to an ideal. It seeks to determine the supreme ideal involved in human conduct. It seeks to teach us how we can pass correct judgments upon human conduct, consider it as right or wrong, with reference to the supreme ideal of human life. Ethics is the science of the ideal involved in human life (Sinha, 2009).

Neher and Sandin (2007) note that: "In a technical sense, ethics is a branch of the field of philosophy, which is concerned about judgments on right and wrong actions. Beyond the discipline of philosophy, many fields include the study of and applications of ethics to their domain. Ethics refers to a systematic method for making judgments concerning voluntary actions of people." Neher and Sandin highlight several aspects of the definition thus:

- First, ethics is intended to provide us with a system so that the decisions or judgments one makes can be justified to others and to oneself in a clear and objective manner.
- Second, ethics is concerned with judgments about actions that can be determined to be right or wrong according to the principles of this method.
- Third, the judgments are to be made about actions, in which the actors appear to have a choice; they could have done otherwise.
- And, fourth, the actions are seen as intentional: the persons seemed to know what they were doing and intended to do what they did. Thus, ethics often involves the balancing of competing rights when there is no "correct" answer.

A case in point is a student who promises to remain silent when a classmate confides that he has cheated. If a teacher attempts to solicit testimony from that student regarding her friend's nefarious behaviour, the student must then weigh the value of loyalty to the friend (a moral virtue) against commitment to the truth - another moral virtue (Day, 2006).

Once in a while, ethical decisions involve more than one moral rule. For example, most of us have been taught that stealing is wrong; we have also been taught that human lives are highly valued. What if a loved one required medication to live and we had no money to buy that pharmacy? Would we be morally justified in doing so? Does the value of a human life outweigh the harm done by stealing the medicine? Or is stealing always wrong, regardless of the motivation? From the foregoing therefore, it is obvious that ethics is a set of values, principles and standards guiding an individual, a group or professionals' conduct or actions, especially when confronted with two or more compelling situations. Ethics, in short, may be seen as being concerned with that which holds society together or provides the stability and security essential to the living of human life (Black *et al*, 1999).

Self-Assessmentexercise

From your understanding of the presentation above, give your own definition of ethics?

Differences between Law and Ethics

Ethics is not the same as law, and ethical constraints are not the same as legal rules. Ethics articulates what we ought to do in order to be moral individuals and professionals, while law concentrates on the bottom line below which we should not fall. Ethics deals with ideal behaviours, while law deals with minimum standards. There is a common tendency today to equate ethical standards with legal standards, and for victims of unethical behaviour to seek legal remedies for perceived ethical lapses. This is a false equation and a fundamental misconception of the relationship between law and ethics. For instance, invasion-of-privacy laws widely permit the publication of information that, for reason of ethics, taste, compassion or professionalism, some news media would not publish or broadcast (Black et al, 1999). Not all moral issues can be, or should be, legally codified. The law permits many immoralities that transgress against friends and enemies alike, such as breaking of promises, uttering of unkind words, and certain forms of deception. In the course of our lives we often offend the feelings of others, an act for which the law provides no restitution to the offended party. A high school student, for example, might break his date at the last minute, but the lady kept in waiting cannot resort to the courts for redress of her tearful ordeal. Even in a litigious society it would be undesirable to open the floodgates to such deep interference into individual relationships (Day, 2006).

Nevertheless, legal obligations are based on moral ones. The criminal and civil statutes codify some of our most important moral obligations for example, proscriptions against killing, stealing, raping, or maliciously defaming another's reputation. Most of these statutes involve punishing direct harm to others, but some laws are based on moral principles that are not concerned with the well-being of others. Laws regulating sexual behaviour between consenting adults and prostitution fall into this category. The moral justification for such laws is not widely shared within society, and thus compliance is less certain. Nevertheless, a fundamental distinction between our legal code and moral obligations is that legal violations involve prescribed penalties and ethical indiscretions do not. But if the laws themselves are based on moral respect, are there circumstances when we are warranted in breaking a law? Does our ethical system provide for such waivers of our moral obligations? Civil disobedience, in which citizens intentionally ignore laws that they feel are unjust, has received some moral respectability in recent years, particularly since the nonviolent civil rights demonstrations led by the Reverend Dr. Martin Luther King, Jr., in the 1960s. Most ethicists agree, however, that the legitimacy of civil disobedience depends on (1) the moral agent's true belief that the law is unjust, (2) nonviolence, and (3) the willingness of protesters to face the consequences of their actions. In addition, some people justify civil disobedience only if the legal avenues of redress have been explored. For example, an environmental group, having exhausted all legal avenues to prevent the disposal of nuclear wastes at a site within their community, might resort to acts of civil disobedience to bring its concerns to the public's attention. In such cases, even when legal questions have been settled, the moral issues persist. A just law might be violated in emergency situations or when higher moral principle is involved. For example, we would not think a husband immoral for running the red light to get his pregnant wife to the hospital in time for the delivery of their baby. On a more serious level, media practitioners may occasionally feel obligated to violate a just law if they believe that they must do so because of a more significant moral obligation.

Hence, ethics is the foundation for all laws but not all laws are based on ethics. Most laws are ethical but not all ethics are written in law. Violation of all legal rules can be redressed in a law court while not all ethical violations can be compensated Okoye (2008) provides the following differences between law and ethics: a)

Law is imposed by the outer society, while ethics is self-imposed and self-enforced (e.g. by a professional body for its members). b) Law has a definite effective date while ethics has no effective date. c) Law can expire or be repealed, but ethics is continuous. d) Law has more formal institutions, such as the legislature, police, judiciary, (the courts, tribunals, court-martials, etc) penitentiary (prison, reformatory, etc), but ethics has less formal institutions for its formulation and enforcement. Indeed, the chief enforcer of ethic is the conscience. e) While morality protects a way of life by tabooing immoral action even before it takes place, laws only provide recourse after the deed has been done (Caster, 1983). There is a close relationship between law and ethics as both are attempting to restrain or constrain the media to behave responsibly, but the purpose of the law is always to set the limits of behaviour, to identify those things we must do (or, often, must not do). Ethics set out those things that we ought to do or not do. Think of a hen's egg – the hard outer shell represents the law – an easy-to-detect boundary between the white and the yolk is a much softer boundary, and although it sits within the hard shell of the law, it can easily be pushed in one direction or another, depending upon our desire and beliefs. The law has a more powerful effect on people than a code of conduct. A person's own moral code may supersede the law every time, but a professional code can only be for guidance this means that when there are conflicts between the law and professional practice, the law will almost always take precedence (Frost, 2007).

Self-Assessmentexercise

Explain the relationship between law and ethics.

Importance of Ethics to the Society

Every society needs a system of ethics or morals for peace, stability and cohesion. Without ethics, morality and law, society, according to the common saying will be brutish and short. It is a system of ethics that guide personal, interpersonal and public relationships. Without ethics, there won't be law and without law, there will be anarchy in the society. It is a system of ethics that the society uses as a guide in judging and assessing conduct and actions.

Day (2006) explains five reasons why every society needs a system of ethics. The reasons are:

The need for social stability

First, a system of ethics is necessary for social intercourse. Ethics is the foundation of our advanced civilisation, a cornerstone that provides some stability to society's moral expectations. If we are to enter into agreements with others, a necessity in a complex, interdependent society, we must be able to trust one another to keep those agreements, even if it is not in our self-interest to do so (Olen, 1988).

The need for a social hierarchy

Second, a system of ethics serves as a moral gatekeeper in apprising society of the relative importance of certain customs. It does this by alerting the public to (1) those norms that are important enough to be described as moral and (2) the "hierarchy of ethical norms" and their relative standing in the moral pecking order. All cultures have many customs, but most do not concern ethical mores. For example, eating with utensils is customary in Western countries but the failure to do so is not immoral. Standing for the national anthem before a sporting event is a common practice, but those who remain seated are not behaving unethically. There is a tendency to describe actions of which we disapprove as immoral, although most of our social indiscretions are merely transgressions of etiquette. A system of ethics identifies those customs and practices of which there is enough social disapproval to render them immoral.

The need to promote a dynamic social ecology

Three, an ethical framework serves as a social conscience, challenging members of a community to examine ethical dimensions of both public issues and private concerns and to aspire to elevate the quality of the moral ecology. However, the goal should not be the ideal society (which is impossible) but a decent society. What should be avoided are claims of infallibility. Ethics is not a science, and trial and error are inevitable. In a not-so-perfect society, some compromises and balancing are required because not every claim deserves equal attention.

The need to resolve conflicts

Four, a system of ethics is an important social institution for resolving cases involving conflict claims based on individual self-interest. For example, it might be in a student's own interest to copy from a classmate's term paper. It is in the classmate's best interest to keep her from doing so. Societal rules against plagiarism are brought to bear in evaluating the moral conduct inherent in this situation.

The need to clarify values

Finally, a system of ethics also functions to clarify for society the competing values and principles inherent in emerging and novel moral dilemmas.

Some of the issues confronting civilisation today would challenge the imagination of even the most ardent philosopher. A case in point is the controversy over the cloning of humans, a scientific breakthrough with unimaginable ethical consequences. Ethicists have already begun passionately debating this issue in the hopes of clarifying competing moral values and affording some time for reasoned reflection before such scientific experimentation becomes commonplace.

Self-Assessmentexercise

Can a society survive without an agreed system of ethics? Justify your position.

MEDIA LAWS: REPUTATION AND DIGNITY OF PERSONS

The essence of this unit is to provide an understanding on the meaning, forms, proof and defenses against defamation and its remedies. It is also intended that you will understand, after going through the unit, the reasons why defamation should be avoided and how it can be evaded.

Objectives

At the end of this unit, you should be able to:

- define and explain in detail the law of defamation
- explain the two major forms of defamation
- identify the essential elements of defamation (requirements for proof of defamation)
- highlight the defenses against defamation
- enumerate the remedies for defamation.

Main Content

Definition and Explanation of Defamation

The media, while discharging its functions of informing, entertaining and educating the public has, as an obligation to ensure that it does not infringe on the rights of individuals by publishing words that are capable of causing them harm, injury, hatred or rejection by right-thinking members of the society. The issue is therefore in two folds. According to Article Global Campaign for Free Expression (2000) "The society has to allow freedom of expression and the free flow of information - including free and open debate regarding matters of public interest, even when this involves criticism of individuals- are of crucial importance in a democratic society, for the personal development, dignity and fulfillment of every individual, as well as for the progress and welfare of society, and the enjoyment of other human rights and fundamental freedom." The media, on the other hand has to ensure that it is "Mindful of the importance to individuals of their reputations and the need to provide appropriate protection for reputation" (ibid,). The freedom to publish news, which is enjoyed by the press derives from Article of the Nigerian constitution which accords the same right to other individuals. The freedom is a qualified one and is subject to any law which is reasonably justifiable for the purpose of protecting the rights, reputation and freedom of other persons (Nylander, 1969). According to Justice Dore in Swindler (1955), "Any written or printed article published of and concerning a person without lawful justification or excuse and tending to expose him to public contempt, scorn, obloquy, ridicule, shame or disgrace, or intending to induce an evil opinion of him in the mind of right thinking persons, or injure him in his profession, occupation or trade is libelous and actionable, whatever the intention of the writer may have been. The word need not necessarily impute actual disgraceful conduct to the plaintiff; it is sufficient if members of public rendered him contemptible and ridiculous".

The constitution of Nigeria also clearly explains what defamation is. Section 391 of the Nigerian Penal Code states that: "Whoever by words either spoken or reproduced by mechanical means or intended to be read or by signs or by visible representations makes or publishes any imputation concerning any person intending to harm or knowing or having reasons to believe that such imputations will harm the reputation of such person, is said ... to defame that person."

Articles of the Nigerian Criminal Code are quite plain on this issue: "Defamatory matter is matter likely to injure the reputation of any person by exposing him to hatred, contempt or ridicule or likely to damage any person in his profession or trade by an injury to his reputation. Such matters may be expressed in spoken words or in any audible sounds, or in words legibly marked on any substance whatever, or by any sign or object signifying such matters otherwise than by words, and may be expressed whether directly or by insinuation or irony. It is immaterial whether at the time of the publication of the defamatory matter; the person concerning whom such matter is published is living or dead."

Forms of Defamation: Libel and Slander

Actionable defamation may take the form of libel or slander. Any publication of defamatory matter in a permanent form is libel at common law. It is libel to publish printed or written words, a picture or effigy which carries a defamatory meaning. Slander, on the other hand, is a publication of defamatory matter by spoken words or in any transitory form, whether audible or visible, and it may take the form of significant sounds, looks, signs or gestures (Nylander, 1969). According to Crone (2002:4), the distinction between libel and slander is relevant only to the issue of damages. Damage is presumed in cases of libel. In cases of slander the claimant has to prove certain loss, unless the allegation falls within one of four exceptions where damage is presumed:

1. An allegation that the claimant has committed a crime punishable by imprisonment.
2. An allegation that the claimant is suffering from a contagious or infectious disease.
3. An allegation that the claimant is an unchaste woman or is a woman who has committed adultery.
4. An allegation that is likely to damage the claimant's business or profession.

On his part, Nylander (1969) believes "There is one important difference between libel and slander. A libel is actionable *per se,* i.e. without the necessity of proving special damage. With five exceptions, no action will lie for slander unless the plaintiff proves that he has suffered special damage. Special damage means actual and definite temporal loss- for instance, loss of employment or the refusal of persons to enter into contracts with the plaintiff as a result of the slander.

Libel

Bowles and Borden (2004) note the following about libel: "Libel is a false statement that exposes people to hatred, ridicule or contempt, lowers them in the esteem of their colleagues, causes them to be shunned or injures them in their business or profession." Generally, libel falls into one of two classifications: (1) libel *per se*, words that are defamatory on their face and thus presumed to damage reputation; and (2) libel *per quod*, words that are not ordinarily defamatory but become damaging by facts or circumstances extrinsic to the story. Examples of libel *per se* include words that falsely accuse someone of committing a crime or having a loathsome disease. An example of libel *per quod* would be the publication of an incorrect date for the granting of a divorce so that it appeared that someone had remarried before the divorce became final.

Types of libel

There are two major types of libel: 1. Criminal libel 2. Civil libel The *Free Legal Dictionary* by Farlex sees criminal libel as "Any intentional false communication, either written or spoken, that harms a person's reputation; decreases the respect, regard, or confidence in which a person is held; or induces disparaging, hostile, or disagreeable opinions or feelings against a person. Defamation may be a criminal or civil charge. It encompasses both written statements, known as libel and spoken statements, called slander."

Crone (2002) says "A criminal libel must be in permanent form. The words must tend to vilify a person and to bring them into hatred, contempt and ridicule...criminal libel differs from civil libel in a number of respects. The accuracy or truth of a statement in criminal libel will not necessarily protect its maker from punishment. 'The greater the truth the greater the libel' is a phrase that is rooted in this branch of the law. It has always been recognised that the truth is more often to arouse fury than obvious falsehood. Unlike civil libel, those accused of criminal libel must establish that the words were true and that they were punished for the public benefit."

Crone adds that "Despite the availability of the laws of defamation, a person may think it advantageous to pursue his case for libel in the criminal court instead of, or as well as, the civil courts. The penalties for the maker of a serious libel are harsher for criminal libel than those imposed in the civil courts. An embittered individual may get far more satisfaction from the thought of sending a reporter, broadcaster or editor to jail than from pursuing an action for damages."

Slander

Slander occurs when an individual or group's reputation is attacked through spoken words or gesture, especially believed to be false and malicious but presented as fact. Kayne (2012) says, "Slander is the spoken or transitory form of defamation of character, a legal term that refers to a falsehood presented as true which could harm the reputation of a person or entity. Slander also encompasses body gestures as in the case of sign language…In short, slander is temporarily uttered or gesticulated…Slander is a tort, or civil law, meaning a civil lawsuit can be brought against someone who is accused of slander." For an individual to be successfully sued and found guilty of slander, the plaintiff has to establish that the accused actually uttered those words, that the words were overheard by a third party, that the words are false and that those words identify the plaintiff, and they have a malicious intent. In Nigeria, slander actionable *per se* falls into five classes:

1. Statements imputing the commission of a criminal offence punishable by imprisonment
2. statements imputing certain contagious or infectious diseases
3. statements imputing promiscuity to a woman or girl
4. statements imputing unfitness or incompetence or calculated to disparage a person in any office, profession, trade or business
5. statements imputing that a person is an *osu*.

Self-Assessmentexercise

Distinguish clearly between slander and libel.

Essential Elements of Defamation

Articles of the Nigerian Criminal Code, state that "Defamatory matter is matter likely to injure the representation of any person by exposing him to hatred, contempt or ridicule or likely to damage any person in his profession or trade by an injury to his reputation. Such matters may be expressed in spoken words or in any audible sounds, or in words legibly marked on any substance whatever, or by any sign or object signifying such matters otherwise than by words, and may be expressed whether directly or by insinuation or irony…". Defamation can be either of libel or slander. When defamatory words are printed or legibly marked on any substance or audible words are recorded in a retrievable format, then it is libel. On the other hand, when spoken words, signs and gestures, with malicious intent and/or false claims about a person or entity's character are overheard or seen by a third party is slander. Nylander (1969) writes that "the following elements are common both to libel and slander and must be proved by a plaintiff in order to succeed in an action of defamation:

1. The statement must be defamatory
2. It must refer to the plaintiff
3. It must be published maliciously.

For a statement to be regarded as defamatory, the words must clearly depict the plaintiff in a way that will generate or arouse hatred, scorn, ridicule, contempt and cause him harm in his profession and relationships and lower him in the estimation of right-thinking members of the society. If the words do not clearly and overtly depict defamation, then the plaintiff will have to prove that beyond the overt meaning, the words or the way it has been used has injured his prestige and image in the opinions of the public and it is thus defamatory. To do this, the plaintiff has to allege innuendo. A plaintiff pleads innuendo, according to Nylander (1969) by "…giving the meaning which he attributes to the words and proving the existence of facts and circumstances which would convey such a meaning to the person to whom the words were published." Nylander (1969) says "An innuendo may be true or false. A true innuendo is one which derives support from extrinsic facts, but a false one is only implied from the words themselves."

On reference to the plaintiff, it has to be clearly proved beyond doubt that it is the plaintiff that is identified in the story or statement with the defamatory words. If the name of the plaintiff is used, then it would be easy. But if more than one person bears the name, the plaintiff will have to plead innuendo to establish the fact that the words were actually referring to him. On the other hand, if no name were used, the plaintiff may establish that the personality painted, the symbols and signs, position, character and other elements in the statement are enough to lead reasonable people to conclude that they refer to him. Publication is one of the most important, if not the most important element of defamation that is required to be established. Before an individual can win a case of defamation, he has to establish that the words were published to a third party. It can be through a print medium, a broadcast medium or in the case of slander, word of mouth. To prove that a statement is defamatory, in the case of libel, Bowles and Borden (2004) say " A person who sues for libel must prove the following:

- the statement was published
- the plaintiff was identified in the statement
- the statement was defamatory • the statement caused injury
- the publisher was at fault in publishing the statement."

Publication

Publication is usually obvious in cases involving the mass media. Strictly speaking, publication has occurred when at least one person other than the defamed person has received the material. In media cases, courts have usually, but not always, held that publication has not occurred until the material reaches its intended audience. In other words, media personnel can discuss a potentially libelous item during the production process without fear of a successful libel lawsuit. However, in 1980 an Illinois jury found the Alton Telegraph liable for material that was never published. Publication resulted, the jury decided, during the newsgathering stage. In an attempt to verify accusations of wrongdoing by a local building contractor, reporters wrote a memo about the wrongdoing to a government official.

Identification

Identification may be established even though the plaintiff is not named in the story, if people reasonably understand that the statement refers to the plaintiff. An address or title might be sufficient for people to identify the plaintiff.

Individuals cannot sue successfully just because they are members of a large group that has been defamed. For example, the statement "all lawyers are crooks" would not be sufficient identification for an individual lawyer to bring a lawsuit. But an attorney might be able to prove individual identification or harm by the statement "All lawyers at the XYZ Law Firm are crooks." No exact number exists for deciding how small a group must be before any single member can claim to have been libeled. A "rule of 25" grew out of a libel case in the 1950s, but subsequent court decisions allowed members of groups larger than 25 to sue when individuals were closely identified with the group. Although published statements may identify and damage the memory of a deceased person, the dead cannot sue, and relatives may not sue on their behalf.

Defamation

Defamation is another part of the plaintiff's burden of proof. The plaintiff must persuade the court that the offending statement carried a "sting", meaning that it harmed the plaintiff's reputation. Evidence about a plaintiff's reputation before and after publication is admissible. In a few instances, courts have decided that plaintiffs were "libel proof" because their reputations were already tarnished beyond the possibility of further damage. In most cases involving the mass media, the plaintiff must also prove that the offending statement was false. True statements that harm people's reputation are not actionable as libel, although they may be actionable as an invasion of privacy. Thus, the accurate claim that someone has been arrested and charged with murder is not actionable, even though the person may subsequently be acquitted of the charge. Minor inaccuracies will not defeat the defense of truth so long as the part of the statement that carries the sting is true. For example, a libel case would not be decided on inaccurately reporting the place of arrest of the murder suspect so long as the suspect was accurately identified and the charge accurately reported.

Self-Assessmentexercise

What factors must be present to establish defamation?

Defenses against Defamation

There are numerous defense options to the mass media and individuals against defamation. The following are identified in Nylander (1969):

- justification
- fair comment
- privilege
- unintentional defamation
- apology and payment into court
- accord and satisfaction: release
- res judicata
- statutes of limitation
- volenti non fit injuria

Justification

Crone (2002) writes that "Justification protects the freedom to tell the truth. In order to raise the defense of justification successfully, the defendant must prove that the defamatory statement is true in both substance and fact, or is substantially true. In cases where writers or broadcasters are sued over factual pieces, justification will often be the only plausible defense. In principle, this should not be something that causes concern, as truth and accuracy are supposed to be bywords for the professions of journalism and broadcasting. In practice, success in raising the defense of justification is measured not by whether the piece is true but whether the defendant can prove that the piece is true. Because the law presumes that the defamatory statement is false, the defendant has the onerous task of overcoming this presumption by proving that the statement is true." That is why Nylander (1969) says that "If the defendant can prove that the statement is true, he has a complete defense to the action even if he made the statement maliciously; 'For the law will not permit a man to recover damages in respect of an injury to a character which he does not or ought not to possess.' The onus of proving a plea of justification lies on the defendant. In its formal form, the plea is stated as follows: 'The words complained of are true in substance and in fact'...If the statement contains an innuendo, the defendant must justify not only the primary meaning of the words, but also the innuendo." That is why, according to Bowles and Borden (2004), "True statements that harm someone's reputation are not actionable as libel, although they may be actionable as invasion of privacy."

Aggravation

One of the major concerns a defendant frequently has to face when pleading justification is that the plea itself exacerbates the damages. A claimant is perfectly entitled to argue that the defendant not only published defamatory material and refused to apologise, but also persisted in the damaging and libelous allegations right up to the moment the jury delivered its verdict. In the event that the jury does not accept the plea of justification, the very fact that the defendant chose to enter such a defense can operate as an aggravation of the original libel and become a reason to award a greater amount in damages than would otherwise be called for Crone (2002). An unsuccessful attempt to justify a defamatory statement will aggravate damages. There seems to be no authority, however, that an award may be increased merely because a defendant, acting without malice and fully believing in his plea, has failed to justify the statement Nylander (1969).

Fair comment

According to Bowles and Borden (2004), "Fair comment protects opinion about public interest or things that have been put on public display. The doctrine of fair comment allows reviewers, for example, to publish scathing reviews of plays, movies, books, restaurants and the like. Copy editors should ensure either that opinion in a story is based on generally known facts or that the factual basis for such opinion is stated in the story...Copy Editors must eliminate opinion that relies for its support on the existence of undisclosed information unless the editor knows that such information is accurate." Fair comment allows a person to publish a statement of opinion or comment on a matter of public interest provided it is done without malice. It protects the freedomto voice an honest opinion Crone (2002). Nylander (1969) notes that "It is a defense to an action of defamation that the words complained of are fair comment made in good faith and without malice on a matter of public interest and, if sued for defamation, may plead the defense of fair comment or its alternative, usually called the 'rolled-up plea'. The requisites of the plea of fair comment are: 1. The matter commented on must be of public interest 2. It must be an expression of opinion and not an assertion of fact 3. The comment must be fair, i.e. it must be based on facts accurately stated 4. The comment must not be malicious. Malice will destroy a plea of fair comment Nylander (ibid).

The 'rolled-up' plea is a plea of fair comment and not one of justification *Odutola* [1960].

Privilege

There are certain occasions when the law recognises that there ought not to be liability for defamation in the interest of public policy or of the community. Such occasions are deemed by the law to be privileged Nylander (1969). Privilege can be either absolute or qualified.

Absolute privilege

Absolute privilege "is the strongest defense available to the libel defendants. Where it is applicable it will succeed, no matter how false and defamatory the statement and no matter how malicious the writer or broadcaster Crone (2002). The occasions of absolute privilege, according to Nylander (1969) are classified as follows: 1. Judicial privilege, e.g. statements made in proceedings before superior and inferior courts are absolutely privileged, provided it has some reference to the inquiry in hand. The privilege extends to other tribunals recognised by law, provided that they are exercising judicial functions. 2.

Legal professional privilege protects absolutely any communication a client and his legal advisers. 3. Official privilege will include communications made by one officer of state to another in the course of his official duty, and military reports. 4. Parliamentary privilege will protect statements made in the House of Representatives, House of Assembly and reports, papers, votes and proceedings ordered to be published by them. 5. Statutory privilege. The Defamation Act, 1961 and similar state enactments provide that a fair and accurate report in any newspaper of proceedings publicly heard before any court exercising judicial authority within Nigeria is, if published contemporaneously with such proceedings, privileged; but this does not authorise the publication of any blasphemous or indecent matter. The protection given to newspapers by this section is extended to broadcast reports from a broadcasting station within Nigeria.

Qualified privilege

Nylander (1969) says "Qualified privilege, on the other hand, may only be pleaded if the publication was made honestly with respect to what is stated and the means by which it is stated. Here lies the distinction between absolute and qualified privilege. Malice defeats a defense of qualified privilege, but it is irrelevant in cases of absolute privilege. Actual malice does not necessarily mean personal spite or ill-will and it may exist even though there is no spite or desire for vengeance in the ordinary sense. Any indirect motive other than a sense of duty is what the law calls malice. Malice means making use of the occasion for some indirect purpose." Instances of qualified privilege include: 1. Statements made in the performance of a duty, legal, moral or social. 2. Statements made in the protection or furtherance of an interest, private or public. A person whose character has been attacked by the press is entitled to reply in his own defense in the press; and if, on answering such attack, he makes relevant defamatory statement about the person who attacked him, it will be privileged provided it is made bona fide. 3. Statements made in the protection of a common interest, e.g. in family matters, a bishop's charge to his congregation. 4. Reports in a newspaper or broadcast Nylander (ibid).

Unintentional defamation

Nylander (1969:30) notes that: "The Defamation Act (1961) has introduced a completely new form of defense, which subject to certain conditions will constitute a complete answer to proceedings for defamation in cases of unintentional defamation. This defense is only applicable if the words were published innocently and there has been an offer of amends as stipulated in the section. Words are deemed to have been published innocently if the publisher proves: 1. That he did not intend to publish them of and concerning the complainant, and did not know of circumstances by virtue of which they might be understood to refer to him; or that the words were not defamatory on the face of them, and he did not know of circumstances by virtue of which they might be understood to be defamatory of the complainant. 2. In either event, that he exercised all reasonable care in relation to the publication."

A defendant who is pleading unintentional defamation is by law expected to publish a correction or retraction of the defamatory content and an apology to the aggrieved party. The law equally expects him to notify recipients of the defamatory matter through all reasonable and practicable means to inform them that the words are alleged to be defamatory of the aggrieved party.

Accord and satisfaction: release

Okoye (2008) explains that accord and satisfaction means a situation "... where there is a mutual settlement between the two parties to the satisfaction of both of them." It must be noted, however, that a release under seal, by way of accord and satisfaction in respect of one joint tort-feasor, discharges the others because the action is one and indivisible. Thus, in an action against the author, printer and publisher of a libel, a release of any one of them will amount to a release of all the others Nylander (1969).

Res Judicata

The import of the principle of *Res Judicata* implies that if a plaintiff files a case of defamation against a defendant and the case is tried, regardless of its outcome, it is presumed that the case is concluded and the plaintiff cannot therefore file a fresh case, based on the same defamatory words, against the same defendant. Nylander (1969) says that "It must be noted, however, that each separate publication of defamatory words give rise to a separate cause of action. A plaintiff might well bring an action against the writer of a defamatory letter to the press under the heading 'Letters to the Editor' and later bring another action in respect of the publication in the columns of the newspaper against the writer and the editor. Selling back numbers of a newspapers or periodical, which has either already been the subject of libel proceedings or is known to contain libel proceedings which has gone unnoticed, will constitute a fresh publication on which an action can be founded."

Statutes of limitation

The law sets aside a period (from the date of publication of a defamatory matter) after the expiration of which a plaintiff cannot sue for damages.

An action for defamation must be brought within six years after the publication of the words complained of. The Limitation Decree, 1966, which applies to the former Federal Territory only, provides, however,that an action claiming damages for slander cannot be brought after the expiration of three years from the date on which the cause of action accrued. For the purpose of limitation of actions, time does not commence to run against a plaintiff under disability. But once the disability ceases, time begins to run Nylander (ibid)

Volenti non fit injuria

Also known as leave and license and consent to publication, *Volenti non fit injuria* means that a plaintiff will not be entitled to sue for defamation if he had previously expressly consented or implied consent to the publication of the matter he regards as defamatory. Crone (2002) is of the opinion that "As one would logically expect, if a person consents to the publication of certain statements he is not then entitled to sue for libel because of the publication. The evidence of consent must be clear and unequivocal. Whatever authorisation the claimant is said to have given should be seen to refer to the publication of the defamatory matter." Nylander (1969) cites an interesting case; "*Chapman v.Ellesmere*, the plaintiff, a trainer, complained about the publication of certain statements about him in the *Racing Calender*. Lord Justice Slesser, in the Court of Appeal, pointed out that the doctrine of *Volenti non fit injuria* applied to this publication as the trainer had undertaken to submit to the rules and regulations of the Jockey Club which was entitled to publish their decisions in the *Racing Calender*."

Self-Assessmentexercise

What defenses can a defendant present to bail himself out of a charge of defamation?

Remedies for Defamation

Okoye (2008) writes that "If a case of defamation has been established and accepted by the court, then the plaintiff is entitled to one or a combination of the following remedies: (a) Damages (b) Injunction, which may be interim, interlocutory or perpetual (c) Publication of retraction or correction

(d) Publication of apology and offer of amends."

Damages

In law, damage is an award or a grant that a judge or the court orders to be paid (usually in money) to a plaintiff after a loss or injury to him after the defendant(s)' action has been established.

Types of damages

Crone notes that: "Damages for defamation can fall under three possible headings: 1. Compensatory damages 2. Aggravated damages 3. Exemplary damages. The first two are broadly concerned with compensation, and the third is aimed at punishing the defendant.

Compensatory damages

Compensatory damages aim to put the claimant back in position he would have been had the defamatory material never published. Under this heading the claimant is entitled to recover the monetary equivalent of everything he had lost and suffered as a result of the defamation. There are two components to the compensatory award. Special damages amount to a sum equal to the actual financial or material loss suffered by the claimant. Damages for distress and injury to reputation are an intangible loss, and are more difficult to calculate. The jury must assess the effect of the defamation on the claimant's feelings.

Aggravated damages

Aggravated damages are awarded where the behaviour of the defendant has somehow added to the hurt and injury to the claimant that resulted from the mere publication of the defamatory words. Various factors may give rise to an award under this category of damages. Anything that looks like a campaign of vilification, even if many of the derogatory things said about the claimant are true, might qualify, as would repetition of the defamation after the original complaint is made. Failing to publish the claimant's denial or explanation, or making no attempt to check the defamatory allegations with him, could also be said to aggravate the injury. Similarly, failing to apologise and persisting in a plea of justification are normally put forward with some success as arguments for awarding aggravated damages.

Exemplary damages

In certain circumstances, the jury in a libel action may decide that the defendant should be liable not only to compensate the claimant for the wrong committed but should also suffer punishment for the way he has behaved. The appropriate course in such cases is to make an award of exemplary damages. They are a purely punitive measure that will only apply where the jury are satisfied that the defendant showed a cynical disregard for the feelings of the claimant by knowingly publishing the defamatory statement in the hope of profiting from it. In *John v Mirror Group Newspapers* (1997), Elton John was awarded exemplary damages because the *Mirror* deliberately published for profit a defamatory statement about him.

Self-Assessmentexercise

Explain the remedies for defamation?

Highlight the media roles towards upholding state security?

STATE SECURITY AND THE MASS MEDIA

It is sadden that the pages of Nigerian dailies recently are bloody with news about killings, bombings, armed robbery, inter-tribal wars, religious chaos, curfew, suicides, accidents, lootings, bribery, boarder dispute, and many others. All these are pointers to the state of security in the country.

Objectives

At the end of this unit, you should be able to:

- define state security
- identify the organ(s) that provide state security
- state the relationship between state security and national security
- explain the roles of the media in safeguarding state security.

Main Content

Understanding State Security

Nigeria presently is in a state of insecurity because of the happenings you have read above. It therefore implies that security secured state is the one that is void of the menace of threat to life. Every Nigerian especially in the northern part of the country is a working ghost because of the fear of bomb or gun attack.

Security simply means freedom from danger, fear, anxiety or uncertainty. Security is not limited to freedom from danger but it also deals with economic well-being i.e. job security because 'a hungry man is an angry man'. Freedom to socialise is also part of state security i.e. protection against social disorder, health hazards and other social threats. According to Imobigbe (2003), security is a condition of being protected from, or not being exposed to danger. A secured state therefore is one that is reasonably free from, or not expose to external aggression and internal sabotage. Security of a state can be categorised into two: internal and external. Whether internal or external, what is important for a state is to ensure that it embarks on policies that guarantee both.

Internal Security

Internal security is concerned with the protection of lives and property of every citizen and even the foreigners living within the state against internal crises and threats. Imobigbe states further that the security of a state is affected at the domestic level by the nature of its internal socio-political and economic circumstances, the manner its affair are run by its political elites and by the degree of commitment of its citizenry to national development and welfare.

External Security

The nature of a state external security is concerned with its relationship with the external environment. A state external affairs determine the benefit, support, aids, or otherwise it gets from outside. It implies that a state that has good relationship with others is likely to be secured than the one that does not have good record with neighbours.

Imogbe added that:

At the external level, a state's security is affected by the nature of the geo-political circumstances surrounding it, as well as by the nature of its foreign policy and the manner it conducts its relations with other countries.

Self-Assessmentexercise

How can Nigeria becomes more secured as a nation?

Between State and National Security

The two terms are used interchangeably. National security does not mean security of the people in power alone. Unlike what is the case in the country, in which national security is defined by the number of security officers guiding a politician or a political office holder. National security is concerned with ensuring public safety, protecting public interests and public and private property.

Self-Assessmentexercise

Can you make any difference between state security and national security?

Who Provides State Security?

a. The state

The security of a state is vested in the hand of the government of the state. The state must protect the people within the state and the entire territory from any hazard whether internally or externally. It must formulate policies that would be of public interest and at the same time ensure justice and even development as this would avail it the opportunity of carrying every segment along. It must use the security agencies in its custody such as The Nigerian Police, Nigerian Army, The Nigerian Navy, The Nigerian Custom and others to ensure peaceful coexistence within the state and to protect the state against external aggression.

b. The citizenry:

Every Nigerian also has roles to play in upholding the security of the state. This could be ensured by love for the state, respect for laws, and being loyal and having belief in the state. Besides, the citizen must not expose his or her state to hatred or harbour hatred of which would have negative implication on the development of the country.

Self-Assessmentexercise

In what ways do you think Nigerians can support government to ensure security of the country?

The Media in Safeguarding State Security

The roles of the media in protecting national security of a state cannot be overemphasised. Through the slogan of the media profession that "The pen is mightier than the sword," it is understandable that the media has the power to make peace and at the same time make wars or fuel crises.

That is why the media professionals are guided by the journalistic principle to ensure that the state is secure through the following:

- That the media would not publish or broadcast any information that undermines public safety and public interest.
- That the media would not publish or broadcast any information that would degrade or ridicule the culture and the traditions of the people of the state.
- That the media would not publish or broadcast classified information which may expose the state of security of the country to the outsiders.
- That the media would not publish or broadcast untrue information for

financial gain or any other reason.

- That the media would expose individuals, groups or organisations that break law and order through their reports. vi. That the media would support development within the state by reporting developmental programmes.

PRIVACY

Privacy entails the right of an individual to have physical, psychological and emotional space for her/himself in the society within the ambience of the law. The role of the media however is to ensure disclosure to the public, information they deem newsworthy and/or important for the public good about individuals, corporate bodies and government. This unit is dedicated to explaining the law of privacy and how the media can effectively perform its function of informing the public of information it deem necessary without running the risk of infringing on the right of individuals "to be left alone".

Objectives

At the end of this unit, you should be able to:

- define privacy
- list the four popular areas or aspects of privacy
- highlight the likely defenses for a suit on the infringement on an individual's privacy.

Main Content

Understanding Privacy

Section 37 of the 1999 Constitution of the Federal Republic of Nigeria provides that "The privacy of citizens, their homes, correspondence, telephone conversations and telegraphic communication is hereby guaranteed and protected."

But it does not define privacy and neither does any other part of the 1999 Constitution. The deliberations on what really constitute privacy and the breach of it is not limited to Nigeria. From Europe to America, defining privacy and its violation has been a controversy. Privacy has been defined as "The right to be left alone."(Cooley, 1888) It is also known as "The right of the individual to be protected against intrusion into his personal life or affairs, or those of his family, by direct physical means or by publication of information" (Calcutt Committee; 1990). Privacy suits occur when an individual feels that he has been wrongly portrayed in the media, especially in a way that causes him emotional distress, humiliation, shame, suffering or anguish. The individual may be a public figure or he may be a private person who has generated public interest through his actions or his involvement in a tragedy or any other event or incident that is of human interest. "Although the concept of libel has its roots in English common law of the Middle Ages, the law of privacy is a 19th century American development. Before 1890, no American court had recognised a right of privacy.

In 1890, an article entitled "The Right of Privacy" by Samuel D. Warren and future Supreme Court Justice Louis Brandeis was published in the *Harvard Law Review*. Although there is little evidence to support the assertion, the two Boston lawyers claim inspiration for the article from gossip in the press about the social affairs of the wealthy Warren family. Warren and Brandeis argued that the growing excesses of the press required the courts to consider granting private individuals protection against the hounding media. In essence, "The Right of Privacy" attempted to establish a common law right of privacy using property rights, defamation, and breech of confidence as its basis. The authors argued that property owners should be allowed to apply the same right of protection of their houses and lands from trespass to the protection of their private lives" (Creech, 2003). "Warren and Brandeis argued, "Instantaneous photographs and newspaper enterprise have invaded the sacred precincts of private and domestic life; and numerous mechanical devices threaten to make good the prediction that 'what is whispered in the closet shall be proclaimed from the house-tops'" (Pember, 2003/2004).

However, the law of privacy is only limited to individuals. Corporate bodies or companies cannot sue for invasion of privacy based on the assumptions that such corporate entities have impersonal entities without personal sensitivities that can be wounded.

Self-Assessmentexercise

Why is there a controversy over the definition of privacy? Trace the history of the "Right of Privacy."

Aspects of Privacy Law

Invasion of privacy is a multifaceted tort that is designed to redress a variety of grievances. These include the commercial exploitation of an individual's name or likeness, the intrusion on what might be called our private domains, the revelation of intimate information about someone, and the libel-like publication of embarrassing false information about a person.

Appropriation

Appropriation is defined as taking a person's name, picture, photograph or likeness and using it for commercial gain without permission. Illegal appropriation occurs when consent is not obtained before using someone's name, picture, or likeness to advertise a product, to accompany an article sold, or to add "luster" to a company name. Courts have held, however, that the incidental use of a person's name or picture in a book, film, magazine, or other medium is not an invasion of privacy. If a name or likeness is not published for commercial gain, it cannot be appropriation (Creech, 2003). It should be noted, however, that stage names, pen names, pseudonyms and so forth count as real names in the eyes of the law. If the name of the rock star Elton John is used in an advertisement for dental floss without his permission, the suit cannot be defended on the basis that because Elton John's real name is Reginald Kenneth Dwight, his "name" was not appropriated illegally. Only the names of people are protected under appropriation. The names of businesses, corporations, schools and other "things" are not protected under the law. However, the use of a trade name like Kodak or Crest can create other serious legal problems…a photograph, a painting and a sketch- anything that suggest to readers and viewers that the plaintiff is pictured-is a likeness. federal courts in New York State ruled that a sketch of a black sitting in the corner of a boxing ring was, for purposes of an invasion-of-privacy suit, the "likeness" of former heavyweight champion Muhammad Ali. The boxer looked a little like Ali, and the sketch was accompanied by a verse that referred to the boxer as "the Greatest" (Pember, 2003/2004).

In *Onassis v. Christian Dior*, Jackie Onassis was successful in her claim against Christian Dior's advertising series that used a model who strongly resembled the former first lady to sell their line of clothing. Citing *Negri v. Scering*- in which silent film star Pola Negri objected to the publication of a scene from one of her movies so captioned as to appear that she endorsed use of the antihistamine drug Polaramine- the Supreme Court of New York noted that 'if a picture is a clear and identifiable likeness of a living person, he or she is entitled to recover damages suffered by reason of such use'" (Creech, 2003). Pember (2003/2004) outlines examples of actions that can be regarded under appropriation as commercial use.

They are:

1. Use of a person's name or photograph in an advertisement on television, on radio, in newspapers, in magazines, on posters, on billboards and so forth.
2. Display of a person's photograph in the window of photographer's

shop to show potential customers the quality of work done by the studio.

3. A testimonial falsely suggesting that an individual eats the cereal or drives the automobile in question.

4. Use of an individual's name or likeness in a banner ad or some other commercial message on a web site.

5. The use of someone's likeness or identity in a commercial entertainment vehicle like a feature film, a television situation comedy or a novel.

The appropriation tort encompasses two legal causes of action. One is the right to privacy, and the other is the right of publicity. The differences between the two are small but important. The right to privacy protects an individual from the embarrassment and humiliation that can accrue when a name or picture is used without consent for advertising or trade purposes.

The right to publicity on the other hand, protects individuals from the exploitation of their names or likeness for commercial purposes. In other words, someone is making money by using another individual's name and photo. The right to privacy protects a personal right; the right to be free from such humiliation or embarrassment. The right to publicity protects a property right; the economic value in a name or likeness.

For instance, a regular Nigerian may wake up to see his or her picture on the box of Dangote noodle packs. He or she may argue that he/she suffered embarrassment and humiliation with such use but it will be difficult to claim that Dangote used his/her picture to sell the product because Nigerian children will buy and eat Dangote noodles because he/she eats it. But if Kanu Nwakwo or Funke Akindele's picture were used, either or both can claim right to publicity because they may believe that Nigerian children may buy the product if it is believed that they eat it.

Therefore, ordinary citizens can claim right to privacy while the famous can claim right to publicity. It is therefore important to note that the right to privacy dies with the death of an individual, but the right to publicity may live on. Only the living can claim that their right to privacy has been intruded upon. But if a famous person were to have heirs, the principle of descendibility will apply. That is, permission must be sought or payment for licensing must be made before the use of a name, picture or image of a late but famous person for commercial purposes. If this is not done, the heirs to the estate of late public figures can sue.

Intrusion

Intrusion involves the encroachment, invasion, or trespass by an individual on the solitude, seclusion or personal affairs of another. Intrusion can occur either physically or with the use of technological equipment or gadget. "Examples of intrusion consist of unreasonable searches; eavesdropping on conversations; surveillance by cameras, telescopes, or other devices; telephone harassment; peering into windows; and wiretapping...To be considered intrusion, the act clearly must encompass prying into matters that are of no public concern, and such prying must be judged offensive by a reasonable person" (Creech, 2003).

Intrusion is different from the other three privacy tort categories in an important way: Intrusion involves the collection of data about someone; the other three involves the publication of information about an individual. In an intrusion case, if the information has been gathered illegally, an intrusion has taken place. It doesn't really matter what the defendant does-if anything-with the data. The legal wrong takes place when the material is gathered. Under appropriation, publication of private facts, and false light privacy, it is the publication of the data that creates the legal wrong. How the information has been gathered is generally immaterial to those causes of action (Pember, 2003/2004).

One key concept to the tort of intrusion is the phrase "reasonable expectation of privacy".

If an act of intrusion occurs when the plaintiff is deemed to expect that he has a reasonable expectation of privacy, then, an intrusion can be deemed to have occurred. However, if a person is in a public place or in a situation where the court does not regard him as having any reasonable expectation of privacy then, information gathered in those situations will be deemed legal and no intrusion would have occurred.

Pember (2003/2004) cites the following cases to show that there is no expectation of privacy in public places: "A pharmacist in Seattle, Wash., sued KING-TV for invasion of privacy after the television station photographed the interior of his pharmacy through the front window. The druggist had been charged with cheating the state out of Medicaid funds. He refused to talk with the reporters after the charges were made, so the KING-TV camera operator placed the camera against the outside of the store's front window and photographed the druggist as he talked on the telephone. The filming was done from the exterior of the building, from a place open to the public.

The court ruled that an intrusion must be something that an intrusion must be something that the general public would not be free to view. In this case, any passerby could have seen what was recorded on film by the KING-TV camera operator. There was no unwarranted intrusion. American Airlines flight attendant Beverly Deteresa sued ABC for secretly recording a conversation she had with ABC producer Anthony Radziwill. The plaintiff worked the flight that O.J. Simpson took to Chicago the night that Nicole Brown Simpson and Ronald Goldman were killed. Radziwill asked Deteresa to appear on television as the two talked at her front door. She declined, but Radziwill secretly taped the conversation and instructed a camera crew across the street to videotape the discussion between the producer and the flight attendant.

A brief segment was later shown on ABC news. The 9th U.S. Circuit Court of Appeals affirmed a lower-court decision granting a summary judgment to the television network. There was no reasonable expectation of privacy when the plaintiff was talking with a journalist in plain sight of anyone who passed by on the public street. It is just unreasonable for individuals to expect privacy in other settings where people gather. A woman sitting in a restaurant complained of intrusion after a television news crew videotaped patrons sitting in the room. The Iowa Supreme Court ruled that someone sitting in a restaurant could not have a legitimate expectation of privacy. It is worthy of note that when intrusion occurs, it can be through the use of technological equipment like tape recorders, hidden cameras and others. There has been much debate on whether it is allowed or ethical. And different cases have been won or lost on the use of hidden recording devices.

In 1992, the Society of Professional Journalists and the Poynter Institute for Media Studies drafted guidelines for the use of hidden cameras.

These guidelines outlined in the American Journalism Review state that hidden cameras should be used only:

- When the information is of profound importance.
- When all other alternatives for obtaining the same information have been exhausted.
- When the individuals involved and the news organisations apply – through outstanding quality of work as well as the commitment of time and funding-the excellence needed to pursue the story fully.
- When the harm prevented by the information revealed through deception outweighs any harm caused by the act of deception.
- When the journalists involved have conducted meaningful, collaborative and deliberate decision to justify deception. Pember however notes that "the guidelines say that winning a prize, beating the competition, getting a story cheaply, doing it because others have done it

> or doing it because the subjects of the story are unethical are not sufficient reasons to justify the use of hidden cameras.

Worthy of note is the discussion on intrusion and the publication of stolen or illegally obtained materials. A number of times, journalists come across stolen or obtained illegally newsworthy materials. Past cases have proved that a journalist may not be liable if they are not involved in the theft or illegal acquisition and if they are not aware it was stolen. However, journalists are still expected to be careful with the use of such materials as its use may still constitute liability.

Publication of private (embarrassing) information about individuals

The third privacy tort is the publication by the media of private, truthful, non-defamatory but embarrassing information about an individual. Creech (2003) writes that "Sometimes an invasion of privacy case can be brought against the media for the publication of truthful, non- defamatory facts that are embarrassing to an identified individual. Generally these facts must be communicated to a widespread public, be private in nature (rather than newsworthy), and be highly offensive and objectionable to a reasonable person.

The plaintiff in a private facts case carries the burden of proving each element. Failure to convince the court of any one of these three parts of the law means the lawsuit is doomed (Pember, 2003/2004).

Publicity

For a private fact case to be established, it is essential that the plaintiff shows that the 'private' information was communicated to a large number of people. When a story is published in the media, it is taken for granted that it has already been publicised and that a large group of people are now aware of the information.

Private facts

A plaintiff in a private fact case will also have the burden of establishing that the information published about him are indeed private and they were not known to the public prior to that time. "If a large segment of the public is already aware of supposedly intimate or personal information, it is not private. Oliver Sipple, who deflected a gun held by a woman who tried to assassinate President Gerald Ford, sued the San Francisco Chronicle after a columnist noted that Sipple was a homosexual and that that may be the reason Ford has never thanked his benefactor for his heroic act. But Sipple's suit failed, in part at least, because his sexual orientation was hardly a secret in San Francisco. A California Court of Appeals noted that Sipple routinely frequented gay bars, marched in parades with other homosexuals, and openly worked for the election of homosexual political candidates, and that many gay publications had reported stories about his activities in the homosexual community. That he was a homosexual was not a private fact, the court ruled. A court in Massachusetts ruled that because the plaintiff in a private action had told three other persons about some personal information, the information was not a private fact for purpose of an invasion of privacy lawsuit" (Pember, 2003/2004). It is also worthy of note that documents and files and indeed all pieces of information that are considered to form part of public record, like court files, health records, police files and others can be published by the media without fear of liability. So should the names of rape victims or those of individuals who are sexually assaulted be published? There is a lot of contention on this. But the media should be guided more by ethics than by legislation on this issue.

Highly offensive legitimate public concern

After establishing that private facts about an individual have been publicised and to a large segment of the community, the plaintiff must also establish that the publication of the material is offensive to a reasonable person. It is the responsibility of the jury, or better put, it is a jury question to determine whether a material is offensive to a reasonable person or not. Pember (2003/2004) observes that "Frequently, courts are faced with the real dilemma that while revelation of the material was extremely offensive and embarrassing, its publication was of great importance for the public. Except in extremely unusual circumstances, the press will win such cases. The judiciary places great weight on the role of the press as an agent to inform and enlighten the public on matters of interest and importance. Judges have ruled time and again that it is the responsibility of the press to bring such "newsworthy" information to the people. And courts have been hesitant to define narrow limits on what the public needs to know or on the kinds of information in which the people have a genuine interest. And remember, the publication of the material must be offensive to a reasonable person. The feelings of a hypersensitive person or someone who is especially sensitive do not count." Creech (2003) cites the following cases:

- In 1964, in *Daily Times Democrat v. Graham*, Flora Bell Graham won a $4000 judgment against the Culiman County, Alabama *Daily Times Democrat*. The paper had published a picture of Graham taken as she emerged from a Fun House at a county fair. The 44-year-old housewife's skirt had been blown over her head by air jets, exposing her legs and underpants. Although the picture had been taken in a public place, the Alabama Supreme Court found the picture offensive to modesty and decency because it revealed private information in which the public had no legitimate interest.

- Certainly, *Time* magazine crossed the line when it photographed hospital patient Dorothy Barber against her will. Barber had a rare disease that caused her to lose weight even though she ate a great deal of food. *Time* referred to Barber as "The starving glutton" and "Insatiable Eater Barber" who "eats for ten." In *Barber v. Time* Inc., the Missouri Supreme Court found the story to be an invasion of privacy and noted that privacy rights include the receipt of medical treatment without "personal publicity".
- Stories dealing with matters of public concern are generally not subject to successful invasion-of-privacy claims. When the *Washington Post* printed an article about heroin addiction and included the photograph of Monica Little, who had been interviewed as part of the story, she sued for privacy invasion.

Little contended that although she had agreed to be interviewed, she had used false name and her family did not know that she was an addict. The use of a photograph had damaged her anonymity. She claimed that the Post had intentionally caused her emotional distress. In *Little v. Washington Post*, the U.S. District Court for the District of Columbia ruled against Little, stating that the public interest supports dissemination of accurate information about the risk of drugs and drug addiction, and that she waived her privacy rights when she agreed to the interview. In short, the *Post* did not go beyond the limits of her consent.

False light

The false-light tort involves the publication of false information that is highly offensive to an ordinary person. False-light invasions of privacy are similar to libel, but the important distinction is that the false light is non-defamatory. Libel actions are instigated to protect persons' reputations (i.e., the way they are viewed by society). False-light privacy actions stem from a person's right to be left alone and is based on the way people view themselves. Emotional distress is often the basis for false-light privacy suits. Unlike libel, false-light invasions of privacy actually may embellish one's reputation. When an unauthorised biography of famous baseball pitcher Warren Spahn portrayed him as a war hero, Spahn was able to bring a successful suit in

Messner Inc. v. Warren E. Spahn. Even though the material was flattering, the "gross misstatement of fact" portrayed the former pitcher in a false-light, thereby causing him emotional distress. False-light claims often result from dramatisations and fictional accounts of real-life incidents (Creech, 2003). There are three important elements in the tort:

The material is substantially false; the false statement or material is offensive to a reasonable person; the defendant who published the false material was at fault (Pember, 2003/2004). A 96-year-old Arkansas resident sued the *Sun* for using her photo to illustrate a totally fabricated story about a 101-year-old female newspaper carrier who had to give up her route because she was pregnant. Plaintiff Nellie Mitchell's photo had been published 10 years earlier in another tabloid owned by the same company in a true story about the Mountain Home, Ark. woman. But the editors at the *Sun* needed a picture to illustrate their phony story and simply used Mitchell's, undoubtedly thinking she was dead. A U.S. District Court jury awarded the elderly woman $1.5 million in damages. The simple rule for writers who want to be dramatists is this: If you change the facts, change the names and don't use photos of real people (Pember, 2003/2004).

In *Cantrell v. Forest City Publishing Co.* (1974), according to testimonial given in court, the story contained a number of inaccuracies.

It implied that reporters had spoken with Mrs. Cantrell in her home and that the home was untidy and her children were poorly clothed. Mrs. Cantrell charged that the story made them the objects of pity and ridicule. In reality, Mrs. Cantrell had not been present when reporter Joseph Eszterhaus came to call. Eszterhaus spoke with one of her children, while a photographer snapped some pictures.

Writing for the Supreme Court, Justice Potter Stewart noted: "There was no dispute during the trial that Eszterhaus...must have known that a number of the statements in the feature story were untrue. In particular, his article plainly implied that Mrs. Cantrell had been present during his visit to her home and that Eszterhaus had observed her "wearing the same mask of non- expression she wore at the funeral." These were "calculated falsehoods," and the jury was plainly justified in finding that Eszterhaus had portrayed the Cantrells in a false light through known or reckless untruth" (Creech, 2003).

Self-Assessmentexercise

Distinguish clearly among the four forms of invasion of privacy

Defense against Invasion of Privacy

The basic defenses against invasion of privacy suits are consent and newsworthiness. Others can be legitimate public interest and the use of public record.

If an individual had given consent for an interview or the use of his name or picture, he can no longer sue for invasion of privacy. Consent can be clearly stated (by word of mouth or the signing of a document) or it can be implied. For instance, Pember (2003/2004) cites the *Schifano v. Greene Country Greyhound Park, Inc.* case in which "Sam and Joseph Schifano sued the Greene County Greyhound Park, a dog racing track, for including their photo in an advertising brochure for the facility. The plaintiffs, who visited the park often, were photographed while they sat with several other persons in what is called The Winner's Circle, a section of the park that can be reserved by interested groups of spectators.

There was no written consent for the use of their picture, but there was ample evidence that park officials had told the plaintiffs why they were taking the pictures and gave them a chance to leave if they did not want to be in the picture. "Plaintiffs, neither by objecting nor moving, when those options were made available by park employees,consented to having their photograph taken at the park," the Alabama Supreme Court ruled in 1993". It is however worthy of note that consent does not always work as defense even if it was given by the plaintiff. Pember (2003) states three clear instances: i. Consent given today may not be valid in the distant future, especially if it is gratuitous oral consent. ii. Some persons cannot give consent. E.g. under age, psychologically deranged etc. iii. Consent to use the photograph of a person in an advertisement or on a poster cannot be used as defense if the photograph is materially altered or changed.

Newsworthiness is another strong defense in an invasion of privacy suit. If a story or event is newsworthy, this argument is likely to supersede embarrassing facts cases of invasion of privacy. "When a temporarily deranged man in Idaho ran nude out of his house brandishing a gun, a local television station filmed the event. On regaining his senses, the man filed an embarrassing privacy suit against the TV station. He claimed that the station could have edited the film so that he was not pictured nude. Although he won the initial judgment, in *Taylor v. KTVB, Inc.,* the Idaho Supreme Court ordered a new trial because the event was newsworthy" (Creech, 2003).

Public interest can also be a defense against a privacy suit. A good example is the case of *Little v. Washington Post,* cited earlier where the U.S. District Court for the District of Columbia ruled against Little, stating that the public interest supports dissemination of accurate information about the risk of drugs and drug addiction, and that she waived her privacy rights when she agreed to the interview. The use of public record can also be a defense in a privacy suit. Information already in the public domain or in public records can be published by the media. When newsworthy private facts are part of the public record, suit cannot be brought (Creech 2003).

LAW AND ETHICAL REGULATION OF THE NEW MEDIA

This unit explores the new media, the challenges that accompany its regulation and the implications of publishing defamatory or indecent materials through the Internet or infringing on the copyright of author's work on the Internet.

Objectives

At the end of this unit, you should be able to:

- explain the various aspects of the new media
- enumerate regulations against indecent publication on the Internet
- state the implications of publishing defamatory materials on the Internet
- write on copyright infringement on author's work on the Internet.

Main Content

New Media in Nigeria: The Challenges of Regulation

The media are the channels of communication that allow information to be passed to a large, heterogeneous and widely dispersed audience. Until the 19th century, the known media of communication, which are now referred to as the traditional mass media are; newspapers and magazines, radio, television, and film.

With the advent of the computer came new channels of communication that involve the transmission of information, also to a large heterogeneous audience, but through the use of digital technology, usually the Internet. These media are popularly referred to as the 'new media' and there are different forms of new media channels but almost all are accessible only using new and recent technologies like the desktop computers, laptops, smart phones, and tablets all linked to the Internet. Information is available on the Internet through websites, news groups, chat forums, bulletin boards, e-mails, blogs and social networking sites. A plethora of laws are available to protect private individuals and corporate bodies from the activities of the media and check the commission of civil and criminal offences using the traditional media. However, there are a lot of challenges when it comes to the protection of the rights of individuals from publications on the Internet or remedying violations of rights committed on or via the Internet. This is because there is a dearth of laws on Internet regulation in Nigeria, and indeed the world over. Besides, the global nature of the Internet makes it very cumbersome and almost impossible to regulate its use and this probably explains why a lot of individuals publish whatever they deem fit with reckless abandon on the Internet as it is regarded as a regulation-free zone. So pathetic is it that in September 2011in Nigeria, a video was posted on the Internet of an alleged female student of Abia State University in South East Nigeria who was gang-raped by five male students. The ordeal (based on the video recording) lasted for about an hour and at a point, the victim became suicidal, asking that she be killed. I do not know which is worse, the fact that she was raped or the fact that the rapists found it exciting enough to share their atrocity with the world! Some people who watched the video commented (on chat forums) that she was not a student but a street hawker. I ask: does anyone deserve to be raped? In any case, the essence of the illustration is just to show one fact; people the world over see the Internet as a no-law zone and a 'space' in which they can do as they please! Unfortunately, this is not the case. There is regulation in the world and the new media and indeed the Internet is not exempted. The laws that apply to the traditional media also apply to the new media and violations executed on the Internet can be redressed.

There are no specific laws on the new media in Nigeria but there are laws that regulate the media that can be extended to proceedings on their violations if and when they occur on the Internet. The statutes that seek to regulate violations committed using the Internet or the new media are more concerned with cyber crimes or financial crimes, not intellectual property or other civil rights.

In all, it is obvious that Nigeria is far behind in legislating on crimes and offences that can be committed using the Internet and until this is done, proceedings on violations of rights committed via the Internet may not be instituted. This is a big loop-hole that will encourage the violation of civil and intellectual property rights and an impairment of creativity. Surprisingly, the new media is in wide use in Nigeria. Almost all traditional media organisation have a website on which they publish and/or broadcast the messages and audio and/or video messages that have been earlier published or that are simultaneously published in the new media. It is therefore advisable for these media organisations, individual journalists or authors and private persons and organisations who use the new media to apply existing media law and ethics to their publications on the Internet in order not to be culpable as a judge or court may derive a law or principle to try criminal and/or civil violations on/via the Internet pending the time that Nigeria will derive contemporary laws to address this area. In dealing with the Internet and media laws, we will have to depend on cases from the West as there is a scarcity, if not an absence of such litigations in Nigeria.

Self-Assessmentexercise

Why do you think there is a dearth of Internet or new media specific laws in Nigeria?

Internet and Defamation

We have learnt that "defamation is a communication which exposes a person to hatred, ridicule, or contempt, lowers him in the esteem of his fellows, causes him to be shunned, or injures him in his business or calling". (Phelps and Hamilton, 1996) In a proceeding for defamation, an element that must be proved is publication, and publication occurs when a third party, (other than the defamer and the one who is defamed) is exposed to the defamatory message.

According to Overs (2002) "Those working in the media should apply the existing legal principles of defamation to any material published in new media format in order to avoid being sued for defamation."

International Nature of Internet Defamation

The nature of the Internet is delicate, so delicate is it that whatever is published automatically is available to be read, heard, viewed and downloaded worldwide. This increases the impact of defamatory messages published online. This provides the prospective claimant the opportunity to choose where to issue proceedings and what law to use. This is due to the fact that an action for defamation can arise in the country where the information is downloaded and viewed as well as in the country where it is posted online. Claimants will just have to confirm the law and the opportunities and challenges of the respective countries and the provisions they have on defamation via the Internet.

In Overs (2002), "the courts are beginning to recognise the complex issues involved in defamatory statements published on the Internet and read in other jurisdictions. In 2000, the House of Lords held that a Russian businessman could sue a United States magazine called *Forbes* in England in respect of alleged defamatory statements published on the magazine's website (*Berezovsky v Michaels (2000*). In the case of *Gutnick v Dow Jones (2001)* the Australian Supreme Court allowed Gutnick, an Australian, to sue Dow Jones, a United States company, for defamation in Australia in relation to an article published by Dow Jones on its website. The court rejected the contention by Dow Jones that the proceedings should take place in the United States because the article was only intended to be read there." If an individual or body corporate however issues proceeding in another jurisdiction, they must worry about enforcement as there are courts that do not recognise judgments in other jurisdiction if there is no mutual agreement or joint law between them and the issuing jurisdiction.

Self-Assessmentexercise

Why is defamation on the Internet actionable?

Internet and Copyright

Copyright is a law that protects intangible property. It seeks to prevent people from publishing and reproducing the works of others without their consent and permission.

Copyright subsists in every original literary, dramatic, musical or artistic work and it belongs to the author of the work or the individual who commissions and/or pays for it. Copyright is infringed with the unauthorised publication, production, reproduction or copying of an author's original work without his consent or permission.

There are domestic laws in every country of the world to protect the copyright in works published in their jurisdictions. However, the Internet makes works (print, multimedia) available to everyone worldwide and the copyright law that protects these works in the countries where they are posted does not protect them in other countries (jurisdictions) the world over where they will be assessed. Even the Nigerian Copyright Decree No 47 of 1988 (See Section 2 (1a&b)) protects only copyright in works printed or published: in Nigeria, by Nigerian authors, by persons domiciled in Nigeria, or body corporate incorporated under the laws of Nigeria. The modification to the Nigerian Copyright law: Copyright Act CAP. 68 LFN 1990 has not altered this section. "For international copyright protection under the Universal Copyright Convention the formula ©, the name of the copyright owner and the date of first publication must be placed on a work" (Overs, 2002). The global nature of the Internet means that the international protection of copyright is of considerable importance. Two international treaties on copyright, the Berne Convention and the Universal Copyright Convention, provide for possible world-wide protection of copyright for authors of original material. Many countries, including the United Kingdom and the United States, are signatories to both conventions. In addition, the WIPO (World Intellectual Property Organisation) co- ordinates and administers international treaties relating to intellectual property protection (ibid). Different continental organisations are also working hard to collaborate on the protection of copyright of authors in their domain. "There is a little harmonisation of copyright laws throughout the member states of the European Union. In an effort to provide a more uniform system of regulation, the European Union has recently approved two directives that promote and facilitate the exchange of information in new media formats. The Copyright Directive (2002/29/EC) was approved in 2001 and is aimed at ensuring that all works protected by copyright are adequately protected throughout the European Union. The E-commerce Directive (2000/31/EC) was approved in 2000 and is aimed at harmonising certain legal aspects of 'information society services' in Europe, in particular electronic commerce" (ibid).

Another important aspect of copyright and the Internet which the media must note involve the aspect of contract. When full time employees write or produce (broadcast) for a media organisation, the organisation can publish it in print or broadcast version and still publish it on the Internet because the copyright belongs to the employer. However, when a media organisation commissions a freelance journalist to write or produce a multimedia product for it, it must ensure it is clearly spelt out that the work will be used in the traditional media as well as the Internet so as not to be culpable as the freelance journalist may sue for infringement if the agreement is not clear.

Sometimes, a media organisation which is recently hosted on the Internet may post pre-existing works and contributions on its pages. As stated earlier, if the contributions are from full time employees, there will be no problem. But if the pre-existing contributions are from third parties, it is important to secure their consent/permission before posting such works on the Internet in order to avoid an infringement proceeding.

Self-Assessmentexercise

Does the Berne Convention have any impact on the Nigerian copyright law?

Internet and Morality

The laws still affect publications on the Internet as such publications of any article are capable of corrupting persons who are likely to read, see or hear it. In Nigeria, Obscene Publications Act No 15 of 1961, Children and Young

Persons (Harmful Publications Act, 1961, Child's Right Act of 2003 and Trafficking in Persons (Prohibition) Law Enforcement and Administration Act, No. 24 2003 are some of the laws that can be evoked to combat the publication of indecent and obscene material on the Internet in Nigeria. A lot of them forbid the publication of indecent and obscene articles but they are not specific to the Internet. The Child's Right Act of 2003 now makes publication of pornographic pictures of children an offence. In the United Kingdom, under the Obscene Publications Act 1959, as amended by the Criminal Justice and Public Order Act 1994, a person who makes obscene material available for transmission or downloads or communicates obscene material by electronic transmission commits an offence.

"It is not possible to access the Internet without an Internet service provider. As a result, the Internet Service Providers have been targeted

by law enforcement agencies and action groups for providing access to obscene material. For example, in Germany in 1997 the local manager of CompuServe was prosecuted in connection with child pornography on the Internet, which was hosted on CompuServe's servers. However, the Government and the European Union support self-regulation by Internet service providers rather than the passing of specific obscenity legislation. Under article 15 of the E-commerce Directive, Internet service providers will not be obliged to monitor the information and content transmitted and stored on their systems, although they will be required to remove unlawful material from their sites if it is brought to their attention" (Overs, 2002). Adebiyi (2009) says "The dissemination of pornography, via the Internet has raised numerous legal questions. The major issues that need to be examined are in respect of the liability of the author of the material and the additional liability of the network service provider." Adebiyi (ibid) cites the "American case of *State of New York v. BuffNet*, An Internet service provider (ISP) pleaded guilty to the misdemeanour charge of knowingly providing access to child pornography. A two-year investigation found that ISP, BuffNet, knowingly hosted a child pornography newsgroup called "Pedo University". The police notified BuffNet that they were hosting illegal content, yet BuffNet failed to remove the newsgroup from its servers. Police then seized the ISP's servers. BuffNet was levied a $5000 fine, and removed the obscene content."

Self-Assessmentexercise

In what respect does the mass media law in Nigeria relevant to social media?

CONCLUSION

Law is one of the key elements that shape society. The functions of laws are numerous. Law holds the society firm to save it from falling apart. It therefore implies that if there is any lapses in law, it make proportional impact in the growth and development of the society.

The law of defamation exists not just to check the press, but also to protect the rights of individuals in the society. The media must ensure that they do not impinge on the rights of individuals and organisations in their role as watchdogs of the society.

Ethics is the foundation of morality and law in every society. The culture, civilisation, customs and religion of a people determine the values they will regard as ethical and the ones they will see as abominable. It is necessary, if not mandatory for every society to have a generally accepted level of ethics or standards in order to ensure stability, peace and progress.

The security of a state is the first priority of the government, the citizens and every stakeholder in the country. A secure state is already half-way to development because such a state would have cordial relationship with the neighboring countries and thereby enjoy mutual benefit with them

The right to privacy seeks to protect the individual. The media must ensure that in the discharge of its duties of informing the public and acting as watchdogs, it does not intrude into the lives of the citizens.

There are no much law regulating the legal and social atrocities committed on the Internet and little or nothing is being done to address this grave challenge in Nigeria. Adebiyi's (2009) comment captures the situation completely: "Much of the international work has so far been centered in western European and OECD countries; the potential extent of computer crime is as broad as the extent of the international telecommunication systems. All regions of the world must become involved in order to prevent this new form of criminality. Ensuring the integrity of computer systems is a challenge facing both developed and developing countries. It is predicted that within the next decade, it will be necessary for developing nations to experience significant technological growth in order to become economically self-sufficient and more competitive in world markets. As dependence on computer technology grows in all nations, it will be crucial to ensure that the rate of technological dependence does not outstrip the rate at which the corresponding social, legal and political frameworks are developing. It is important to plan for security and crime prevention at the same time that computer technology is being implemented."

SUMMARY

From the discussion above, you should understand that law protect individuals and the state, it preserves life and property; it promotes the administration of justice, it preserves social welfare; and it brings about change and transformation. All these are tantamount to development in a society.

In this unit, we examined defamation, its definition, essential elements, defenses, and remedies. We distinguished libel from slander, noting that slander occurs when an individual or group's reputation is attacked through spoken words or gesture, especially believed to be false and malicious and libel as a false statement that exposes people to hatred, ridicule or contempt. The essential elements of defamation, amongst others are publication, identification, and defamation. Defenses against libel include justification, fair comment, privilege, unintentional defamation, accord and satisfaction: release and many others.

Finally, we identified remedies for defamation, which include damages, publication of apology, and offer of amends.

Ethics is a system of moral or respectable conduct that guides the actions of individuals and organisations in an organised society. Ethics is different from law as not all ethical values are enforceable by the courts but most laws have their foundation in ethical standards. Society needs to have a system of ethics to ensure stability and cohesion.

In this unit, the focus was on the media roles in ensuring the security of the state. Mass media play key roles in this respect and some of the roles form the major discussion in this unit Privacy is "The right to be left alone" (Cooley, 1888). It is also known as "The right of the individual to be protected against intrusion into his personal life or affairs, or those of his family, by direct physical means or by publication of information" (Calcutt Committee; 1990). There are four privacy torts: Appropriation, which is the use of a person's name or likeness for commercial use without permission or consent; intrusion, which is the invasion of an individual's solitude to illegally gather information about him/her; publication of embarrassing private facts about a person which are of no legitimate public concern and the publication of information that put a person in false light. Consent, newsworthiness, legitimate public interest and the use of public record are the available defenses in a privacy suit.

We have discussed the Internet and how defamation, obscene publication and copyright infringement can be committed on the Internet. The Internet, by making information posted on it available to the whole world simultaneously publishes the information posted on it automatically, an important element in defamation and obscene publication cases. Media organisations and individual authors must ensure that they apply the regular media laws in their publications on the Internet as they do while publishing in traditional media.

TUTOR-MARKED ASSIGNMENT

Law can save any society from falling apart. Do you agree?

What methods can be adopted by a media house to ensure it avoids lawsuits and charges of defamation?

A system of ethics is a cover-up for unofficial censorship. Discuss

If you have just been given license to establish and operate a radio station in Nigeria, in what ways can you support the struggle for the protection of the state security?

Interview a soft-sell magazine editor on his or her paper's policy on privacy and the procedure he or she employs in avoiding privacy suits

Will regulation of the Internet hinder the freedom of expression? Interview a member or executive of the Nigerian Union of Journalist for his/her opinion, on the question.

REFERENCES/FURTHER READING

1. Brown, S. (2008). Crime and Law in Media Culture. New York: Bell and Bain Ltd.
2. Elias, T. O. (1969). Nigerian Press Law. London: Evans Brothers Ltd.
3. Makowsky, R. C. (2010). The Discovery of Society. New York: McGraw-Hill.
4. Oloyede, B. (2008). Free Press and Society: Dismantling the Culture of Silence. Ibadan: Stirling-Horden Publishers Ltd.
5. Oyakhilomen, G. I. (2006). Nigerian Legal System I. Kaduna: National Open University of Nigeria.
6. Oyakhilomen, G. I. (2009). Introduction to Law. Kaduna: National Open
7. University of Nigeria
8. Article Global Campaign for Free Expression (2000). Defining Defamation- Principles on Freedom of Expression and Protection of Reputation, London. Retrieved from http://www.article.org/data/files/pdfs/standards/definingdefam ation.pdf on February 2, 2012.
9. Bowles, D. A. & Borden, D. L. (2004). Creative Editing. (4th ed.). Belmont, USA: Wadsworth/Thomson.
10. Criminal Libel. The Free Legal Dictionary by Farlex. Retrieved from

http://legal-dictionary.thefreedictionary.com/Criminal+libel on February 3, 2012. Crone, T. (2002).

11. Law and the Media (4th ed.). Oxford, Great Britain: Focal Press. Fakayode, E. M. (1977) The Criminal Code Companion. Nigeria: Ethiope Publishing.
12. Kayne, R. (2012) What is Slander? WiseGeek: Clear answers for Common Questions. Retrieved from http://www.wisegeek.com/what-is-slander.htm on February 10,. Nylander, A. V. J., (1969) "Defamation and the Press." In: T. O. Elias Nigerian Press Law. Lagos: University of Lagos and Evans Brothers Limited. Okoye, I. (2008). Media Law and Ethics, Lagos: National Open University of Nigeria.
13. Swindler, W. F. (1955). Problems of Law in Journalism. Westport, Conn.: Greenwood Press.
14. Black, J., Steele, B., & Barney, R. (1999). Doing Ethics in Journalism. (3rd ed.). Massachusetts: Allyn & Bacon. Bowles, D. & Borden, D. (2004). Creative Editing. (4th ed.). Belmont: Thomas Wadsworth.
15. Caster. H. (1983). "The Problems of Ethics in the Mass Media." A paper presented at the Nigerian Press Council National Workshop held at Aja, Lagos, Nigeria from April 9-12, 2006.
16. Christians, C. G., Mark, F., Kim B. R., & Kathy, B. M. (1998). Media Ethics: Cases and Moral Reasoning. (5th ed.). New York: Longman
17. Day, L. A. (2006). Ethics in Media Communications. (5th ed.). Belmont: Thomas Wadsworth.
18. Frost, C. (2007). Journalism Ethics and Regulation. (2nd ed.). Essex: Pearson Education Limited. Neher, W. W., & Sandin, P. J. (2007).
19. Communicating Ethically: Character, Duties, Consequences, and Relationships. Boston: Pearson Education, Inc.
20. Olen, J. (1998). Ethics in Journalism. Upper Saddle River, NJ: Prentice-Hall.
21. Okoye, I. (2008). Media Law and Ethics. Lagos: National Open University.
22. Sinha, J. (2009). A Manual of Ethics. Kolkata: New Central Book Agency Ltd.
23. Imobigbe, T. A. (2003). *Nigeria's Defence and National Security Linkages: A Framework of Analysis.* Ibadan: Heinemann Education Books Nigeria Plc. Elias, T. O. (1969).
24. *Nigerian Press Law.* London: Evans Brothers Ltd.
25. Mojaye, E. M. (2012). "The Press, Politics And Journalism." *Journal of*

Communication And Media Research, 41 - 49.

26. Sambe, J. A. (2004). *Mass Media Law And Ethics in Nigeria* . Ibadan: Caltop Publications Nigeria Ltd.
27. Creech, K. C. (2003). *Electronic Media Law and Regulation*. (4th ed.). USA; Elsevier Science (Focal Press).
28. Cooley, T. M. (1888). *A Treatise on the Law of Torts*. Chicago: Callaghan & Co.
29. Lissit, R. "Gotcha." *American Journalism Review*, 17, March 1995,
30. *Onassis v. Christian Dior (NY Sup.Ct., 1984) 10 Med.L.Rptr at 1861.*
31. Pember, D. R. (2003/2004) Mass Media Law. New York: McGraw-Hill.
32. Report of the Committee on Privacy and Related Matters 1990 Cmnd. 1102, London: HMSO at 7.
33. *Schifano v. Greene Country Greyhound Park, Inc.*, 624 So. 178 (1993).
34. Spilsbury, S. (2000.). *Media Law*. London: Cavendish Publishing Limited.Warren, S. D. & Brandeis, L. D. (1890). "The Right of Privacy," *Harvard Law Review* 4. Pg. 193-220.
35. Adebiyi, A. (2009). *Internet Crime: The Nigerian Perspective.* Presented at the 1st Annual Conference on Cyber Security by the Anti-Money Laundering and Cyber Security Coalition.
36. Children and Young Persons (Harmful Publications Act, 1961.
37. Child's Right Act of 2003.
38. Copyright Decree No 47 of 1988.
39. Creech, K. C. (2003). *Electronic Media Law and Regulation* (4th ed.). USA: Focal Press (Elsevier Science).
40. Obscene Publications Act No 15 of 1961 Overs, E. (2002). "Copyright." In: T. Crome (Ed.). *Law and the Media* (4th ed.). Oxford: Focal Press.
41. Phelps, R. & Doughlas H. (1996). *Libel.* New York: Macmillan.
42. Spilsbury, S. (2000) *Media Law*. London: Cavendish Publishing Ltd.
43. Trafficking in Persons (Prohibition) Law Enforcement and Administration Act, No. 24 2003.

Chapter 9

JOURNALISM STUDENTS AS COMMUNITY NEWS PROVIDERS: THREE CASE STUDIES AND AN ANALYSIS OF INTELLECTUAL PROPERTY ISSUES RELATED TO STUDENTCREATED CONTENT

INTRODUCTION

So many news outlets; so little news. That could be the headline for the Federal Communications Commission's 2011 report The Information Needs of Communities by Steven Waldman, which describes in detail the landscape of commercial and nonprofit media and the regulatory landscape in which they operate. The digital revolution has spawned a proliferation of online sources of information, but Waldman's research documents a concomitant decline in news reporting, particularly that pertaining to state and local governments. Citing numerous previous analyses and case studies, the report summarizes the evidence:

- In just four years, from 2006 to 2010, the workforce in daily newspaper newsrooms dropped by nearly 25 percent to 41,600, which was roughly the size of the daily newsroom workforce before Watergate (40).
- Statehouse news bureaus have shrunk, by one estimate by as much as one-third, with more than 50 newspapers nationally terminating statehouse coverage altogether between 2003 and 2009, according to data compiled by the American Journalism Review (44-45).
- The number of regional reporters working in Washington also has shrunk, with more than half of the states now having no reporter in the nation's capital (50).

The FCC report quotes Bill Girdner, owner and editor of a California wire service that covers legal issues, who explains succinctly why all of this matters. When journalists aren't present, he said, "others control the information process" (48). The FCC report contains a plethora of recommendations, but of particular interest to journalism educators is its endorsement of the idea that journalism schools should take a more active role in producing journalism for their communities (355).

To that end, Part I of this document reports on the results of research conducted under a Knight Foundation grant to examine efforts by journalism classes at the University of Nebraska-Lincoln to provide news content for specific audiences, particularly those that historically have been underserved. A companion grant to the University of Texas at Austin supported research on similar J-school community news efforts in Texas. Additionally, Part II of this report, supported by the Knight Foundation grant, is an examination of intellectual property issues related to having students provide community news. John Bender, a professor in the UNL College of Journalism and Mass Communications, explores copyright and public records issues as they pertain to student-created news content and also comments on whether establishing such news-generating projects as 501(c)3 entities has merit.

The idea that journalism schools can and should be engaged in providing community news is not a new one. The FCC report describes numerous such efforts, some of which have been ongoing for decades, largely in urban settings on the east and west coasts (194-196). But these reports, focusing on efforts in Nebraska and Texas, will add new dimensions to the discussion. Specifically, the UNL community news efforts shed light on serving the unique needs of the underserved refugee and rural communities, particularly those with weekly newspapers, which are not addressed in the FCC report. The three case studies examined in this report are:

- Nebraska Mosaic, News and Information for Lincoln's New Americans. This website, cojmc.unl.edu/mosaic/, aims to reach Lincoln's refugees and the broader community with stories about refugees and their experiences. It also aims to provide opportunities for refugees to contribute their own stories and to learn more about navigating their new environment.
- Nebraska News Service. This news bureau provides state government news coverage to small dailies and weeklies throughout the state and to about a dozen radio and television stations.
- UNL-Seward County Independent partnership. For nearly three decades, students from UNL summer school reporting classes have worked at the weekly Seward County Independent as part of their course, providing Fourth of July coverage and special projects that the four-person editorial staff of this community newspaper otherwise would not have time to accomplish.

This report offers a detailed examination of each project, describing the origins of each one, how it works and how its stakeholders see it. It also attempts to assess these projects in connection with the FCC report's recommendations and addresses questions of the long-term sustainability of efforts like these to fill the community news gap. Finally, this report offers some observations about possible best practices that seem to have evolved from these projects or, at the very least, pitfalls to avoid. Journalism programs interested in embarking on community news operations may wish to consider some of these common threads and practical ideas. Expanding research on these kinds of operations at other schools in other regions also may prove fruitful as a way to compile lessons learned so journalism educators more broadly could benefit.

The Case Studies

Methodology

The three case studies reported here are based on two dozen interviews with a wide variety of stakeholders reflecting various aspects of each of the projects. The interviews sought to explore the following themes:

- The extent to which stakeholders perceive a need for increased news coverage
- Specific details of how each project was started and how it operates
- Whether the content being produced appears to meet perceived needs
- Stumbling blocks the projects have encountered
- What it would take to make the projects more successful

Graduate student Charlie Litton conducted all of the interviews from February through April 2012, and all were either audio or video recorded. Interviews were either face-to-face or by telephone in circumstances when face-to-face interviews were impossible. Many of the interviews conducted for the Nebraska News Service case study took place during the Nebraska Press Association's annual spring conference, which several hundred editors and publishers attend. Litton was able to arrange individual interviews with editors who subscribe to the Nebraska News Service while they were attending the conference. His interview schedule also took him to several communities around the state to visit editors and other stakeholders. A list of the interviewees and the time and location of each interview appears as an appendix to this report. All direct quotes and paraphrased information attributed to specific interviewees are taken from the interviews unless otherwise noted. No attempt was made to locate and interview systematically any of the students who have participated in these community news projects, and indeed, the FCC report does not directly address the impact on students from participating in such projects. Most published discussions of 8 J-schools as community news providers assume a positive impact on student learning, but the views of some of the faculty members interviewed for this report raise questions about the educational merit of these programs. So the educational value of these efforts should be analyzed more systematically than is done here as journalism programs seek to embark on similar efforts. Likewise, these case studies do not attempt to determine in any systematic way the impact of these projects on their intended audiences, a research task that at best is problematic in any case. Nonetheless, the stakeholder interviews contain significant anecdotal evidence that suggest what kind of impact these projects have had.

[Author's note: Litton served as a graduate student assistant and a class member for the Mosaic project and also was a reporter for the Nebraska News Service. Additionally, I have taught the Seward summer school class since 2000 and also serve as NNS bureau chief. We both have an insider's advantage or disadvantage in conducting this qualitative research, depending on one's point of view. But as journalists trained to be skeptical, I believe we have brought an analytical mind to bear in distancing ourselves from our own experiences and examining what our sources told us about these three community news projects. Readers, of course, are free to come to their own conclusions.]

Mosaic: News and Information for Lincoln's New Americans

How it got started; how it works

No one knows how many refugees live in Lincoln. Or in Nebraska, for that matter. But the federal Office of Refugee Resettlement reports than since 2000, some 6,100 refugees have been resettled in the Cornhusker State. Last year alone, 738 refugees from 13 countries found new homes in Nebraska, whose total population is about 1.8 million. Refugee resettlement nationally dipped dramatically after 9/11, but the numbers have been growing, and Lincoln has resumed its historic role as a refugee resettlement community, largely because of the low cost of housing and low unemployment that makes it easier for newcomers to get a foothold. While federal data account for the states where refugees are initially settled, no one tracks what happens to them thereafter. Refugees, like most residents of the United States, are free to pick up and move. They hear of better jobs or better weather or bigger communities of their fellow countrymen and pull up stakes for a new home. It's this secondary migration that makes it difficult to know precisely how many people in any given community could be classified as refugees. In Lincoln, Nebraska, population 258,379, another way to look at the refugee population is to consider the Lincoln Public Schools' English Language Learner program. In the 2011-12 school year, the district served 2,212 English language learners, who spoke a total of 56 languages other than English. Twenty years ago, the program served just 388 students. And a school official who has been with the district for 30 years recalled that in those days, non English speakers almost exclusively spoke Vietnamese or Cambodian, a reflection of post Vietnam refugee resettlement. While Spanish is now the most common non-English home language of Lincoln ELL students, most of the children who speak Spanish are likely immigrants, according to school officials, while those who speak Arabic, Karen or Vietnamese, for example, are likely refugees or the children of refugees. (For more information on refugee numbers in Nebraska see "Just how many refugees are there in Nebraska?" by Emily Nohrat Nebraska Mosaic, cojmc.unl.edu/mosaic/).

In the fall of 2010, the UNL College of Journalism and Mass Communications set out to reach three groups of these hard-to-count refugees with a $25,000 grant from J-Lab: The Institute for Interactive Journalism at American University. The idea was to create sources of news and information for communities that either had lost their voices or never had one. While most grantees defined community in terms of geography, the UNL grant focused on three communities of refugees new to Lincoln: Iraqis, Sudanese and Karen, a beleaguered Christian ethnic minority largely from Burma and Thailand. In 2011, the Lincoln Community Foundation was awarded a $24,000 grant for the project from the Knight Community Information Challenge, which the foundation matched with $24,000. The first grant was used to fund initial research, buy video and audio equipment, pay for website development and cover various miscellaneous expenses. The second grant is being used to take the project out into the community, including work with a family literacy class at an elementary school and to pay refugees to produce stories for the website.

The project grew out of a fall 2009 multimedia journalism class that associate professor Tim Anderson taught with another faculty member in which they assigned their students to read Mary Pipher's book "The Middle of Everywhere: The World's Refugees Come to Our Town." The book documents the lives of refugees from all over the world who have made Lincoln their home. Students in the multimedia class were expected to devote half of their assignments to stories related to immigrants and refugees. So many engaging stories emerged that Anderson was convinced more could be done.

The following spring, when J-Lab announced its New Voices grant competition, Anderson and several other UNL journalism faculty members started brainstorming ideas and settled on a proposal to focus on immigrants and refugees. Anderson said J-Lab liked the idea but considered it too broad, so the planners suggested "refugee communities in Lincoln," which was again deemed too broad. Eventually the college suggested refugees from Iraq, Sudan and former Soviet bloc countries. Iraqi refugees began arriving in Lincoln in the aftermath of the first Gulf War, and the second wave of refugees continues today. Sudanese refugees have been in Lincoln longer than many other refugee groups, and Nebraska has more Sudanese refugees than any other state, with most of them living in Omaha. But refugees from the former Soviet bloc countries posed a number of problems. The planners heard anecdotal accounts of ethnic conflicts among various groups of those refugees and didn't want to have to deal with that complication as the project was getting underway. At the same time, the planners learned from representatives of a local government agency that works with refugees that a new group, the Karen, were beginning to arrive from Burma. The project planners were intrigued with the idea of focusing on a brand new refugee group alongside the Sudanese and Iraqis, who were more settled in Lincoln, so the Karen replaced the former Soviet bloc refugees as one of the three initial groups on which the project would focus.

While immigrants as well as refugees could be the audience for a website that offers "News and Information for Lincoln's New Americans," the project consciously started out focusing specifically on refugees, who are here not necessarily by choice. In some cases they might prefer to be home with their families, but for most, even visiting their homeland would be perilous.

The project sought to identify the information needs of the three refugee groups and figure out how best to reach them and address those needs. To accomplish that, the college offered a cross-disciplinary course for advertising and journalism majors to lay the groundwork, largely through a series of focus groups, and their findings were not surprising. Refugees clearly are underserved by traditional media, which tend to focus on the invariably dramatic tales of refugees coming to the United States, if they cover refugees at all. But for their part, refugees aren't interested in those stories, which, to them, are all too familiar. Instead, the student researchers found, the refugees would really rather learn the basics about navigating their new home, stories local media seldom tell, but which historically have been the staples of the foreign language press once common in large urban centers. Indeed, that is also what the American penny press of the 1830s and 1840s did for rural Americans and immigrants arriving in cities. (See, for example, Karen Halttunen's "Confidence Men and Painted Women" and Michael Schudson's "Discovering the News.")

The research phase also identified unique information needs some refugees have. If, for example, you lived for decades in a dirt-floored refugee camp hut without running water, as did most of the Karen refugees, your information needs will include things like why sweeping the floor and discarding spoiled food from the refrigerator is a good idea now and then. An array of community agencies, many driven by volunteers, attempt to help meet refugees' needs, but access can by limited by the diffuse nature of the services. So one of the major goals of the Mosaic project became collating information about the various agencies and services available to assist the newcomers.

Language barriers and lack of computer savvy also make it difficult for refugees—and non-English-speaking immigrants, for that matter—to contend with the Department of Motor Vehicles, police and fire departments, and other commonplace American bureaucracies. Even the federal food stamp program, for which many refugees qualify, is accessible only through a daunting online application form written in English. The student researchers found that people in the three refugee communities generally did not have easy access to computers or smart phone technology and that the best way to reach refugees was by radio, preferably in their native language. Despite the research findings, however, terms of the initial grant required Mosaic to create an English-language website to reach its target audience. After the first semester's research phase that involved advertising as well as journalism students, subsequent semesters of the Mosaic class have exclusively enrolled journalism students, graduate as well as undergraduate. Beginning in October 2011, the students met once a week with refugee families participating in Arnold Elementary School's after-school Community Learning Center family literacy class, which proved to be a mutually beneficial opportunity for the students to break out of their comfort zone and for the refugees to practice their conversational English.

The public launch of the Mosaic website came on Nov. 3, 2011, with a program on the UNL campus that an estimated 50 people attended, including about a dozen Karen and Iraqi refugees. Promotional efforts since then have been limited to word of mouth, but visits to the site have grown steadily. Anderson, who teaches the Mosaic class and manages the site, reported the site had 1,500 views in January, 2,800 in February and 2,834 in March. On average, visitors spent 3.4 minutes on the site in January, compared to 5.39 minutes in March. Anderson plans to embark on broader promotional efforts to reach Lincoln residents in general through avenues such as buying ads on city buses.

The website does, indeed, reflect the mosaic of newcomers who have made Lincoln their home, with stories, videos and photos about them and their experiences. By the end of May 2012, a total of 97 stories had been posted and the 22 videos on the site had received more than 1,400 views. Stories on the site profile several ethnic restaurants, explain how a Karen couple came to open an Asian food market, and describe experiences of refugees voting in their first American election. The website also includes a number of examples of the kind of information aimed at helping newcomers acclimate to the community and solve real problems. One story describes a training program for refugee and immigrant women who want to become licensed child care providers. Another describes training offered by StarTran, the local public transit service, to teach people how to use the bus system. Still another features a small business loan program for refugees started by a prominent retired Lincoln banker.

One Mosaic project resulted in two videos that explain how to prevent and treat bed bug infestations. The videos were produced in English and translated into Arabic, French, Burmese and Karen, using translators from the refugee community. French was chosen as a target language because most African refugees know either Arabic or French or both. Creating the bed bug videos was a complicated process because a sentence that might have taken eight seconds to read in English turned out to take 12 or 13 seconds in Arabic and 15 seconds in Burmese and Karen, which meant that the audio tracks couldn't just be swapped. Instead each video had to be recut specifically for each language.

Stakeholders' views: Pluses, minuses and academic considerations

In some respects, Mosaic is like any startup in the digital arena. As Anderson put it, you have to be willing to "fail early and often." Making a mistake with an online publication, he noted, isn't nearly as consequential as it might be for a print publication. While "failure" would be an overstatement to describe some stakeholders' assessments, a number of shortcomings were identified, some of which are related to the peculiarity of being required by terms of a grant to create a website for audiences whose knowledge of and access to computers is limited. People who don't have computer access at home can use the Lincoln city library system's computers available for public use, but library hours may not always be convenient, and user time may be limited when many library patrons are waiting. Moreover, according to Liz Heusman, job training coordinator for the Center for People in Need, when refugees do use the Internet, they do so as a way to stay connected with their homeland, seeking news, pictures and other information from or about wherever they used to live. And they want it in their native language. "If they see it's in English, then they think it's not for them," Heusman said.

Faris Pirali, a Kurdish Iraqi refugee forced to leave his homeland because he worked with the U.S. military in Iraq, echoed Heusman's concern. Because the Mosaic site is in English, it contains little worth sharing. One exception, he noted, was the bed bug videos. He said he watched them not because he cared about bed bugs but because he saw there was an Arabic version. Heusman, too, cited the bed bug videos as one of the most successful Mosaic projects to date because they were available in Arabic, French, Burmese, and Karen, in addition to English. Language accessibility is significant, she said, because it "makes them feel a part of what's being offered."

An early version of the website included an automated translation feature, but Anderson said he wasn't satisfied with the results of the computer-generated translations and plans to address the language barrier in the coming year. In addition to the language issues, Heusman suggested the stories on the site need to be simpler and more about basic needs, such as food, shelter, safety, jobs and transportation, again a reflection of the content typical of foreign language newspapers in American cities at the turn of the last century, when waves of European immigrants turned to newspapers in their native tongues to acclimate to their new home. Heusman also suggested more engaging photos of the refugees' home countries, which don't currently exist on the site. Her comments raise interesting questions about the nature of the refugees' experiences and the intended nature of the website. For example, are the newest refugees with the most to learn the most important target audience? And how would the length of time refugees have lived in Lincoln or their degree of acclimation to America affect their interest in the site?

Several stakeholders commented on the apparent lack of a marketing strategy for the Mosaic website, and some suggested that the early market research conducted by the advertising students failed to identify a critical aspect of how the refugee community communicates. The array of state and local agency staff, people who work for or volunteer with numerous nonprofit organizations that aid refugees, and specific refugee community leaders like religious figures and people who work as translators for Lincoln Public Schools all are resources for reaching refugees. But they weren't initially identified as part of a marketing strategy to spread the word about Mosaic

In addition to the challenge of spreading the word into the refugee community, several stakeholders identified the challenge of reaching the broader community of non-refugee Lincoln residents. Dayna Kranawitter works for the Lincoln Housing Authority as site supervisor for the Arnold Community Learning Center and service coordinator at the Carol Yoakum Family Resource Center. She considers the Mosaic website a valuable resource that brings "perspective on a part of our population." She said she wishes others in Lincoln would visit the site and read the stories because it would help eliminate public ignorance about refugees and immigrants. If people understand what the refugees go through, it might help "change their world view." But Kranawitter noted that she's motivated to read the stories on the Mosaic site, whereas others who might benefit from learning more about their refugee neighbors probably don't care enough to go to the site to learn more anyway. What people read in traditional media about refugees is limited. "It had to be a sensational story or a tragedy before they're represented," she said. (The morning she was interviewed, the Lincoln Journal Star carried a story about a Karen refugee who allegedly stabbed his girlfriend with a knife.) "It's such a one-sided portrayal," she said. Moreover, Kranawitter noted, even though she works with refugees and immigrants, she's far from a daily visitor to the Mosaic site because it "is competing for my attention with so many other things."

Initial plans to reach the broader the community included an arrangement with the Lincoln Journal Star, the city's daily newspaper, to publish some of the students' stories. But so far, the only story published was about refugee children whose parents can't help them with homework because of their limited English skills. That hasn't hurt Mosaic's attempt to reach refugees, because they don't rely on the Journal Star in the first place. But, as Anderson noted, "The secondary audience is the larger community and that has been hurt by not being published."

Despite shortcomings the stakeholders identified, the Mosaic project also has experienced some serendipitous, if unintended, consequences. One feature of the site, an interactive map that introduces and explores many features of the city, was a professional project created by graduate student Litton, co-author of this report. In presenting a testing version of the map application to the family literacy class at Arnold Elementary School, Litton said it became clear that the map and the Mosaic site could be used as a training tool for refugees and immigrants to acquire critically important computer and Internet skills. Both UNL's Anderson and Arnold's family literacy teacher indicated they are developing curriculum ideas to make that work.

Initial plans to involve refugees as volunteers in contributing to the site ran aground on the realities of refugees' lives, jobs, children and other obligations. "We learned very quickly that didn't work," Anderson said. Instead, several refugees were recruited as freelance writers who are paid $50 per story for contributions to the Mosaic site. Anderson calls them not citizen journalists but "para-journalists," analogous to paralegals who free up time for lawyers to do other work. For Pirali, the Iraqi refugee, the opportunity represents a chance for personal growth. Pirali said he had wanted to work at a newspaper, but in Iraq, he never had the chance to do so. Now, in writing for Mosaic, he also can learn more about English, America and the people who live here, said Pirali, who describes his trek to America in a Mosaic article. Whatever its value to Pirali, other refugees and their advocates in the community, Mosaic also is a journalism class, and as such, illustrates some of the challenges of students being community news providers. Importantly, the quality of their work is not an issue. Kranawitter, in fact, was surprised to learn that most of the Mosaic students were undergraduates. Her first impression of their professionalism and their work led her to the mistaken belief that all were graduate students. "Tim [Anderson] does a good job of making sure the students have a real passion or interest in exploring a different culture," she said. It also, however, reflects the value of rewriting drafts of stories and of a commitment to publishing only professional-quality work.

In its first semester as a joint course with eight advertising and eight journalism students, the two advertising and journalism faculty members at the helm challenged students with starting something from scratch. And not all the students reacted favorably to the lack of structure and what many apparently saw as unclear expectations.

After moving beyond the research phase that first semester, the Mosaic course has been offered only to journalism students, and a total of 13 undergraduate and graduate students have been enrolled in the subsequent two semesters. Anderson scheduled the three-credit-hour Mosaic course to meet from 12:30 p.m. to 5:30 p.m. on Wednesday afternoons, figuring it would create a block of time for busy students, overcommitted with courses and work schedules, to accomplish some of the reporting for their assignments. But that made it difficult to keep up with students' progress. So for the fall 2012 semester, the course will meet two days a week for shorter periods of time. The course is not offered during summer school, but one undergraduate and two recent master's degree recipients are working for the site this summer. Anderson said he has struggled with the sometimes slim volume of content students create. A teacher could demand 12 stories each semester, but "that limits you" in the kinds of stories students can produce. Requiring six stories each semester from each student creates additional options for stronger stories that might take more reporting time, but in turn, results in less content for the website, a particular concern for a news site, which should not appear static. The challenge is finding a workable balance between features and profiles or more enterprise or investigative pieces. Also, particularly at the beginning of a semester, weeks can go by before new stories are ready to post. So keeping the site active and looking fresh is a challenge that adds a layer of complexity to managing the site, publishing stories and balancing demands placed on students.

Whatever its limitations and challenges, the Mosaic course has created a significant benefit for everyone involved, several of the stakeholders emphasized. The original intent of the grant that initially funded the Mosaic project was to create voices for the voiceless, and, in a perhaps unexpected way, it has in the personal interactions between refugees and college students. Take the Mosaic class's awkward first visit to the community learning center at

Arnold Elementary School as an example. The students were uncomfortable; the refugees skeptical. To the Americans, it was doubly intimidating to realize they were trying to talk to someone who had a horror-story background and barely spoke English. But by the time the afternoon ended two hours later, the room was loud with conversation and laughter. And one of the refugees took the opportunity to sell Avon products to some of the American girls. It became a running joke that makeup was the international language. The simple act of meeting an American, having a conversation in English, and sharing their stories represents a major milestone for the refugees, said Liz Heusman of the Center for People in Need. Having to meet and interact with an American can be a frightening prospect for these newcomers, but successfully engaging with the Mosaic students represents to the refugees an empowering experience.

Nebraska News Service

How it got started; how it works

When the Nebraska Legislature convened in January 2011, two new faces, representing the fledgling Nebraska News Service, were in the section of the chamber reserved for reporters. The next day, one of the reporters, a University of Nebraska-Lincoln journalism student, was thrilled to see her page-one byline in the Norfolk (Neb.) Daily News, circulation 15,960, one of the state's important medium-sized dailies serving northeast Nebraska. Spring semester classes weren't yet in session, but the Nebraska News Service, which had been the wisp of an idea six months earlier, was officially under way. Five students were accepted into the NNS class that first semester, nearly doubling the size of the regular Nebraska statehouse press corps. To understand the significance of that, Allen Beermann, executive director of the Nebraska Press Association, provided some background. Beermann has been at the NPA for the past 18 years and before that served as Nebraska's Secretary of State from 1971 to 1995. He knows his way around the statehouse.

Beermann recalled that in his early career in state government, a hallway near the legislative chamber comprised a press row of sorts, where you could find three or four reporters from the Omaha World-Herald, the state's largest newspaper, three or four reporters from the Associated Press and a couple of United Press International reporters as well. Those days are long gone. The World-Herald has three reporters in its Lincoln bureau who regularly cover state government, but sends additional reporters as needed; the nearest AP bureau is in Minneapolis, and the UPI is gone altogether. The local Lincoln Journal Star covers the statehouse, but it has never had significant circulation beyond Lincoln and the surrounding counties. Moreover, Beermann said, the

World-Herald, which once prided itself on being a statewide newspaper that covered a Main Street 500 miles long, ceased delivery in the western half of the state in 2009, and is widely perceived by people in "greater Nebraska" as being uninterested in covering anything beyond the concerns of Omaha and the University of Nebraska-Lincoln. Ellen Mortensen, editor of the Custer County Chief in Broken Bow, Neb., reflected that view. "We kinda feel like we're in the desert," she said, suggesting that WorldHerald editors think the state's western border "ends in Lincoln." (The World-Herald in recent years has purchased five small dailies and 12 weeklies in the Omaha metro area and throughout the state and operates its own news service, transmitting news and feature stories drawn from its company-owned properties.)

Smaller newspapers and news consumers in Nebraska historically relied on this handful of major news sources to provide their state government news, but as those sources have shrunk, the smallest dailies and weeklies—and their news consumers—have been left out in the cold. As far as Beermann is concerned, the Nebraska News Service, created to cover state government, fills a pressing need. "It's filling a great void," he said, "and I think an important one." Beermann also offered a wider historical context. Current technology allows for cheap, easy delivery of news. As recently as 10 years ago, Beermann said, a wire service like the NNS might have had to rely on a fax machine to transmit stories, a significant impediment to their use. "Now it's instantly useful to the newspaper," he said. "If they like the story, they just plug it in." The NPA was an early supporter of the statehouse news bureau idea, in large part because the press association and the UNL journalism college have a long track record of collaboration. "When you're working together, it's a lot easier than working apart," he said, noting that not all state press associations and their state journalism schools have such a collegial relationship. Creating a statehouse news bureau is not a new idea.

Associate professor Tim Anderson, then the UNL journalism sequence (department) head, contacted at least three similar programs at Maryland, Michigan State, and Arizona State during UNL's discussion phase of the project. And in years gone by, UNL journalism students in public affairs reporting classes occasionally wrote state government stories of local interest for particular papers. The NPA also once briefly experimented with hiring students as interns to cover legislative sessions. But the college had never established an ongoing statehouse news service.

As Dean Gary Kebbel tells the story, he made a "seminal" trip to Seward, Neb., in one of his first weeks as dean in the summer of 2010. He realized the college should take advantage of the rare geographic proximity of a journalism college situated just blocks from a state capitol. Kebbel sounded out the publisher of the weekly Seward County Independent about whether there would be interest in more statehouse news, and the idea took off. (The weekly paper has had a long collaboration with UNL detailed in the last case study in this report.) Kebbel and others emphasized that the idea of the journalism college creating a program to cover state government for news organizations throughout the state was in keeping with the long-standing tradition of service embodied in the Morrill Act of 1862, which created the landgrant university system. Establishing the news service fits in with the university's overall mission because it's part of "helping people in the state," Kebbel said. "It's sort of in our DNA." And as a practical matter, the news service also helps address a perception by some Nebraskans that the state university mostly serves Lincoln. "It would be good for the university to show that's not true,"

Anderson said Support from the NPA, which provided access to its mailing list of papers throughout the state, was critical. Beermann, with his extensive statehouse contacts, was instrumental in "smoothing the road" with the clerk of the Legislature, who "was not a particular fan at the start," Kebbel recalled. Cooperation of the legislative clerk was essential because he issues press credentials, which give reporters virtually open access to the legislative chamber. But he was initially cool to the idea because of previous negative experiences with journalism students. Too often they dressed and acted unprofessionally when in the statehouse on class assignments and didn't seem to bother learning anything about the legislative process. The clerk ultimately agreed to issue daily credentials, but not permanent credentials, to NNS reporters. And he provided helpful background briefings for the NNS reporters before the legislative session began.

The dean, associate dean, journalism sequence head, and faculty member assigned to head up the news service met periodically in the fall to talk about how the three-credit-hour class would work. The dean also applied for a $130,000 grant from the Ethics and Excellence in Journalism Foundation to hire a person who would promote the news service around the state. Plans also were put in place to establish the news service as a tax exempt 501(c) entity allowing it to accept donations for equipment and other needs that arise and also to attempt to create a legal separation of sorts between the news service and the university, itself a state government agency. Initial discussions were predicated on the notion of charging a modest fee for clients to subscribe to the news service, but at one point, shortly before invitation letters were to be sent out, sequence head Anderson suggested the college offer it for free, at least at the start. To the planning group, that seemed much easier than trying to figure out an appropriate way to price an unknown product to potential clients of widely varying size. The planners also thought it was important to let editors at the state's two largest newspapers, the Omaha World-Herald and Lincoln Journal Star, which are the only two providing regular statehouse coverage, know about the plan. Both were cool to the idea, and a top editor at the World-Herald dismissed the notion that student reporters could competently cover state government. To date, neither has joined the news service. Nonetheless, the NNS client base has a total circulation of about 300,000, not counting the potential audiences of the 10 radio stations and four television stations that subscribe

In December 2010 the college invited subscriptions with letters describing the Nebraska News Service to 156 weekly newspapers, one monthly, 18 dailies, 50 radio stations and 11 television stations that were members of the Nebraska Press Association or Nebraska Broadcasters Association. The letters included a tear-off slip at the bottom asking people to provide an email address, to list state senators in their circulation areas, and topics of particular interest to their readers. By the opening day of the legislative session in January 2011, the news service had acquired more than 40 clients. Also in December, the clerk of the Legislature met for an hour with the five students enrolled for the first semester of the Nebraska News Service, who sought to make a positive impression by their professional attire and deportment. He described protocols for reporters covering the Legislature and its committees, including the unusual access reporters have to go onto the floor and buttonhole lawmakers when the Legislature is in session except when a vote is in progress. The five students and the bureau chief (Quinlan) then went to the coffee shop in the Capitol and determined who was available to cover the opening day, which was during the UNL winter break, fixed the naming convention for g-mail addresses each student would use, and exchanged cell phone numbers. Sequence head Anderson designed a logo and printed business cards for everyone, and the journalism college office staff member who is the keeper of keys had keys made so each student could have access to a small storage room/library that was to become the NNS office. Dean Kebbel recalled, "My overall surprise was how fast and easy it was to get this going."

To him, the speed with which the news service was stitched together and the relatively little planning that went into it is part of its success. "I'm glad we threw it together so fast, because we didn't have time to think about how it wouldn't work and why it wouldn't work." When the second semester of the 2010-11 academic year--and the legislative session--got underway, the news service reporters met as a class on Friday mornings to make plans for the following week and hear guest speakers on various aspects of state government, such as the director of the Nebraska Accountability and Disclosure Commission and the legislative director of Common Cause Nebraska. Each student took on a beat covering specific topics and the legislative committees that deal with those issues and was responsible for staying on top of issues of particular interest to the more rural areas of the state, which most NNS clients serve. One student who was more interested in editing than reporting took on the duties of establishing the client data base and creating a large map of the state showing each legislative district, its lawmaker and the NNS clients in the district. She also wrote a style guide for the news service, created a schedule showing when each student was available to work, gave a first read to stories, and, by the end of the semester, when the client base had grown to more than 80, she did some basic analysis of the client news organizations, their circulation sizes, their Web presence and the like. She also covered legislative hearings when no one else was available to do so. Students wrote their stories in Google Docs and shared them with the bureau chief, who then edited them, asked for changes as needed, and emailed them to the clients. Editors at small weekly newspapers typically are overwhelmed with things to do and not enough time to do them, so the decision was made to send stories to them directly rather than sending them a link to some other site or otherwise creating even one more step standing in the way of using NNS material. Additionally, one of the news service reporters created a Web page where news organizations can sign up for the service, but NNS purposely did not create a website to publish stories. Doing so would, in effect, put the news service in the position of competing with its own clients. Nebraska News Service sent out 90 stories covering its first legislative session. The semester ended while the Legislature was still in session, but to continue providing coverage, the dean obtained a $10,000 donation from an alumnus to pay two reporters and the bureau chief for five more weeks of coverage until the Legislature adjourned. In the fall 2011 semester, three students were enrolled in the class and each identified subject areas of state government they planned to cover. But a special session of the Legislature was called to address the controversial Keystone XL oil pipeline proposal, and most of the NNS efforts were devoted to covering that issue, particularly aspects of the economic claims being made by pipeline proponents, which weren't being covered by other news media. In its third semester of existence, only one reporter joined the news service, which, as the stakeholders' comments detailed below indicate, sharply limited the extent to which legislative activity could be covered. Even so, the reporter filed 31 stories throughout the 60-day legislative session for the more than 100 clients being served. She also wrote short versions of each story suitable for on-air use by NNS broadcasting clients. After the session ended, she researched, reported and wrote stories about all 10 major and minor U.S. Senate primary candidates, except one who wouldn't schedule an interview. The stories became ran as full-page election previews in a number of papers before the state's May 15 primary.

Stakeholders' views: Pluses, minuses and academic considerations

Interviews for this case study as well as informal, unsolicited feedback from NNS clients suggest that to many editors, the service clearly fills a void. Rob Dump, who owns a half dozen weeklies in the northeast corner of the state, said he canceled AP service four years ago for budgetary reasons, which left him with what he considered the distasteful option of running state senators' opinion columns as his only real source of state news. "I would never run them," he said. "And then I had to resort to running them." Indeed, scanning weeklies from across the state makes clear the sources of content not locally produced by staff or community correspondents are almost entirely freebies: columns from the governor's office, columns from state senators, columns from U.S. senators and representatives, summaries of calls for service from the county sheriff's department, articles by the local cooperative extension agents and the like. To John Weare, managing editor of the Alliance Times-Herald in Nebraska's western Panhandle, a free service that offers capable and competent state news coverage represents an opportunity to provide more for his readers. At the very least, NNS stories fill space. One paper ran nine NNS-bylined stories in a single issue during the first legislative session the student reporters covered. Editors never called into question the accuracy of NNS stories. In fact, Custer County Chief editor Mortensen was under the mistaken impression that the stories she received were not written by students because the quality was so good it seldom needed any editing. Kent Warneke, editor of the Norfolk Daily News, said the NNS stories are on par with those from the AP and the World-Herald's news service.

The NNS stories are accurate, interesting to read and comprehensive. Warneke said he chooses from among his various news sources depending on factors like whether area senators are quoted in one story or whether one better explains how an issue will affect Nebraskans, and he will sometimes combine stories from the various sources into a single, comprehensive piece. All of it adds up to more information for readers. "If I had to rely on the AP for state coverage, whoa, it'd be slim pickings," he said. Warneke noted that his was the first daily to publish an NNS story, and he never had any misgivings about the quality of work the news service would produce. He has hired university students as interns for many years and has come to expect a certain quality of work from them, he said, noting that he wouldn't hesitate to tell a colleague who didn't have experience with UNL students and was concerned about using student work to "give it a chance." Deborah McCaslin, publisher of the Custer County Chief and an ardent supporter of the news service, told graduate student Litton, "I love, love, love it," when he called her to arrange an interview for this project. And that was before he even told her why he'd called. McCaslin said she couldn't do without the news service and has reserved a spot on page A3 every week so her readers will expect statehouse news and know exactly where to find it.

To her, NNS reporters' ability to cover legislative hearings represents "feet on the ground, ears in the room" assuring that open meetings are truly public. Laws that require open public meetings are one thing, but if news outlets fail to cover them, such meetings effectively become closed, she said. McCaslin suggested the notion that readers don't care about state government news is a chicken and egg argument. Perhaps readers don't care "because no one knows about it," she said, suggesting that by regularly carrying statehouse news, she's helping people become more involved in the process. McCaslin offered anecdotal evidence supporting that. She said she's noticed that when state senators and politicians visit Broken Bow for coffees and meet-and-greet sessions, people have begun to ask more pointed questions of their lawmakers. She's heard them ask, "Well, I read in the paper…" and she knew they were referring to NNS stories carried in the Custer County Chief. McCaslin is planning a reader survey for June to gauge the popularity of various features of the paper, including the NNS. But she said it won't matter what the readers think; she's planning to stick with the service. "If the numbers aren't high enough, then we'll advertise more for it." Mortensen, McCaslin's editor, dismissed suggestions that perhaps state news wasn't local enough for community newspapers, given the trend toward hyper-local coverage, which has long been a staple of weekly papers. "Just the opposite,"

Mortensen said. "They (readers) appreciate knowing what's going on." McCaslin's enthusiasm for state government news contrasts with that of several other editors interviewed, who said their main focus is stories with local interest. An editor at one weekly characterizes news judgment there by saying that if it didn't happen in the county, it's not news. Nonetheless, that paper has published most NNS stories this year. Many of the stakeholders interviewed for this case study reserved their greatest enthusiasm for Anthony Roberts, who was hired in September 2011 under the grant from Ethics and Excellence in Journalism Foundation. Originally conceived as a position for someone to travel the state promoting the news service, the job description was redefined after it became apparent that the news service was selling itself. What was also apparent was that while the college wanted students to create multimedia content for its clients, the clients' technical capabilities to use such content varied widely. Some had an active Web presence and at least one was unable to open email attachments. So the job was recast for someone to serve as a multimedia coach, working individually with client news organizations to help them improve their abilities to use multimedia content on their websites. Roberts, himself an honors graduate of the UNL journalism college, has the rare ability to speak both English and technology, and has built a large fan-base for the news service as he has reached out to help existing clients and has recruited others to join. Weekly newspapers in particular take varied approaches to using the Web. Some update regularly with breaking news; others only weekly when the printed paper is published. Some have limited content and use the Web mainly as a teaser to drive readers to the printed paper.

Many use the Web to sell copies of photos, frequently of local high school athletic events, that aren't published in the paper. But interest in e-editions is growing in large part because of threatened closure of local post offices that deliver weekly papers to subscribers. The issue is a complicated one because in some parts of the state, access to high-speed broadband Internet service remains problematic. And further complicating the technology picture in small newsrooms is the reality of never having enough time to accomplish what they want to accomplish, much less embark on something brand new. Some of the larger daily papers in the NNS client base have capable Web and social media gurus on their staffs, and they have also been receptive to visits from Roberts to learn even more. Roberts has clearly filled a niche for the state's papers. "I can't even overstate the value of technical assistance," he said. "They're so close and so far. There's a deficiency or a complete lack of training budgets." Roberts said he has found that the client newspapers' staff members know enough about their content management systems to publish, but not enough to do anything complicated. "It helps to have someone show you how to get started." And getting people up to speed on the basics is easy, particularly in a one-on-one, client-specific setting. He cited as example the paper in Chadron, in the far northwest corner of the state, 424 miles from Lincoln. Roberts said the Chadron staff was regularly publishing videos after about three hours of tutoring. "For the most part, no one is embarrassed for not knowing this stuff, nor should they," he said. "How would they know if no one told them…Who has time in the news business to go out and learn this stuff on their own? Very, very, very few. Everybody needs a little catalyst, a kick in the pants, so to speak."

The biggest stumbling block for Roberts' services as a multimedia coach is editors' time. At a prearranged visit to one weekly, the editor told him when he arrived, "You know, if you really want to help, you can leave." She wasn't trying to be mean; she was just trying to cope with a suddenly busy breaking-news day. He left. Editors interviewed for the case study uniformly sang Roberts' praises. Rob Dump of the Cedar County News and five other northeast Nebraska newspapers identified two major reasons for Roberts' success over other, more formal technology training opportunities for editors and publishers. First, such training sessions are available primarily at the Nebraska Press Association conventions, where the trainings often are geared to papers of a particular size.

That means much of what is discussed isn't necessarily what smaller papers may be ready or able to produce. And second, Dump said he might find value in what he learns at a conference, only to discover he can't make practical use of the information because he does not have the same equipment at his office. "Then you're stuck," he said. With Roberts making house calls, both of those issues are instantly resolved: editors can start at whatever level of expertise with whatever technology they already have. And if something doesn't work right, Roberts can adjust on the fly. "He was right there, 'OK, let's go to plan B,'" Dump said, adding: "It's invaluable for him to come to our shop." The NPA's Beermann, another Roberts fan, said the state association had addressed papers' technology needs only "in a non-organized way." The NPA has helped some members with starting websites and sent out "visitation teams" to help. But he said the UNL journalism college is in the best position to offer the kind of multimedia coaching Roberts is providing. For his part, Roberts credits the NPA with being "instrumental in helping me spread the service across the state."

Some editors, he said, "might not have called me back otherwise, but did so on the recommendation of Allen Beermann because they respect him." While generous with their praise of the news service, many stakeholders are also quick to cite its shortcomings, generally phrased as suggestions for improvement. First, they say, recruit more students so you can do more work. Dean Kebbel and others expressed surprise that there was not more interest among journalism students in applying for the news service, but Kebbel acknowledged that part of the problem was a mushrooming number of special topics and elective classes that, in effect, dilutes the pool of top candidates. Out-of-the-way office space also contributes to lack of awareness about it among students. Stakeholders all agreed that better marketing to students, citing the value of getting clips to build a portfolio rather than the importance of public affairs reporting, is essential to keep it going. To publisher Rob Dump,

"That's job number one; recruit a bigger staff." Editor Steve Frederick of the Scottsbluff Star-Herald called for more feature stories, especially about local people. "Hometown papers care about hometown people," he said. "It doesn't matter if they lived here 30 years ago." Several editors said they wanted a weekly or daily digest of upcoming stories, and others wanted the option of requesting specific stories. (Editors regularly have been invited to suggest stories, and a handful have made special requests, which have been honored, except once when no student was available to cover a specific event.) Editor John Weare in Alliance suggested a variant of individual papers' requests. His idea is that the news service and a client could work together on an enterprise project and then make the double-bylined story available to the rest of the NNS clients. "We'd like to do that, give our writers more exposure" he said. "I'd like to see it happen."

Norfolk Daily News editor Kent Warneke said providing photos and video would be an appropriate next step for the news service. "If it's going to grow, grow it slowly," he advised. "Visual is the next logical step in my mind." Roberts pointed out that the staffing shortage means there will be a shortage of multimedia pieces, which take longer to produce than a straightforward text story. Kebbel noted that one drawback to more multimedia content is that costs associated with video cameras and computer editing software will go up. While a major draw of the news service is that it's free, charging a fee for it hasn't been ruled out. But former sequence head Anderson said he doubted a pay schedule would generate enough revenue to offset all the costs. Beermann said his main concern was with student journalists covering the Legislature. He said he feared that the news service could "very easily get derailed" if a student misconstrued sensitive or complicated legislation and inaccurate stories were published. "But I think Mary Kay (Quinlan) has been very careful about that," he said. As with the other case studies examined in this project, the Nebraska News Service, whatever its value as a community news provider, is still a college credit course. But as a class expected to produce professional content, it raises some important academic questions, as Anderson points out. "When you add the publication component you cannot tolerate even B student work," he said. In regular classwork, students get their grades and then move on to the next assignment, "but when publishing is the goal, somebody's got to take that B-minus and turn it into an A paper." More students creating more content, in turn, translate to more work for faculty, he noted. Moreover, the imperative of creating professional, publishable work with upper-level students suggests the critical importance of the college having a demanding lowerlevel curriculum that prepares students to be competitive as NNS reporters.

The news service reporters were advised not to take more than 12 credit hours, including the three credits for the news service, so they would have 15 or more hours a week during the normal business day that they could commit to being available for NNS assignments. But because they have other classes, it isn't always possible for a reporter to be available, particularly not at a moment's notice. Beermann highlighted another concern: the reality of student turnover. A new crop of students every semester means the news service cannot build institutional memory the way a newsroom does. From an academic standpoint, this raises the question of whether NNS could become a two-semester course, or whether students could at least have the option to repeat the class if they chose to do so. Dean Kebbel raised another academic reality that affects a college's effort to embark on something new. It's difficult, he said, to ask faculty to take on experimental projects where there is no guarantee of success. "Faculty want to know the end result before they start," he said. "Tenure track teaches you not to take risks....It's a huge problem." This case study suggests that further detailed analysis would be in order comparing various approaches to journalism colleges' statehouse bureaus, if other schools were tempted to establish such operations. The Nebraska News Service's early success may, in fact, be attributable to several accidents of geography and history over which no college can exert total control:

- It's a mere five-block walk between the Nebraska Capitol and UNL's Andersen Hall, which houses the journalism college;
- Nebraska's unique one-house legislature, with just 49 members and a tradition of openness, is unusually accessible and operates with minimal staff
- Most state agencies have offices either in the Capitol or in nearby downtown buildings;
- Nebraska has just one major state university with the only accredited journalism program
- The state's press association, for the most part, reflects a collegiality that helped spur enthusiasm for the news service. In short, the lack of planning that went into the Nebraska News Service, suggests that simply the chemistry of the people and place may have much to do with its success.

UNL-Seward County Independent Partnership

How it got started; how it works

Twenty-nine years ago, long before the FCC report on the information needs of communities called for colleges to play a role in filling those needs, UNL journalism faculty and students embarked on what would become a long-term effort to immerse college journalists in a community newspaper, augmenting local news coverage and providing students with clips and course credit. It got off to a rocky start, one of the original professors recalled, but has taken on a life of its own, as far as some of the stakeholders are concerned. Even in the early years, it was recognized as innovative, winning a merit award in 1984 for a Creative and Innovative Community Journalism Program from the National Association of Summer Sessions. Retired professor Alfred "Bud" Pagel taught the advanced reporting classes that, along with editing and photojournalism classes, produced a laboratory newspaper during the regular academic year. During the summer, the journalism students used the facilities of the Daily Nebraskan, the independent campus newspaper, for the course's lab paper operation.

But for reasons Pagel said he no longer remembers, the Daily Nebraskan's facilities became unavailable in 1983, which forced the faculty members to find another way to offer the hands-on course. Pagel said he pitched the idea of a summer internship program of sorts to the newspaper in Syracuse, Neb., about 32 miles from Lincoln. He said he thought the best way to get the paper to participate was to offer the idea as a way for the editor to get a week of vacation. Syracuse jumped at the idea, but to Pagel's dismay, the entire editorial staff went on vacation, leaving the students and teachers with an entire newspaper to publish and very few ideas on how to do it. Even worse, the Syracuse operation assembled and printed three newspapers, and all three publications fell on the students' (and faculty members') shoulders. "We got them all out, but it just about killed us," Pagel recalled. Beyond that, the problem with Syracuse was that the community, with a population of about 1,800, and its newspaper were a little too small to handle the influx of six or seven reporters. So the next year, they went to David City, with a population of more than 2,500. But David City is a 100-mile, two-hour round trip from Lincoln and proved to be too far to be practical for making a daily drive there. So the next year, Pagel said he approached Charlyne Berens, who, with her husband, owned and published the Seward County Independent, and "we convinced her somehow to do it." Pagel said the arrangement with Seward was a "perfect" fit. Everyone on the staff bought into the idea; at about 25 miles from the UNL campus, the town is an easy daily drive; and with a population then approaching 6,000, it was large enough to support additional reporters. Plus, the paper welcomed the additional help necessary to cover a stupendous Fourth of July festival that is said by organizers to draw in 40,000 people. (Stephanie Croston, the paper's current sports editor, who has been the point person for the partnership for nearly a decade, said July 4 is "the only holiday in Seward.)

Retired professor Jack Botts, who taught the editing classes that worked with Pagel's reporters, said it's important to understand the context in which the outreach to community newspapers took place. He recalled that William Hall, who was the director of what was then UNL's School of Journalism, began a push in the early 1960s to create more contacts within the state's press by starting a program in which journalism classes went to predominantly daily newspapers throughout the state for two days at a time and produced the papers. Classes traveled as far as McCook, some 228 miles from Lincoln, and Scottsbluff, nearly 400 miles away in the western Panhandle. Botts credited those years of contact with the state press as a primary reason that Nebraska's journalism school became a college in 1979. When then-director R. Neale Copple sought to split the J-School off from the College of Arts and Sciences, all those contacts became useful, Botts recalled. There was doubt that the Board of Regents could be convinced to create a college of journalism. So Botts said Copple charged his journalism faculty with contacting everyone they knew in the state, newspaper editors and broadcasters, urging them to "rain phone calls, telegrams or whatever" in support of a journalism college. "Within a week they said OK. They were really just inundated with calls and demands," Botts said. "That's the main reason for maintaining contact with the state press." By the time the school became a college, the two-day stints at daily papers had been dropped because of the strain of traveling long distances, including almost getting snowed in occasionally in distant towns. Students instead got hands-on publishing experience with a laboratory newspaper that involved four five-hour lab sessions every Tuesday and Thursday for students enrolled in advanced reporting, news editing, senior editing and photography, an arrangement

Botts said gave the students "a lot of experience and a lot of work." There were "enormous teaching moments in the labs that you don't get on these trips out through the state." Pagel indicated that the program never would have been attempted in the first place if the students weren't up to the task of gaining that experience by collaborating with a weekly newspaper during summer school. Still, the faculty and newspaper editor installed a system to ensure a quality product. He said the students' copy was put through a rigorous editing process. He gave all copy a first edit, then it went to Botts and his copyediting students for a second round of editing, and finally it landed on the editor's desk. And everyone agreed at the outset, that the editor was the boss and had the final say. "It sounds like it would be extremely hard work, but it wasn't," he said. In the intervening years, the program has evolved in several ways. It no longer includes editing or photography classes; only reporting students participate, but they are also expected to take photos with all their stories, just as reporters at any weekly newspaper would. Where the students work during their sojourn in Seward has also changed. In the early years, the class worked out of an un-air-conditioned upstairs space in the paper's historic building on the courthouse square, which participants remembered as miserably hot. That space was later air conditioned and transformed into the paper's newsroom, forcing the editor to find alternate locations. Once, it was a nearby corner storefront whose tenant had vacated. Another summer it was a former restaurant most easily reached down the alley behind the newspaper building. And still other summers, it was the basement of a local bank in the next block. Ultimately, the newspaper office was renovated, and the newsroom moved back downstairs, making the air conditioned upstairs space available for up to nine reporters and one teacher. Enrollment in the class has varied considerably over the years. In recent years, as few as five and as many as a dozen have signed up. But the current space limitation means enrollment now cannot exceed nine students.

The class has also experienced changes in technology that have made logistics easier. In the early computer days, the class had to spend at least half of one day simply transporting computers, monitors and printers to the assigned workspace, a process considerably eased now that students provide their own laptop computers. And photography, particularly on the Fourth of July, is much easier with digital cameras than it was in the days when film had to be developed, often on deadline, by a Seward County Independent staff member. What hasn't changed is the general approach to determining what the students will do. First, they are expected to contribute significantly to the annual July Fourth coverage, and beyond that, they work on stories that sometimes include spot news, but always also include working on special sections or assignments that the Seward County Independent staff doesn't have time to do. Marcia Goff, who succeeded Berens as editor when the Berenses sold the paper in 1990, noted that when the students arrived every summer, it essentially doubled the newspaper's staff. Many of the stories they were assigned essentially were ideas that came up during the day-to-day operation of the paper. It became a list of story ideas they wanted to do, but couldn't, largely for lack of time. "You get a lot of work done that might not get done otherwise," she said. Goff said that while she always started out with a list of story ideas, she also encouraged students to find their own. If they came up with a story, she let them run with it, under her guidance, and if she wasn't satisfied with the results, she might add one of her own reporters to the story and give it a double byline.

Students enrolled in the summer school class, now known as Reporting II in the college's curriculum, meet for three hours on Monday, Wednesday and Friday mornings on campus covering the regular curriculum for the course during the first three weeks of the five-week summer session. One of those mornings usually includes a field trip to Seward to meet the editor and to get an introduction to county government from the county clerk and county sheriff. For the last two weeks, the students and teacher travel daily in university cars to Seward, leaving the journalism college around 8 a.m. and returning around 5 p.m. The July Fourth assignments can start as early as the anvil firing and flag raising at 7:30 a.m. and go until the end of the fireworks, which start at 10 p.m. Students provide their own transportation on the Fourth, and because they are required to work on the holiday, they usually are given a day off class one morning during the first part of the session. The nature of the assignments varies from year to year. The editor (Croston) and faculty member (Quinlan) usually meet in April to start making plans for the summer. To the extent possible, the students are involved in brainstorming story ideas, often around a particular theme. But sometimes, the editor has particular projects that need to be completed and there is less flexibility for student input on story ideas. The projects have included stories analyzing census data after county-level figures become available, a series that focused on religion in Seward County, and profiles of the county's volunteer fire companies. Students also have written stories about county residents who run Internet businesses, created a slideshow of women at the senior center who do hand quilting, and a covered spot news story about a Girl Scout troop in a nearby town that sponsored a Harry Potter-inspired Quidditch tournament for local youth.

Publisher Kevin Zadina said one of the reasons the program works is that story assignments are carefully selected based on his staff members' "good grasp on the community." That's important, Croston added, because "we don't want to set them up to fail." Students often rely on Croston and others at the paper for suggestions of sources, since no one expects them to know the community. Because of the community's size, many people students need to interview are within walking distance in the Seward business district. Students are expected to manage their own schedules and turn in stories throughout the two weeks. The faculty member in charge reads them first and asks for changes, as needed, and the stories are then sent to Croston, who often requests changes to conform to the paper's style or suggests an additional source to interview. Students are told from the outset that the editor is the boss, and she has the final say on how a story will be handled. On the final Friday of the two-week stint, no one can leave until the editor has signed off on all the stories and photos students have produced. Even though many UNL journalism students work at the independent campus newspaper, the Seward internship often is a first-time experience of working for a professional editor, which, for some, can be hard to grasp. One student, after being asked several times to do some more interviewing for a story, told the teacher and editor, "But I like it this way." The story was never published

Stakeholders' views: Pluses, minuses and academic considerations

The stakeholders exhibited widespread agreement that the Seward internship is a valuable opportunity for students to experience community journalism, something that may get short shrift in journalism education. Retired editor Goff recalled: "Every year, I had the feeling that there were a certain number of the students who came in expecting to go to The New York Times or The Washington Post on their first job, and seeing that as the only journalistic goal that they had. Community newspapers were just kind of out there, and unimportant and unprofessional. I think that many of them changed their minds after being around for a couple of weeks and seeing what went on and how it operated and why it was important." Goff suggested that programs such as the one in Seward could go a long way toward creating better journalism in communities because they could encourage some to choose it as a career path, not just in Nebraska, but everywhere. "My feeling is that community journalism is among the very most important parts of what J-schools should be about," she said. Professor John Bender, who taught the summer school class in the 1990s, said the students' immersion in the last two weeks of the class—coupled with the fact that they cannot take any other summer school courses at the same time—contributes to a degree of focus that they otherwise might not be able to achieve.

The result, he suggested, is better journalism. Pagel said the students benefit from the work experience, however brief. "Everything they learn on the first job, they learn there (in Seward), only you can't get fired," he said. "You could get flunked, but not fired." Students also benefit from their exposure to community members, many of whom take an almost nurturing role in dealing with the interns. Sherry Schweitzer, Seward County clerk, is a regular speaker for the reporting class, explaining how county government works in Nebraska, which out-of-state students and those not from rural areas seem to struggle to understand, she said. She also has an extensive knowledge of the city and the region and is a go-to person when students need leads for sources on stories. "I'm glad to be a contact person".

Schweitzer said. "I know where to steer them." Clark Kolterman, an English teacher at Seward High School, is chairman of the July Fourth events, and often serves as a source for the students. He explained that members of the community are willing to help the young reporters, partly because they're proud of their community and proud of their hometown newspaper, to the point where they almost take some small claim of ownership in it. Rhoades Publishing Inc. in Blair, Neb., owns the Seward County Independent and a number of other weekly newspapers, but that doesn't diminish local residents' sense that it belongs to them, Kolterman indicated. "People take a real identity in a paper in a small community, too," he said. "It's not the guy in Blair who owns it. It's not his paper; it's Seward's paper. So they want the paper to be successful and they want the paper to be right." Students also benefit, of course, from adding to their portfolios of published work. And at least one student in recent years decided after her two weeks in Seward to change her major, concluding that journalism just wasn't for her. The two weeks during which the students invade the newspaper can be stressful and disruptive for the staff's normal routines. But stakeholders agreed that the paper, with its fulltime newsroom staff of four, including editors, benefits. Some stories simply wouldn't get done, and the July Fourth coverage would be much thinner. "We couldn't cover the Fourth of July without them," Croston said. Kolterman said there's no real comparison to the Fourth coverage before and after the Seward internship program began. He's in a position to know. Kolterman has been involved with the July Fourth festivities for more than 40 years, beginning when he was chairman of the parade committee in 1969, while he was still in high school. "When that intern program came, the coverage was so much better because they had the manpower to do it," he said. "Before, we had to feed them all the articles." Today, the coverage is much different, he said, and it's his impression that the paper usually takes two issues (two weeks) to publish all the photos and stories the interns and full-time staff generate.

One of the biggest improvements, he said, is in the quality of photojournalism, which might be related to improved camera and printing technology as much as better student work. Nonetheless, he said, there was a time when "you had to read the captions to know what was in the picture." Kolterman said he considers the internship program "a win-win for everyone" and said he believes the program could be replicated elsewhere. "The wheel's been invented…It's been invented here. I would just try to emulate what they did here." But the Seward internship arrangement is not without problems. Goff recalled an important lesson from the early 1990s when a professor allowed 17 students to be in the Seward summer class. And he made matters worse by requiring everyone to write 10 stories in two weeks. Goff said that meant she needed to come up with nearly 200 story ideas and then faced the logistical nightmare of reading and editing 170 stories. That never happened again. Several stakeholders commented on the practical limitations of a two-week internship. Students have neither the necessary background nor time to cover city or county government meetings or engage in any meaningful accountability or investigative reporting. Government meetings are filled with jargon and acronyms and can be confusing, particularly to someone who lacks historical context, Goff said. "It's like coming in on the third act of a three-act play." County clerk Schweitzer agreed. "Government sometimes works slow," she said. In just two weeks, there just wouldn't be much to cover. That means the students are best suited for feature or historical assignments, Goff said, which is not necessarily bad. "Those are about people," she said. "They're [the readers'] friends and interested in reading about them. So those are always popular and well read."

Croston suggested that adding a third week to the Seward internship experience might make it possible for students to cover a government meeting and get an even better sense of community journalism. Sometimes the students' inexperience—or inability—leads to mistakes. Bender and Croston both recalled an incident in which a student "garbled some pretty important facts" about a local manufacturing company, Bender said. Croston recalled it was her first year working at the paper, in 1998, and one of her first tasks was to go back and re-report and re-write the student's story. Bender said the student's shoddy journalism on that story provided a valuable lesson in community journalism. Even though a business profile may be more of a "soft" story, and may not seem as demanding, "at the same time they are real stories and they are stories that are going to be read and people care about," Bender said. "From that you can understand or learn that you gotta get it right, that people do pay attention, they do care. If you take a "halfassed attitude toward your work… there is going to be a price to pay" for a young reporter, and that's a valuable learning experience, he noted. Pagel said that every once in a while he had to deal with a weak student, like one he recalled as "dead lazy and not very good when she did work." Schweitzer recalled one year when the assignments included profiles of county officials. The student who wrote about her said that at the end of every day she liked to kick back a cold beer on her porch. Schweitzer said that wasn't true. "I don't even have a porch." She said she got a lot of ribbing about that, but seemed to take it in stride. Publisher Zadina and Croston agreed that such episodes never threatened to kill the program largely because they are uncommon. Some of the stakeholders cited intangible, but nonetheless significant, downsides to the community newspaper experience.

Berens, now the associate dean of UNL's journalism college, recalled that when she was editor at the Seward County Independent, one of the UNL professors, whom she did not identify, made her want to "run the other way" because he "wanted to tell me everything I should be doing." Small town newspaper people sometimes are defensive and don't appreciate outsiders coming in with a condescending attitude, she said. "We live here. We know what's best for our community," she said. "Don't come in here telling us how to practice journalism….You don't want to come in saying you have all the answers." In reality, not all community newspapers are created equal. While retired professor Pagel recalled the paper in Syracuse, the first summer class location, as being too small and too far, Botts, the retired editing professor, recalled it as basically a lousy newspaper. "We found out that this wasn't a good example, not a good place to do that" because the owners "didn't care what went into the paper and that wasn't good," he said. Botts added that he always wished David City had been about 20 miles closer to Lincoln.

"They had a more dedicated journalistic attitude," he said. "In Seward it always appeared as if they were learning every day what to do." Botts said he disagreed with some of the news judgments the Seward staff made, particularly because they seemed inclined to back away from a story that might hurt a local advertiser, which he said wasn't the case in David City. "Print it, that's what they'd (David City editors) say," Botts said. "As long as you spell all those Bohemian names right." The students themselves sometimes pose another challenge if they don't understand the professional behavior and appearance that are expected, despite faculty members' efforts to explain what's appropriate. Pagel famously told his students in writing: "Remember, I know where you live. Screw up and I will follow you home and rip out your heart."

That was necessary, he said, because "anytime you start thinking college students are mature, you're making a big mistake." Kolterman echoed the importance of students carrying themselves professionally. "They need to dress equal to or better than the people they are interviewing," he said. Seward, he noted, is a predominantly conservative, Missouri Synod Lutheran community where "tattoos are still not the norm and multiple piercings should be under your hat." The student interns "need to look as quasi-normal as possible," he said. From a strictly academic standpoint, the arrangement with the Seward County Independent leaves something to be desired, several of the professors involved with the program said. "I hope they don't consider it a big teaching thing," retired professor Botts said. "As far as teaching writing, editing and photography, I don't think it had a whole lot of value….As a teaching tool it was far inferior to the labs paper, I thought." That was also true, he said, of the earlier program in which students sojourned out to publish a small daily newspaper somewhere in the state for two days. "There were enormous teaching moments in the labs that you don't get on these trips out through the state." Bender agreed. The Seward program, he said, is "just not an environment in which you can really get into a lot of the ethical issues, technical issues, reporting kinds of issues that provide…those teachable moments." In part, he suggested, that's because the story assignments tended to be features simply because they were more doable given the limitations of time. Moreover, stories written for special sections often weren't published until long after the students left, which also tended to limit their educational value for the students.

The summer school class also faces challenges in offering experiences comparable to Reporting II sections during the regular academic year. As the journalism curriculum has evolved, Reporting II students now work on multimedia skills and produce video assignments suitable for Web publication. The options for doing that are more limited in Seward, mainly for lack of time. In recent years, however, the summer school classes have produced slideshows for the paper's website, giving students some experience in telling stories visually. Alongside the academic limitations, there is at least one academic advantage for students enrolled in the Seward summer class, beyond seeing their stories in print. The limited class size and intensive work environment mean students essentially get one-on-one tutoring with the faculty member. The teacher can sit down with each student and critique a draft of a story or discuss a student's plans for an interview, which can be particularly useful both for the student who is struggling as well as the more talented student who can be challenged to improve even more. Whatever the limitations, after nearly three decades the UNL-Seward County Independent partnership seems to have evolved into what Berens, the associate dean and former editor, called a symbiotic relationship. "We all benefitted," she said. "It wasn't like we were doing them this big favor or the other way around." To publisher Zadina, though, the balance tips more toward benefitting the students. The Seward County Independent is happy to have the extra copy, but it's not critical to their survival. "Community newspapers are here to stay," Zadina said, "and that represents an opportunity for students."

CONCLUSIONS

Metrics-motivated, data-driven managers will find little reassurance in these case studies. Two of them are too new to draw conclusions about their long-term prospects, and the third has never been subjected to any attempts to measure its value in anything other than anecdotal terms. Nonetheless, the accounts of these three efforts by the UNL journalism college to be community news providers offer some insights that could help others who decide to take on similar projects, in keeping with the FCC report's recommendation. And the fact that one of them has been in existence for nearly three decades sheds some light on what it takes to make such efforts sustainable. The recommendations highlighted in the following sections are derived from the experiences of all three projects examined in this report. While they are not offered as a prescription for success, they suggest considerations that other colleges and community news organizations should keep in mind when embarking on similar efforts.

Planning

These case studies offer an interesting juxtaposition of projects with a significant amount of planning and those without. It's clear both approaches can work. The first Mosaic class was designed to undertake the research and planning phase of the project, but the class itself was, of necessity, less structured than some students could deal with. But a great deal of planning went into creating the website itself, including, importantly, identifying the target audience. This characteristic, in fact, is one all three projects share. Mosaic narrowly defined its audience to a manageable segment of the refugee population in Lincoln. The Nebraska News Service defined its target audience as news organizations in the state that want statehouse news coverage. And the target audience in the case of the Seward project is the Seward County Independent and, by extension, its readers. Community news projects would seem likely to have a greater chance to succeed, in other words, if they have a specific audience in mind, not just some vague idea that there's a shortage of news coverage student journalists can fill.

Beyond identifying the audience, successful projects seem to be figuring out how to reach that audience. Mosaic was hampered by a grant requirement to create an Englishlanguage website, illustrating, perhaps, a key weakness in the prevailing enthusiasm for all things digital. In this case, it led to a mistaken one-size-fits-all notion of communicating with an underserved population that has limited Internet access and a different way of using the Internet when it is available. In the case of the news service, reaching the audience was accomplished in a simple, direct way, by emailing clients the stories students produced, including accommodating one client who couldn't open email attachments. Working successfully with entities outside the college, which appears to be an element that makes these projects succeed, requires getting buy-in from partners. In the case of Mosaic, it means ongoing links with various community institutions that work with refugees and that provide helpful insights and contacts in the refugee community. For the news service, it means cultivating cooperation with the clerk of the legislature, the Nebraska Press Association, and editors who support the news service by using its stories. (Interestingly, however, the news service found it was not hampered by lack of support from the state's largest news organizations.) And for the college's partnership with the Seward County Independent, it means making space available for students to work and having the key editor agree not to go on vacation while the students are there, perhaps the most important lesson faculty learned the first time they attempted such an arrangement. Beyond that, clear ground rules need to be established at the outset affirming that the local editor maintains control and has the final say on content.

These three case studies also suggest that another planning element to consider is the role in the journalism curriculum these news-providing efforts will fill. Indeed, playing a clear role in the curriculum would seem to be an important factor in the Seward partnership's longevity. The summer school class fulfills a reporting course requirement for journalism majors, although it faces a challenge of assuring that the summer content is analogous to that offered in the regular academic year. Mosaic and the news service were created as upper-level electives, but discussions are underway to tweak them in such a way that they would fulfill expectations for a senior-level capstone course, assuring them a place in the curriculum. Beyond that, it would seem that creating community news in journalism colleges might best be done through the structure of specific classes rather than a more vague approach in which providing community news became an add-on expectation for a variety of different classes. It is generally much easier to hold people accountable when their mission is clearly focused, as it is in these three case studies. Colleges embarking on such efforts need to remain aware of the realities of dealing with students who, in most cases, are not able or willing to turn over their entire lives to the mission of creating community news. They have other classes, jobs, and, increasingly, families who all legitimately demand part of their time, all of which argues for making sure a college keeps its community news efforts in perspective. Yet another common thread among all three cases is the apparent approach of remaining vague when it comes to determining success. Dean Kebbel remarked on the need for faculty to be willing to take on experiments like these community news operations whose outcomes are uncertain. Dealing with that uncertainty, he suggested, could be a significant challenge, because tenure-track faculty members tend to be risk-averse. Of course, one of the advantages of proceeding with little planning may be that there are likely to be fewer concrete expectations for results.

But just as not all students are prepared to deal with ambiguity, neither are all faculty members, tenured or not. Finding the right people to take on such projects is surely an important part of the planning process.

Executing

All three of these projects suggest that one of the most critical elements of their success lies in committing to create professional quality content. Stakeholders interviewed for the Mosaic and news service projects both expressed surprise that the content was largely produced by undergraduates. Custer County Chief editor Deb McCaslin repeatedly emphasized that the quality is critical. If the stories NNS students produced needed a lot of editing or additional work, they simply wouldn't be used. That's true in Seward as well, although the Seward case study illustrates a corollary to the principle of creating professional quality work. That is: Students should not be given assignments beyond their ability. Or as Seward sports editor Stephanie Croston puts it: "We don't want to set them up to fail." Related to creating professional quality content is the expectation that students will be adhering to professional appearance and behavior. Making such expectations clear at the outset never guarantees that college students will follow them. But to the extent students are engaged in professional activities outside their comfort zones, they need to know what is expected of them, whether that means wearing a long-sleeved shirt to cover up offending tattoos in conservative Seward, Neb., or knowing a female reporter shouldn't offer her hand in greeting to a Muslim man unless he first offers his. It also needs to be made clear to students involved in providing community news that they should be expecting constructive feedback. Working with a student to make a story

Executing All three of these projects suggest that one of the most critical elements of their success lies in committing to create professional quality content. Stakeholders interviewed for the Mosaic and news service projects both expressed surprise that the content was largely produced by undergraduates. Custer County Chief editor Deb McCaslin repeatedly emphasized that the quality is critical. If the stories NNS students produced needed a lot of editing or additional work, they simply wouldn't be used. That's true in Seward as well, although the Seward case study illustrates a corollary to the principle of creating professional quality work. That is: Students should not be given assignments beyond their ability. Or as Seward sports editor Stephanie Croston puts it: "We don't want to set them up to fail." Related to creating professional quality content is the expectation that students will be adhering to professional appearance and behavior. Making such expectations clear at the outset never guarantees that college students will follow them. But to the extent students are engaged in professional activities outside their comfort zones, they need to know what is expected of them, whether that means wearing a long-sleeved shirt to cover up offending tattoos in conservative Seward, Neb., or knowing a female reporter shouldn't offer her hand in greeting to a Muslim man unless he first offers his. It also needs to be made clear to students involved in providing community news that they should be expecting constructive feedback. Working with a student to make a story

Remaining Open to Change

The cases examined here suggest that community news efforts can be launched with only the vaguest planning outlines. And while there may be merit in Dean Kebbel's advice to "go in stupid," it does not necessarily follow that continuing to be stupid is advisable. Shooting from the hip may be a way to get started, but once a community news project is underway, it probably pays to think about avoiding rash judgments as the project evolves. Establishing a solid framework and taking a lesson from the tortoise and the hare are approaches more likely to lead to a sustainable project than looking for the flashy, one-time headline.

To that end, Mosaic and the Seward project illustrate the importance of being willing to critique what you do and make adjustments accordingly. Mosaic teacher Anderson has given thoughtful consideration to how much content students should be expected to produce. He was also willing to reconsider the notion that refugee volunteers could be recruited to contribute to the Mosaic website and turned instead to paying them as freelancers. And the Mosaic team recognized a serendipitous opportunity to use a feature of the site itself as an Internet training tool for refugees, something no one had anticipated. Likewise the Seward project learned the hard way that allowing 17 students to enroll in the summer school class, however well intentioned, was completely unmanageable. Perhaps the most interesting example of a change in course can be seen in the grantfunded position of multimedia coach for the Nebraska News Service. The position initially was conceived as someone who would travel the state drumming up clients for the fledgling operation. But when it became clear that the news service was attracting clients without much promotion, the job was recast to meet a different need that subsequently had been identified. UNL's journalism program, like most, is committed to having its students master multimedia reporting skills. But when it became apparent that many NNS clients weren't able to use much multimedia content, the job was redefined and a person was hired to work with NNS clients to improve their multimedia capabilities. The widespread enthusiasm among the Nebraska press for the multimedia coach's services suggests that such a service could be something journalism colleges could consider offering, independent of any link to providing content.

Ongoing Challenges

Whatever the merits of journalism colleges providing community news, these case studies make one thing abundantly clear: college-based community news operations are not a silver bullet that will compensate for the dramatic reduction in daily newsroom staffs and consequent shrinkage of what journalists deem important public affairs reporting, as the FCC report documents. But that doesn't mean they aren't worth doing. As the three cases examined here suggest, programs that link journalism colleges to their communities in a collaborative, collegial manner can provide news and feature content that otherwise wouldn't be available and give students opportunities they otherwise wouldn't have. But they face some very real challenges. One of those challenges—being tied to the academic calendar—likely could be addressed with sufficient resources to pay faculty and student interns to continue the services through the summer, for example. Indeed, The Information Needs of Communities calls on foundations and philanthropists to "help fund journalism-school 'residencies' for recent graduates" who could run year-round community news programs staffed by journalism students (355). The idea might be worth examining. Students are, by definition, transient, which poses another challenge that may be insurmountable. It's the reason news organizations would be unwise to hope that studentprovided news can make up for shrinking reporting budgets. As transients, students generally have a limited storehouse of knowledge about communities they might be expected to cover.

Briefing manuals and garden-variety research can help fill the storehouse a bit. So can faculty running the program, whose institutional memory can help steer student reporters along the right track. But community news projects that are tied to specific college courses inevitably would see students pass the class and move on after a semester or two, making way for a new crop of reporters who have to start up the learning curve.

Clearly, such newcomers can create content. They probably can cover speeches and press conferences and committee hearings and public meetings. And they no doubt can write a wide array of feature stories and profiles of interesting or important figures in the community. Some of them will be able to mine stories from publicly available data that no one else has bothered to look at. But what none of them is likely to be able to do is spend a year or two or three trolling the halls of the courthouse or statehouse or city hall, developing sources—and stories—the way the best beat reporters have always done. And that is the kind of journalism that student-created content is unlikely ever to replace. Perhaps a bigger challenge relates to issues raised by two faculty members about the educational merits of such content-providing classes. Such arrangements may not, in fact, be the best way to teach journalism, a question that deserves further study. A journalism program that decided to embark on or expand such efforts might be well advised to have serious discussions about the college's priorities and how to balance journalism education with public service, if it decides to adopt such a mission.

Final Comments

The FCC's report, The Information Needs of Communities, endorses the much-discussed idea of journalism schools adopting a teaching hospital or medical residency approach, in which students actually do journalism while they are learning it (194-196, 355). The report documents the tens of thousands of students enrolled in hundreds of journalism programs around the country, suggesting that they constitute a rich resource for creating community news if such programs adopted the learning-by-doing approach of teaching hospitals.

But the case studies described in this report suggest that the medical residency analogy may be misplaced. For one thing, the medical residents providing patient care in teaching hospitals already have a medical degree, usually following four years of medical school. And even getting into medical school is an intensely selective process in which a premium is placed on high test scores.

Medical residents, in short, are unlikely to tell a supervising physician "but I like it this way" when being advised how to render patient care. Perhaps a more apt analogy for journalism education could be found in our teachers' colleges, which have evolved methods for gradually placing undergraduate students in increasingly responsible positions in elementary and secondary classrooms under the supervision of full-time cooperating teachers. Students in teachers' colleges may start out observing various classrooms. Then they may engage in presenting individual lessons or conducting classroom activities several times a week, followed by feedback from a cooperating teacher or university supervisor.

Ultimately, their training usually culminates in an immersive, semester-long, professionally supervised student teaching assignment. Such a model, in short, might provide inspiration for undergraduate journalism education. Indeed some elements of the case studies examined here already reflect parallels with the teacher education model, such as the immersion, however limited, that students experience at the Seward County Independent or the one-on-one feedback students in Mosaic or the news service get as their stories are shaped for publication. Whatever model journalism educators envision as a way to reshape their operations and create community-focused programs to fill gaps in news coverage, these case studies offer a powerful reminder never to discount the value of intangibles that may emerge: the student who changes her major because she decides journalism is the wrong field for her; the student who goes on to work in community newspapers; the student who learns what happens when you make a serious mistake in a story; the student who encounters a refugee who has survived unspeakable horrors; the refugee who encounters an American student and successfully communicates her dreams for tomorrow. Journalism educators should be prepared to accept that the possible outcomes of such community focused programs are likely to include those that are entirely unquantifiable, even life-altering, which perhaps constitutes a strong argument for doing them

INTELLECTUAL PROPERTY ISSUES AND STUDENT-CREATED CONTENT

Economic and social changes have constricted the reach of American journalism in the early 21st century. Many news organizations have cut staff and newspapers have reduced their size. Some television stations have been expanding the amount of time they devote to news, but even in such situations, they are largely recycling the same number of stories. As a result, what journalism is available through commercial media is increasingly reactive and superficial. Investigative reporting and reporting that requires journalists to devote large amounts of time to a single topic are increasingly rare. The consequence is that Americans are learning less about their safety, livelihoods and government and business decisions that may affect their lives.1 One possibility for filling the gap in public information is to call on the journalism programs at colleges and universities around the country to provide some of the reporting that commercial media are no longer doing.2 This possibility raises a number of questions related to copyright and public records law. This essay attempts to answer some of those questions.

Basic Copyright Principles

The place to begin this examination is with the basic provisions of copyright law: what is protected by copyright; when and how is it protected; what is not protected; and who is presumed to own the copyrights to the materials created. The federal copyright law as amended in 1976 expressly protects "original works of authorship fixed in any tangible medium of expression."3 This short phrase includes two key concepts that are central to understanding how copyright law works: originality and fixation. The report of the House Judiciary Committee, which accompanied the bill on its passage, states that "originality" does not require that the work exhibit great novelty or aesthetic value.4 In one of the more important recent cases on copyright, the U.S. Supreme Court re-emphasized that point. The court said:

To qualify for copyright protection, a work must be original to the author. Original, as the term is used in copyright, means only that the work was independently created by the author (as opposed to copied from other works), and that it possesses at least some minimal degree of creativity.5 Even a routine paper written by a student would satisfy this low standard for originality. So long as the student had not copied the material from another, it would possess sufficient originality to qualify for copyright protection, even if the content were banal and the research or investigation superficial. The other requirement for copyright protection is that the work be fixed in a tangible medium of expression, including any medium now known or later developed that would allow another to perceive the work either directly with one's own senses or with the aid of some mechanical device.6 Before the 1976 revision of the law, works enjoyed statutory copyright protection only if published, but the revision applies statutory protection to any work fixed in a tangible medium, regardless of whether it has been published.

The House report explains that the work—whether it is words, pictures, sounds or any other copyrightable matter—must be recorded on some stable medium. In the case of written words, that might mean nothing more than recording them on a piece of paper. Or, as is more common now, recording them on the hard drive of a computer or on a CD-ROM or some other magnetic medium. In the case of images, it would be recording them on a memory card or tape. Even if the material in question were a live broadcast, say of a legislative hearing, the material would be eligible for copyright protection so long it was being recorded at the same time it was being broadcast.7 An assignment written by a student would be fixed in a tangible medium if the student wrote it on paper or saved in on a computer disk or even submitted it through email or Blackboard or a similar course management program, because the assignment probably would be recorded on some computer server and, therefore, exist on a tangible medium.

Clearly, almost all student work would qualify for copyright protection on the basis of its originality and its having be fixed on a tangible medium of some kind. The next question is the ownership of the copyright. The answer seems to be equally straightforward: The student owns the copyright. The statute provides that ownership of the copyright in a work initially goes to the author or authors of the work.8 In a law review article written before the adoption of the 1976 changes to the copyright law, Robert B. Carpenter concluded, "Preliminarily, there does not appear to be any general impediment in the law of copyright that would prevent a student from securing copyright in a qualified work under either common law or federal statute."9 Carpenter's main reservation was that much student work was never published, but he was writing at the time when unpublished works enjoyed only common law protection.

One might argue that a student paper is akin to a work for hire. Ownership of the copyright in a work for hire goes to the employer.10 The copyright in a news story prepared for a newspaper or a television station, for example, belongs to the owners of the newspaper or station, not to the reporter who researched and wrote the story. What case law exists, however, suggests that the work-for-hire doctrine does not apply in the case of student works. In 1979, David Quinto, a second-year student at Harvard Law School, wrote an article for the Harvard Law Record on the experiences of law students on their summer jobs. The Legal Times of Washington, D.C., later republished 92 percent of Quinto's article without his permission. The managers of The Legal Times believed that Quinto's article was a work for hire and that the copyright belonged to the Harvard Law Record, and they obtained permission from the editor of the Record. 11 The court, however, concluded that Quinto's article was not a work for hire. It would be difficult to envision a case where it is more clear than it is here that the article was a contribution to a collective work and not a work for hire. It is uncontested that plaintiff received no compensation for his article, that the idea to write it was entirely his, that he was not a party to an express contract for hire and was free to engage in other writing activities for pay, that he had no regular working hours and that neither the interviews nor the initial writing occurred at In the case of a contribution to a collective work, such as a collection of essays or short stories, or in some cases, magazines or newspapers, the copyright in each individual contribution belongs to the contribution's author or authors.13

In order for a work to be considered for hire, it must have been created by an employee within the scope of his or her duties. If a school were to claim ownership of the copyright in student works, it would have to show that there is an employment relationship between the school and the student and that the work was created within the scope of that relationship. But students are not employed by their schools. Even in situations where the student may hold a work-study job or some similar employment, the duties of such jobs do not include the preparation of papers or assignments for academic credit.14 After reviewing the facts of the typical student-instructor relationship, Carpenter concluded, "A student author, then, should not be treated as an author for hire under the current statutory application of that doctrine."15

In Community for Creative Non-Violence v. Reid,16 the U.S. Supreme Court used the law of agency to determine whether a work was a work-for-hire or the creation of an independent contractor. James Earl Reid had executed a sculpture for the Community for Creative NonViolence depicting the plight of the homeless. Reid was paid for the sculpture, and after its completion both CCNV and Reid filed competing applications for a copyright.

A federal district court held that the sculpture was a work-for-hire, so the copyright belonged to CCNV, but an appellate court reversed and said the copyright belonged to Reid.17 The Supreme Court said the general common law of agency used the following factors to determine whether one party was an employee of another:

- the skill required;
- the source of the instrumentalities and tools;
- the location of the work;
- the duration of the relationship between the parties;

- whether the hiring party has the right to assign additional projects to the hired party;
- the extent of the hired party's discretion over when and how long to work;
- the method of payment;
- the hired party's role in hiring and paying assistants;
- whether the work is part of the regular business of the hiring party;
- whether the hiring party is in business;
- the provision of employee benefits;
- and the tax treatment of the hired party.18

Few of these factors would favor a university or college in a copyright dispute with a student. The school may have some control over the student's discretion in the execution of the work and may be able to assign additional work (at least for the duration of the course), but the important factors pertain to payment, benefits, tax treatment, provision of tools and instrumentalities, and the location where the work is performed. All are irrelevant to the student-school relationship or favor the student. The original owner of the copyright to a student-produced news story, therefore, is the student, not the school. The next question is whether there is a transfer of copyright to the school as a condition for the publication of the work.

II. Transfer of Ownership

Sec. 201 of the copyright law provides that owners may transfer all or part of their exclusive rights to others by sale or by inheritance.19 The exclusive rights of owners include the right to prepare copies of the original work, to distribute copies of the work, to prepare derivative works, to display the work and to perform the work.20 The House report said each of these rights may be owned separately and may be conveyed separately.21 The author of a novel, for instance, has the right to prepare a derivative work based on that novel, such as a play or a movie. But the author could sell that right to another, allowing that person to prepare the derivative. Rights are also divisible by time and place. A television station owns the exclusive rights to broadcast a network show for a given time and region. Owners of these partial rights may also sue to defend them.22 The owner of the right to prepare a screenplay based on another person's novel would have the right to sue for infringement any other person who prepared a screenplay. Another part of Sec. 201 says transfers of copyrights must have been voluntary. No government body or official or other organization can expropriate, seize or transfer a person's copyrights. The House report says the purpose of this provision "is to reaffirm the basic principle that the United States copyright of an individual author shall be secured to that author, and cannot be taken away by any involuntary transfer." This section seems to foreclose the possibility that one may presume that students have transferred the copyright in their work simply by enrolling in a class or by having their work published by the college or university.

This issue came up when four Virginia and Arizona high school students sued iParadigms LLC, the operator of the anti-plagiarism program Turnitin. The company contracts with schools which then require students to submit their papers to Turnitin. Students must sign up with Turnitin before they can submit their papers. As part of the sign-up process, they have to agree, by clicking on an "accept" button, to Turnitin's terms, which include giving it a perpetual license to store and use the submissions. The program stores, with the approval of the school, all papers that are submitted. It then produces an originality report on each submission. Instructors can ask to see the entire copy of an earlier paper if they want it to evaluate whether any detected similarities are the product of plagiarism. The students claimed iParadigms had infringed on the copyrights in their papers by storing them and reproducing them as part of subsequent reports on whether papers written by other students had been plagiarized. The federal district court that heard the iParadigms case ruled in favor of Turnitin, holding that the "clickwrap" agreement constituted a valid contract and that, in any event, Turnitin's use of the student papers was protected by the fair-use defense in copyright law.26 In spite of the ruling, however, some legal scholars believe the district court erred on both the contract and on the application of the fair-use defense. One scholar, Stephen Sharon, said contracts involving minors can be voided in most states when the person reaches.

Also, for a contract involving a minor to be binding, the minor must have received some benefit, but the students who must submit papers to Turnitin, receive no benefit. The benefits all accrue to the school or the instructor.

Although students would have the copyright in any news stories they produced for news organizations operated by or in cooperation with an academic journalism program, both the students and the school (and other parties involved) might benefit from an explicit agreement. The agreement should allow the school (or the news organization that is collaborating with the school's journalism program) first-time rights to publish or broadcast the students' work. The agreement might convey the school and collaborating news organization more rights, but by conveying at least these rights the school and news organization could sue to protect the copyright, if necessary. Students should retain at least some rights to their work. If the school and collaborating news organization have only first-time publication rights, then the students would be free to republish the work later. The likelihood their work would have great commercial value is slight, but leaving students that opportunity may give them an incentive to perform better. They should at least have the right to reproduce the work for distribution to potential employers or to display it on a personal webpage. In any event, an explicit agreement would avoid confusion, litigation, and bad feelings if disagreements arose later.

III. Use of Student Work by Other News Organizations

Any journalistic works created by students would probably be published in some form, and today, that would include publication on the Web. The publisher might be the students' college or university, or it might be a commercial news organization collaborating with the school in providing a forum for student work. Such publications would be licensed by the agreement between the students, the school and the collaborating news organizations. However, once the information is on the Web, others would have the opportunity to access it and even republish it. This might violate the exclusive rights of the copyright owners unless the use fell within the scope of the fair-use defense. The fair-use defense is a judicially created doctrine dating to at least 1841.28 But in 1976, Congress incorporated the defense in the copyright statute.29 Fair use allows one to make unlicensed use of another's copyrighted work "for purposes such as criticism, comment, news reporting, teaching ..., scholarship, or research." No use, not even those listed in the statute as qualifying as fair use, is presumptively fair. In every instance, a court must determine whether a use is a fair one by applying four factors:

- the purpose and character of the use, including whether it is commercial or noncommercial;
- the nature of the copyrighted original;
- the amount and substantiality of the portion used;
- and the effect on the potential market for the original and any likely derivatives.

Further complicating the picture is the doctrine that copyright does not protect facts, only expression. The Supreme Court has said, "[F]acts do not owe their origin to an act of authorship.... The first person to find and report a particular fact has not created the fact; he or she has merely discovered its existence." This does not mean that a work that is based on facts alone cannot be copyrighted; rather, the copyright protects only the way the facts are expressed, not the facts themselves. A history of the Civil War, for instance, would have copyright protection for the manner in which the author described the facts. The same would be true of a news story. As a result of the doctrine that facts cannot be copyrighted, a competing news organization may take the facts that another news organization has reported, rewrite them so that they are expressed in a different manner, and republish them without violating the copyright of the organization that first reported the information. Ethically, the second news organization should credit the first for having initially collected and published the information, but the law does not require giving credit. Copyright law may offer only limited protection, but another legal concept may be more helpful in protecting, at least temporarily, the work of student journalists: unfair competition. The U.S. Supreme Court applied this concept to a news piracy case dating from the early 20th century. The Associated Press and the Hearst-owned International News Service were competitors in the business of providing national and international news to newspapers around the country. The AP sued INS alleging the INS had bribed employees of AP papers, induced AP members to sell it news in violation of their contract with the AP, and stolen news from bulletin boards and published it verbatim or with slight revision. The AP claimed no copyright in its news stories, but it did argue that INS had unfairly appropriated news the AP had gathered and used it to its own commercial advantage.

The Supreme Court described the news business in the following terms: What we are concerned with is the business of making [news] known to the world.... That business consists in maintaining a prompt, sure, steady, and reliable service designed to place the daily events of the world at the breakfast table of the millions at a price that, while of trifling moment to each reader, is sufficient in the aggregate to afford compensation for the cost of gathering and distributing it, with the added profit so necessary as an incentive to effective action in the commercial world.... The parties are competitors in this field; and, on fundamental principles, applicable here as elsewhere, when the rights or privileges of the one are liable to conflict with those of the other, each party is under a duty so to conduct its own business as not unnecessarily or unfairly to injure that of the other.

the AP was disseminating was of greatest value, and this amounted to unfair competition on the part of INS.

It may seem strange that the key technology of the early 21st century would revive and give new significance to a court decision from the early 20th century, yet that is what has happened. INS v. AP has existed in textbooks for the last 40 or more years as something of an oddity, and not a central part of media law. But the Internet has made it possible for a Web site operator, whether affiliated with a traditional news organization or not, to collect and repackage news from organizations that have invested large amounts of money in reporters to gather and write that news. A Web operation based on the West Coast could gather information from the Web sites of East Coast newspapers and make it available to readers and viewers essentially at the same time it was available through the Web sites of the creating news organizations. The pervasiveness of the theft of news has led one prominent media law attorney to suggest the adoption of a "hot news doctrine."40 Only a few states have explicitly recognized the hot-news doctrine from INS v. AP, but if more recognized it, the doctrine might prove useful to traditional news organizations losing revenue to aggregators and pirates. Another possibility would be for Congress to recognize the doctrine, thereby making it uniformly applicable throughout the country.

The most relevant case on this point since INS v. AP is National Basketball Ass'n v. Motorola, Inc., which involved the real-time distribution of basketball scores over pagers by Motorola's SportsTrax operation. The NBA argued that SportsTrax was engaged in unfair competition and infringing on its rights in the "hot news" of the basketball scores. Motorola contended any hot-news claims had been pre-empted by the federal copyright law.

The federal appeals court said a claim based on the hot-news doctrine might be sustainable if (i) a plaintiff generates or gathers information at a cost; (ii) the information is time-sensitive; (iii) a defendant's use of the information constitutes free riding on the plaintiff's efforts; (iv) the defendant is in direct competition with a product or service offered by the plaintiffs; and (v) the ability of other parties to free-ride on the efforts of the plaintiff or others would so reduce the incentive to produce the product or service that its existence or quality would be substantially threatened.

The appeals court concluded, however, that the NBA was unable to satisfy these factors and ruled in favor of SportsTrax and Motorola.

Between the fair-use defense and the doctrine that facts cannot be protected by copyright, the main limitation on the piracy of news stories prepared by students is that the user not appropriate the expression as well as the facts. So long as another Web site does not take the students' stories verbatim or nearly verbatim, then the republication would be considered fair use. The hot-news doctrine, which has limited scope at present, offers some additional protection against Web sites or others who routinely pirate fresh news that others have gathered and prepared for publication.

IV. Protecting the Records and Sources of Student Journalists

A problem allied to the intellectual property issue but involving different legal provisions is the vulnerability of unpublished information compiled by student journalists to requests for records under state public records laws. This might include unpublished drafts of the stories that are eventually published, instructor comments on those drafts, notes of interviews and the names of sources, audio and video tapes of interviews and unpublished photographs and video or audio recordings. Such requests could expose student journalists to hostile publicity and expose any confidential sources and information the students obtained in the course of their reporting. For students attending a private college or university, the answer is fairly simple: The students' records are not public. State colleges and universities, however, usually are considered public bodies or public agencies that are subject to the open records laws of their states.44 Even though the state-supported universities and colleges may be subject to public records laws, at least two legal barriers protect the confidentiality of unpublished records of student journalists. The first of these legal barriers is the federal Family Educational and Privacy Rights Act (FERPA). Part of this law requires that students and parents have access to their educational records. Another part, however, prohibits the release of educational records to third parties without the consent of the students or their parents. The relevant provision prohibits making federal money available to any educational institution that has the policy or practice of releasing educational records to any individual, agency or organization without the consent of the student or parents. The law defines educational records to include any records, files or documents that contain information directly related to the student and are maintained by the educational institution or someone acting on behalf of the institution. That definition would seem to include most if not all of the materials a student journalists might compile in the course of reporting a story. It would protect that information regardless of whether it was in the possession of the student48 or the instructor. It would also protect any unpublished drafts of a story, which presumably would have the instructor's comments and criticisms and the grade assigned to the work.

A possible second barrier is the public records law of the individual state. Every state has a public or open records law. The laws vary greatly from state to state, but all contain at least a few exemptions. In some cases, the state law contains an explicit exemption for the educational records of students. The first exemption in the Nebraska Public Records law, for example, says that personal information in records regarding current, prospective or former students is exempt from disclosure. Texas exempts from disclosure personally identifiable student records held by a state-supported school. The provision is explicitly designed to bring Texas law into agreement with FERPA. Oregon has an exemption that would seem to apply most clearly to the work of student journalists completed as part of an academic course.

The provision exempts "[w]ritings prepared by, or under the direction of, faculty of public educational institutions completed in connection with research." Maryland has a similar provision, though not quite as clearly on point as Oregon's. The Maryland law exempts records of research projects carried out at state institutions.52 Some state laws do not specifically exempt student records, but they may contain broad privacy exemptions that could apply to student records. California, for instance, says that "[p]ersonnel, medical or similar files" are exempt if they contain information the disclosure of which would constitute an unwarranted invasion of privacy.53 Virginia also exempts scholastic records containing information about identifiable individuals.54 As with the federal FERPA, the state public records laws would seem to apply to many of the records students might compile in the course of reporting on a story for a school-affiliated publication. Any drafts, notes or other materials the student might share with the instructor would clearly be educational records. They are part of the work the student is required to submit in order to receive academic credit for the course. The fact that a finished, edited version of the material might later be published does not make the drafts, which contain the instructor's comments, corrections and criticisms, public records. Even if the state law does not include an exemption for student records, a general privacy exemption, like that in California, would likely apply. The comments an instructor might make on a student's story would be highly personal and confidential. The disclosure of that information would constitute an unwarranted invasion of personal privacy. Another scenario could lead to the disclosure of some of the information student reporters might gather. This involves a situation in which a grand jury or court or legislative committee

subpoenaed the reporter's information in connection with an investigation into a criminal matter.55 The U.S. Supreme Court has said there is no First Amendment right for a journalist to withhold confidential sources or information from a grand jury investigating criminal activity.56 Nevertheless, in many jurisdictions, journalists possess a privilege to withhold confidential sources or information or both under some circumstances. Forty states and the District of Columbia have shield laws which allow reporters to withhold information.

Some states have absolute shield laws; others qualify that protection. Some shield laws apply to student journalists, and others do not. In a state where a shield law does not protect student journalists, the student may be marginally more at risk than a professional reporter. Elsewhere, however, the student journalist would be in exactly the same position as the professional. Student status would probably have no effect on the outcome of any litigation over the subpoena. Would a journalistic enterprise run by a college or university have more protection from disclosure of records and other information if it operated as a separate entity, such as a 501(c)(3) nonprofit organization?

There is some reason to believe that it would add little, if any, to the protections already described above, although the answer may vary with the laws of the particular state. Just because an organization is a private entity does not mean all records it holds are exempt from disclosure under a state public records law. In 2001, the Cincinnati Enquirer sought records pertaining to cost overruns in the construction of a new football stadium. The city and Hamilton County had contracted with a private company to oversee the construction, and the relevant records were held by the private company. The Ohio Supreme Court said that records of private entities may be subject to the state's Open Records Law if the entity prepared the records to carry out a function ordinarily carried out by a public office, the public office was able to monitor the private entities performance, and the public office had access to the records for the purpose of monitoring the work.57 The court held that these criteria applied to the records the Enquirer sought.58 This reasoning quite probably would not apply to a journalistic enterprise run by a state university or college. Gathering, writing and publishing news is not a function ordinarily carried out by any state entity, so it would be difficult to argue that the news gathering operation was functioning as an agent of state government.

V. CONCLUSIONS

The intellectual property created by student journalists gathering news published by a university or college class belongs to the student. Students cannot be presumed to transfer their ownership of that property simply because they are receive a grade or the opportunity to have their work published. Nevertheless, both students and the school (and any private news organization that is involved) might benefit from an explicit agreement between all parties giving the school and private news organization first-time publication rights. This would clarify the relationships among the parties and give all of them an interest in protecting the intellectual property. The school or the private news organization conceivably could insist on a transfer of more, or even all, intellectual property rights in the story. Universities and colleges, however, should be mindful of the unequal bargaining position of the students and should try to protect the students' interests.

Because news stories are reporting facts and facts cannot be copyrighted, the copyright protection they enjoy is limited to the manner in which the facts are expressed. That would allow the copyright owners to sue for infringement if another organization used the students' work verbatim or nearly verbatim. The owners might also be able to sue under an unfair-competition theory, at least in some states. The educational setting in which the student journalists are working would protect most, if not all, of their unpublished materials from disclosure under state public records laws. The materials probably would be exempt either because of the federal FERPA law or exemptions to the state public records laws or both.

REFERENCES

1. Ball, Rick. Meet the Press: Fifty Years of History in the Making. New York: McGraw-Hill, 1998.
2. Barnhurst, Kevin G. and John Nerone.The Form of News: A History. New York: Guilford Press, 2001.
3. Beasley, Maurine Hoffman, and Sheila Gibbons. Taking Their Place:
4. A Documentary History of Women and Journalism. Washington, DC: American University Press, 1993.
5. Bernstein, Mark and Alex Lubertozzi. World War II on the Air. Naperville, IL: Sourcebooks, Inc., 2003.
6. Blanchard, Margaret A., ed. History of the Mass Media in the United States, An Encyclopedia. Chicago: Fitzroy Dearborn Publishers, 1998.
7. Brennen, Bonnie and Hanno Hardt, eds. Picturing the Past: Media, History and Photography. Champaign, IL: University of Illinois Press, 1999.
8. Briggs, Asa. The BBC: The First Fifty Years. Oxford: Oxford University Press, 1985.
9. Briggs, Asa and Peter Burke. A Social History of the Media from Gutenberg to the Internet.
10. Malden, MA: Blackwell, 2001.
11. Bliss, Edward. Now the News: The Story of Broadcast Journalism. New York: Columbia University Press, 1991.
12. Broussard, Jinx Coleman. Giving a Voice to the Voiceless: Four Pioneering Black Women Journalists. New York: Routledge, 2004.
13. Burke, Peter and Asa Briggs. A Social History of the Media: from Gutenberg to the Internet. Malden, MA: Blackwell, 2001.
14. Burns, Eric. Infamous Scribblers: the Founding Fathers and the Rowdy Beginnings of American Journalism. New York: Public Affairs, 2006.

15. Campbell, Joseph. The Year that Defined American Journalism. New York: Routledge, 2006.
16. Cannadine, David. History and the Media. New York: Palgrave Macmillian, 2004.
17. Chadwell, William Robert. Horace Greeley: Champion of American Freedom. New York: New York University Press, 2006.
18. Clark, Roy Peter and G. Stuart Adam. Journalism: The Democratic Craft. New York: Oxford, 2006
19. Cloud, Stanley and Lynne Olson. The Murrow Boys: Pioneers on the Front Lines of Broadcast Journalism. Boston: Houghton Mifflin Company, 1996.
20. Clowse, Barbara Barksdale. Ralph McGill: A Biography. Macon, GA: Mercer University Press, 1999.
21. Copeland, David A. Debating the Issues in Colonial Newspapers. Westport, CT: Greenwood Press, 2000.
22. Cronkite, Walter. A Reporter's Life. New York: Knopf, 1996.
23. Crowley, David. J. and Paul Heyer. Communication in History.
24. Boston, MA: Allyn and Bacon, 2003.
25. Danky, James Philip, et al, eds. African-American Newspapers and Periodicals: A National Bibliography. Cambridge, MA: Harvard University Press, 1999.
26. Downs, Robert Bingham and Jane B. Downs. Journalists of the United States. Jefferson, NC: McFarland & Company, 1991.
27. Eaman, Ross Allan. Historical Dictionary of Journalism. Lanham, MD: Scarecrow, 2009.
28. Ehrlich, Matthew C. Journalism in the Movies. Urbana: University of Illinois Press, 2004.
29. Emery, Michael, Edwin Emery, and Nancy L. Roberts. The Press and America:
30. An Interpretive History of the Mass Media, 9th ed. Boston: Allyn and Bacon, 1999.
31. Engelman, Ralph. Friendlyvision: Fred Friendly and the Rise and Fall of Television Journalism.
32. New York: Columbia University Press, 2009.
33. Fang, Irving E. Alphabet to Internet: Mediated Communication in Our Lives. St. Paul, MN: Rada Press, 2008.
34. Fanning, Kay. Kay Fanning's Alaska Story. Kenmore, WA: Epicenter

Press, 2006.

35. Farrar, Howard. The Baltimore Afro-American, 1892-1950. Westport CT: Greenword Press, 1998.
36. Fedler, Fred. Lessons from the Past: Journalists' Lives and Work, 1850-1950. Prospect Heights, IL: Waveland Press, Inc., 2000.
37. Fellow, Anthony R. and John Williams Tebbel. American Media History. Belmont, CA: Thomson/Wadsworth, 2005.
38. Folkerts, Jean, and Dwight L. Teeter, Jr. Voices of a Nation: A History of Mass Media in the United States.
39. Needham Heights, MA: Allyn & Bacon, 1997.
40. Frank, Reuven. Out of Thin Air: The Brief Wonderful Life of Network News. New York: Simon & Schuster, 1991.
41. Ghiglione, Loren. CBS's Don Hollenbeck: An Honest Reporter in the Age of McCarthyism.
42. Washington, DC: Library of Congress, 2008. Godfrey, Donald G. Methods of Historical Analysis in Electronic Media. Mahwah, NJ: Lawrence Erlbaum Associates, 2005.
43. Gomery, Douglas. A History of Broadcasting in the United States. Malden, MA: Blackwell, 2008.
44. Graham, Katharine. Personal History. New York: Knopf, 1997.
45. Harnett, Richard M. and Billy G. Ferguson. Unipress: United Press International: Covering the 20th Century. Golden, CO: Fulcrum Publishing, 2001.
46. Harrison, S.L. Cavalcade of Journalists 1900-2000. Miami, FL: Wolf Den Books, 2002.
47. Hartsock, John C. A History of American Literary Journalism: The Emergence of a Modern Narrative Form.Amherst, MA: University of Massachusetts Press, 2000.
48. Haskell, Harry. Boss-Busters & Sin Hounds: Kansas City and Its Star. Columbia: University of Missouri Press, 2007.
49. Haynes, Gary. Picture This!: The Inside Story , and Classic Photos of UPI Newspictures. ,New York: Bulfinch Press, 2006.
50. Hewitt, Don. Tell Me a Story. New York: Public Affairs, 2001.
51. Hoffman, Joyce. On Their Own: Women Journalists and the American Experience in Vietnam. Cambridge MA: Da Capo Press, 2008.
52. Hollis, Daniel Webster. The Media in America. Santa Barbara, CA: ABC-CLIO, Inc., 1995.

53. Hudson, Frederick. Journalism in the United States from 1690-1872. New York: Routledge, 2000.
54. Huntzicker, William. The Popular Press, 1833-1865. Westport, CT: Greenwood Press, 1999.
55. Humphrey, Carol Sue. The Press and the Young Republic, 1783-1833. Westport, CT: Greenwood Press, 1996.
56. Hutton, Frankie and Barbara Straus Reid, eds. Outsiders in 19th-Century Press History. Bowling Green: Bowling Green State University Press, 1996.
57. Kitch, Carolyn L. Pages from the Past: History and Memory in American Magazines. Chapel Hill, NC: University of North Carolina Press, 2005.
58. Kotler, Johathan and Miles Beller. American Datelines: Major News Stories from Colonial Times to the Present. Urbana, IL: University of Illinois Press, 2003.
59. Knudson, Jerry W. In the News: American Journalists View Their Craft. Wilmington, DE: Scholarly Resources, 2000.
60. Kuralt, Charles. A Life on the Road. ew York: G.P. Putnam's Sons, 1990.
61. Langman, Larry. The Media in the Movies. Jefferson, NC: McFarland & Company, 1997.
62. Lee, Alfred McClung. The Daily Newspaper in America: The Evolution of a Social Instrument.
63. New York: Routledge, 2000.
64. Lewis, Jon E. The Mammoth Book of Journalism: An Anthology of the 100 Greatest Newspaper Articles.
65. New York: Carrol & Graf., 2003.
66. Library of America. Reporting on Civil Rights. vols. 1-2. New York: Library of America, 2003.
67. Lutes, Jean Marie. Front Page Girls: Women Journalists in American Culture and Fiction. Ithaca, NY: Cornell University Press, 2006.
68. McPherson, James Brian. Journalism at the End of the American Century, 1965-Present. Westport, CT: Praeger, 2006.
69. Mills, Eleanor, Kira Cochrane and Naomi Wolf. Journalistas: 100 Years of the Best Writing
70. and Reporting by Women Journalists. New York: Carroll & Graf Publishers, 2005.
71. Mindich, David T. Z. Just the Facts: How Objectivity Came to Define American Journalism. New York: New York University Press, 1998.

72. Munson, Eve Stryker, and Catherine A. Warren, eds. James Carey: A Critical Reader. Minneapolis: University of Minnesota Press, 1997.
73. Murray, Michael D., ed. Encyclopedia of Television News. Phoenix, AZ: The Oryx Press, 1999.
74. Ness, Richard. From Headline Hunter to Superman: A Journalism Filmography. Landham, MD: Scarecrow Press, 1997.
75. Newton, Eric, ed. Crusaders, Scoundrels, Journalists: The Newseum's Most Intriguing Newspeople. New York: Times Books, 1999.
76. Nord, David Paul. Communities of Journalism: A History of American Newspapers and Their Readers. Urbana: University of Illinois Press, 2001.
77. Perry, James M. A Bohemian Brigade: The Civil War Correspondents. New York: John Wiley & Sons, Inc., 2000.
78. Pride, Armistead S. and Clint C. Wilson. A History of the Black Press. Washington, DC: Howard University Press, 1997.
79. Rafferty, Anne Marie. American Journalism 1690-1904. New York: Routledge, 2000.
80. Raymond, Joad. The Invention of the Newspaper: English Newsbooks, 1641-1649.
81. New York: oxford University Press, 1996.
82. Reporters of the Associated Press.Breaking News: How the Associated Press has Covered War, Peace, and Everything Else.New York: Princeton Architectural Press, 2007.
83. Ritchie, Donald A. American Journalists. Oxford: Oxford University Press, 1997.
84. Sachsman, David B., et. al, eds. The Civil War and the Press. New Brunswick, NJ: Transaction Publishers, 2000.
85. Seib, Philip M. Broadcasts from the Blitz: How Edward R. Murrow Helped Lead America into War.
86. Washington,DC: Potomac Books, 2006.
87. Serrin, Judith and William Serrin. Muckraking!: The Journalism that Changed America.
88. New York: New Press, 2002.
89. Shepard, Alicia C. Woodward and Bernstein: Life in the Shadow of Watergate.Hoboken, NJ: J. Wiley, 2007.
90. Sims, Norman, ed. Literary Journalism in the Twentieth Century. New York: Oxford University Press, 1990.

91. Sloan, William David. The Early American Press, 1690-1783.Westport, CT: Greenwood Press, 1994.
92. ----. Perspectives on Mass Communication History.Hillsdale, NJ: Lawrence Erlbaum, 1991.
93. Sloan, W. David and Lisa Mullikin Parcell, eds. American Journalism: History, Principles, Practices.Jefferson, NC: McFarland & Company, 2002.
94. Sloan, W. David, James G. Stovall, and James D. Startt.The Media in America: A History, 4th ed. Northport, AL: Vision, 1999.
95. Smythe, Ted Curtis. The Gilded Age Press. Westport, CT: Praeger, 2003.
96. Sorel, Nancy Caldwell. The Women Who Wrote the War. New York: Arcade Publishing, 1999.
97. Spencer, David Ralph. The Yellow Journalism. Evanston, IL: Northwestern University Press, 2007.
98. Stacks, John F. Scotty: James B. Reston and the Rise and Fall of American Journalism. Boston: Little, Brown & Company, 2003.
99. Sterling, John Michael. Stay Tuned: A History of American Broadcasting. Mahwah, NJ: Lawrence Erlbaum Associates, 2002.
100. Startt, James D., and W. David Sloan. Historical Methods in Mass Communication. Hillsdale, NJ: Lawrence Erlbaum Associates, 1989.
101. ----. The Significance of the Media in American History. Northport, AL: Vision Press, 1994.
102. Sterling, Christopher H., ed. Encyclopedia of Journalism. Thousand Oaks, CA: SAGE Reference, 2009.
103. Sterling, Christopher H., and John M. Kittross. Stay Tuned: A Concise History of American Broadcasting.Belmont, CA: Wadsworth, 1990.

CITATION

CHAPTER 1

Udomisor, I. and Udoh, A. (2015) Professional Demand of Objectivity and Its Effect on Media Objectivity in Conflict Management in Journalism. Advances in Journalism and Communication, 3, 1-9. doi: 10.4236/ajc.2015.31001.

CHAPTER 2

Günther Pallaver / Theo Hug; Political Journalism under Pressure; http://www.medienimpulse.at/articles/view/207

CHAPTER 3

Umeogu, B. & Ifeoma, O. (2012). Sycophancy and Objective Journalism. Advances in Applied Sociology, 2, 159-166. doi: 10.4236/aasoci.2012.23022.

CHAPTER 4

D. Weisenhaus; Media law education for journalists in Hong Kong; http://ro.uow.edu.au/cgi/viewcontent.cgi?article=1050&context=apme

CHAPTER 5

Ifeoma Dunu* and Gregory Obinna Ugbo; The Nigerian journalists' knowledge, perception and use of the freedom of information (FOI) law in journalism practices; DOI: 10.5897/JMCS2013.0377

CHAPTER 6

Caroline Fisher (2015) The disclosure dilemma: Returning to journalism after political media advising, DOI:10.1080/22041451.2015.1042425

INDEX